Inclusion and Exclusion Through Youth Sport

'We can reach far more people through sport than we can through political or educational programmes. In that way, sport is more powerful than politics. We have only just started to use its potential to build up this country. We must continue to do so.'

Nelson Mandela

Nelson Mandela's statement reflects a widely held view that sport can contribute in unique and far-reaching ways to the delivery of important social outcomes. But is this really the case? Can sport bring people from different backgrounds together, and in so doing act as a force for social transformation and change? In the language of policy makers and practitioners, can sport contribute to social inclusion or could it be argued that sport acts to marginalise and disadvantage some groups in society? In other words, could sport reinforce, rather than challenge, social inequality?

Focusing on youth sport as a touchstone sector of sport in society, this book examines the theoretical and empirical bases of arguments for the role of sport in social inclusion agendas. Authors are drawn from around the world and offer critical perspectives on assumptions underpinning the bold claims made about the power of sport. This book represents the most up-to-date and authoritative source of knowledge on inclusion and exclusion in youth sport. As such, it is essential reading for those who want to use sport to 'make a difference' in young people's lives. It is, therefore, recommended for students, researchers, policy makers and practitioners working in sports development, sports coaching, sport studies or physical education.

Symeon Dagkas is a lecturer in the School of Education, Department of Sport Pedagogy, University of Birmingham, UK. His research interests lie in intersectional issues in sport participation through the examination of multiple layers of disadvantage including socio-economic factors, ethnicity, gender and religion.

Kathleen Armour is Professor of Education and Sport in the School of Education, and Head of the Department of Sport Pedagogy, University of Birmingham, UK. Her main research interest is career-long professional learning for teachers and coaches, and its impact on young people's learning in physical education and sport.

Routledge studies in physical education and youth sport

Series Editor: David Kirk

University of Bedfordshire, UK

The *Routledge Studies in Physical Education and Youth Sport* series is a forum for the discussion of the latest and most important ideas and issues in physical education, sport, and active leisure for young people across school, club and recreational settings. The series presents the work of the best well-established and emerging scholars from around the world, offering a truly international perspective on policy and practice. It aims to enhance our understanding of key challenges, to inform academic debate, and to have a high impact on both policy and practice, and is thus an essential resource for all serious students of physical education and youth sport.

Also available in this series

Children, Obesity and Exercise: A practical approach to prevention, treatment and management of childhood and adolescent obesity
Edited by Andrew P. Hills, Neil A. King and Nuala M. Byrne

Disability and Youth Sport
Edited by Hayley Fitzgerald

Rethinking Gender and Youth Sport
Edited by Ian Wellard

Pedagogy and Human Movement
Richard Tinning

Positive Youth Development Through Sport
Edited by Nicholas Holt

Young People's Voices in PE and Youth Sport
Edited by Mary O'Sullivan and Ann MacPhail

Physical Literacy: Throughout the Lifecourse
Edited by Margaret Whitehead

Physical Education Futures
David Kirk

Young People, Physical Activity and the Everyday
Living Physical Activity
Edited by Jan Wright and Doune Macdonald

Muslim Women and Sport
Edited by Tansin Benn, Gertrud Pfister and Haifaa Jawad

Inclusion and Exclusion Through Youth Sport
Edited by Symeon Dagkas and Kathleen Armour

Sport Education: International Perspectives
Edited by Peter Hastie

Inclusion and Exclusion Through Youth Sport

Edited by
Symeon Dagkas and Kathleen Armour

Routledge
Taylor & Francis Group

LONDON AND NEW YORK

First published 2012
by Routledge
2 Park Square, Milton Park, Abingdon, Oxon OX14 4RN

Simultaneously published in the USA and Canada
by Routledge
711 Third Avenue, New York, NY 10017

Routledge is an imprint of the Taylor & Francis Group, an informa business

First issued in paperback 2013

British Library Cataloguing in Publication Data
A catalogue record for this book is available from the British Library

Library of Congress Cataloging in Publication Data
Inclusion and exclusion through youth sport /
edited by Symeon Dagkas and Kathleen Armour.
    p. cm. — (Routledge studies in physical education and youth sport)
    1. Sports for children. 2. Sports for children—Social aspects.
    3. Physical education for children. 4. Physical fitness for youth.
    I. Dagkas, Symeon. II. Armour, Kathleen M.
    GV709.2.I575 2011
    796.083-dc22
    2011006183

ISBN: 978-0-415-57803-5 (hbk)
ISBN: 978-0-415-85798-7 (pbk)
ISBN: 978-0-203-85239-2 (ebk)

Typeset in in Times New Roman
by Swales & Willis Ltd, Exeter, Devon

Contents

List of figures and tables

Figures

Tables

Notes on contributors

Kathleen Armour is Professor of Education and Sport, and Head of the Department of Sport Pedagogy at the University of Birmingham, UK. Her research focuses on career-long professional development for teachers and coaches to help them to meet the needs of diverse learners in physical activity, physical education and sport.

Laura Azzarito earned her PhD in Kinesiology at Louisiana State University, USA, receiving the 2004 Josephine A. Roberts LSU Distinguished Dissertation Award in the Arts, Humanities, and Social Sciences. Her research examines the links among young people's construction of the body, identity and inequality issues from a socio-cultural and pedagogical perspective. Currently at Loughborough University, Laura has published numerous academic articles and book chapters in PE and sport pedagogy, sociology of sport, qualitative methods and curriculum studies. In 2009, she received the American Association of Health, Physical Education, Recreation and Dance fellow status award for her scholarship. Laura is currently conducting visual research projects with young people in urban, multicultural school PE contexts. This research is being funded by the Economic and Social Research Council, UK and The British Academy.

Tansin Benn is a Professor in the School of Education, Department of Sport Pedagogy, College of Social Sciences, and President of the IAPESGW 2009–2013. Her specialist research and publications field is the interface of gender, ethnicity, religion and physical education/sport. Her research into the life experience of British Muslim women in teacher training started in the 1990s and has involved work linking policy, theory and practice at national and international level. She recently authored with Gertrud Pfister and Haifaa Jawad a new book *Muslim Women and Sport*.

Mark Bruner is an Assistant Professor in the School of Physical and Health Education at Nipissing University in North Bay, Canada. His line of research focuses on the social factors that influence participation and personal development in youth sport.

Lisette Burrows is an Associate Professor at the University of Otago's School of Physical Education in New Zealand. She draws on post-structural theoretical resources to examine how health imperatives are being recontextualised in and around homes and schools in the context of an avowed obesity 'epidemic.' She is also interested in the meanings children advance about their own and others' health and fitness and, more generally, in the place and meaning of physical culture in the lives of young people. All of her work is informed by a recognition that physical and health education are normalised practices that derive from developmental, racialised, gendered and classed assumptions that do not necessarily serve all well.

Colleen Coakley is a master's student in the School of Kinesiology and Health Studies at Queen's University in Kingston, Canada. Her research interest is in the area of youth sport. She has coached all levels of ice hockey, from beginner to the university level.

Mike Collins was first a geographer and town planner, then a researcher at LSE, and a teacher-researcher at Loughborough; he is now Visiting Professor at the University of Gloucestershire's Centre for Sport Spirituality & Religion. His specialities are the social and economic impact of sport, sport and social capital, sports development. He is the author of *Sport & Social Exclusion* and *Examining Sports Development.*

Jean Côté is Professor and Director in the School of Kinesiology and Health Studies at Queen's University in Kingston, Canada. His research interests are in the areas of children in sport, sport expertise and coaching.

Symeon Dagkas is a Lecturer in the Department of Sport Pedagogy, School of Education, at the University of Birmingham, UK. His research interests centre on intersectionality and the cumulative effects of social disadvantage including socio-economic factors, ethnicity, gender and religion. He has a particular interest in the role of families in physical activity engagement.

Paul Downward PhD is Senior Lecturer and Director of the Institute of Sport and Leisure Policy in the School of Sport, Health and Exercise Sciences. He has recently published a book on the Economics of Sports, following up an earlier monograph on the Economics of Professional Team Sports. He is currently embarked on a study of the economic determinants and impacts of sports participation in the UK. He has also published widely in the philosophy and ethics of economics, and applied microeconomics.

Michael Gard is an Associate Professor in Charles Sturt University's Faculty of Education, Australia. He teaches and writes about dance, sport and the science of human health. He is the author of two books: *The Obesity Epidemic: Science, Morality and Ideology* (with Jan Wright) and *Men Who Dance: Aesthetics, Athletics and the Art of Masculinity.*

Donna Goodwin is an Associate Professor in the Faculty of Physical Education and Recreation at the University of Alberta, Canada. She is also the Executive Director of The Steadward Centre for Personal & Physical Achievement, a research centre that also provides instruction in disability fitness, sport development and physical activity for children, teens, and adults.

Peter J. Hay is a Lecturer in the School of Human Movement Studies at the University of Queensland, Australia. His research focuses on the constitution and consequences of ability in movement and educational contexts and understanding the conditions of assessment efficacy in these contexts.

Grant Jarvie is Vice-Principal and Professor at the University of Stirling, UK. He is currently advisor to governments on both higher education and sports policy. He was awarded an Honorary Doctorate in 2009 in recognition for his efforts to forge international cooperation and academic developments between universities. He is an Honorary Professor of the University of Warsaw. He has held established chairs and been head of departments at research centres in different UK universities including Stirling, Warwick and Heriot-Watt. His research has covered aspects of sport, health and education in other countries including Denmark, China, South Africa, Kenya, Taiwan and France.

Haifaa Jawad is Senior Lecturer in Islamic and Middle Eastern Studies, School of Philosophy, Theology and Religion, University of Birmingham, UK. She is associate editor of *The American Journal of Islamic Social Sciences* and the *Journal of the Study of Islam and Christian-Muslim Relation.* Haifaa has recently authored a book with Tansin Benn and Gerturd Pfister entitled *Muslim Women and Sport* and she is currently working on *The Contribution of European Converts to Islam: Britain as a Case Study*, for Continuum International.

Tess Kay is Professor of Sport and Social Sciences at Brunel University, UK, and former director of international sport research at the Institute of Youth Sport, Loughborough University. She has conducted extensive research in the UK and internationally into the relationship between sport, leisure and social structure, with particular emphasis on inclusion, diversity and development. Her publications include *Fathering through Sport and Leisure* and *Understanding Sport in International Development*.

Kelly Knez is a research scientist at ASPETAR, the Qatar Orthopaedic and Sports Medicine Hospital, Doha. Her current research seeks to move beyond white, Western ways of understanding young Muslim women's engagement in sport and physical activity.

Doune Macdonald is Professor of Health and Physical Education and Head of the School of Human Movement Studies, The University of Queensland, Australia. She has recently co-edited with Jan Wright, *Young People, Physical Activity and the Everyday*.

Ann MacPhail is Senior Lecturer in the Department of Physical Education and Sport Sciences at the University of Limerick, Ireland. Ann's main teaching and research interests revolve around physical education, teacher education, young people in sport, curriculum development in physical education, teaching, learning and assessment issues within school physical education, methodological issues in working with young people and ethnography. Ann is associate editor for *Physical Education and Sport Pedagogy* and is co-editor, with Mary O'Sullivan, of *Young People's Voices in Physical Education and Youth Sport*.

Nate McCaughtry is an Associate Professor in the Department of Kinesiology, Health and Sport Studies at Wayne State University, USA, where he is the Coordinator for the Physical Education Pedagogy programme. He is Director of the Detroit Healthy Youth Initiative, a long-term urban school physical activity and nutrition education partnership. His research focuses on socio-cultural issues in physical education, as well as teacher learning and development. (http://coe.wayne.edu/kinesiology/bio.php?id=42229)

Jaleh McCormack has been managing a research company for the past decade, conducting contract research for Ministries of Health and Education and project managing academic projects focusing on young people's understandings of health, sport and physical activity. She is currently a doctoral student at the School of Physical Education, University of Otago, New Zealand, investigating how families, and parents in particular, are negotiating health imperatives in a context where obesity concerns are paramount.

Louise McCuaig is Health, Sport and Physical Education Programme Coordinator at The University of Queensland, School of Human Movement Studies. She is a passionate teacher educator whose current projects focus on health literacy and education across the lifespan, health education teacher education and student transition.

Alison Nelson is an Occupational Therapy Practice Educator with the University of Queensland's Children's Life Skills Clinic and the Workforce Development Coordinator for the Institute for Urban Indigenous Health. She recently completed her doctorate exploring the place and meaning of physical activity in the lives of young urban Indigenous Australians.

Kimberly Oliver is an Associate Professor in the Department of Human Performance, Dance & Recreation at New Mexico State University, USA, where she is the Director of the Physical Education Teacher Education Program. Her research focuses on inquiry-based curriculum and the examination of what influences girls' sense of self and enjoyment and participation in physical activity. (http://education.nmsu.edu/departments/academic/perd/kimberly.html)

Bonnie Pang is a PhD candidate of Human Movement Studies, The University of Queensland, Australia. Her research centres on the socio-cultural lives of Chinese young immigrants and draws on ethnographic methods to interrogate issues related to in/exclusion and equity in their physical activity engagements.

Danielle Peers is a doctoral student in the Faculty of Physical Education and Recreation at the University of Alberta, Canada, who researches at the intersections of Critical Disability Studies and Physical Cultural Studies. She is a Paralympic medalist in wheelchair basketball, a filmmaker and an active volunteer in her sport, art and activist communities.

Simona Rasciute PhD is Lecturer in Economics in the School of Business and Economics, University of Loughborough, UK. Her main research interests are discrete choice econometrics, but she has published widely on sports participation and its impacts, and Foreign Direct Investment.

Doug Risner is an Associate Professor at Wayne State University's Maggie Allesee Department of Dance. His research and teaching centre on critical perspectives in dance education and training. He is the author of *Stigma and Perseverance in the Lives of Boys Who Dance* and is editor-in-chief of the *Journal of Dance Education.*

Deborah Tannehill earned a BSc in Physical Education, Master's in Guidance and Counseling, and PhD in Physical Education Teacher Education at Washington State University, Seattle University, and University of Idaho respectively. Before joining the Sport and Exercise Sciences Department at the University of Limerick as a Research Fellow in 2005, Deborah was Assistant Dean and Professor of Physical Education at Pacific Lutheran University in Tacoma, Washington for seven years. Prior to that Deborah was Professor of Physical Education Teacher Education at The Ohio State University where she taught and conducted research for eleven years. Currently a Senior Lecturer, Deborah is Course Director of the Graduate Diploma in Education–Physical Education, Course Director of the MSc in Teaching Physical Education, Physical Activity, and Sport, and Co-Director of the Physical Education, Physical Activity and Youth Sport (PE PAYS) Research Centre in the Department of Physical Education and Sport Sciences at the University of Limerick.

Ian Wellard is based at Canterbury Christ Church University, UK, where he is a Reader in the Sociology of Sport and Physical Education and Associate Director of the Centre for Sport, Physical Education and Activity Research (SPEAR). His main research interests relate to body practices, gendered identities and sport. Much of this research has been generated through ethnographic studies, which draw upon qualitative and reflexive approaches to the ways in which embodied identities are constructed and negotiated. Recent publications include *Sport, Masculinities and the Body* and *Re-thinking Gender and Youth Sport* as well as numerous articles relating to his research in international journals.

Preface

Youth sport is the foundation of sport in society, therefore what happens in this sector of sport matters. It is often argued that sport can contribute much to social inclusion agendas yet, at the same time, some of the practices that prevail in sport result in exclusion and marginalisation for some young people. This book considers this conundrum by critically examining the arguments underpinning social inclusion claims made about sport. Drawing on detailed conceptual analyses and examples from empirical studies, leading scholars from around the world offer a range of perspectives on the causes of exclusion and marginalisation, and on the practical and pedagogical steps that can be taken towards greater inclusion.

This collection of essays on 'Inclusion and Exclusion Through Sport' represents an up-to-date and authoritative discussion on the core issues in the context of youth sport, as part of the *Routledge Studies in Physical Education and Youth Sport*. It is an invaluable text for those involved in sport provision and pedagogy who believe in the power of sport and who want to deploy it to make a difference in children's lives; especially those children and young people who tend to be left out. There is something in this book for students in the broad field of sport who are trying to grapple with some of these issues for the first time; researchers trying to break new ground; policy makers who are striving to develop inclusive sport; and professionals and practitioners in physical education and youth sport who are attempting to meet the diverse needs of the young people they encounter. For all these groups, this book will raise questions and offer insights and challenges.

Acknowledgements

We want to thank our colleagues from around the world who have contributed chapters to this volume. Your patience throughout the process is much appreciated. We would also like to extend our gratitude to the many young people whose 'stories' are represented in this volume. It is only through the hearing and telling of such stories that we can begin to appreciate the range of youth positionalities and experiences. Understanding difference, and respecting the needs of children and young people whoever they are, and whatever their needs, are the first steps towards developing advanced pedagogies of inclusion in physical education and youth sport. Finally, we would like to thank Routledge for supporting this project.

Introduction

Symeon Dagkas and Kathleen Armour

Questions and assumptions

Engagement in sport has been highlighted as an effective means of combating social exclusion both in national government policies and by the World Health Organization. The EU Commission in its White Paper on Sport (EC, 2007) argued that all EU residents should have access to sport regardless of social, religious, cultural or ethnic background, and that sport can promote social integration and inter-cultural dialogue.

The optimistic view that sport can contribute – in unique and far-reaching ways – to the realisation of a range of positive social outcomes has been promoted around the world by New Labour and neo-Conservative governments. Yet, questions have been asked about whether there is sufficient robust evidence to support such optimism. Is it true that sport can bring people from different backgrounds together, acting as a force for social transformation and change? In other words, are sport and physical education able to live up to claims that they contribute to social inclusion? Or, would it be more accurate to claim that sport and physical education marginalise and disadvantage some groups within society? Is there any sense in which they reinforce, rather than challenge inequities? Could it even be argued that we, as researchers, contribute to the process of 'othering' in society by identifying specific groups as 'youth at risk' and targeting them for special attention? Questions such as these, that is, questions at the very heart of social inclusion/exclusion agendas, are at the heart of the essays presented here.

This book is part of the *Routledge Studies in Physical Education and Youth Sport* series which provides a forum for academic debate, discussion and furthering of knowledge and understanding of key issues of inclusion and exclusion in, from and through sport, school and club settings. This book has been written for students, researchers and practitioners (teachers, coaches and sport developers). Its core purpose is to 'map' young people's experiences of sport and physical education from an inclusion/exclusion perspective. The challenges inherent in the language of inclusion/exclusion are identified in different ways by different authors and, in this introduction, we present an overview of some of the key issues. For example, authors have identified youth positionalities and subjectivities in relation to issues of geographic location, gender, race, social class, ethnicity, sexuality and sport. In some chapters it is argued that exclusion and inclusion discourses should not be understood as a binary; for example, Macdonald and colleagues (in Chapter 1) interrogate the ideas of inclusion and exclusion which sets the 'tone' for the rest of the book. More specifically they highlight the 'false binary of in/exclusion', arguing that 'one is never fully excluded from the discourse of sport, although some might be excluded from the practice of sport'.

The contested nature of debate around exclusion and inclusion through sport is illustrated vividly in this book. As with all edited texts, the chapters in this book can be read in the order presented, or different chapters can be selected as required. It is worth noting, however, that the book has been designed to identify complexities around issues of *exclusion* in Part I, followed by suggested solutions for *inclusion* in Part II. Readers might find it helpful, therefore, to access some of the chapters in Part I in preparation for reading those in Part II. The chapters are organised into two sections: Part I: 'Understanding Exclusion'; and Part II: 'Moving Toward Inclusion'. Part I reflects the belief that exclusion can be 'seen' in the case of specific youth groups in society. This belief is supported by evidence from case study research that makes 'visible' exclusive practices. Part II consists of chapters that offer accounts of inclusive practices that have been developed in and through sport, physical education and community sport. Despite differences in interpretation and political or ideological standpoint, the book accepts that 'othering' and marginalisation are part of sport-related policies and practices in many countries in the Western world. Young people themselves may feel they have been excluded from something they would like to access; but it is possible that the process of marginalisation is largely unrecognised. It is also important to remember that our assumptions about exclusion should always be open to challenge. Assumptions about the value of certain types of sport for different groups, for example, are always a reflection of our own positionality in the vast global enterprise that is sport. In essence, therefore, the chapters in this book caution against easy (lazy) advocacy and challenge us to subject our own beliefs to critical questioning before making assumptions about others.

Sport settings

Young people engage in sport in a range of settings – mainly school, community and sports club. Although these settings are contextually different, they also overlap in numerous ways, not least in the sport practices that define them.

There is obviously a close relationship between physical education and youth sport, although they are not synonymous. Bailey (2005) argues that at the most superficial level, the distinction between the two is simply that 'sport' refers to a range of activities, whereas physical education is located in school. Physical education also refers to specific curriculum areas that are closely associated with formal pedagogic outcomes, whereas youth sport is a broader term that can, and sometimes does, embrace physical education. Inclusion and exclusion can be identified in both settings and, in some chapters, authors have drawn upon examples from both to illustrate their arguments.

Part I: Understanding exclusion

Whereas it is not suggested that sport is some kind of panacea, there is widespread societal support for the idea that children and young people, whatever their abilities, have much to gain from participation in high-quality physical education and sport (Armour, 2011). Governments have often viewed sport as a tool for social integration and the youth sport inclusion agenda tends to focus on 'disaffected' youth or 'youth at risk' with the purpose of developing 'healthy' and 'responsible' citizens (EC, 2007, p. 3). The intention in this book is to initiate dialogue and provide a platform for the creation of pedagogical environments where teachers, coaches and policy makers can listen to youth voices in order to understand *old challenges* in *new ways*.

In Part I of this book, the term '*pedagogies of exclusion*' is used to refer to specific pedagogical environments and discourses that can act as barriers to youth participation and engagement in sport and physical education. A range of characteristics are implicated in the development of '*pedagogies of exclusion*' such as economic resources, gender, race, ethnicity, religion and sexuality. In these chapters, formal pedagogical environments are identified as barriers to youth participation in/from/through sport, and pedagogies of exclusion are related to the quality and nature of teaching; for example, the syllabus, teachers' attitudes and knowledge, and issues linked to coaching and parental supervision.

In Chapter 1, Doune Macdonald, Bonnie Pang, Kelly Knez, Alison Nelson and Louise McCuaig interrogate the concepts of exclusion and inclusion. Using Foucault's concepts of discourse and power, they explore inclusion and exclusion within the context of sport as a biopolitical practice. In challenging the complexity of inclusion and exclusion as conceptual and practical terms, they are able to challenge the in/exclusion binary, arguing for an understanding of both concepts from different positionalities. In Chapter 2, Mike Collins interrogates the concept of exclusion and examines social exclusion through an economic lens. He draws on data from the UK to substantiate the existence of exclusion based on economic resources. Lack of resources shapes young people's choices, attitudes and consumption of physical activities and sport. Issues of child poverty, structural inequalities and impact on sporting participation are explored and comparisons are drawn with other national contexts. Paul Downward and Simona Rasciute, in Chapter 3, examine definitions and concepts underpinning discussions of social exclusion and sport from the non-economic, social scientific literature. More specifically they discuss the development of social capital and interrogate the concept of social exclusion. In Chapter 4, Grant Jarvie provides accounts of recent key social divisions and forms of social inequality that have impacted and continue to impact on sport and sport participation.

The next four chapters identify specific social and cultural characteristics as forms of youth exclusion through sport. In Chapter 5, Laura Azzarito argues that rethinking gender requires recognition of ongoing inequalities that shape young women's experiences of sport and which are obscured by current global, neo-liberal 'gender-neutral' claims. She problematises the ways in which the hidden curriculum operates in the context of school physical education at the local level, and she draws upon a narrative of a young girl to illustrate the ways in which the local/global hidden curriculum informs embodiment and performance of sport in her everyday life. Peter Hay, in Chapter 6, offers a social critical explanation of physical 'ability'. He argues for a social constructionist view of ability that draws attention to those aspects of sport that influence the inclusion and exclusion of young people in a movement culture. He maintains that ability is viewed as the value of one's embodied dispositions with reference to the structuring charac- teristics of social fields. In Chapter 7, Ian Wellard discusses sexuality as a form of exclusion. He considers ways in which different sexualities are presented and experienced in sport settings, and he highlights the need for sexuality to be exam- ined alongside broader definitions of gendered performance and the body. In Chapter 8, Symeon Dagkas and Tansin Benn discuss the concept of embodiment of faith *and* culture by looking at the ways in which Muslim girls relate to physical education and school sport. They identify exclusionary pedagogies through Mus- lim girls' positionalities and subjectivities as well as considering Muslim parents' voices and teachers' practices. The chapter concludes by challenging both educa- tion and community systems that fail to provide suitable learning environments for participation in sport and physical activity.

Chapter 9 turns our attention to health and the role of physical activity and sport. Lisette Burrows and Jaleh McCormack interrogate the relationship between youth sport and obesity imperatives expressed in public health promotion policy, school- based physical activity initiatives, and the testimonies of young people and their teachers. Drawing on discourse analyses of the data from ethnographic projects in schools in New Zealand, they illustrate some of the ways in which teachers and pupils link sport and health imperatives (including weight loss) in their talk and practice. Finally, they point to some of the problematic consequences of framing sport as a health-enhancing and/or fat-busting tool.

Part II: Moving towards inclusion

According to Collins (2004), inclusion is about equal opportunities for all young people regardless of their social, cultural and demographic characteristics. Sport as a 'social inclusion' tool has been used in policies around the globe to address issues of deprivation, (dis)ability, and health. Creating inclusive pedagogical environments is, however, a challenging task, as the authors of these chapters testify.

At the forefront of any efforts to provide effective, inclusive learning experi- ences is the need to understand youth voices and subjectivities which are, them- selves, evolving and are shaped by socially constructed discourses. In this sense, any discussion on 'inclusion' needs to begin with critical reflection on the use of the term in contemporary society. Accepting that youth subjectivities are in flux means that it is imperative to view inclusion as a complex series of actions that are, to some extent, context dependent in their structure and format. This second part of the book, therefore, seeks to identify inclusive pedagogic practices as a response to Part I, where exclusion was presented as a contested concept, and was defined through young people's voices and discourses.

In Chapter 10, Ann McPhail discusses young people's voices in sport in the context of gender, perceived competence, sexuality and the role of significant others in youth sport participation. She argues it is imperative that the voices of young people inform and help to create appropriate, worthwhile and meaningful sporting provision. In Chapter 11, Kimberly Oliver and Nate McCaughtry claim that working to transform physical activity inequity requires researchers, teachers and students to collaborate on the key issues. Through reflective narratives, these authors demonstrate specific instructional strategies they have used with young girls to help them identify, critique, and transform inequities that threaten their enjoyment and/or opportunities to be physically active. Finally they critically discuss implications for teaching, teacher education and research. Jean Côté, Colleen Coakley and Mark Bruner, in Chapter 12, consider effective practice in a different way by using the concepts of effective versus efficient youth sport programmes. These authors present guidelines for improving the experiences of youth sport participants. Essentially, they argue that increasing the amount of deliberate play within and beyond organised sport, encouraging sampling during childhood, and emphasising developmentally appropriate outcomes will lead to lifelong involvement in sport for greater numbers of young people.

In Chapter 13, Donna Goodwin and Danielle Peers view sport as a complex and socially constructed site that can reflect, (re)produce and potentially resist attitudinal hierarchies, ambivalence and stigmatisation. They examine three interrelated planes of sport experiences for youth experiencing disability: sport structures of inclusion/exclusion, experiences of inclusion/exclusion, and cultural contexts of inclusion/exclusion. This examination leads them to reflect on inclusion as a socio-cultural phenomenon. Chapter 14 discusses pedagogical constraints in physical education learning and teaching environments that have led to parental exclusion of Muslim girls from physical education and school sport. Haifaa Jawad, Tansin Benn and Symeon Dagkas identify a multiplicity of factors that influence the learning experiences of Muslim girls such as the degree of religiosity in the local community, the school's degree of control over local facilities, educational demands and teachers' and head teachers' strategies to overcome parental concerns.

Tess Kay, in Chapter 15, examines ways in which sport is being used to promote youth inclusion in the poorest and most populous regions of the globe: the 'Majority World'. This chapter provides a brief overview of the emergence of sport as an international development policy tool, and raises a series of critical questions about its role in youth inclusion. Chapter 16 raises a series of issues related to how curricula might be designed to meet the needs of greater numbers of children and young people around the world. Deborah Tannehill considers ways in which the use of curricula choice can increase opportunities for engagement in physical education and physical activity. Finally Michael Gard and Doug Risner look back through history at some of the ways in which dance has been used for explicit social outcomes, and then look forward to what might be possible in the future. They argue that it is more useful to focus on the specificity of dance as an embodied experience, rather than trying to turn into something else to make it more 'acceptable' to greater numbers of young people. These authors maintain that knowing *why some people dance* is at least as important as understanding *why others do not* if greater participation and inclusion are our goals.

The debate continues

At the Australian Association for Research in Education conference in December 2010, a symposium was presented on a range of issues around exclusion through sport. The symposium led to a lively debate among those scholars in the audience; mainly researchers in physical education and youth sport from around the world. Some researchers argued that in/exclusion is a discourse that is largely created in and through research outputs, and that it is highly dependent on the ways in which researchers portray youth situational subjectivities. At the same time, there was agreement that monoculture (Western) perspectives on sport provision and physical education can contribute to pedagogies of exclusion. It was agreed that as researchers and scholars, we are committed to providing evidence-based outputs that can inform future policy and stimulate the development of inclusive practices. Teachers and coaches have a professional responsibility to meet the needs of all young people no matter what their cultural and personal characteristics, but researchers have responsibilities too. Mary O'Sullivan (2007, p. 16) claims that educational researchers have responsibilities to 'inform important educational problems or issues; enrich the body of knowledge in our field; communicate findings appropriately; and contribute to the development of good social order'. Furthermore, as Macdonald and colleagues maintain in Chapter 1, 'stakeholders cannot ignore the constant processes of socio-cultural change or the challenges and opportunities these bring'. What this debate seems to signal is the imperative to continue these discussions and to critically interrogate our practices as scholars, researchers, teachers and coaches, and sport developers. The need to continually research youth experiences, understand youth subjectivities and hear youth voices appears to be at the root of developing more inclusive practices that can include those who currently feel marginalised in, from and through sport.

References

Armour, K. (2011) *Introduction to Sport Pedagogy for Teachers and Coaches: effective learners in physical education and youth sport*. London: Routledge.
Bailey, R. (2005) Evaluating the relationship between physical education, sport and social inclusion. *Educational Review*, 57 (1): 71–90.
Collins, M. (2004) *Sport and Social Exclusion*. London: Routledge.
Commission of the European Communities (2007) *White paper on sport*. Brussels: (COM(2007) 391 final).
O'Sullivan, M. (2007) Research quality in physical education and sport pedagogy. *Sport, Education and Society*, 12 (2): 245–260.

Part I
Understanding exclusion

1   The will for inclusion

Bothering the inclusion/ exclusion discourses of sport

*Doune Macdonald, Bonnie Pang,
Kelly Knez, Alison Nelson and
Louise McCuaig*

Introduction

> The barriers for many people and the impact of our changing lifestyles on Australians' engagement with our sports and physical activity need to be examined so the system can be opened to all.
>
> (Commonwealth of Australia, 2009, p. 36)

> The national PESSYP (Physical Education and Sport Strategy for Young People), has received significant investment. The focus of this work has been further enhanced by the successful London Olympics 2012 bid; and the ongoing concerns over the health of the nation – which is seen as critical and has raised both the recognition of the role of PE and community sport and its importance in terms of access to provision.
>
> (Sport England, 2005; Partnerships for Schools, 2009)

Worldwide, governments extol the virtues of sport for the benefit of the individual and society. Indeed, for many, participation in sport provides pleasure, a sense of achievement, companionship, identity, health outcomes, income etc. but there is more to sport than this. Sport is an embodied cultural practice that is invested with several interrelated biopolitical purposes beyond individual fulfilment, such as health promotion, social cohesion, and nation-building. The discourses of sport, often articulating assumptions about sport's inherent worthiness, permeate contemporary societies such that it is nearly impossible to sit outside the circulation of these discourses. Schools, families, community organisations, businesses, the media, government policies and associated services are all invested in the idea that the population should participate in sport. Thus, there is an enduring and omnipotent belief that non-participants, those 'excluded' from sport engagement for whatever reasons, should become participants such that they are 'included'. Given this *will for inclusion*, we suggest that one is never fully excluded from the discourses of sport, although some individuals might be excluded from the practices of sport. This is the first position we take in this chapter.

Our second position, following from the first, is that inclusion and exclusion discourses of sport are not a binary; that is, in practice, children and young people move across a spectrum of engagement that may take them to a point of non-participation from the sporting practice (but not from the discourses). We suggest that this spectrum of engagement involves the circulation of power between the young people and the sporting contexts in which they are included/excluded. Thus, data are presented following two themes: *choosing exclusion*, where children and young people resist sport participation and *being excluded*, where children and young people are 'othered' in sporting contexts resulting in them becoming non-participants. Regardless of the level of engagement, we conclude that most children and young people in developed countries operate within the discourses of sport though not necessarily through physical engagement.

Those readers who are familiar with the work of Michel Foucault will have noticed reference to his concepts and thinking in the paragraphs above. Foucault's work provides us with ways of understanding discourse/s, power, inclusion and exclusion practices, and positioning sport as a biopolitical practice, replete with the associated technologies exercised by individuals and governments. In short, Foucault offers a theoretical platform from which to understand imperatives in relation to sport. What follows is a focus on discourse/s and how they may be manifested as biopolitical power. While discourse/s are historically and culturally specific, we have made an assumption (backed by international research) that there are also global similarities in the discourses of sport.

Discourse/s and biopolitical power

Discourse was a concept that Foucault revisited over the course of his writing and its meanings and interpretations have shifted over time. In *The Archeology of Knowledge*, Foucault wrote that discourse comprises 'practices that systematically form the objects of which they speak' (1972, p. 49). Around the same time, Foucault (1971) explained that in societies the production of discourse is controlled, selected, organised and redistributed by procedures that aim to provoke a sense of power, direction and danger.

According to Carrabine (2001, p. 275), discourses may be understood as 'functioning as sets of socially and historically constructed rules designating "what is" and "what is not."' Discourses then provide possibilities for what can be thought, giving a 'solidarity and normality which is difficult to think outside of' (Mills, 1997, p. 17). As such, discourses are frequently repeated and take on a naturalness, or even a truth, that perpetuates their credibility (Ball, 2007). As sets of sanctioned statements which have institutionalised force, discourses such as those that shape how we think about sport have a profound influence on the way that individuals think and act (Mills, 2004). Take, for example, a policy position 'Sport For All'. Here, the inherent 'goodness' of inclusion in sport is unquestioned and an oppositional stance unthinkable. Sporting practices that accurately conform to the rules of (sport/exclusion) discourse are likely to be ratified.

Discourses also generate subject positions; they generate how people see themselves and the way people go about their lives (Jose, 1998). Consistent with the ways in which Foucault came to see power operating, subject positions or subjectivities shift as individuals engage with multiple and shifting discourses. Such discourses can be associated with, for example, sport participant, student, or family member as they are framed by gender, race, religion, socio-economic status etc. It follows that children and young people are not stable entities and have the potential to assume subject positions that are not predictable, consistent or concurrent with the expectations of the group to which they belong (e.g. where boys may not have an interest in sport). This approach to the self as shifting, unstable, contradictory etc. is pertinent to our discussion as it introduces the notion that while children and young people may be immersed in the discourses of sport, they can also resist them in unexpected ways that challenge the in/exclusion binary.

In his work, Foucault was interested in who or what sat outside the dominant discourse through procedures such as acts of exclusion (e.g. sexuality) and classification (e.g. ability). Paradoxically, exclusion is 'one of the most important ways in which discourse is produced' (Mills, 2004, p. 60). In examining the mechanisms of exclusion, Foucault (1972–73) argued in *The Punitive Society*, that exclusion was not a definitive position one was put into or took up but a continua of aims, relationships and operations of power. Yet, exclusion discourses in/through/from sport generate subject positions such as the non-participating, 'problem' individual and group. Following Foucault, we argue that exclusion discourses need to take account of the shifting positions of children and young people; that they as individuals or members of a (problem) group may move fluidly across the sporting landscape and so sedimented readings of their position should be avoided.

The potential for individuals to move across subject positions and perhaps resist dominant discourses such as those associated with the imperatives to be a sport participant can be further explained using Foucault's understanding of power.

> There are manifold relations of power which permeate, characterise and constitute the social body, and these relations of power cannot themselves be established, consolidated nor implemented without the production, accumulation, circulation and functioning of a discourse.
>
> (Foucault, 1980, p. 93)

In *Discipline and Punish* (1979) and the *History of Sexuality* (1984), Foucault sought to understand power as something beyond the power of the state, describing it, says Paras (2006, p. 64), as 'an enigmatic entity that was visible and invisible, present and hidden, but most importantly "invested everywhere"'. For humans, power simultaneously produces forms of behaviour, including resistance (e.g. choosing not to participate in sport), as well as restricting behaviour (e.g. boys-only teams) (see Mills, 2004). In particular, Foucault sought to explain power in the context of the new government rationality, *liberalism*. Liberalism can be considered as the art of government in managing populations, individuals and 'the question of truth' (i.e. the production and control of objective knowledge about, for example, healthy weight or sport participation patterns) (Paras, 2006, p. 93).

In the *Birth of Biopolitics*, Foucault (1978–79) analysed the governance of others and oneself; a form of power he termed 'biopower' that was 'situated and exercised at the level of life' (Rabinow and Rose, 2006, p. 196). Foucault saw biopower as having two poles: the individual body and the species body 'around which the organisation of life was deployed' (Foucault, 1984, p. 139). The emergence of biopower was marked by the 'explosion of numerous and diverse techniques for achieving the subjugation of bodies and the control of populations' (Foucault, 1984, p. 140). Theoretically, Foucault employed biopolitics as a process for understanding 'the formation of subjects, both as individual consciousness and as members of a given social and political community' (Jose, 1998, p. 3). In the context of this discussion on sport, the concepts of biopower and biopolitics alert us to ask questions such as, 'What advantages does the government see from sports participation by individuals and society?' or 'How are we persuaded to become sport participants?'

The disciplinary power required to govern both individuals and populations is more successful when it conforms to the 'natural' order of things (and a good example here are the discourses of 'sport for all'). It also follows that 'The *individual*, no longer seen as the pure product of mechanisms of domination, appears as the complex result of an interaction between outside coercion and techniques of self' (Paras, 2006, pp. 94–95) given the interrelationship between the individual and the population to which they belong. However, Harwood (2009, p. 19) emphasises that 'while disciplinary power can be characterized as making "docile bodies," these are not bodies at the total mercy of a sovereign form of power'. Markula and Pringle (2006) have examined sport as a disciplinary power looking at its intersection with practices such as exercise, fitness, self-stylisation, and self-care, to which we could add citizenship, health, sociability, workforce participation, performance and the like. Sport is thus fulfilling the biopolitical endeavour begun 'in the eighteenth century to rationalise problems presented to governmental practice by the phenomena characteristic of a group of living human beings constructed as a population' (Foucault, 1997, p. 73). Through various techniques (including our field's research on exclusion in/from/through sport), the government seeks to render the population knowable, to understand population patterns of behaviours, and thereby find direction for interventions.

Dominant discourses on exclusion in/from/through sport

Within academia, there has been a growing body of research into inclusion/ exclusion in/from sport and this knowledge, with its authoritative status, is powerful within the in/exclusion discourses. A cursory review of the literature that follows suggests that the body of research generally takes the line that some children and young people are excluded from sport on the basis of largely structural factors such as gender and sexuality, race and ethnicity, social class, or (dis)ability. This body of work functions as an underpinning structure of sport discourses (and thereby 'truths') and is implicated in how exclusion is talked about and understood. Further, as articulated by Foucault (1978–79, p. 18), academic research as a regime of truth 'constitutes these practices as a set bound together by intelligible connection and, on the other hand, legislates and can legislate on these practices in terms of true and false'. To extend this position, the type of research outlined below, accompanied by large scale, statistical data sets often collected by governments, is integral to the biopolitical strategies for legislation, policy-making, and intervention at the societal level and more subtle steering of the practices of the self by the individual (see Rabinow and Rose, 2006).

Exclusion discourses framed by questions relating to gender (see Chapter 5 this volume) and, more recently, sexuality serve to remind us of the centrality of the body and, more particularly, biological sex for understanding exclusion in/from/ through sport. For example, Clark and Paechter (2007) conducted a study with 10- to 11-year-old students at two state primary schools in London, focusing on the involvement of boys and girls in playground football. The study revealed that boys possessing particular knowledge and expertise in the sport excluded both non-footballing boys and girls. This hegemonic masculinity has been and continues to be identified in a range of research suggesting that the practices of sport are entrenched with a particular masculinist culture that discourages participation by young men and women who do not conform to appropriate heterosexual norms (Hemphill and Symons, 2009; Wellard, 2006; see also Chapter 7 this volume). The high value attributed to the embodiment of particular sporting skills and dispositions has also generated exclusion discourses concerning dis/ability. A survey conducted in England (Finch *et al.*, 2001) found that young people who have disabilities were less likely to participate in out-of-school sporting activities. Moreover, Bailey's (2005) review suggested that the barriers that young people with disability encountered in relation to sports included self-consciousness, low levels of self-confidence, and negative school experiences.

Discourses of race, ethnicity and exclusion in/from/through sport are increasing within the sport exclusion literature as global migration patterns underpin new cultural interfaces. Research reports the social exclusion of young people based upon language difficulties, unfamiliarity with mainstream sport, different sets of skills and abilities, and verbal harassment by peers. As well as research that argues other young people find sport fun, healthy and a touchstone to the dominant culture (e.g. Doherty and Taylor, 2007; Millington *et al.*, 2008; Taylor and Doherty, 2005), race-based exclusions intersect with gender to further accentuate the (dis)engagement patterns in sport by those 'othered' as ethnic minorities; for example, young men and women may hold firm views on participation in 'appropriate' 'masculine' and 'feminine' sports (Elling and Knoppers 2005; Millington *et al.*, 2008). The complex interplay of race, ethnicity, religion (e.g. Islam) and gender results in ethnic minority girls often reportedly having the lowest participation rate among all groups (e.g. Australian Bureau of Statistics, 2006; Bailey *et al.*, 2005; Elling and Knoppers, 2005).

The uptake of particular sports and the corresponding exclusion in/from/ through sports, also has a reported socio-economic or social class dimension that frequently intersects with the exclusion patterns outlined above (e.g. Swanson, 2009). Participation in sport for children and young people, particularly sport that occurs outside schooling, is an expense that many families cannot afford (Lee, 2010; Macdonald and Wright, 2010). Where this problem occurs, research suggests that although some families have a will for inclusion, exclusion occurs because of structural barriers (club fees, transport, uniforms, equipment etc.). With low socio-economic status may also come family dislocation and instability and these impact upon the family regimes that are often required to support junior sport participation (Macdonald *et al.*, 2005; Nelson, 2009).

While recognising the value of research into exclusion and sport in informing policies and practices that seek to promote inclusion, we make the following observations. Research is powerful in shaping the exclusion discourses because in our society research discourses have been invested with truths that shape what can be asked and what outcomes can be recommended. Second, the nature of the research process and its dissemination in journal articles, book chapters, reports, conference presentations etc. necessitates boundaries around what has been asked and shared, often reinforcing foci on particular 'groups' of the population and this can result in artificial classification. Further, the 'group' as a focus of study, may then be rendered as a 'problem' requiring specific strategies to assist their inclusion and thereby comply with the aspirations of the state. We also note that much of the research in English-speaking countries on in/exclusion and 'others' has been conducted through the lens of a white, Western way of knowing. Lastly, as we will explore in the next section, research discourses, in their seeking to know/explain, may also risk oversimplifying the complexities of the in/exclusion positions of children and young people.

Interrogating exclusion

The following data are derived from three projects, one in Hong Kong and two in Australia, all of which had the goals of understanding the place and meaning of physical activity (including sport) in the lives of young people. The data, viewed through the lens of biopolitics, help us to 'bother' those discourses of exclusion that suggest exclusion sits in opposition to inclusion and/or that exclusion is some-thing that happens *to* children and young people. Each data set was derived from a series of semi-structured interviews conducted by an author of this chapter. The Hong Kong participants were 12 young people (aged 10–12 years; 6 males and 6 females). The Australian, urban Indigenous cohort comprised 8 girls and 6 boys (aged 11–15 years), while the Australian resident Muslim girls were 14–16 years old across the years of data collection. Following our reading of Foucault's work on discourse/s and biopolitics, we were interested in exploring decision-making and dilemmas around sport participation at the level of the young person and their family. What follows are brief excerpts from the three data sets that serve to challenge the in/exclusion binary and its associated discourses.

Choosing exclusion

Children and young people reported interests and priorities that precluded their engagement in both informal and formal physical activity and sport.

> My greatest interest is not to excel in badminton or sport. Instead, I would like to excel in my academic studies. I think studies, and not sport will affect

my future . . . My father thinks that money is the most important thing. For him, money is related to everything in the world. He said that sport is not important. Instead the most important thing is having good academic results. He says if I study well and get a decent job, then I will be able to take care of myself.

(Ching, Hong Kong Chinese, girl)

A similar position was held by Hong Kong Chinese boys. For example, Cheuk explained:

Sport is not important and I do not want to waste time on things other than studying. I already do not have enough time for my homework; I sleep very late at night and do not get enough rest. What more if we talk about time for sport.

(Hong Kong Chinese, boy)

In the majority of the Hong Kong families interviewed, children and young people absented themselves (or were directed by parents to refrain) from sporting commitments that could interfere with their academic priorities. As discussed elsewhere (Ha *et al.*, 2010), this pattern of participation can be explained in part through Confucian principles. Confucian principles steer families to prioritise academic achievements before other activities, which would lead the child into a successful career and future prospects. The implication of the child's academic results is that it becomes an evidence or benchmark of having responsible parents and being a filial child.

For Muslim girls, cultural values and the way these interplay at times with religiosity and/or gender shape their participation in sport. Below, we introduce Jasmine who used to play interschool sport, especially netball, and currently enjoys riding her bike, but who also had substantial responsibilities at home, that included looking after her younger siblings and helping with the house chores.

Int.:   And um, do you play any sport.
Jasmine: I do lots of cycling, I enjoy cycling, you know, just getting out there and ride, just cycling, you don't have to do stunts or anything like that, and you know just let my hair out, feel the wind through my hair and stuff. But I had to quit that because I got so many homework, and now I don't have time.
Int.:   Because you've got what sorry?
Jasmine: Homework, and my Mum, now she goes 'you are growing older, you have more responsibilities now', you know, cooking, ironing, make lunches. When I was younger it's like, you know my Mum used to do everything, but now, there's more members of the family, I got lots more responsibilities.
Int.:   Okay, and how do you feel about that?
Jasmine: Oh sometimes I'm a bit peeved off at my Mum but then, I'm happy

because I look at my other cousins in Bangladesh they're sometimes starved, they don't have food, and I actually, I don't compare myself to people richer than me, I compare myself to people worser than me, at least I'm not in Africa, starved to death, or in Iraq bombed every day. So I actually feel lucky sometimes that I am living in this country where people are not in prison and stuff like that.

Jasmine went on to say that she does not play club sport as 'Mum doesn't let me, she doesn't like sports, that's why.'

Zeena too suggested the low priority for sport in her cultural context:

Zeena: This year, um I played netball.
Int.:   And do you play that competitively for a club or in a school?
Zeena: No, just in school. I think, um, I have become less physically active, I don't know, I guess because I study and stuff and my parents are not that interested in sports. They don't want me to do sports, they don't think it's, it's not good for a girl to do sports.

Jasmine and Zeena, as with Ching, give us an insight into the breadth and complexity of family cultures that can shape patterns of sport participation.

Alana, who self-identified as a Palestinian living in Australia, talked in terms of her own sport participation 'choice' based upon her interpretations of Islam, including the wearing of a head scarf.

Int.:   And the stuff that you are doing, the past week, is this the same as what you were doing this time last year?
Alana: No. Last year, first of all, the homework was much easier, and you didn't really have to worry about it, and secondly, I wasn't wearing the scarf, so it made a big difference.
Int.:   Tell me about that.
Alana: Well, before, like last year, when I wasn't wearing the scarf, and my Mum says 'Hurry up' if we were going somewhere, I'd just wear anything, quickly, and now I have to find a scarf and stuff. And when I didn't wear the scarf, I could swim and everything. It's not like my Mum forced me, I wanted to wear it. But things changed, you have to get used to it, you have to like, act more mature, you can't just swim and stuff, it just doesn't look good, or sound good. That's what changed sort of. At home nothing really, but at school, you get changed, and the sports uniform, I still wear half-sleeved, but I don't feel comfortable. I don't play as much as I did last year. But I still muck around.

Alana, as with her Muslim friends, alluded to the biopolitical (and gendered) discourses around the imperative to be physically active and maintain a particular body shape that sits in tension with their interpretations of 'appropriate' sporting activities:

Int.:   Why is your Mum, why are your Mums concerned about your bodies?
Alana: About marriage, you know . . .
Ranya: You know, they think 'What are we going to do with you when you grow up? No-one will want you.'
Alana: And they say you will grow fat, and you will be ashamed of going outside. And when you're female, and you get ashamed because your clothes don't fit you properly and everybody looks at you just because you are fat, and everything. That's what they (mothers) are concerned about, you know.

The Australian Indigenous young people with whom we talked often had clear preferences around activities in which they would like to participate. They often had strong allegiances to particular football codes and, for a variety of reasons, firmly repudiated other sports or codes.

Soccer Girl (Indigenous Australian, girl):	Yeah. Friends come and say 'come and play touch football' but I don't like it. I love soccer.
Int.:	So what happened with athletics that Yani was taking you over to at QEII?
Soccer Girl:	I only did javelin and we just ran.
Int.:	But it's finished or you just aren't going any more?
Soccer Girl:	Not going, I just decided to quit.
Int.:	What kinds of physical activities do you do?
Jayden (Indigenous Australian, boy):	None really. Just what we have to do.
(later):	I play soccer in my backyard. I teach my sister how to do soccer tricks and all that.
(later):	exercising? . . . I don't need to. Look at my bones.
(later):	I don't like football . . . hate that stupid game.
(later):	I just sleep in and don't want to exercise . . . rather watch TV . . . play Play Station or ride my bikes.

Jacobi, a young Indigenous woman, recalled:

> when I was a little kid I used to swim a lot and I used to always go around here and I came first I remember and I won a medal. But I was only little. And I always think, 'Oh I want to do swimming again but I'm just too slack.'

The language of self-deprecation used by Jacobi was frequently employed by the Indigenous young people when talking about non-participation. 'I didn't run this year. Cos I was too slack' (Tannika, Indigenous girl). Jacinta described herself as, 'I guess sometimes being lazy cos I don't want to do things' but she did not want to be 'one of those potato couches'.

The voices of the Indigenous, Asian and Islamic young people remind us that despite the dominant discourses of sport participation, young people for a variety of reasons (academic priorities, family responsibilities, religious interpretations or lack of interest) may choose not to participate. We note, however, that their decisions are nuanced in that there is rarely a complete renunciation of all sporting participation (i.e. their exclusion from participation is not complete). In any reduction or repudiation of their participation, they remained mindful that this choice should be balanced against societal expectations of the virtues of sport participation.

Being excluded

Children and young people talked about circumstances and experiences when they had wanted to be involved in sport participation but found themselves unable to participate or were sufficiently uncomfortable that non-participation was a consequence. Difficulty in accessing sporting facilities and opportunities was a recurring theme. Here, Cheuk and Soccer Girl allude to safety concerns:

> We could not play badminton by ourselves without any adult accompanying us in the estate park.
>
> (Cheuk, Chinese Hong Kong, boy)

> Um nowhere to run around. There's nowhere to run around in our yard. Our yard is too small . . . and there's nowhere really to exercise. Mum doesn't really like us running around outside . . . 'cos people might catch you.
>
> (Soccer girl, Indigenous Australian, girl)

Another, limiting factor is where children and young people rely on parental support in terms of time, transport or funding.

> I would like to do more sport but my father needs to work very late on weekdays. During weekends, he would rather sleep and rest at home than do sport with me.
>
> (Lok, Chinese Hong Kong, boy)

Int.:   So what normally stops you from going?
Sanae: When it's hot.
Int.:   Yep. So who decides that? Does mum decide that or do you decide that?
Sanae: Mum. Mum decides when it's too hot to go and to catch the bus . . . Mum's supposed to be getting a car soon so she can put us into sports again.

The cost of access to facilities drove exclusion in some cases:

Kerrey (Indigenous Australian, girl): We used to do Little Athletics and soccer and we had trophies and all that.
Int.: So why did you stop doing Little 'A's last year?
Kerrey: 'Cos we moved and we had to find a new club to do it and mum's just trying to find one.

Int.:	So the pool obviously costs money and the squash centre. Is that an issue for you guys? Like is that a problem?
Kerrey:	Um sorta, like we rarely go there.
Int.:	Yep.
Kerrey:	Yeah we'll just go to the beach.
Int.:	So you choose things that don't cost as much?
Kerrey:	Yeah just go to the beach or go down to the park and play yep. So yeah and ride our bikes.
Int.:	When, can you tell me about a time when it (money) has stopped you?
Soccer Girl:	Um well this year we weren't able to do athletics cos we done soccer.

Access to equipment was another problem:

> I haven't really asked Uncle B but sometimes Miss M lets us borrow her football. Depends on the boys, 'cos last time we borrowed it, the class borrowed it, the boys were supposed to take it back and they wouldn't so I don't think Miss M will let us use it again . . . and that sucks 'cos then we haven't got a football.
>
> (Jacinta, Indigenous Australian, girl)

In the 'Choosing exclusion' section above, we argued that for cultural reasons, some young people may choose to exclude themselves from participating in sport. Here, we extend this argument with examples of how, at times, cultural pressures/ mores are sufficiently strong that they dismiss the possibility of participation, even when the intent is there.

> I asked them if I could do this Basketball training thing, it's like Thursday afternoon, and I asked my parents and they were like 'no, no, no', and then I asked my Dad and he said okay but we don't want to drop you off because of Ramadan, and that's cool because my friend's parents can drop me off, and then he was okay with that and then no one came, only four people turned up. You can't make a basketball team out of four people. But he was prepared to, I think I'll wait until I am in year nine. I can't do Saturday sports because of Saturday (Islamic) school. I am very busy with my life.
>
> (Zeena, Islamic Australian, girl)

Int.:	So what's happened with Two Indig [an Indigenous touch football team], because you don't play for them anymore do you?
Julie (Indigenous Australian, girl):	Two Indig. Um, ever since Uncle Ricky [the coach/organiser] passed [died] they've never carried on the team. So that's why.
Int.:	Is that out of respect for him or is it just because they haven't had time or been able to get it organised?

Julie: I think that's out of respect, yeah. Just the girls just wouldn't,
                    couldn't, do it any more.

Literature suggests that racism can drive exclusion from sports participation
(Lovell, 1991; Taylor and Doherty, 2005). The following two examples of racism
were clearly at the levels of systemic exclusion and resulted in pressure directed
at them as Indigenous individuals. In these two cases the racism was challenged
by the young people involved yet we understand that for many, their will to be
involved was overridden by racism.

Julie: In sport we had to get picked to go to Met East (district) . . . me and my
            cousin T, we were like, the only two girls that never got picked.
Int.:   Was everybody else white?
Julie: Yeah and it was possible for the whole team to get picked and we were
            the only ones that never got picked. And then next year we still had the
            same coach and we never got picked again. We were the only two and I
            told (the PE teacher at school) and he went and seen them and that . . . so
            that's when we went to Met West.
Int.:   And then you got picked?
Julie: Yeah.
Int.:   Have you ever experienced racism?
Talia: On the touch field when I'm playing touch. Lot of times.
Int.:   Oh OK. So what's happened? Can you tell me something that's
            happened?
Talia: Oh well like when you're winning or like if you touch someone they'd be
            like 'oh you black dog' stuff like that.
Int.:   Really!
Talia: (nods). Happened a few times.
Int.:   Yeah? How do you feel when that happens?
Talia: I dunno, like just really angry and stuff.
Int.:   And what do you normally do? Like what's your response?
Talia: Well like I usually say stuff back but my coach just says it's just part of the
            game.

Our point here is that despite the children and young people's interest in
participating, factors such as cost, geographical dis/location, cultural constraints
and racism render participation difficult or inaccessible. Again, the circulating
will for inclusion was sometimes strong, reminding us of the need for caution
in approaching issues of inclusion and exclusion. In particular, these data draw
attention to the structural features framing sport (travel, fees, timing, coaching
behaviours) that can preclude inclusion.

Conclusion

According to national statistics, the majority of children and young people in
developed countries participate in sport (e.g. Australian Sports Commission, 2009).

This majority reflects the success of sport in its various iterations (school-based, club, community etc.) in giving children, young people and their families sporting experiences that are inclusive and this should be recognised and valued. We also argue that this majority reflects how most citizens are complicit in circulating the dominant discourses of sport, having been co-opted into the contemporary, societal *will for inclusion*.

The biopolitical discourse of the 'goodness' of sport is sufficiently pervasive (and persuasive) to ensure that those who are not included (through choice or alienation) are positioned as a 'problem' to be addressed through research and alternative policies and practices. Australia's newly released report on *The Future of Sport in Australia* (Commonwealth of Australia, 2009) continues with the tradition of listing 'nine areas' (including 'women'; 'our young people'; 'Indigenous communities'; 'the disadvantaged'; 'people with disabilities'; 'migrant communities') for which 'specific strategies will be required to understand and remove existing barriers to participation and to create inclusive environments where participation can grow' (p. 36). It can be argued that this approach serves to reproduce a biopolitically predetermined group membership where the classification of 'the group', such as those outlined above, is spurious and potentially limiting. That said, while some children and young people who fall into these categories may not be regular sport participants, *few sit outside the pervasive discourses of sport*.

This work reinforces the importance of alternative narratives regarding young people's engagement with sport in challenging the moral binary that invariably positions individuals as good/bad in relation to their sport practices and non-participation as a deficit/problem. Teachers in school communities can provide students with opportunities to gather and explore the range of reasons why young people do or do not participate in sport and position this within the context of the barriers and facilitators (competing discourses) operating within their lives. More specifically, teachers can assist in challenging the damaging stereotypes around participation patterns and the 'othering' of 'groups' as a problem. Researchers can continue to disseminate these alternative narratives through teacher education and professional development sites to challenge simplistic, elitist and individualistic perspectives, counter the dominance of moral overtones, and incite engagement with broader notions of well-being.

Many of the chapters to follow will outline the experiences of those individuals and groups who have been excluded and the policies and strategies deployed to seek to include them. This is important work, particularly for those children and young people for whom sport could meet their needs and interests but who find themselves excluded from participation. We argue, however, that whether they are participating in sport or not, most children and young people are implicated in the discourses of sport. In these discourses, exclusion is not 'acceptable' in our societies. Moreover, individuals move fluidly, or hold simultaneous contradictory positions, across the inclusion/exclusion continuum as the discourses of sport clash and intersect with other discourses related to, for example, gender, religion, family, ethnicity, school achievement, work and the like. This complexity behoves those working in the field of in/exclusion and sport research to understand how discourses operate, particularly those associated with the biopolitical imperative to be part of the active, 'sporty' citizenry, and take a questioning approach to the false in/exclusion binary.

References

Australian Bureau of Statistics (2006) *Migrants and Participation in Sport and Physical Activity*. ACT: Commonweatlh of Australia.

Australian Sports Commission (2009) *Participation in Exercise, Recreation and Sport Survey, Annual Report*. ACT: Commonwealth of Australia.

Bailey, R. (2005) Evaluating the relationship between physical education, sport and social inclusion. *Educational Review*, 57 (1): 71–90.

Bailey, R., Wellard, I. and Dismore, H. (2005) *Girls' Participation in Physical Activities and Sports: Benefits, patterns, influences and ways forward*. Online: www.icsspe.org/documente//Girls.pdf (accessed 7 August 2010).

Ball, S.J. (2007) *Education plc: Understanding private sector participation in public sector education*. London and New York: Routledge.

Carrabine, J. (2001) Unmarried motherhood 1830–1990: a genealogical analysis. In Wetherell, M., Taylor, S. and Yates, S (eds) *Discourse as Data: a guide for analysis*. London: Sage Publications.

Clark, S. and Paechter, C. (2007) 'Why can't girls play football?' Gender dynamics and the playground. *Sport, Education and Society*, 12 (3): 261–276.

Commonwealth of Australia (2009) *Independent Sport Panel Report. The Future of Sport in Australia*. Online: www.health.gov.au/internet/main/publishing.nsf/Content/crawford-report-full (accessed 7 August 2010).

Doherty, A. and Taylor, T. (2007) Sport and physical recreation in the settlement of immigrant youth. *Leisure*, 31 (1): 27–55.

Elling, A. and Knoppers, A. (2005) Sport, gender and ethnicity: practices of symbolic inclusion/exclusion. *Journal of Youth and Adolescence*, 34 (3): 257–268.

Finch, N., Lawton, D. and Williams, J. *et al.* (2001) *Disability Survey 2000: survey of young people with a disability and sport – findings*. York: University of York Social Policy Research Unit.

Foucault, M. (1971) *Madness and Civilization: a history of insanity in the age of reason.* London: Tavistock.

Foucault, M. (1972) *The Archaeology of Knowledge*, trans. A.M. Sheridan Smith. London: Tavistock Publications.

Foucault, M. (1972–73) La société punitive. Lecture course delivered at the Collège de France, Paris. Unpublished text edited and prepared by Jacques Lagrange, Archives of the Bibliothèque Générale du C.

Foucault, M. (1979) *Discipline and Punish: the birth of the prison*, trans. A. Sheridan. New York: Vintage Books.

Foucault, M. (1984) *The History of Sexuality, Volume 1: an introduction*. Harmondsworth, Middlesex: Peregrine, Penguin Books.

Foucault, M. (1978–79) *The Birth of Biopolitics: lectures at the College de France, 1978–1979*. Hampshire: Palgrave Macmillan.

Foucault, M. (1980) Prison Talk. In C. Gordon (ed.) *Power/knowledge: Selected Interviews and Other Writings 1972–1977*. Harlow: Harvester.

Foucault, M. (1997) The birth of politics. In Rabinow, P. (ed.) *Ethics, Subjectivity and Truth: the essential works of Foucault*, vol. 1. London: Penguin Books.

Ha, A., Macdonald, D. and Pang, B. (2010) Parental perspectives on physical activity in the lives of Hong Kong Chinese children: the interplay of Confucianism and postcolonialism. *Sport Education and Society*, 15 (3): 331–346.

Harwood, V. (2009) Theorizing Biopedagogies. In Wright, J. and Harwood, V. (eds) *Biopolitics and the 'Obesity Epidemic': governing bodies*. London and New York: Routledge.

Hemphill, D. and Symons, C. (2009) Sexuality matters in physical education and sport studies. *Quest*, 61 (4): 397–417.

Jose, J. (1998) *Biopolitics of the Subject: an introduction to the ideas of Michel Foucault*. Australia: NTU Press.

Lee, J. (2010) Australian young men's meanings of physical activity and health: An exploration of social class and schooling. In Kehler, M. and Atkinson, M. (eds) *Boys Bodies: speaking the unspoken*. New York: Peter Lang.

Lovell, T. (1991) Sport, racism and young women. In Jarvie, G. (ed.) *Sport, Racism and Ethnicity*. Basingstoke: Falmer Press.

Macdonald, D. and Wright, J. (2010) Young people, physical activity and the everyday: the life activity project. In Wright, J. and Macdonald, D. (eds) *Young People, Physical Activity and the Everyday*. London: Routledge.

Macdonald, D., Rodger, S. and Abbott, R. *et al.* (2005) I could do with a pair of wings: Perspectives on physical activity, bodies and health from young Australian children. *Sport Education and Society*, 10 (2): 195–209.

Markula, P. and Pringle, R. (2006) *Foucault, Sport and Exercise: power, knowledge and trans-forming the self*. Abingdon: Routledge.

Millington, B., Vertinsky, P. and Boyle, E. *et al.* (2008) Making Chinese-Canadian masculinities in Vancouver's physical education curriculum. *Sport, Education and Society*, 13 (2): 195–214.

Mills, S. (1997) *Discourse*. London: Routledge.

Mills, S. (2004) *Discourse: The New Critical Idiom*. 2nd edn. London: Routledge.

Nelson, A. (2009) Sport, physical activity and urban Indigenous young people. *Journal of Australian Aboriginal Studies*, 2009/2: 101–111.

Paras, E. (2006) *Foucault 2.0 Beyond Power and Knowledge*. New York: Other Press.

Partnerships for Schools (2009) PE and School Sport in BSF. Online: www. partnershipsforschools.org.uk/documents/BSF_PE_Sport_Factsheet_102009.pdf (accessed 8 August 2010).

Rabinow, P. and Rose, N. (2006) Biopower today. *BioSocieties*, 1: 195–217.

Sport England (2005) *Spatial planning for sport: the policy context*. Online: www. sportengland.org/search.aspx?query=spatial+planning+for+sport%3a+the+policy+cont ext (accessed 7 August 2010).

Swanson, L. (2009) Soccer fields of cultural [re]production: Creating 'good boys' in suburban America. *Sociology of Sport Journal*, 26 (3): 404–424.

Taylor, T. and Doherty, A. (2005) Adolescent sport, recreation and physical education: experiences of recent arrivals to Canada. *Sport, Education and Society*, 10 (2): 211–238.

Wellard, I. (2006) Able bodies and sport participation: social constructions of physical ability for gendered and sexually identified bodies. *Sport, Education and Society*, 11 (2): 105–119.

2 Understanding social exclusion and sport for children

Mike Collins

Introduction: the concepts of social exclusion and child poverty

Social exclusion is a term that only entered the policy vocabulary in the mid-1970s, but was soon adopted by the European Commission and then many governments, most notably of the UK. Poverty is said to be a state, but exclusion is a process. EU researcher Commins (1993) described poverty as lack of access to four basic social systems: democracy, welfare, the labour market, and family and community. People do move in and out of poverty (see below), but I see poverty as the core of exclusion (first in Collins et .al, 1999; then in Collins, 2003). Poor people lack money and material resources – most have low self-confidence and lack power, they often have poor health, live in high-crime, low-cohesion environments with high unemployment and have poor transport, leisure and other facilities. All these factors are described in the UK government's seminal policy paper *Bringing Britain Together* (Social Exclusion Unit, 1998). Other factors have exclusionary potential in their own right, but really bite when they are combined with poverty. These are explored by other authors in this book.

If exclusion is a process, the question then is: who is doing the excluding? Well, sometimes exclusion results from wider issues in society and community, sometimes it is caused by people in positions of power, and sometimes it is down to citizens themselves. In reviewing the literature on the processes of exclusion for the UK government, I identified the following factors:

1 Four structural factors in the external environment which require over-arching policies.
2 Two mediating factors; for example, the attitudes of managers/gatekeepers of leisure resources and labelling by society, which is particularly likely to happen to youth, especially if they are viewed as lazy, troublesome or deviant.
3 Six personal factors that are often subjective and require person-centred policies.

I looked at the strength of impacts of the various factors on eight groups, three of which are children, youth in general and young delinquents (see Table 2.1). The strength of each factor is shown by the number of crosses.

Table 2.1 Multiple constraints and exclusion in children's sport and leisure

Group excluded	Youth		
Constraint/exclusion factor	Children	Young people	Young delinquents
Structural factors			
Poor physical/social environment	+	+	++
Poor facilities/community capacity	+	+	++
Poor support network	+	+	++
Poor transport	++	++	++
Mediating factors			
Managers' policies attitudes	+	+	++
Labelling by society	+	++	+++
Lack of time structure	+	+	++
Lack of income	+	+	++
Lack of skills/personal social capital	+	+	+++
Fears of safety	++	++	++
Powerlessness	++	++	+++
Poor self/body image	+	+	++

Source: Collins, 2003, Table 3.1

In this short chapter, focusing on the UK, section two outlines recent government policy on social exclusion affecting children, section three covers its implications for their sport and leisure, and section four looks at ideas from other countries and the latest UK data.

Social exclusion is complex, and the previous New Labour government in the UK decided to dedicate a unit in the Cabinet Office to it to ensure cross-departmental action. They continued to monitor progress annually, as did many external observers. The reason for the political urgency of Tony Blair's New Labour government was that under Mrs Thatcher's three conservative governments, the proportion of poor people had quadrupled to 24 per cent of adults, 46 per cent of single parents, and 30 per cent of children by the early 1990s. It is important to remember that even in an advanced economy, poor people generally have larger families than the more affluent, including immigrants until they get to the second or third generations. Poverty was, therefore, a major structural issue, which Minister Peter Mandelson described as 'a scourge and waste' and 'the greatest social crisis of our times' (Mandelson, 1997, pp. 6, 9). The core measure of poverty was income and across the European Union (EU) the threshold for poverty was set at 60 per cent of contemporary median income taking into account housing costs. The main strategies in UK policy, as in the EU itself, were to get people into work, provide better welfare benefits especially for families, and to improve access to and standards of education.

Of course, the great bulk of research and policy reports focus on the poor people below the EU threshold, but in a neglected study, Barry (2002, p. 17) suggested there is an upper threshold for the affluent that is more difficult to define 'the lower divides those who habitually participate in the mainstream institutions from those who are outside them . . . the upper is the one that divides those in the middle from those who can detach themselves'. These latter are the people who, in sport, can afford to choose private sports and fitness clubs and specialist holidays for themselves and their children, in order to obtain privacy and avoid crowding, and to get specialist personal coaching and attention. As a result of the policies described later in this chapter, this group has been growing and indeed they are the most active and the highest spending; yet little is known about them because they and their suppliers are coy about spending and especially profit, and virtually all research is proprietary (i.e. owned by commissioning organisations which often consider it commercially sensitive).

For adults, it is clear that poverty is compounded by age, gender, ethnicity and/ or disability, and this is still most clearly shown in Sport England's equality index (see Table 2.2). There is a problem, however, in that because British respondents are wary of giving details of their income in surveys, we have to use social class as a slightly loose surrogate for adults. For children, however, the main annual surveys of PE and sport participation in school do not ask about parents' jobs or income (indeed many children do not know this), so we have to use data from smaller studies. The new DCMS (2007) *Taking Part* survey of children showed that during the four weeks prior to the survey, 93 per cent of children had under-taken some sport out of school. Most claimed they had participated for an hour, on average, on three days a week although there was no measure of levels of exertion. (See later section on scepticism about self-report data.)

Poverty, exclusion and children in the UK under New Labour

The information in this section has to be viewed against twenty-five years of mainly rightward moving politics in most advanced economies in the twenty-two nation-strong Organisation for Economic Cooperation and Development, and of growing social inequality in these nations. In a lecture to commemorate Beveridge, the founder of Britain's welfare state, former prime minister Tony Blair (1999, p. 17) made a now famous pledge: 'Our historic aim will be for ours to be the first generation to end child poverty. It is a 20-year mission, but I believe it can be done.' The mission was soon spelled out in concrete targets: to reduce child poverty by a quarter by 2004–05, and by half by 2010. This was the marker,

Table 2.2 Sport England's Equality index, 2002

Each group indexed against males without a disability, the highest participant rate (60.3% participation=100)

All DE male	75		
DE without disability	65	DE 16–19	84
White majority, all ages	56	DE 25–29	64
DE ethnic minority	46	DE 30–44	50
DE female	45	DE 45–59	30
DE adult with disability	35	DE 60–69	24

Note: social classes D and E are semi and unskilled workers.

above all, by which the success of Tony Blair's social policy would be judged by researchers, press and public.

By the time of Blair's pledge, poverty had become more complex, affecting more groups than in the 1970s when it had been overwhelmingly a problem of the old and the sick. By the 1990s, poverty also included the unemployed (with the decline of the sunset industries) and large numbers with only low pay. This latter group included new groups with no or few qualifications; that is, 75 per cent of disabled people, over 56 per cent of Black and Ethnic Minorities (BEM), people in service and in low skill manual jobs. Many low paid people on the fringes of the labour market rotated in and out of work and welfare payment entitlements, making the welfare system cumbersome and costly. Data showed that the issue was ubiquitous, with even affluent areas including poor minorities and some areas of public or private rented housing having high concentrations of poverty and exclusion. Hence the policy paper *Bringing Britain Together* (Social Exclusion Unit, 1998) started by focusing on the 333 most needy urban estates. Area-based policies were introduced; for example, New Deal for Communities, and Action Zones for education, health, transport – even briefly for sport (e.g. Sport England, 2008). Yet poverty and exclusion were as prevalent in rural areas as urban areas, but they were less obvious because they were geographically scattered. Consequently rural poverty was more difficult to combat because it involved smaller numbers of people and often greater unit costs (e.g. Slee *et al.*, 2001).

Since 1979 child poverty rose dramatically because:

- 20 per cent lived in workless households (cf. 8 per cent of adults);
- 22 per cent lived with single parents (cf. 10 per cent);
- Feinstein (1998) had already shown that social class affected educational development, even before age 4.

New Labour's policy to address child poverty had two streams, to (i) eradicate income poverty and (ii) improve related public services (education, health and childcare). The plans for each term of government were as follows.

Term 1 1997–2001

- Childcare tax credit (70 per cent of costs) relieving parents of some income tax and improving provision in deprived wards.
- Increased income via Working Families' Tax Credit and Children's Tax Credit.
- Child Trust Funds provided at birth and Universal Child Benefit payments.
- Surestart outreach programmes for under 5s in most deprived wards, including play provision, health advice/special needs.

Term 2 2001–05

- Preventive services including specialist Children's Centres.
- Child Tax Credit, Working Tax Credit replaced WFTC and CTC, and removed

earlier barriers (together these increased benefits by 60 per cent in real terms, £11bn, plus £3bn on early years education and childcare).

Term 3 2005–07

- 2006 Childcare Act projected provision of 3,500 Children's Centres by 2010, and Extended School programmes of care and community use before and after teaching hours.
- 2007 Welfare Reform Act extended Child Benefit to women in their third trimester, but produced extra conditions before lone parents could benefit.

Term 4 2007+ under a new prime minister, Gordon Brown

- Increased CT Credit.
- More delivery via local authorities, Housing and Council Tax benefits (delivering £0.9bn, although Hirsch (2006) and others thought £4bn was needed) and reduced support for Children's Centres.

Before taking over from Tony Blair, Gordon Brown had been chancellor of the exchequer since 1997 and so central to the child poverty reduction policies, describing the issue as 'a scar on the soul of Britain' (*Guardian*, 17 March 2000). Moreover, ethnic minority children formed 25 per cent of those in poverty, although they only make up 15 per cent of the child population (Platt, 2009). Between 1998–99 and 2006–07, the number of poor children indeed was reduced by 400,000, or 8 per cent, but this is still a long way from the 25 per cent target set for 2010. However, the rise in median incomes affected by large increases for the top 10 per cent resulted in shifting the poverty benchmark and so fewer additional children benefitted after 2005. Children of lone parents gained most during this period, but the risk of poverty in workless households remained at 77 per cent (Stewart, 2009a). Increases in provision of childcare services oversupplied the poorer end of the market, and fewer BEM and poorer parents took advantage of them, finding them unaffordable. Nonetheless, Stewart's (2009a, p. 69) judgement was 'poor children are far better off . . . than they would be had policies been left unchanged from 1997. Perhaps it was unrealistic to expect the damage done during the 1980s to the life chances of today's parents could be undone in the same timeframe.'

Child poverty and its impact on sport and physical activity

Sport is not costless, and so those on low incomes are constrained in what they can provide, especially if they have several children. Those on the lowest incomes cannot afford holidays, take few day trips, and engage less in regular sports activities outside schools in clubs and leisure centres.

Supporting earlier studies, the latest school sport survey (Quick, 2009) reported on the number of schools that had reached the government's target for children to be engaged in three hours a week of physical education and school sport both in and outside the curriculum. The survey showed:

- fewer schools in deprived areas achieved the target of three hours in curricular and extra-curricular sport and PE;
- schools reaching three hours had fewer children receiving free school meals (the educational measure of poverty);
- fewer schools with higher proportions of BEM children achieved three hours;
- fewer schools with higher proportions of children with Special Educational Needs (SEN) achieved three hours.

The results of this survey seem to confirm that structural social inequity is reflected in levels of sports participation. This finding was also illustrated in Collins and Buller's (2000, 2003) surveys in Nottinghamshire, England. They were able to relate participation to poverty in three levels of courses aimed at improving participation and performance. These very cheap eight-week training courses ranged from basic (Go for Gold), intermediate/improver (Champion Coaching) and linking to the club coaching system (Performance Resources). Referral could be by teacher, coach, parent or the children themselves. Table 2.3 shows a consistent, strong social gradient over these three levels, over the whole county, and over several years, reflecting the same patterns found by Quick's 2009 survey using similar Champion Coaching data in NW England. Bell (2010) found similar patterns of inequity of take up.

In terms of wider and longer-term benefits of sport, some researchers argue that participation helps enhance children's educational performance. For example, it has been argued that increasing physical fitness and ability can aid concentration, improve confidence and self-esteem and produce better relations with classmates and teachers (e.g. Sibley and Etnier, 2003; Spence *et al.*, 2005). Reviewing the data, Coalter (2007) would go no farther than saying that sport participation appears to do no harm. The UK government set up specialist colleges for science, arts and sport – 400 of the latter, with some extra finance. The academic results for sports colleges (and to a smaller degree other specialist colleges) suggested they had an above average improvement in exam results, although it is not clear whether this is as a result of enhanced sport provision or as a consequence of

Table 2.3 Start early, but even low cost is not enough! Young residents and participants in areas of social need in Nottinghamshire

Level of deprivation	% in Go for Gold	% in Champion Coaching	% in Performance Resources	% Notts population
Below average	92	87	91	71
Moderate	5	4	4	11
Serious	2	7	**4**	**10**
Extreme	1	2	**0.3**	7
Base	951 in 4 sports	751 in 9 sports 1994–98	315 in 3 sports 1995–99	994,000

Sources: Collins and Buller 2000, 2003

some extra focused teaching, coaching, and minor facility improvements (Houlihan and Wong, 2005). One interesting programme is *Playing for Success*, where under-performing children were put into apparently glamorous, professional soccer, cricket or rugby club settings, and offered incentives alongside classes in literacy, numeracy and IT skills (though not generally the opportunity to meet the professional sports stars). Dramatic short-term improvements in these skills were evidenced, greater than being achieved in conventional school settings (Sharpe *et al.*, 1999). Improvements were also apparent in small-scale programmes for youth at risk of committing crime (Nichols, 2007). These results imply that developing good relations with credible mentors who have skills and time is a vital issue. DCLG *et al.* (2008) suggested that some communities, with close internal ties and a lack of wider ones, a sense of isolation and a history of economic decline, produced children with lower aspirations for life, including leisure.

In a systematic review of twenty-six studies worldwide, Dobbins *et al.* (2009) showed that physical activity in school *did*:

- increase time spent in PE (confirmed in English schools by Quick, 2009);
- increase oxygen uptake and cardiovascular capacity;
- reduce blood cholesterol;
- have some effect on lifestyles.

But it *did not*:

- reduce heart rate or Body Mass Index;
- reduce time spent watching TV, except in the short term for primary pupils;
- increase time spent on PE outside school.

The continuing rise in children's obesity levels has generated something of a moral panic. It has been claimed that one-third of all children are now either obese or overweight without intervention, this could rise to two-thirds by 2050 (Butland *et al.*, 2007). Clearly this trend has implications for a whole range of health, clear social and financial outcomes. However, Dollman *et al.* (2005) stated that, unlike for adults, research cannot attribute among children how far this rise in obesity is due to claimed reductions in physical activity levels and how far to excesses in diet. So whereas the overwhelming majority of children still appear to enjoy sport, the authors speak of 'activity toxic environments' outside the school gates that restrict opportunities, especially for disadvantaged children. It is for this reason that HM government has embarked on a cross-departmental strategy (CGOU, 2008) involving sport, medical, planning transport and environmental services.

Green *et al.* (2005) suggested there is 'new condition of youth', whereby youth is a longer life stage than previously. Whereas increases in the range of leisure activities available and broader PE curriculum provide a basis for wider choices, participation is still structured by class. The main difference is not between *whether* or not young people play sport, but *how often*. On this measure there are enduring differences by gender, ethnicity and disability (see also Platt, 2009).

Parental involvement in sport tends to be associated with socio-economic status, and both degree of encouragement and role modelling, and how such encouragement and modelling are received by youth is important (Welk *et al.*, 2004). Scheerder *et al.*'s (2005) longitudinal study from 1969 to 1999 for 13 to 18 year olds in Belgium confirmed this relationship. Shropshire and Carroll (1997) found that fathers' involvement in sport was an influence on a sample of 10 to 11 year olds, but not that of the mothers. More fundamentally, Basterfield *et al.* (2008) argued that the Health Survey for England (HSE) self-report questions greatly over-estimated the actual volume of health-conferring moderate or vigorous daily physical activity (MVPA). Where accelerometers were used for a week with 6 to 7 year olds, it was found that, on average, they did only 46 minutes of MVPA compared to 146 minutes as claimed in the HSE questionnaires. This is a concern because it is the latter data that are used as the basis for policy effectiveness (see also Dobbins *et al.*, 2009).

If class and income are important influences, the price of leisure services is also pertinent. UK leisure centre prices were low until the 1980s (and still are relative to some EU countries). In 1989, however, the Audit Commission (1989) argued that the non-user local taxpayers should bear a smaller proportion of costs and users should bear a greater share. Since then prices have generally risen ahead of inflation under pressure from overall local authority budget-making, and leisure services do not have legislative protection as an essential local service. In practice, children get a relatively small share of space in leisure centres, except in swimming pools. Most local authorities offer leisure cards, giving discounted access to a package of leisure services, especially for people on welfare benefits and their children and senior citizens, though often they can only claim these at off-peak times (Collins, 2003).

In 2009, the then minister for sport introduced a new policy of free swimming for over-60s and under-16s to promote participation. There was a surge of use by both groups (Bolton, 2010, pp. 242–255). Recent government monitoring (PWC, 2010) made it clear that the schemes attracted more new swimmers amongst children (50 per cent) but only 21 per cent amongst over-60s, among whom most were 'free riders', getting swims for nothing which they previously paid for. The government cancelled the programme after a year as poor value for money. An associated problem is that transport to leisure facilities can be as or more expensive than entry fees, and transport timetables can limit access. Offering gym membership for free is a joint policy in the midlands of England, Birmingham City Council and the National Health Service (NHS) locally. The aim is to provide fitness facilities to the whole of the city's 1.1m population and the initial success of the scheme in one deprived area among poor and BEM populations lead to its extension citywide, and many others are watching its progress. One possible explanation for the wide take-up could be that the gym/fitness facilities had more spare capacity than the leisure centres and pools. However, the former government's ambition to make all public sports facilities free by 2013 seems an unattainable aim. Apart from economic barriers, there are too few facilities to meet targets for increasing participation, *let alone* extend it. At the time of writing, the current Minister for Sport Hugh Robertson has admitted that, as permissive rather than mandatory local services, culture sport and libraries are likely to 'take a huge hit' in budget cuts, which are sure to have a regressive effect on poor households.

Bailey (2008) stressed that for sport and PE to have a positive effect on social exclusion, several important conditions were necessary: adequate accessibility, credible leadership, involving youth in decisions about the programmes, emphasising social relations and focusing on specific learning processes and outcomes. In order to achieve this, joined-up policies across many central departments and local authorities and agencies would be needed (see also Shaw *et al.*, 2001) and this is notoriously difficult to deliver.

International comparisons and latest UK data

How does the UK compare to other places, especially Europe? In 1997 the UK had compared badly with the other OECD countries on poverty and inequality. In 2008, UNICEF, the United Nations Children's Fund, placed the UK below all other countries on measures of material well-being, education, family and peer relationships, risk-taking behaviour and subjective well-being, and ranked it the middle only for health and safety. To be fair, much of the data came from 2001–02 and so missed some improvements that had been made in the intervening period, but this was a public relations blow to New Labour after the policy efforts listed in section two. Stewart (2009b) concluded that UK would have risen several places in any UNICEF survey based on later data because of better participation in 15–19 education, improved literacy/numeracy, health behaviour and subjective well-being. However, income inequality has worsened, and so has the proportion of children in poverty. Stewart (2009b) argued that there are a number of reasons for this: childcare costs are still relatively high and of poor quality by EU standards, higher incomes lead to pressure on house prices, and the problems of low income remain due to a very low National Minimum Wage.

The Spirit Level (Wilkinson and Pickett, 2009, p. 23) compared inequality and a host of social indicators for twenty-two advanced economies. It showed that with reference to the UNICEF index, child well-being achieved higher scores the more equal states (Figure 2.1). It can be seen that the UK was ranked the fourth most unequal. These authors also showed that the UK did relatively badly in child obesity/overweight, maths and literacy scores at age 15, teenage pregnancies and birth rates, conflict between children, and social mobility (Wilkinson and Pickett, 2009, pp. 93–4, 106, 123–4, 139, 161). This lack of social mobility in Britain was confirmed by the Organisation for Economic Cooperation and Development (2010, p. 195), with a more persistent intergenerational wage gap between those whose fathers had tertiary education and those who had poor secondary education than any other European country other than Italy and Portugal.

Harriet Harman, the then minister for women and equality, commissioned the most searching analysis of inequality entitled *The Anatomy of Economic Inequality in the UK*. In her foreword she states:

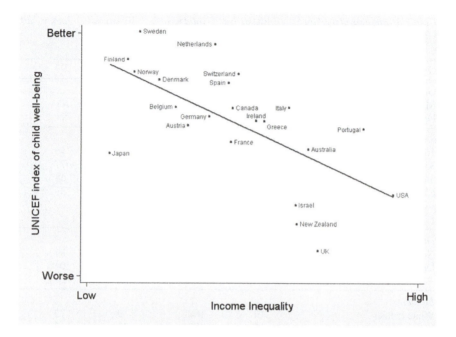

Figure 2.1 Child well-being and income inequality (reproduced with permission, the equalitytrust.org.uk)

We know that disadvantage can come from your gender or ethnicity; your sexual orientation or your disability; your age or your religion or belief or any combination of these. But overarching and interwoven with this is the persistent inequality of social class – your family background and where you were born . . . This report . . . shows clearly how inequality is cumulative over an individual's lifetime and is carried from one generation to the next.

But [it] also shows that public policy intervention works. It has played a major role in halting the rise in inequality which was gaining ground in the 1980s. Public policy has narrowed gaps in educational attainment, narrowed the gap between men and women's pay and tackled poverty in retirement.

The . . . Panel Report shows the key stages in people's lives where public policy intervention is most important and most effective – during the pre-school years, at the transition from education to the workplace and re-entering the labour market after having children.

(Hills *et al.*, 2010, p. iii)

Table 2.4 displays selected findings from this report, focusing on the disparities in personal incomes and the even greater ones in wealth, and on the differences between the top and bottom tenths of the population (the 90:10 ratio where this can

Table 2.4 Differences in wealth between and within groups

Cols 2, 3 % of overall median Cols 4, 5 90:10 ratio	Weekly net individual incomes	Total wealth	Weekly net individual incomes	Total wealth
Overall median/all	£223	£205	4.2	97
Gender				
Male	126	Na	4.3	Na
Female	81	Na	4.2	Na
Selected ages				
16	43	6	—	46
35	131	86	9.7	77
50	118	14	12.2	68
65	79	1	5.9	37
		15		
		0		
Disability				
Not disabled	112	10	10.6	84
DDA&WLD	65	3	7.2	104
		97		
Ethnicity				
White British	101	108	9.2	72
Indian	97	99	32	57
Pakistani	59	47	*	N/a
Bangladeshi	56	7	159	N/a
Black Caribbean	97	37	4.0	183
Black African	98	10	4.1	N/a
Chinese	92	32	6.4	N/a
Selected occupational classes				
Higher managerial/professional	242	220	4.1	25
Routine	101	36	3.2	92
Housing tenure				
Social housing	69	9	2.6–2.7	42
Private rented	93	12	3.7–5.0	86
Owned outright	90	201	4.6	7
Owned via mortgage	134	132	3.8	12
Area Deprivation (England)				
Most deprived tenth	76	16	3.3	104
Least deprived tenth	129	253	4.5	19

Source: Hills *et al.*, 2010, tables S4, S5

Note: * ratios cannot compute because 10 percentile is zero.

be calculated). So, for example, compared with the median household income of £393 a week in 2008 (giving an EU poverty benchmark at 60 per cent of £236), the bottom tenth received £191 and the top £804. The gap between these two groups widened from three times in the 1960s and 1970s to four times in the 1990s.

Median wealth was £205,000 (personal possessions, housing financial assets and private pensions), but the poorest tenth had only £8,800 while the top boasted £853,000. The report found that some of the gaps between men and women and ethnic groups are closing, but black and Pakistani children did less well at school, went to less prestigious universities, and obtained lower class degrees, while their adult counterparts had a 'pay penalty' in the labour market. The table shows the gaps associated with disability, with living in social housing, and especially in neighbourhood differences; and this affected children. In Scotland, for example, the 90:10 difference in educational performance at 16 was equivalent to crossing half the overall range.

The Panel stressed two matters

1   The impact of social class thus: 'rather than being fixed at birth . . . from age 3 to age 14, differences in assessment related to family income, father's occupation and mother's education widen at each stage' (Hills *et al.*, 2010, p. 22).
2   Economic disadvantage is reinforced across the life cycle: 'The evidence shows the long arm of people's origins in shaping their life chances, literally from cradle to grave. Differences in wealth in particular are associated with opportunities to buy houses in the catchments of the best schools, or to afford private education with advantages for children that continue through and beyond education' (2010, p. 31).

From the point of view of children, the report points to the need for policy action on early years, performance of low income pupils, provision for special educational needs and Travellers' (Roma/Romany) children, and the inequalities between neighbourhoods. Early results from Millennium Cohort study (of children born in 2000) showed that children whose parents read to them and played with them were more likely to flourish in primary school in all respects; and the social gradient of parents reproduced itself (R. Williams, *Guardian* 17 Feb 2010, p. 10). For these reasons, Kirk (2005) argued that educational resources should be focused on Key Stage 2 pupils (9 to 11 year olds).

For those in the bottom 20 per cent in tables of income, wealth and poverty, all of these data blunt government claims that 'sport can make a unique contribution to tackling social exclusion in our society' (DCMS, 2000, p. 39). Moreover, it has not been a priority for local authorities to invest in staff or new facilities except in schools or as part of Olympics planning. This has been the case for the last four UK governments, despite much rhetoric to the contrary such as: 'now [there is] a shift from sport for good to sport for sport's sake . . . LAs drive local provision and are the key partner, particularly for Sport England' (DCMS, 2008, p. 19).

Conclusion

For the Western world, the challenges of narrowing the poverty gaps are huge in mixed but laissez-faire economies that reward success and have only moderate

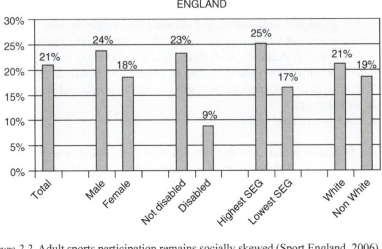

Figure 2.2 Adult sports participation remains socially skewed (Sport England, 2006)

redistribution through taxes, like the UK. Added to this are the problems to be faced in countering the health and social costs in adulthood of youth obesity in cultures of a sedentary majority. In the UK, which has relatively low social mobility, these challenges are even greater. Hills *et al.* (2010, p. 2) began their summary report on inequality by saying 'Britain is an unequal country, more so than many industrialised countries and more than it was a generation ago.' In this situation, the disparity of resources within and between groups highlighted in Table 2.4 must be reflected in opportunities for participation in a leisure activity such as sport, and while the curriculum differences are small, once more choice comes in at Key Stage 4 (age 14), the gaps, partly by choice, partly as a result of resource shortage, show up (Quick, 2009). Laudable as current PE and sport policies are, and substantial though the benefits of PE and sport are (Bailey, 2006), the sector can flourish only if wider social policies are stronger. Given the scale of challenge to reduce material inequality and its consequences in mainstream social policy, and the continuing fight to reduce expenditure and public debt, it is unlikely that inequality in sport as a non-mandatory field will reduce, as Active People data for 2006–08 showed for community participation (Figure 2.2), and the English Sports Council (1998) for elite players. With poor families generally having poorer diets and larger obesity issues, this remains a major education, health and social challenge.

References

Audit Commission (1989) *Sport for Whom? Clarifying the local authority role in sport and recreation.* London: HMSO.

Bailey, R. (2006) PE and sport in schools: a review of benefits and outcomes. *Journal of School Health*, 76 (8): 397–401.

Bailey, R. (2008) Youth sport and social inclusion. In Holt, N.L. (ed.) *Positive Youth Development Through Sport*. London: Routledge, pp. 89–96.

Barry, B. (2002) Social exclusion, social isolation and the distribution of income. In Hills, J., Le Grand, J. and Piachaud, D. (eds) *Understanding Social Exclusion*. Oxford: Oxford University Press, pp. 13–22.

Basterfield, L., Adamson, A. and Parkinson, K. *et al.* (2008) Surveillance of physical activity in the UK is flawed: validation of the Health Survey for England physical activity questionnaire. *Archives of Disease in Childhood*, 93 (12): 1054–1058.

Bell, B. (2010) Building a legacy for youth and coaching: champion coaching on Merseyside. In Collins, M. (ed.) *Examining Sports Development*. London: Routledge, pp. 139–166.

Blair, A. (1999) Beveridge revisited: a welfare state for the 21st century. In Walker, R. (ed.) *Ending Child Poverty: popular welfare for the 21ˢᵗ century*. Bristol: Policy Press.

Bolton, N. (2010) Promoting participation and inclusion? The free swimming initiative in Wales. In Collins, M. (ed.) *Examining Sports Development*. London: Routledge.

Butland, B., Jebb, S. and Kopelman, P. *et al.* (2007) *Foresight – Tackling Obesities: future choices*. London: Department of Innovation, Universities and Skills.

Coalter, F. (2007) *A Wider Social Role for Sport. Who's keeping the score?* London: Routledge.

Collins, M. (2003) *Sport and Social Exclusion*. London: Routledge.

Collins, M. (ed.) (2010) *Examining Sports Development*. London: Routledge.

Collins, M. and Buller, J. (2000) Bridging the post-school institutional gap: Champion Coaching in Nottinghamshire. *Managing Leisure*, 5 (4): 200–221.

Collins, M. and Buller, J. (2003) Social exclusion from high performance sport: are all talented young people being given an equal opportunity of reaching the Olympic podium? *Journal of Sport and Social Issues*, 24 (4): 420–442.

Collins, M., Henry, I. and Houlihan, B. *et al.* (1999) *Sport and Social Exclusion*. London: DCMS.

Commins, P. (1993) *Combating Social Exclusion in IRELAND 1990–94: a midway report*. Brussels: European Commission.

Cross Government Obesity Unit (2008) *Healthy Weight, Healthy Lives: a cross government strategy for England*. London: Central Office for Information.

Department of Communities and Local Government and Department for Children Schools and Families, and Cabinet Office (2008) *Aspirations and Attainment Amongst Young People in Deprived Communities*. London: CO.

Department of Culture Media and Sport (2000) *A Sporting Future for All*. London: DCMS.

Department of Culture Media and Sport (2007) *Taking Part: Headline findings from the child survey*. London: DCMS.

Department of Culture Media and Sport (2008) *Playing to Win: a new era for sport*. London: DCMS.

Dobbins, M., DeCorby, K. and Robeson, P. *et al.* (2009) School-based physical activity programs for promoting physical activity and fitness in children and adolescents aged 6–18. *Cochrane database of systematic reviews*, 1: DOI: 10.1002/14651858.CD007651.

Dollman, J., Norton, K. and Norton, L. (2005) Evidence for secular trends in children's activity behaviour. *British Journal of Sports Medicine*, 39: 892–897.

English Sports Council (1998) *The Development of Sporting Talent*. London: ESC.

Feinstein, L. (1998) *Pre-school Educational Inequality? British children in the 1970 cohort*, No 404. London: Centre for Economic Performance, London School of Economics and Political Science.

Green, K., Smith, A. and Roberts, K. (2005) Young people and lifelong participation in sport and physical activity: A sociological perspective on contemporary PE programmes in England and Wales. *Leisure Studies*, 24 (1): 27–43.

Hills, J., Brewer, M. and Jenkins, S. *et al.* (2010) *An Anatomy of Economic Inequality in the UK: Report of the national Equality Panel.* London: London Government Equalities Office/Centre for Analysis of Social Exclusion.

Houlihan, B. and Wong, C. (2005) *Report on 2004 Survey of Specialist Sports Colleges.* Loughborough: Institute of Youth Sport.

Kirk, D. (2005) PE, Youth sport and lifelong participation: the importance of early learning experiences. *European Physical Education Review*, 11 (3): 239–255.

Mandelson, P. (1997) *Labour's Next Steps: Tackling social exclusion.* London: The Fabian Society.

Nichols, G. (2007) *Sport and Crime Reduction: The role of sports in tackling youth crime.* London: Routledge.

Organisation for Economic Cooperation and Development (2010) A family affair: Inter-generational social mobility between OECD countries. In OECD, *Going for Growth.* Paris: OECD.

Platt, L. (2009) *Ethnicity and Child Poverty.* London: HMSO.

Price Waterhouse Coopers (2010) *Evaluation of the Free Swimming Programme.* London: Department of Media Culture and Sport.

Quick, S. (2009) *PE and School Sport Survey 2008–9.* London: TNS-BMRB for Department of Children Schools and Families.

Scheerder, J., Taks, M. and Vanreusal, B. (2005) Social changes in youth sports participation styles 1969–1999: The case of Flanders. *Sport Education and Society*, 10 (2): 321–341.

Sharpe, C. (1999*) Playing for Success: National Evaluation.* Slough: National Foundation for Educational Research.

Shaw, M., Dorling, D. and Gordon, D. *et al.* (2001) Putting time, person and place together: the temporal, social and spatial accumulation of health inequalities. *Critical Public Health*, 11 (4): 298–304.

Shropshire, J. and Carroll, B. (1997) Family variables and physical activity: Influence of parental exercise and socio-economic status. *Sport Education and Society*, 2 (1): 95–116.

Sibley, B. and Etnier, J. (2003) The relationship between physical activity and cognition in children: A meta-analysis. *Pediatric Exercise Science*, 15: 243–256.

Slee, W., Curry, N. and Joseph, D. (2001) *Removing Barriers, Creating Opportunities: Social exclusion in countryside leisure in the UK.* Cardiff: Countryside Recreation Network.

Social Exclusion Unit (1998) *Bringing Britain Together*. London: Cabinet Office.

Spence, J., McGannon, K. and Poon, P. (2005) The effect of exercise on global self esteem: A quantitative review. *Journal of Sport and Exercise Psychology*, 27 (3): 311–334.

Sport England (2002) *Sports Equity Index*. Online: *www.sportengland.org*.

Sport England (2006) *Active People Survey 2*. Online: *www.sportengland.org*.

Sport England (2008) 3D: *Driving Change, Developing Partnerships, Delivering Outcomes*. Online: www.sportengland.org (accessed 10 August 2008).

Stewart, K. (2009a) A scar on the soul of Britain: Child poverty and disadvantage under

New Labour. In Hills, J., Sefton, T. and Stewart, K. (eds) *Towards a More Equal Society? Poverty, inequality and policy since 1997*. Bristol: Policy Press/Joseph Rowntree Foundation, pp. 47–69.

Stewart, K. (2009b) Poverty, inequality and child wellbeing in international context: still bottom of the pack? In Hills, J., Sefton, T. and Stewart, K. (eds) *Towards a More Equal Society? Poverty, inequality and policy since 1997*. Bristol: Policy Press/Joseph Rowntree Foundation, pp. 267–290.

UNICEF (2008) *Child Poverty in Perspective: An overview of child well-being in rich countries*, Report Card 7, Florence: Innocenti Centre.

Welk, G., Babkes, M. and Schaben J. (2004) Parental influences on youth sport participation. In Coelho e Silva, M. and Malina, R. (eds) *Children and Youth in Organised Sports.* Coimbra: Coimbra University Press, pp. 95–122.

Wilkinson, R. and Pickett, K. (2009) *The Spirit Level: why more equal societies almost always do better*. London: Allen Lane/Penguin.

3 Sport and social exclusion

An economic perspective

Paul Downward and Simona Rasciute

Introduction

This chapter has three main objectives, which are reflected in its structure. The first is to briefly examine some definitions and concepts underpinning discussions of social exclusion and sport from non-economic, social scientific literature and which have been discussed elsewhere in this volume.[1] The second is to present the evidence from literature examining sports participation and its impacts, as well as some evidence from recent surveys on sports participation, to describe the current situation in the UK. The data will be used to draw comparisons between the 16 to 18-year-old age group, and older age groups.[2] The third objective is to interpret the social exclusion literature and this informal and non-inferential empirical analysis from an economic perspective.

Throughout this chapter, it will be argued that conventional approaches to economic analysis would interpret the empirical analysis of sporting participation differently from the social science literature and, in so doing, challenge the existence of 'social exclusion' and the effectiveness of policies to promote inclusion. Whilst policy ineffectiveness is also noted from the social science perspectives, the scepticism in economics lies at the core of the theoretical explanation of social interactions and social capital formation rather being based on the practical constraints facing policy, or limitations of the evidence base used to inform policy.

Social science, social exclusion and sport

Conceptual issues

This section very briefly reviews what is meant by social exclusion in sport drawing on ideas from the widely cited work of Collins and Kay (2003) and Coalter (2007). In a review of the origins of the concept of social exclusion, and its relevance for sport, Collins and Kay (2003) argue that discussions of social exclusion have their basis in a long-standing general social policy concern with poverty. Poverty is not confined to a particular *level* of material well-being, but is something that adjusts over time and can be understood in relation to changing socio-cultural norms. Understandings of poverty changed following the work of writers such as Townsend (1979, 1987), Lister (1990) and Scott (1994) who helped to shape a discourse around exclusion. Partially as a consequence of such work,

> The European Commission's Poverty III programme was concerned to integrate the 'least privileged' into society and, before its completion, the rhetoric had moved to a concept of 'social exclusion.'
>
> (Collins and Kay, 2003, p. 6)

Despite such arguments, Collins and Kay (2003) suggest that the common denominator of social exclusion is poverty. Indeed, they argue explicitly that it is low relative income that 'underpins the exclusion experienced by people' (p. 2). This perspective goes hand-in-hand, therefore, with a basic normative proposition that

> Sport for all who want it, is still a worthy and worthwhile objective for anyone who believes in a just society and equal opportunities of citizenship and . . . a feasible one.
>
> (Collins and Kay, 2003, p. 253)

This naturally begs the question of how exclusion comes into being.

The mechanisms by which social exclusion or inclusion operate can be understood as deriving from social interactions and, in particular, the reduction in or accrual of social capital respectively (see Chapters 6 and 12 in this volume). Coalter (2007), for example, charts how government thinking has tended to emphasise the ways in which policy mediums such as sport can promote the production of social capital, by promoting social inclusion through developing personal skills and enlarging individuals' social networks (as, for example, stressed in UK government documentation such as DCMS (1999), Scottish Office (1999) and DCMS/Strategy Unit (2002)).

But what exactly is social capital? There are, important conceptual variances in the literature on social capital, with the three main contributions stemming from Bourdieu (1997), Coleman (1994) and Putnam (2000). In the former case, social capital is linked to the building of durable networks of relationships for elites that work to their mutual advantage. In this regard, social capital is linked directly to the accumulation of economic and cultural capital; that is, the economic, knowledge and skill resources possessed by individuals. Coleman (1994) by contrast does not view social capital as something that helps to reproduce an elite but, rather, the family and community relationships and organisation that affect the ability of individuals (particularly the young) to develop their human capital. Resonating with Bourdieu's cultural capital, this is explained as the education, employment skills and expertise possessed by individuals. A methodological contrast between the two approaches drawn by Coalter (2007) is that the former focuses more on the processes by which inequalities are reproduced, whereas Coleman adopts a rational choice perspective in which individuals collude out of self-interest. As will be shown later, Coleman's approach resonates more strongly with the economic approach.

Finally, Putnam (2000) conceptualises social capital as the property of aggregate structures, such as communities, cities or regions; it is the networks that hold together these *aggregate* entities. An important feature of this approach is that it emphasises how trust, developed through social capital, helps to make communities and societies more efficient. It does this by reducing the need for formal forms of transaction, such as contracts or the formal exchange of ideas, information and resources, while at the same time enabling the collective pursuit of objectives. In this respect 'social capital is not just a public good, but is *for* the public good' (Coalter, 2007, p. 53). Clearly too, there are echoes of an economic approach to Putnam's work. Putnam also places more emphasis on organised social groups than the other theorists. An important feature of Putnam's (2000) analysis worth noting is that it distinguishes between bonding and bridging capital. The former promotes homogeneity between those of similar characteristics and familiarity. In contrast, bridging capital is weaker, and links heterogeneous groups and individuals.[3]

The effect of sport

It is possible to interpret the role of sport in the production of social capital according to each of the dimensions discussed above. Notably, sports clubs are often identified as a manifestation of social capital. Coalter (2007) argues that despite the relative lack of citation in the sports policy literature, Bourdieu's (1997) analysis is useful and can indicate how the membership of sports organisations and choice of sports can be linked to the development of class-based divisions in society. For example, membership of golf clubs helps to facilitate business networking and exchange, but this is not something that is available to all. Coleman's (1994) ideas, by contrast, are more applicable to the self-organisation of individuals into collectives which can help to build human and social capital. The origin and role of voluntary sports clubs can be seen to resonate with this view of social capital (see Downward *et al.*, 2009, and below). Further, Coalter (2007) hints that such a perspective is consistent with Putnam's (2000) analysis. This is because Putnam (2000) argues that a decline in social capital can be charted by the decline in organised US league bowling, and the growth of commercial recreational bowling and organisation. This reduces the regular and sustained meeting of diverse acquaintances.

Based on the above discussions Figure 3.1 attempts to synthesise the logic by which sport can be said to be related to social inclusion.

On the one hand, it is suggested that (lack of) participation in sport either independently, or via clubs and their related activities such as volunteering, can (reduce) raise both social and human capital and thus (reduce) increase social inclusion. On the other hand, social inclusion can condition the ability of individuals to participate in sport directly or via activities connected to sports clubs. Figure 3.1 therefore describes a process of feedback, which could be virtuous or vicious. Policy advocates would seek to intervene at some point in this 'causal chain' to promote a virtuous outcome. An important feature of the causal chain that is not best captured by the figure, however, is that there is an implicit shift in ontological

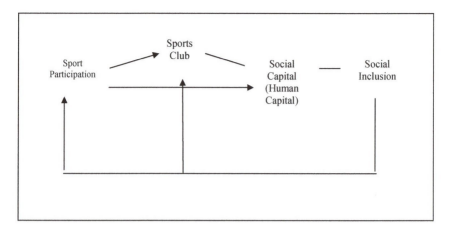

Figure 3.1 Sport and social inclusion

status working from left to right. Individual action as a participant or volunteer in sport has a transformative character, as sport can involve social interactions. It is these interactions that generate the social capital and social inclusion. Without the social interactions – for example, consuming sport as a private individual member of a fitness club – there would be no social inclusion as indicated by Putnam (2000). Coalter (2007, p. 20) provides a logic model to illustrate the point in which it is argued that 'individual, positive outcomes . . . via resultant changes in attitudes and behaviour . . . are assumed to lead to wider impacts.'

The scepticism implicit in this latter comment is actually manifest in Coalter's (2007) view of the policy claims that are made about the impact of sport on social inclusion. In other words, he questions the presumption that voluntary sports organisations can be good at promoting social capital and, by implication improving social inclusion. Further as Downward *et al.* (2009) argue, voluntary sports clubs tend to emerge in contexts of small-scale and heterogeneous interests in which markets and governments cannot meet the needs of citizens. Under such circumstances it seems reasonable to argue that sports club systems may be better at promoting bonding social capital and have limited impact on social inclusion through building bridging capital.[4] This is because the club system might emphasise and consolidate the sentiments of a particular cohort of society. In a sense this is a generalisation of Bourdieu's approach (1997) and perhaps underpins Sport England's historic interest in promoting multi-sport clubs (Horch, 1998).

Patterns and impact of sport participation

The discussion above suggests that theoretical predictions of the determinants and impacts of sport are somewhat ambiguous, and is suggestive of the need to examine the evidence on the patterns and impacts of sports participation.

The evidence base for components of the cycle of interaction presented in Figure 3.1 is varied. There is now a relatively recent but large literature examining the determinants of sports participation. Downward *et al*. (2009) and Downward and Rasciute (2010) provide summaries. Based upon large-scale datasets from a variety of international contexts, correlations motivated by a variety of theoretical perspectives have broadly established that:

- Males participate more in sport than females though, to an extent, this depends on the definition of sport. For example, there are exceptions to this finding for particular 'aesthetic' activities, some winter sports such as skiing, skating and horse riding and games that developed as female sports, such as netball.
- Increasing age, lower incomes and lower indications of socio-economic status, and education are associated with lower participation rates in sports.
- There is evidence that longer work hours and being of a non-white ethnicity are also associated with lower participation rates.
- The same is true of the lack of access to private vehicles and health being self-reported as lower.

It is findings such as these that can be used to support claims that social exclusion reduces sports participation from the perspectives discussed earlier. This evidence can be interpreted as representing the feedback from social inclusion to sports participation as indicated in Figure 3.1.

Interestingly drinking alcohol is typically associated with greater sports participation, but not smoking, which suggests a distinction between elements of health-related social lifestyle behaviours. Finally, a variety of household characteristics also appear to be associated with participation in sport. Being married or a couple with children in the household is associated with less participation unless other family members participate. This is suggestive of household externalities and could be viewed as evidence of social capital effects on sport.

Specific research on the impacts of sport on social capital is more scant but suggests that the impact may be weak or multifaceted.[5] Smaller-scale studies which suggest positive impacts of sport on social capital include Jarvie (2003, see also Chapter 4 in this volume) in Scotland, and Driscoll and Wood (1999) and Tonts (2005) in rural Australia. It is argued in the latter case that both bonding and bridging capital are created. Interestingly larger-scale studies qualify the impacts. For example, Seippel (2006) notes that whilst being a member of a voluntary sport organisation in Norway produces social capital, the effects are stronger if one also belongs to other voluntary organisations. This view is echoed by Delaney and Keaney (2005) who analysed the large-scale European Social Survey (2002), the Home Office Citizenship Survey (2001) and the Time Usage Survey (2000) and found small effects between sports club membership and some measures of social capital, but none between sports participation per se and social capital.

This suggests that it may be the *associational* character of individuals rather than sport which correlates with social capital measurements. In turn, this implies difficulties for simple policy rules which advocate using sports as an intervention as it undermines any sense of causality between the variables. Sports *association* could be an outcome of an associational disposition; that is, one in which social capital measures, such as trust, are simply a part rather than being resultant from activity. The same concerns might be levied at insights from the volunteering literature which tends to suggest that both personal and community development can occur through the act of volunteering (see Downward *et al*., 2005). Further, whilst Nichols (2003) argues that volunteering in sports clubs raises social capital, in part because of the longevity of volunteers, Warde *et al*. (2003) argues that the memberships are less stable than is often argued to be the case with only 32.1 per cent of individuals being a member of a sports club in any one year. Coalter (2007) thus provides a methodological critique of the evidence, suggesting that that there is a lack of strong cumulative evidence to support claims about the effects of sports participation on social inclusion.

Examples of the difficulties in interpreting the evidence can be provided by briefly reviewing the current official data on sports participation in the UK and some emergent economic literature that specifically examines its impacts. Table 3.1 provides the (%) participation rates for the 16–18 age groups and over-18 age groups for three major surveys on sports participation. These include the General Household Survey (GHS), The Taking Part Survey (TPS) and the Active People Survey (APS).

The GHS used to be the main source of data on sports participation for the UK, appending modules on sport to a general survey at roughly three-year intervals. The current data report results from the 2002 wave of the survey, which was the last occasion in which sports data was collected. The survey investigates participation for a wide range (approximately forty) of sports and leisure activities in the four weeks before the interview with respondents took place and for the twelve months before the interview took place. Respondents indicate their participation or not in an activity over these periods. Data on the frequency of participation are also collected for the last four weeks before the interview.

The TPS was a three-year survey commissioned by the government's Department for Culture Media and Sport and conducted by the British Market Research Bureau commencing in 2005. One individual from a randomly sampled household in England was interviewed aged 16 years or older. Data on sixty-seven sports activities identifies participation or not over the last twelve months prior to the interview, in the last four weeks prior to the interview, the frequency in days of participation in the last four weeks, as well as the typical time in minutes of participation in these activities.

The Active People Survey, commissioned by Sport England, is a three-wave rolling survey that was first conducted in 2005, repeated in 2007 and completed in 2010. A private research organisation, Ipsos Mori, conducted the research by a telephone survey of individuals aged 16 or older from randomly sampled households in England. Data on 256 sports activities identifies participation or not in the last four weeks prior to the interview, the frequency in days of participation in the last four weeks, as well as the typical time in minutes of participation in these activities.

The sample sizes are given in brackets in the first row of Table 3.1. The second and subsequent columns report whether or not respondents participated (yes) or not (no) in any of the sports activities investigated for each data set, for the age ranges noted earlier and for the four weeks prior to the survey. The first column indicates the socio-economic dimension of the data investigated with appropriate sub-sample sizes indicated by various rows noted as 'n.' It is with respect to this subsample size that any respective column percentage participation response is calculated. For example, in the second column, for the GHS, of the 628 respondents aged under 18, 40.9 per cent of these respondents were male participants in sport, and 37.3 per cent were female participants in sport. Remaining participants, that were either male or female, did not participate in sport. On some occasions, because of differences in data collection 'n/a' indicates that data were not available.[6] For the number of children, sports and household or individual income variables, the figure reported is the average.

The first consistent pattern in the data is that younger age groups clearly participate in sport more than older age groups. In part this seems to be connected with the naturally greater number of students in that cohort. This is supported by the finding that the differences in participation rates between age groups associated with working are not at all profound, and yet this is also a major factor associated with participation in sport. The second is that incomes are typically higher for participants in sport than non-participants, with the exception of 16 to 18 year olds in the TPS. The third is that the relative drop off of non-white ethnic participation is much greater when comparing 16 to 18 year olds to those aged over 18 years old.

Other patterns in the data are, however, more varied. Male and female participation rates vary across the surveys. Whilst younger males are more likely to participate in any sport, as the literature review above indicates, this disparity with female participation dissipates with age. Further, younger participation coincides generally with the presence of more children in the household, whilst the majority of younger participants are likely to be single. Single participation become less likely as one considers older age groups, which is to be expected, even though participation rates fall overall.

These results suggest a degree of complex cohort and substitution effects between activities. It would seem that 'sporting families' exist and that these families adjust their behaviours over time. Further, in an inferential analysis of the same GHS data, and from an economic perspective, Downward (2007) identifies that activities such as swimming can be female, but family oriented, whereas cycling can be viewed as a male family-oriented activity. In contrast, many team sports and fitness-based sports are more likely to be undertaken by younger single males with a decline in participation over time. In contrast, participation in recreation and more leisure activities grows, with the latter being particularly significant for females (see Downward and Riordan, 2007). Perusal of these results would suggest that the main candidates for drivers of variances in levels of participation overall are likely to be income, as suggested by Collins and Kay (2007) and, potentially, ethnicity with other factors affecting the distribution of participation.

Table 3.1 Patterns of sports participation in England (any sport)

Dataset:	GHS (14 827)				Taking Part 1 (28 117)				Active people 1 (363 724)			
	Yes		No		Yes		No		Yes		No	
Age Group	16–18	>18	16–18	>18	16–18	>18	16–18	>18	16–18	>18	16–18	>18
Male	40.9	29.2	14	16.9	47.5	25.5	4.3	18.9	44	19.6	8.7	21.9
Female	37.3	28.4	7.8	25.6	35.3	25.4	12.8	30.2	29.8	24.3	17.5	34.1
n	628	14156	628	14156	943	27057	943	27057	12599	341326	12599	341326
Married	0	33.9	0.2	24.3	0.2	25.6	0	23.3	n/a	n/a	n/a	n/a
Single	78.2	15.1	21.5	7.4	82.9	15.8	16.9	10	n/a	n/a	n/a	n/a
Separated	0	6	0.2	5	0	6.8	0	7.2	n/a	n/a	n/a	n/a
Widow	0	2.7	0	5.8	0	2.6	0	8.6	n/a	n/a	n/a	n/a
n	628	14156	628	14156	943	27057	943	27057	12330	335387	12330	335387
White British	69	53	17.6	37.6	64.4	43.9	12.8	42	63.8	40.5	21.7	52
Other ethnicity	9.4	4.6	4	4.8	18.8	6.9	4	7.2	10.1	3.4	4.4	4.2
n	628	14124	628	14124	943	27063	943	27063	12330	335387	12330	335387
Working	43.5	40.2	9.4	19.3	36.9	34.1	6.5	20	23.9	30.9	8.9	28.6
Retired	0	9.7	0	14.6	0	8	0	18.7	0	7.4	0	8.2
House keep	0.6	3.1	0.5	3.7	1.4	3.4	1.4	4.6	0.2	2.2	0.4	3.2
Student	27.8	1.1	9.6	0.5	33.1	1.1	6.2	0.5	44.1	1.1	13.8	0.7
Unemployed	4.9	1.5	1.8	0.8	8.8	1.6	2.1	1	5.2	1.7	2.7	2.8
n	627	14151	627	14151	943	27093	943	27093	12427	337199	12427	337199
Children 5 to 15	0.65	0.39	0.81	0.32	n/a	n/a	n/a	n/a	n/a	n/a	n/a	n/a
Children 0 to 4	2	0.14	2	0.14	n/a	n/a	n/a	n/a	n/a	n/a	n/a	n/a
Num child	n/a	n/a	n/a	n/a	0.84	0.67	0.79	0.66	1.71	1.6	1.73	1.43
n	491	8152	137	6004	784	13617	159	13776	9223	149207	3265	189820
Number of sports	3.3	2.02	n/a	n/a	3.88	2.2	n/a	n/a	2.01	1.54	n/a	n/a

Table 3.1 Continued

Dataset:	GHS (14 827)				Taking Part 1 (28 117)				Active people 1 (363 724)			
	Yes		No		Yes		No		Yes		No	
Age Group	16–18	>18	16–18	>18	16–18	>18	16–18	>18	16–18	>18	16–18	>18
n	**491**	**8152**	**n/a**	**n/a**	**784**	**13625**	**n/a**	**n/a**	**9306**	**150000**	**n/a**	**n/a**
Household Income	84499	72814	63664	46395	n/a	18887	n/a	13569	n/a	31540	n/a	23828
Individual income	n/a	n/a	n/a	n/a	4371	n/a	5667	n/a	32048	n/a	26696	n/a
n	**436**	**7392**	**112**	**5318**	**646**	**11494**	**120**	**10237**	**5010**	**120218**	**1469**	**140948**
Club	n/a	n/a	n/a	n/a	n/a	n/a	n/a	n/a	44.5	45.9	n/a	n/a
n	**n/a**	**n/a**	**n/a**	**n/a**	**n/a**	**n/a**	**n/a**	**n/a**	**9302**	**149980**	**n/a**	**n/a**

As far as the direct impact of sport on social inclusion is concerned, there is little economic evidence to supplement that cited earlier other than an emergent literature in which the impact of sports participation upon individual *well-being* is explored. Well-being in this respect is measured on an ordinal scale in which respondents indicate their happiness with life as a whole, or their satisfaction with life as a whole, or components of it, and is identified with the utility of the individual (Rasciute and Downward, 2010; Dolan *et al.*, 2008).[7] Such measurements are identified by Coalter (2007) as relevant to the analysis of social capital (see also note 4).

In this well-being literature, Becchetti *et al.* (2008) identify significant impacts of sports participation on happiness. Lechner (2009) identifies positive impacts of sports participation on measures of both subjective health and well-being. Lee and Park (2010) find positive effects of physical activity measures on the life-satisfaction of the disabled. Finally, Rasciute and Downward (2010) and Downward and Rasciute (2011) identify similar results exploring the impact of active travel modes, such as walking and cycling, on well-being as well as participation in forms of physical activity generally including sports. Downward and Rasciute (2011) further identify that such increases in well-being are greater with sports offering more opportunity for social interactions; that is, those that include partners or teams. This line of research raises two important but related conceptual questions, which are answered in the next section. The first is 'what exactly does well-being refer to conceptually from an economics perspective?' The second is 'what does the economics approach imply about the processes that link sport to wider social impacts?' Answers to these questions help to reveal how economics treats the concept of social exclusion and interprets evidence such as that just reported.

The economic analysis of social interaction

From an economic perspective, choice reflects individual utility maximisation subject to constraints (Downward *et al.*, 2009). This means that *economic agents*, as individuals, allocate the resources at their disposal to activities in such a way as to make them feel as well off as possible. Utility is thus linked to individual well-being as noted earlier. The allocation of resources in society is consequently viewed as emerging from the interaction between the motives of consumers and the resources that they have at their disposal either directly or purchased from markets. The former will be influenced by their tastes or preferences, which are assumed to be given. The primary resources at the consumer's disposal are the time that they have and then income or skills that they possess (Becker, 1965). An important feature of the latter two constraints is that they are essentially endogenous to the agent's decisions. By allocating time to study, human capital is enhanced through education as an investment decision. By allocating time to work, income is earned which can be used to consume other resources and goods and services. Finally, it may be that both time and income are allocated to the production and then consumption of resources. Sport is a good example of this as equipment needs to be obtained, skills in practice accrued and time spent both performing and practising the activities. Further, it follows that both education and income are likely to be related because investment in the former will contribute to higher long-term income as a reward to the skills available to the agent. The higher remuneration can then be consumed or further invested.

Two important results follow from this analysis. The first is that the economic approach essentially argues that any variation of consumption decisions that can be observed in society – for example as indicated in Table 3.1 – are the results of an expression of individual voluntary choice. This means, for example, that observing low participation rates in sport being associated with low incomes reflects the choices of individuals and is optimal for them. Rational economic agents will only engage in activity if it maximises their utility. This undermines the concept of social exclusion as argued in earlier sections.

The second point, which helps to qualify this argument, is that the economic approach maintains that the impact of such decisions will be confined to an individual's well-being for any consumption activity that involves a *private good*. This is a good that is both rival in consumption and excludable in consumption. This means that the use of resources through sports participation can be limited by the resource owners to those granted access to them, and that this access can be strictly limited; in other words, that property rights can be assigned. Of course the purchase of equipment, the joining of a fitness club and so on represents such activity.

However, as was noted earlier in this chapter, it can be argued that sports – for example, mediated by sports clubs – have been viewed as public goods. In fact this is imprecise. Public goods represent resources that are non-excludable *and* non-rival. In contrast, club goods represent resources that are excludable *but* non-rival. In the former case no market can exist and economists doubt the relevance of pure public goods for policy discussion. In the latter case it can be argued that this is precisely why voluntary sports clubs emerged as distinct from commercial market or government-funded activities. This is because resources in sport are voluntarily shared amongst groups of like-minded people with others being excluded.

It might be argued, therefore, that this provides an argument for supporting social exclusion as a concept that has economic relevance. As noted earlier, can clubs create bonding but not bridging capital? However, this is not the case theoretically as the individual's choice now simply becomes one about *membership* of the club. The presence of club goods of themselves does not support the logical possibility of social exclusion or inclusion. Economic analysis suggests, in contrast, that some agents choose not to be in the clubs and, instead, allocate resources to other activities.

It is extremely important to note here that the economic approach, of logical necessity, does not identify inequity with a lower social welfare than otherwise would be the case. In contrast, the economic approach argues that social welfare is maximised if individual welfare is maximised and that this will inevitably involve some inequity as resources are allocated by individuals. To argue that equity is both relevant and a target for policy, for example, as is suggested by Collins and Kay (2003), and noted earlier, is then simply a value judgement.

At this point it should be further emphasised that the economic approach recognises the importance of social interactions and the possibility that socio-cultural patterns of behaviour are likely to be observed; for example, that ethnic minorities are more likely to drop off sports participation than their white British equivalents and that ageing produces less individuals that practice sport. Yet economists are doubtful about the value of social exclusion as relevant to interpreting these results.

On the one hand, sharing Coalter's (2007) scepticism, Manski (2000) argues that,

> One problem is an unfortunate dearth of clear thinking in the empirical literature. Empirical economists may borrow jargon from sociology and social psychology and write that they are studying 'peer influences,' 'neighbourhood effects,' 'social capital' or some other concept. Yet empirical analyses commonly fail to define these concepts with any precision and often explain only obliquely how the reported findings shed light on the interactions being studies . . . and instead seek only to determine whether statistical associations among the experiences of different persons indicate the presence of some loosely specified form of interaction amongst them.
>
> (Manski, 2000, p. 117)

On the other hand, the theory that is presented by economists undermines the view of social interactions and social capital presented by advocates of policy activism and the social sciences. Manski (2000) summarises the ways in which economics approaches social interaction. Of relevance for this chapter is the mechanism of externalities. These occur (and are implicit in club goods) when the costs or benefits of a given individual's activities directly impinge on another individual other than through normal market transactions. This might occur via the constraints that the agents face or through the direct spillover of their utilities. In the latter case it may well be, for example, that a given individual gets utility from the activities of another individual. This has obvious application to the activities of parents and children, between friends and associational life, charitable giving and altruism as well as harmful activity.[8]

Becker (1974) seminally explores this economic prospect. In this framework, individuals can allocate time and market goods to *invest* in human capital such as personal capital, skills and capabilities, or social capital. Downward and Riordan (2007) argue that this has obvious implications for sports participation. On the one hand, participation in sports activities requires the acquisition of consumption skills. On the other hand, this implies that previous consumption in an activity can *lock-in* future consumption to the same activity. Further, it is possible that consumption of one sports activity may increase the consumption of others because of the possibility of transferring the human capital accrued, such as agility, timing, and hand–eye coordination etc. across different sports. This provides an obvious rationale for why sports consumption is likely to be concentrated in certain groups as indicated in the evidence reviewed in the last section.

This theoretical approach also generalises to individuals investing in characteristics that make them more similar, or less similar to other persons consuming the same activities reflecting social capital formation as discussed earlier. This suggests that socio-economic characteristics may reflect the outcome of choice and, in turn, why participation takes place in particular groups of activities and by particular groups of individuals.

The upshot of this discussion is that whilst economists might employ concepts such as social interactions and social capital, unlike the broader social scientific literature it does not offer an inherent rationale for using sport as a vehicle of social policy. Perhaps more significant, is the view that even if sport was likely to be used as a policy for altering an individual's behaviour in favour of those prescribed by a policy maker, for example, to encourage them to participate in sport more, this is likely to fail because of the 'Coase Theorem.' This theorem suggests that if property rights can be assigned, then an efficient allocation of those resources, that is one reflecting individual self interest, will emerge regardless of the form or initial distribution of those property rights. A simple intuition would be that offering cheaper access to sports facilities for those not wanting to use them would neither affect their behaviour nor provide an incentive for them to trade that right to others who would benefit from access to the facilities as users already. It is clear, therefore, that the economic approach to sport and social exclusion is one that essentially removes a case for active policy intervention and does this because the mechanisms identified in Figure 3.1 are essentially representative of individual choices that are optimal for society because it is comprises self-interested individuals.

In closing, it is worth noting what would need to change in the analysis in order to make the economics approach move towards the sorts of arguments made about social inclusion and sport by other social scientists (and by implication what the latter would have to embrace for a movement in the other direction). Instrumental to achieving such a congruence would involve weakening the axioms of the economists approach. Two possibilities spring to mind. The first is connected with a restatement of individual preferences. The second concerns the treatment of externalities, implied for example in club goods, but which are maintained to being internalised via the 'Coase Theorem'.

In the first case, as noted by Downward and Riordan (2007), *heterodox* approaches to economics drawing upon psychology, sociology and post-Keynesian economics reject the *given* status of individual preferences. If these are affected by the individual's choices and those of others, then it follows that it is difficult to argue that currently observed behaviour is necessarily in the individual's own best interests. It follows that policy action through providing information or resources to individuals to promote their participation in sport may be appropriate. In the second case, if the 'Coase Theorem' is relaxed, because externalities are not internalised by individual choices – for example – that voluntary clubs do not capture all of the benefits and costs that might be available from sport, then again policy activism might be relevant to correct the externalities.[9] It is this argument that is ultimately implied in the UK's Game Plan (DCMS/Strategy Unit, 2002). Significantly, Cauley and Sandler (1980) postulate a series of possibilities in which either the 'Coase Theorem' result or no account being taken of interactions, are special cases, and that, in general, the outcomes depend on the extent of bargaining between agents and their awareness of spillovers.

Conclusion

This chapter has examined the definitions and concepts that tend to underpin discussions of social exclusion and sport from the non-economic, social scientific literature. It has presented evidence from literature examining sports participation and its impacts as well as evidence from recent surveys on sports participation. Both the social exclusion literature and this informal and non-inferential empirical approach has been interpreted and assessed from an economics perspective.

It is argued that whilst economics admits of the process of social interactions developing social capital, and that sport can be a vehicle for this, it is also argued that because of its focus on individual voluntary choice, the concept of social exclusion as a constraint on individual's opportunities is not theoretically meaningful and not amenable to resolution through policy activism. Relaxation of the fundamental assumptions of the approach would be required to move economics closer to other the social-scientific approaches.

Notes

1 At the outset it is acknowledged that the definitions of, and links between, the entities that are being labelled 'social science' and 'economics' are complicated. Some elements of this complexity are suggested in the discussions in Sections 2 and 3. The basis of the distinction drawn upon in this chapter can be better understood with reference to Downward and Mearman (2007).

2 In this respect the chapter has a focus on social exclusion more generally than other contributions because of the nature of the data available.

3 At this point, it is worth noting some imprecision in Coalter's arguments. From an economic perspective, social capital is better viewed as a club good rather than a public good per se. In fact this is imprecise. Public goods represent resources that are non-excludable *and* non-rival. In contrast club goods represent resources that are excludable *but* non-rival. In the former case no market can exist and economists doubt the relevance of pure public goods for policy discussion. It is precisely this feature which can produce a tension between bonding and bridging capital as noted later (see Downward *et al.*, 2009, for more on club goods and sport).

4 Or 'linking capital' as developed by Woolcock (2001) in which vertical links between social groupings are forged.

5 Both Coalter (2007) and Oughton and Tacon (2007) review the evidence. Space precludes details of how social capital is measured. In the larger-scale studies, variables such as generalised trust in society, or political commitment, are employed as well as life satisfaction. The latter source also notes how sports volunteering and supporting sports teams may affect social capital.

6 Club-based participation was collected for the GHS and TPS. However, this was for each individual sport and problems of missing values made the comparisons difficult.

7 Whilst individual utility is purported to be measured there are differences in the interpretation of what utility means. The standard axiomatic approach in economics is that it measures the individual's sole utility. Externalities are, however, possible, as discussed in the next section, when individual agent actions directly affect the well-being of others. Gui (2000) argues that social interactions which are implied in 'relational goods' whereby shared activities and experiences prevail are typically examined by economists by individuals internalising externalities. The 'Coase Theorem' is an example of this as discussed. However, if one was to view such goods as interpersonal experiences, then empirical measures might well incorporate these externalities as 'experienced' utility, which is a broader hedonistic concept (Frey, 2008). More fundamentally if the relationality was such as to transform the experience from being one of an individual to a collective nature, then such measurement would be inadequate as the ontological status of the activity would have changed.

8 Of course it may well be that harm to others also yields utility to selfish individuals. In this regard it is important to note that the economic approach is based upon *self-interest* but not necessarily *selfish* behaviour. Naive critical views of economics conflate these two perspectives.

9 This would also apply if 'relational goods' were viewed as having a social rather than individual character.

References

Becchetti, A., Pelloni, A. and Rossetti, F. (2008) Relational goods, sociability, and happiness. *Kyklos*, 61 (3): 343–363.

Becker, G. (1965) A theory of the allocation of time. *Economic Journal*, 75 (299): 493–517.

Becker, G. (1974) A theory of social interactions. *Journal of Political Economy*, 82: 1063–1091.

Bourdieu, P. (1997) The Forms of Capital. In Halsley, A.H., Launder, H. and Brown, P. (eds) *Education, Culture, Economy and Society*. Oxford: Oxford University Press.

Cauley, J. and Sandler, T. (1980) A general theory of interpersonal exchange. *Public Choice*, 35: 587–606.

Coalter, F. (2007) *A Wider Social Role for Sport. Who's keeping the score?* London: Routledge.

Coleman, J.S. (1994) *Foundations of Social Theory*. Cambridge, MA: Belknap Press.

Collins, M. and Kay, T. (2003) *Sport and Social Exclusion*. London: Routledge.

DCMS (1999) *Policy Action Team 10: Report to the Social Exclusion Unit – Arts and Sport*. London: HMSO.

DCMS/Strategy Unit (2002) *Game Plan: a strategy for delivering government's sport and physical activity objectives*. London: Cabinet Office.

Delaney, L. and Keaney, E. (2005) *Sport and Social Capital in the United Kingdom: Statistical Evidence from National and International Survey Data*. London: Department of Culture, Media and Sport.

Dolan, P., Peasgood, T. and White, M. (2008) Do we really know what makes us happy? A review of the economic literature on the factors associated with subjective well-being. *Journal of Economic Psychology*, 29: 94–122.

Downward, P.M. (2007) Exploring the Economic Choice to Participate in Sport: Results from the 2002 General Household Survey. *The International Review of Applied Economics*, 21 (5): 633–653.

Downward, P.M. and Mearman, A. (2007) Retroduction as mixed-methods triangulation in economic research: reorienting economics into social science. *Cambridge Journal of Economics*, 31 (1): 77–99.

Downward, P.M. and Rasciute, S. (2010) The relative demands for sports and leisure in England. *European Sports Management Quarterly*, 10 (2): 189–214.

Downward, P.M. and Rasciute, S. (2011) An economic analysis of the subjective health and well-being of physical activity. In Rodríguez, P., Késenne, S. and Humphreys, B. (eds) *The Economics of Sport, Health and Happiness: The Promotion of Well-Being through Sporting Activities*. Cheltenham: Elgar Publishing Limited.

Downward, P. and Rasciute, S. (2011) Does sport make you happy? An analysis of the well-being derived from sports participation. *International Review of Applied Economics*, 25 (3): 331–348.

Downward, P.M. and Riordan, J. (2007) Social interactions and the demand for sport: an economic analysis. *Contemporary Economic Policy*, 25 (4): 518–537.

Downward, P., Dawson, A. and Dejonghe, T. (2009) *Sports Economics: Theory, Evidence and Policy*. London: Butterworth-Heinneman.

Downward, P.M., Lumsdon, L. and Ralston, R. (2005) Gender differences in sports event volunteering: insights from Crew 2002 at the XV11 Commonwealth Games. *Managing Leisure*, 10: 219–256.

Driscoll, K. and Wood, L. (1999) *Sporting Capital: Changes and Challenges for Rural Communities in Victoria*. Victoria: Centre for Applied Social Research, RMIT.

Frey, B.S. (2008) *Happiness: A Revolution in Economics*. London: MIT Press.

Gui, B. (2000) Beyond transactions: on the interpersonal dimension of economic reality. *Annals of Public and Cooperative Economics*, 71 (2): 139–169.

Horch, H. (1998) self destroying processes of sports clubs in Germany. *European Journal of Sports Management*, 5 (1): 46–58.

Jarvie, G. (2003) Communitarianism, sport and social capital: neighbourly insights into Scottish sport. *International Review for the Sociology of Sport*, 38 (2): 139–153.

Lechner, M. (2009) Long-run labour market and health effects of individual sports activities. *Journal of Health Economics*, 28 (4): 839–854.

Lee, Y.H. and Park, I. (2010) Happiness and physical activity in special populations: evidence from Korean Survey Data. *Journal of Sports Economics*, 11 (2): 136–156.

Lister, R. (1990) *The Exclusive Society: citizenship and the poor*. London: Child Poverty Action Group.

Manski, C. (2000) Economic analysis of social interactions. *The Journal of Economic Perspectives*, 14 (3): 115–136.

Nichols, G. (2003) *Volunteers in Sport*. Eastbourne: Leisure Studies Association.

Oughton, C. and Tacon, R. (2007) *Sport's Contribution to Achieving Wider Social Benefits: a report for the Department of Culture Media and Sport*. Online: www.parliament.uk/deposits/depositedpapers/2008/DEP2008–0406.doc (accessed June 2010).

Putnam, R. (2000) *Bowling Alone: The Collapse and Revival of the American Community*. New York: Simon and Schuster.

Rasciute, S. and Downward, P.M. (2010) Health or happiness? What is the impact of physical activity on the individual? *Kyklos*, 63 (2): 256–270.

Scott, J. (1994) *Poverty and Wealth: Citizenship, deprivation and privilege*. London: Longman.

Scottish Office (1999) *Social Inclusion: Opening the door top a better Scotland*. Edinburgh: Scottish Office.

Seippel, O. (2006) Sport and social capital. *Acta Sociologica*, 49 (2): 169–183.

Tonts, M. (2005) Competitive sport and social capital in Rural Australia. *Journal of Rural Studies*, 21 (2): 137–149.

Townsend, P. (1979) *Poverty in the UK: A Survey of Household Resources and Standards of Living*. London: Penguin.

Townsend, P. (1987) Disadvantage. *Journal of Social Policy*, 16: 125–146.

Warde, A., Tampubolon, G. and Longhurst, B. *et al.* (2003) Trends in social capital: membership of associations in Great Britain 1991–1998. *British Journal of Political Science*, 33: 515–534.

Woolcock, M. (2001) The place of social capital in understanding social and economic outcomes. *ISUMA Canadian Journal of Policy Research*, 2 (1): 11–17.

4 Sport, new social divisions and social inequality

Grant Jarvie

Introduction

Whenever pondering the dynamics of social divisions or forms of inequality in sport it is always useful to consider questions such as who *is* sport; for example, who plays what, who has access to which forms of sport, and who owns sport? We can also ask questions about the ways in which social structures have provided both continuity and change in sport.

Undoubtedly a global poverty gap continues to define today's world with more than 1.2 billion people living on less than $1 a day and 46 per cent of the world's population living on less that $2 a day (Jarvie, 2007). The poverty gap exists both within and between countries. To put this in some comparative context, for the season 2003–04, the wage and transfer bill of the four English football divisions stood at £1,049 billion, a figure which eclipses the gross domestic product of some small African nations such as Lesotho and Mauritania, and that could wipe out most of the debt of many countries both within and outside Africa. The transfer of sporting capital, in terms of both human and physical forms, helps to sustain social divisions between different parts of the world as well as promote the illusion or myth of social inclusion – a much over-used term. This chapter on sport, social divisions and social inequality acknowledges traditional twentieth-century forms of inequality in sport and considers the ways in which sport today both reinforces forms of social inequality and provides a resource of hope for some people.

This chapter is structured around four themes:

1   social divisions and the 'new tribes' that introduce new forms of inequality in the UK based upon people's attitudes to equality and fairness;
2   sport and social class which questions traditional class barriers in sport while acknowledging campaigns for change – some of which originate outside of the UK;
3   the role of gender and sporting heroines in challenging traditional forms of authority;
4   the impact of the Obama phenomenon in the USA and in particular the part played by sport in making a contribution to what Obama refers to as the audacity of hope.

These four themes are not exhaustive of the all the different forms of social division that permeate sport today. They do, nonetheless, suggest ways in which sport – despite exaggerated claims of impact on social inclusion or exclusion – continues to provide many possibilities within certain limits.

Social divisions and the new tribes

Socio-economic systems differ in the degree to which they constrain the rights and powers of different groups of people in different countries. The social class structure in the United Kingdom is not the same as the class structure in America or Asia. Patterns of interaction between different groups sometimes marginalise, disproportionately, segments of the population. In the United States of America, the class structure at the beginning of the twenty-first century includes an extremely rich capitalist and corporate managerial class that lives to extraordinarily high consumption standards. There have been fluctuating constraints on this group's exercise of economic power. Following the emergence of recession in 2008, their predominance reflects a pattern of interaction between race and class in which the working poor and the marginalised population are disproportionately made up of racial minorities.

The potential coherence of social divisions lies in the notions of hierarchy, social inequality and social injustice that permeate sport. Complex social divisions are not just about the reality of everyday sport, rather they reinforce the fact that whatever categories are used, unequal access to sport tends to impinge continually upon the same categories of people. The gap between rich and poor remains a significant gap and so any discussion of sport and social inequality that relates solely to class, ethnicity, gender, or any singular category risks missing issues of poverty, capability, injustice and the precise nature of the limits and possibilities that are open to different people (Hampson and Hilbery, 2010). No one, single narrative can address every form of oppression, identity or political aspiration but it could be argued that sport should be acutely aware of the sheer range of the multiple axes of power and inequality that are in operation at any one time.

New social divisions are emerging all the time but in the Britain of the twenty-first century, new attitudes towards inequality and fairness might suggest that orthodox forms of inequality are not as important as they were in the twentieth century. It has been argued that new social divisions are emerging and researchers have begun to ask new questions about social inequality (Hampson and Olchawski, 2009). Four fairly equal clusters of opinions and groups seem to be emerging out of this recent research. The 'traditional egalitarians' (22 per cent) support measures to tackle inequality at both the top and the bottom of the social scale. They tend to be older and more heavily weighted towards Labour with 55 per cent in socio-economic group C2DE. The 'traditional free marketers' (20 per cent) oppose measures to tackle inequality at both the top and the bottom of the social scale. They are overwhelmingly in socio-economic groups ABC1 (70 per cent) and are much more heavily weighted towards the Conservatives than the country as a whole. The *angry middle* (26 per cent) support measures to tackle inequality at the top, while opposing measures to tackle inequality at the bottom. They are slightly more weighted towards the Conservatives than the country as a whole and 53 per cent are ABC1. Finally a fourth grouping, the *post-ideological liberals* (32 per cent) support certain measures to tackle inequality at the top (although they have more positive attitudes towards those at the top than Traditional Egalitarians) without having negative attitudes towards those in poverty or being opposed to tackling inequality at the bottom (unlike the traditional free marketers and the angry middle). Most of the new tribes are strongly attracted to a social vision framed around improving the quality of life for all.

Sport and social class

Sport has long been viewed as a graphic symbol of meritocracy despite the fact that sociologists and others have been questioning the substantive basis for such a claim for more than quarter of a century (Huggins, 2009; Jones, 1988; Wright, 2009). Thus, it has been argued that the popular image of sport as an unquestioned democracy of ability and practice is somewhat over-exaggerated if not mythical. Generally speaking, the term 'democratisation' tends to imply a widening degree of opportunity or a diminishing degree of separatism in varying forms of sports involvement. The term has been used to describe the process whereby employees or clients have increasing levels of control over sporting decisions and sporting bodies. The expansion of opportunities in sport has been used at one level to argue that sport, at least in the West, has become more open; yet the reality in Britain is that the extremes of privilege and poverty remain sharply drawn. An emphasis on social class cannot explain all aspects of the development of British sport but there is good reason for believing that sport and social class have been mutually reinforcing categories in British society for a long time.

It is important to ask the question: who plays sport? The figures presented below relate to sports participation and social class in one country towards the end of the twentieth century (Jarvie, 2006). The information drawn from national sports participation date over a ten-year period points to six key findings:

1   that the most popular participatory sports amongst class category AB were curling, cricket, ski-ing, sailing and tennis;
2   that the most popular sports amongst DE category included snooker/billiards/pool, ice-skating/ice-hockey, fishing/angling, dancing and walking;
3   that sports participation in all sports is most popular amongst social class C1 (30 per cent); followed by DE (26 per cent), AB (23 per cent) and C2 (21 per cent);
4   that with reference to particular sports; golf participation by social class is made up of AB (33 per cent), C1 (32 per cent), C2 (20 per cent) and DE (15 per cent); football participation by social class is made up of AB (19 per cent), C1 (32 per cent), C2 (25 per cent) and DE (24 per cent); bowls participation by social class is made up of AB (22 per cent), C1 (32 per cent), C2 (21 per cent) and DE (25 per cent); and athletics participation by social class

is made up of AB (24 per cent), C1 (30 per cent), C2 (24 per cent) and DE (16 per cent);

5   that sports such as squash would appear to be extremely elitist in terms of participation AB (39 per cent) and DE (5 per cent);

6   that sports such as walking AB (24 per cent), C1 (30 per cent), C2 (20 per cent) and DE (26 per cent), swimming AB (26 per cent), C1 (31 per cent), C2 (21 per cent) and DE (22 per cent) and cycling AB (27 per cent), C1 (32 per cent), C2 (20 per cent) and DE (21 per cent) are fairly democratic in terms of participation.

Such evidence is never fully robust but it addresses the question *who is sport* rather than what is sport? Arguments about sport and social class (Huggins, 2009; Jones, 1988) have tended to suggest:

1   that it is possible to identify a leisure class that is involved in the conspicuous consumption of sport;

2   that sport helps to sustain and reproduce status, prestige and power;

3   that the struggle for sport has been influenced by social class;

4   that the practice of sport is socially stratified and differentiated by social class;

5   that sport within and between social classes acts as a hallmark of distinction;

6   that sport is intimately associated with classes that exist on the basis of the differential distribution of wealth, power and other characteristics;

7   that sport contributes to a distinct way of life associated with certain class categories;

8   that social class has contributed to the discourse of colonial sport within and between certain former colonies and nations;

9   that class networks continue to afford capacity and opportunity for some. Sport and social class is not dead but perhaps the monolithic social imagery of class as a driver of change is not as forceful in the twenty-first century as it was in the twentieth century.

There are times in human history when liberalisation in the direction of harmless fun can be absorbed in an upward movement of an optimistic and expansive society. For many in Britain, in much of the second half of the twentieth century, the answer lay in the labour party with both a small and large 'L,' in work itself, in the organisation of people who did the work so that their rewards began to match the value of their efforts and in the progress of a political party that historically represented the working class, the un-represented and those in poverty. This traditional synergy has in part declined. For many, the relationship between sport, class and the lottery in the twenty-first century is just another symptom of decline, a change of focus, a feeling of uncertainty and insecurity in a world in which collectivism and solidarity in many instances has been replaced by irreverence and individualism (Therborn, 2001). It has been argued by Marquand (2004) that the United Kingdom was a nation of subjects who historically felt that they had some control over their fate through elections, security of pensions, representation but that the communities where people lived have now been replaced by a loose collection of individuals living in a global world of uncertainty where even the winnings from the sports lottery are distributed elsewhere. It could even be argued that the UK, along with other nations, has become a nation of ricocheting pinballs in some vast global bagatelle machine in which the anonymous financial bankers of the universe pulled the levers which gave rise to the beginning of an economic recession in 2008.

The national lottery has become an icon of uncertainty, individualism and false hope, which even in sporting terms has failed to supply the financial security and provision that was promised. The number of 'good causes' funded through lottery provision has meant reduced funding for sport in many if not all parts of Britain. A Britain in which some people are doing rather well for themselves while other remain marginalised, disadvantaged within sport and in terms of the opportunities for physical activity. It has been argued that the UK has become a 30/30/40 society, in which the privileged 40 per cent remain comfortable, can access private sporting clubs and have sustained their power in the market place. A further 30 per cent, due to their changing relationship to the market place, insecurity of pension provision and an ageing society, have become marginalised but also increasingly politically active as a result of the changes. Meantime a further 30 per cent remain disadvantaged. In 2005, 25 per cent of children living in Scotland under the age of sixteen continue to live in poverty (*The Herald*, 31 March 2005, p. 2). Thirteen million people live in poverty in the UK, including one in three children (Hampson and Olchawski, 2009). It has been suggested in the Britain of the twenty-first century that while the lottery draws more of a working-class support in terms of distribution, the distribution of prize-money is disproportionately biased towards middle- and upper-class sporting tastes. Thus, it could be argued that while the poorest groups in society have always had to live with insecurity and uncertainty, in the past sport was a traditional avenue of social mobility but even this has been left increasingly to chance.

Yet the relationship between sport, social class and campaigns for social change remains a relevant challenge to equitable, neo-liberal notions of global sport. It would be misleading to suggest that as a major driver of social change, social class is no longer relevant to bringing about transformation in sport. It is evident even in sport that social class cannot be viewed as a static entity. It has a life form that changes as a result of social and historical processes and, as a consequence, finds different forms of expression in political movements that endorse forms of social change in and through sport. Many forms of class conflict have been deflected into anti-immigrant and anti-Muslim campaigns. Many forms of traditional urban and rural forms of social class activism have re-emerged and confronted each other over the fight to ban foxhunting in Scotland and England. The International Labour Organisation in conjunction with FIFA and UNICEF launched the Red Card to Child Labour campaign in conjunction with the 2002 African Nations Cup, while Fabians in the twenty-first century have campaigned not only against corruption in world sport but also the need to develop a more progressive politics of sport that promotes co-operation, mutuality and a fostering of trust between different groups who share such concerns (Katwala, 2004). The traditional work-ing-class game of football struggles through movements that are partially state sponsored, such as supporters' trusts, to gain an increased say in the running of clubs. The very cost of viewing elite football is in itself a barrier to many people. The average price of a season ticket for Manchester United Football Club in sea-son 2009–10 was £730.

In other countries where football is deemed to be important, such as Brazil, governments have taken alternative steps to bring about social change through football. In 2002, Luiz Inacio Lula da Silva was elected President of Brazil. The content of the administration's policies were also influenced by football in that the first two laws that the president signed in May 2002 concerned football. Football in Brazil was one of the key battlegrounds upon which the battle to make the country a fairer place was being fought. Previously, sport had been run by a net-work of unaccountable and largely corrupt figures known as carrolas or *top hats* who had become wealthy while the domestic football scene remained broke and demoralised (Bellos, 2003, p. 32). The public plundering of football was viewed by the president as a continual reminder of the previous administration's failure to stamp out corruption in areas of public life. Lula, in an attempt to force the football authorities to become transparent, ratified a *Law of Moralisation* in sport that enforced transparency in club administration (Bellos, 2003, p. 32). On the same day, Lula sanctioned an ambitious and wide-ranging law known as the 'Fans Statute,' which was a bill of rights for the football fan.

Social class continues to impact upon campaigns for social change in sport and yet this particular expression of social class activism has combined diverse social and political protests with different forms of ideological awareness. While one of the elements of the erosion of deference has been the creation of new forms of rebellious collectivism, the motor of sport and social class as an engine of social change is not dead. It may have shifted geographically. Many of the progressive successes in and challenges for world sport continue to be linked to traditional areas of concern such as poverty and labour. It has been argued that classical irrev-erent collectivism, linked to sport and working-class movements, has passed its historical high point and may even be weakening progressively (Huggins, 2009; Jarvie, 2006). Yet it would be foolish to ignore the continuing significance of social class politics in bringing about social change in sport. There may be less class but there is certainly more irreverence which may also express itself in unac-ceptable forms such as xenophobic violence or crime. It may also still reassert itself in struggles over the ownership and direction of football clubs in the UK (Therborn, 2001).

The very poorest in society are rarely found in the main seats and as John Under-wood writing in the *New York Times* of 20 March 2003 has explained:

> The great damage done by this new elitism is that even the cheapest seats in almost every big-league facility are now priced out of reach of a large seg-ment of the population. Those who are most critically in need of affordable

entertainment, the underclass (and even the lower middle class), have been effectively shut out. And this is especially hateful because spectator sport by its very nature has been the great escape for men and women who have worked all day for little pay and traditionally have provided the biggest number of a sport's core support. As it now stands, they are as good as disenfranchised – a vast number of the taxpaying public who will never set foot inside these stadiums and arenas.

Sporting heroines, feminism and the post-neo-liberal era

It is often suggested that the most widely held view of second-wave feminism is that it demonstrates a sharp contrast between relative success in transforming cultures and relative failure in transforming institutions (Fraser, 2009; Osbourne and Skillen, 2010). This assessment is double edged given that feminist ideals of gender inequality now sit squarely in the social mainstream but have yet to be fully realised in practice. Thus, feminist critiques of sexual harassment, sexual trafficking and unequal pay are widely espoused today but have not eliminated such practices. Contemporary issues of gender justice, just like other forms of social division, need to be concerned with issues of redistribution, recognition as well as representation. Global capitalism is itself at a crossroads given the global financial crisis, and the 2008 election of Barack Obama in the USA may signal a further challenge to the neo-liberal project and it remains to be seen whether the optimism of a further period of transformation is to be realised (Anstead and Straw, 2009). As such, there is a need to continue to link hopes for change for women in and through sport with a vision of hope for a better society or worlds of sport in a post-neo-liberal era.

The very same questions that opened this chapter about 'who *is* sport' are just as important in the context of a discussion of sporting heroines. The figures presented below relate to sports participation by women in one country towards the end of the twentieth century (Jarvie, 2006):

1   the most popular participatory sports amongst women are aerobics (75 per cent), dancing (74 per cent), swimming (60 per cent), yoga (87 per cent) and horse-riding (75 per cent), whilst the least popular sports in terms of participation are football (7 per cent), fishing/angling (8 per cent), rugby (8 per cent), golf (12 per cent) and squash (15 per cent);
2   the most popular participatory sports amongst men are football (93 per cent), rugby (92 per cent), golf (88 per cent), fishing/angling (92 per cent) and squash (84 per cent), whilst the least popular sports in terms of participation are yoga (13 per cent), aerobics (25 per cent), dancing (26 per cent), horse-riding (25 per cent), and gymnastics (29 per cent);
3   women's participation in sports in this country is dominated by four activities while men participate in a much wider range of sports with twelve sports having participation rates of above 5 per cent compared with six such sports for women;

4   sports that have the smallest gender gap in terms of participation include curling (51 per cent M and 48 per cent F = 3 per cent difference), badminton (52 per cent M and 48 per cent F = 4 per cent difference), tenpin bowling (53 per cent M and 47 per cent F = 6 per cent difference), hockey (53 per cent M and 47 per cent F =6 per cent difference) and;

5   that in terms of total sports participation, a gender gap of 4 per cent exists between men (52 per cent) and women (48 per cent).

Arguments about sport and women in the wider research literature (Coakley and Pike, 2009; Hargreaves, 2000, 2004; Kay, 2010) have suggested some or all of the following:

1   that different structures of masculinity and femininity have historically influenced the development of sport;

2   that it is necessary to ask the question 'where are the women in sport?' in order to highlight issues of oppression, marginality and empowerment of women in sport;

3   that gender is a fundamental category through which all aspects of life are organised and experienced including sport;

4   that experiences of gender in sport need to be sensitive and aware of 'other' experiences of sporting struggle outwith mainstream and or colonial gender relations;

5   that body culture and physicality are important facets of gender relations that also need to be explored and explained in terms of social division and social differences;

6   that sport and gender relations have contributed to both reformist, emancipatory and evolutionary aspects of social change; and continuity;

7   that sport and gender remains an important and insightful element of social division in its own right.

Key areas of social change fought for by women in and through sport continue to include the struggle for (Brackenridge, 2004; George, 2010; Hargreaves, 2000):

1   a more representative coverage for women within the Women's International Sports Movement;

2   concerns over the existence and strategies aimed at the amelioration of sexual harassment in sport;

3   raising awareness of women in sport across the world;

4   improved conditions for women in sport;

5   increased representation for women in sport both through the existing structures and new structures;

6   women's health and well-being in all parts of the world;

7   ensuring that the women executives in positions of power listen to and do not distance themselves from ordinary women who are the majority;

8   acknowledge that the culture of movement is different for ordinary women in different parts of the world.

The Women's International Sports Movement has been an effective advocate for change in sport and also a successful conduit between sport and other organisations such as the United Nations. The attempt to speak as one voice for all women may be somewhat utopian, but co-operative work between women in sport has meant that there is a stronger possibility that the international voice of women in sport will be heard within the mainstream of other international movements supporting and advocating for women in different parts of the world. The Women's International Sports Movement often struggled with the question of representation (Fraser and Honneth, 2003). The future of a global sports feminism and the Women's International Sports Movement lay in the potential to unite women across social divisions and differences and as such the future remained international in focus and dependent upon effective coalitions both within sport and between sport and other forms of difference including generations of feminisms.

Over two hundred years ago, in 1792, Mary Wollstonecraft, commenting upon the vindication of the rights of women, noted that it was justice and not charity that was needed in the world at that time. Women and feminist movements have continually questioned male radical leadership of movements for liberation and equality in which traditional gender roles have remained unchanged. Overall, feminism has been a movement of the political Left, in the broadest sense, particularly in Western Europe. Similarly in the Third World, questions have been raised about the masculinist rule of capital as well as patriarchy. Whether or not the contemporary women's movement or other forms of activism involving women's issues provides a prototypical alternative social movement is open to question, but certainly struggles for women's sport have benefited from international support, collectivism and forms of solidarity. Struggles for women's sport and other forms of justice for women have also been sensitive to other traditions of emancipatory internationalism, and in this sense a similarity exists between the labour movement and women's movements. One of the major reasons for the advances, policies and interventions won by women in sport has not only been the heightened sense of forms of common orientation but also the linkage of the women's movement to struggles for women in different parts of the world.

Fraser (2009, p. 114) has recently pointed out that the advantages of contemporary dangerous liaisons between feminism and neo-liberalism based upon a mutual critique of traditional authority may also exist. Such authority as male-dominated forms of sport is a long-standing target of feminist activism. However, traditional authority, in some periods of time, have also appeared to be an obstacle to capitalist expansion and, therefore, in this current moment the two critiques of traditional authority – one feminist and the other neo-liberal – seem to converge. If the feminist critique of sport were to integrate in more balanced way issues of redistribution, recognition and the idea of justice, then perhaps it would be possible to reconnect a feminist critique of sport and social inclusion under capitalism. The current ongoing global recession, and the impending transformation of the public sector in many counties, provide the opportunity to re-direct sport in the direction of social justice more broadly.

Sport and racism in an era of audacity

Arguments about the relationship between sport, racism and ethnicity have tended to rely upon some or all of the following arguments (Armstrong, 2008; Bass, 2002; Johnson, 2010). That sport:

1   is inherently conservative and helps to consolidate patriotism, nationalism and racism;
2   has some inherent property that makes it a possible instrument of integration and harmonious ethnic and race relations;
3   as a form of cultural politics has been central to processes of colonialism, imperialism and post-colonialism in different parts of the world;
4   has contributed to unique political struggles which have involved black and ethnic political mobilisation and the struggle for equality of and for black peoples and ethnic minority groups;
5   is an important facet of ethnic and racial identities;
6   has produced stereotypes, prejudices and myths about ethnic minority groups which have contributed both to discrimination against and an under-representation of ethnic minority peoples within certain sports;
7   that race and ethnicity are factors influencing choices that people make when they chose to join or not join certain sports clubs;
8   needs to develop a more complex set of tools for understanding the limits and possibilities that influence sport, racism and ethnicity and, in particular, the way such categories historically articulate with other categories and social divisions.

In 2000, four broad generalisations were made about sports participation in England (Jarvie, 2006). These included:

1   that Black African (60 per cent) and black Other (80 per cent) men have higher participation rates than the national average for England (54 per cent);
2   that Indian (47 per cent), Black Caribbean (45 per cent), Bangladeshi (46 per cent) and Pakistani (42 per cent) men are less likely to participate in sport than men in the population as a whole;
3   that national participation rates for women (39 per cent) are matched or exceeded by women from Black Other (45 per cent), Other (41 per cent) and Chinese (39 per cent ethnic groups);
4   that women who classify themselves as Black Caribbean (34 per cent), Black African (34 per cent), Indian (31 per cent), Pakistani (21 per cent) and Bangladeshi (19 per cent) have participation rates below the national average for all women.

At the same time, sport has been explicitly involved with campaigns, activism, policies and protests aimed at discrediting explicit racism and the power of colonialism. The struggle for sport has involved drawing attention to the fact that up until the 1960s many black and other peoples of colour in the United States were still denied human and civil rights. The de-colonisation of Africa, the attempt to defeat institutional racism in the United States, the overthrow of apartheid in South Africa and the defeat of US imperialism in Cuba and Vietnam have all implicated sport as an area of activism if not policy intervention (Baas, 2002; Jarvie, 1985; Sugden, 1996).

Some of the most prominent areas of legislation and injustice in sport have grown out of struggles over racism. For example:

1   the period of *apartheid* sport in South Africa from 1948 to 1992 when specific racial legislation which separated the practice of sport by racial groupings gave rise to the international slogan 'You cannot have normal sport in an abnormal society';
2   the practice of *colonialism* in many parts of the world which formed the backcloth to sporting relations between many countries. During the 1960s and 1970s the cricket rivalry between England and the West Indies reflected racial tensions and racism rooted in years of colonial struggle. Terms such as 'White Wash' and 'Black Wash' were used to refer to English or West Indian victories. At the same time sport took on the mantle of symbolic colonial/anti-colonial struggle both between the two teams and in the selection of the West Indian team as is explained in C.L.R. Jame's (1963) classic period account of West Indian cricket;
3   the popularity and worldwide coverage of sport has meant that *sport as vehicle for protest* has been a successful medium for drawing attention to the treatment of black Americans as second-class citizens in the United States of America and in American Sport as evidenced by the Black Power protests at the 1968 Mexico Olympic Games. The extent to which Aborigine's or Inuit peoples have also been marginalised in mainstream Australian or Canadian sport has also been a target for sporting activists. For example, much of the coverage of the 2000 Sydney Olympic Games revolved around the performances of the 400m Olympic Gold Medallist Cathy Freeman and the plight of Aborigines living in contemporary Australia;
4   *legislation* such as the Race Relations Acts of 1976 and 2004 in Britain which provides the legal machinery of the law to investigate and act against racism in all walks of life in Britain, including sport.

Equally there are important historical moments that can symbolise a prejudice, a protest, an ideology or a breaking down of barriers. Sport has been racist but has also provided some of the most poignant anti-racist moments. In 1881, Andrew Watson became the first black player to play for Scotland at football/soccer. In August 1936 Jesse Owens won an unprecedented four gold medals at the Nazi Olympic Games in Berlin. Two years later Joe Louis crushed Max Smelling to signal the end of a period of white supremacy in boxing. In 1967, Muhammed Ali, the world heavyweight boxing champion, condemned the war in Vietnam arguing that he did not have any quarrel with the Vietcong. One year later, in October

1968, American black athletes protested from the Olympic medal rostrum against the treatment of black people in America and elsewhere, notably South Africa. Evonne Cawley (Goolagong) became the first aboriginal Australian to play in a Wimbledon tennis final in 1971, two years before Arthur Ashe became the first black American to win the Wimbledon Men's Tennis Championship in 1973. In 1995 Nelson Mandela, following South Africa's victory in the Rugby World Cup, talked of sport as force that could mobilise the sentiments of a people in a way that nothing else could. Three years later, when Zinedine Zidan lifted the Football World Cup for France, the French president talked of the French football team as being symbolic of the new multi-racial integrated France. In 2001, arguably the world's greatest footballer, Pele, endorsed a worldwide anti-racist campaign in football with the words that racism is cowardice that comes from fear; a fear of difference. In February 2002, Vonetta Flowers became the first African American to win a gold medal at the Winter Olympic Games. In 2006, England bowler Monty Panesar became the first Sikh to represent any nation except India in Test Match Cricket (Armstrong, 2008).

In 1997, when Tiger Woods won the Masters and donned the green jacket that accompanied the winning of the coveted title, golf became thrilling to watch for an entirely new audience. On the hallowed putting greens of Augusta, where Woods would not have been allowed membership a few years earlier, history had been made. Social change through sport had occurred yet at the time, America did not have the language to deal with the change. Not since Lee Elder squared off against Jack Nicklaus in a sudden death playoff at the American Golf Classic in 1968 had a black golfer gained so much televised attention (Bass, 2002). The sports press cast the feat of Woods as breaking a modern colour line, yet no one including Woods himself could fully describe exactly what colour line had been broken. The press conveyed his parental heritage as variously African American, Asian and Native American; others portrayed Woods as a black athlete – a golfer who had brought about change in the same way attributed to the likes of Jesse Owens, Tommie Smith, John Carlos, Muhammad Ali, Tydie Pickett, Louise Stokes, Vonetta Flowers and Alice Cochrane. Woods himself did not consider himself in such terms but embraced a nuanced racial heritage more representative of the melting pot imagery associated with American history and a determining demographic factor of so-called Generation X (Bass, 2002, p. xvi).

As this chapter is being written, the financial crisis of 2008 and beyond continues to unfold and what has been termed an 'age of austerity' has arrived. This focus on austerity is tempered by the 'audacity of hope' reflected in the aspirations of a new American president – President Obama. On the eve of the election for the new president of the United States of America (USA), both Barack Obama and John McCain were interviewed on the half-time show of *Monday Night Football*. Asked the same questions, they differed significantly on only one: if you could change one thing about American sports what would it be? McCain offered something worthy about sorting out the steroid problem while Obama wanted a college football play-off. Obama is not only the first black president of the USA but the first president to identify himself primarily as a basketball fan. Presidents defining themselves as sports fan is not new; Reagan played football at college and Bushes senior and junior were both interested in baseball. Clinton did play basketball at Oxford, but Obama's basketball credentials are particularly strong. It has been widely reported that he shook off Election Day nerves by playing basketball. In his book *Dreams of my Father*, Obama writes 'that I was trying to raise myself to being a black man in America and, beyond the given of my appearance, no one around me seemed to know what that meant' (Obama, 2008, p. 9). One thing it appears to mean is basketball. The dominance of African Americans on the basketball court is so well established and documented that it is rarely comment-worthy. In 2009 the Washington Wizards, Obama's new local team, had fifteen players on the roster, thirteen of whom were African American. Obama's presidency will coincide with an aggressive expansion by the National Basketball Association (NBA) and it hopes to establish a club in Europe within this time. One of the problems it faces is the NBA draft laws which are the American method of dividing up young talent which might just be too socialist for European employment law (Markovits, 2003, p. 28).

Concluding remarks

Traditionally, 'social inequalities' was a term that referred to the differences in people's share of and access to resources and opportunities. The term social inequality in relation to sport and other areas can be thought of in at least three senses:

1   inequality of condition which may refer to variations in factors such as income, education, occupation or the amount of time to spend on sport, exercise and recreation;
2   inequality of opportunity which focuses more on the individual and is concerned with the degree of freedom that people have in moving within and between the restrictions set by a reward structure;
3   inequality of capability which refers to the differences that individuals or groups may have as a result of inequalities in power and capability.

A redistribution of income resources clearly affects different social divisions and people living in different countries but it is what people do with this resource that is important. For social thinkers such as Amartya Sen (2009) the issue of inequality of capabilities – in other words, what people do with resources – is also crucial in that it refers to actions in areas such as literacy, nutrition, access to sport and the power to participate in the social life of the community.

Improving life chances requires a co-ordinated effort and, as such, any contribution that sport can make must also build upon a wider coalition of sustained support for social and progressive policies. The life chances approach to narrowing the gap between rich and poor has a key role to play in producing social change. Such an approach requires the harnessing of a strong political narrative and action plan that fits with an intuitive understanding that life should not be determined by socio-economic position and that people do have choices. The concept of justice rests on the idea that to be genuinely free, an individual needs a capability set. What Sen (2009) argued was that the market economy is not a free-standing institution, nor a self-regulating one. Support is needed from other institutions and also resources of hope. You need supervision from the state, you need supplementation by the state and society to take care of poverty, ill-health, illiteracy, and educational achievement and opportunity. Sport cannot sustain change on its own.

Finally, while it is important to explain and understand economic, social, and comparative explanations of what sport can do for society, the more important intellectual and practical questions often emanate from questions relating to social change. Historically, the potential of sport lies not with the values promoted by global sport or particular forms of capitalism because, as has been demonstrated in this chapter, these are invariably unjust and uneven. The possibilities that exist within sport are those that can help with offering radically different views of the world, perhaps based upon opportunities to foster trust, civic obligation, redistribution and respect for sport in a more socially orientated and humane world.

References

Anstead, N. and Straw, W. (2009) *The Change we Need*. London: Fabian Society.
Armstrong, S. (2008) Is British sport still racist? *New Statesman*, 18 November, pp. 32–34.
Bass, A. (2002) *The Triumph but the Struggle: The 1968 Olympics and the making of the black athlete*. Minneapolis: University of Minnesota Press.
Bellos, A. (2003) The President wins the midfield battle. *New Statesman*, 3 November, pp. 32–34.
Brackenridge, C. (2004) Women and children first? Child abuse and child protection in sport. *Sport and Society*, 7 (3): 322–337.
Coakley, J. and Pike, E. (2009) *Sport in Society*. Boston: McGraw-Hill.
Fraser, N. (2009) Feminism co-opted. *New Left Review*, March/April 56: 97–118.
Fraser, N. and Honneth, A. (2003) *Redistribution or Recognition?* London: Verso.
George, J. (2010) Ladies first? Establishing a place for women golfers in British golf clubs, 1867–1914. *Sport in History*, 30 (2): 288–309.
Hampson, T. and Hilbery, O. (2010) Real Lives. In Hampson, T. (ed.) *Hardest to Reach*. London: Fabian Society, pp. 1–8.
Hampson, T. and Olchawski, J. (2009) *Is Equality Fair.* London: Fabian Society.
Hargreaves, J. (2000) *Heroines of Sport: The Politics of Difference and Identity*. London: Routledge.
Hargreaves, J. (2004) Querying sport feminism: Personal or political. In Giulliannotti, R. (ed.) *Sport and Modern Social Theorists.* Basingstoke: Palgrave, pp. 187–207.
Huggins, M. (2009) Special Issue Sport and Class. *Sport in History*, 29 (4).
James, C. (1963) *Beyond a Boundary*. London: Stanley Paul.
Jarvie, G. (1985) *Class, Race and Sport in South Africa's Political Economy*. London: Kegan Paul.
Jarvie, G. (2006) *Sport, Culture and Society*. London: Routledge.
Jarvie, G. (2007) The Promise and Possibilities of East African Running. In Pitsiladis, Y., Bale, J. and Sharp, C. *et al.* (eds) *East African Running – Towards a cross-disciplinary perspective*. London: Routledge. pp. 24–40.

Johnson, N. (2010) *Separate and Unequal.* London: Fabian Society.

Jones, S. (1988) *Sport, Politics and the Working Class.* Manchester: Manchester University Press.

Katwala, S. (2004) Political footballs. *Fabian Review: The Age of Terror?* 116 (2): 14–16.

Kay, J. (2010) A window of opportunity? Preliminary thoughts on women's sport in post-war Britain. *Sport in History*, 30 (2): 196–218.

Markovits, B. (2003) The Colours of Sport. *New Left Review*, July/August 22: 151–160.

Marquand, D. (2004) *The Decline of the Public.* Oxford: Oxford University Press.

Obama, B. (2008) *Dreams of My Father.* New York: Three Rivers Press.

Osbourne, C. and Skillen, F. (2010) The state of play: women in British sport history. *Sport in History*, 30 (2): 189–195.

Sen, A. (2009) *The Idea of Justice.* London: Allen Lane.

Sugden, J. (1996) *Boxing and Society.* Manchester: Manchester University Press.

Therborn, G. (2001) Into the 21st century. *New Left Review*, 10 July/August: 87–111.

Wright, E. (2009) Class patternings. *New Left Review*, November/December, 60: 101–118.

5 'I've lost my football . . .'

Rethinking gender, the hidden curriculum and sport in the global context

Laura Azzarito

Introduction

Equal-opportunity policies introduced in schools in the late 1970s in the United States and in the 1980s in the United Kingdom have positively influenced young women's rates of participation in school physical education and sport. Despite the promise of equal access to education, however, young women continue to face social and structural barriers to engaging in sports. In the context of the United Kingdom, for example, as Clark and Paechter (2007) have pointed out, the celebration of achieved gender equality in such sports as football reflects a rhetorical acceptance of girls in sport, while hindering the resolution of ongoing inequalities. Gender issues continue to limit many women's opportunities, choices, and embodied experiences in sports, in many different ways. While recreational practices such as walking, swimming, netball and jogging play a significant role in the everyday lives of young women, with regard to participation in organised sport such as football, the proportion of young men aged 16–24 is double that of young women (UK Sport, 2006).

Researchers have suggested that, despite some progress towards gender equity, the widespread notion of gender-appropriate physical activities in school PE and sport persists (Azzarito and Solmon, 2009; Gorely, *et al.*, 2003; Oliver *et al.*, 2009; Scraton *et al.*, 1999). The problem with gender-appropriate physical activity practices is that such sites discriminate against girls' participation in certain sports such as football or rugby (Clark and Paechter, 2007; Paechter, 2003). The social construction of those sports as male domains privileges boys' engagement in those 'masculinising' practices. Football and/or rugby, for instance, are seen as particularly relevant to male identity formation as they emphasise masculine body performances such as forceful actions, physical contact, muscularity, bigness, power, and strength (Gorely *et al.*, 2003). In conventional gender terms, those body performances fixate boys' sense of self as masculine in opposition to girls' feminine behaviour in sport. Although it could be argued that women's participation in sports such as football is met with greater encouragement and acceptance today than in previous decades (Giardina, 2003), many young women either continue to be excluded or occupy marginal positions in such practices. At best, when included or legitimated, young women's body experiences remain framed within the new gendered global order of sport (Azzarito, 2010).

The hidden curriculum, gender(s) and exclusion in the global/local terrain: from social feminist critique to post-feminist claims

A brief historical account of the hidden curriculum

Over the past forty years, much of the research on young women in sport and PE has been concerned with revealing the hidden curriculum as a gender issue in local contexts (Bain, 1975, 1985; Fernandez-Balboa, 1993; Dewar, 1987). Researchers initially conceptualised the hidden curriculum as gendered socio-cultural beliefs, values, knowledge and ways of being that students implicitly learn within the educational process. Social feminism, as a political, cultural and philosophical movement, emerged in the 1970s and 1980s in the struggle for social change by recognising women's oppression in society (Weedon, 1997). Partially in response to social feminist claims, in 1979 the United States enacted significant educational reform (Vertinsky, 1992). Title IX, which categorised gender-segregated PE classes as sexist, promoted equality by mandating co-educational PE classes. Although the legislation aimed to resolve the gender problem quickly, stereotypical gender attitudes and beliefs, unequal distribution of resources and opportunities, girls' lack of prior experiences and traditionally gendered practices continued to negatively influence girls in sport and PE (Azzarito and Solmon, 2005). Recognising gender as a social construct (Dewar, 1987; Theberge, 1987; Vines and Bleke, 1987), later research pointed out how in the enactment of Title IX, 'equal access' did not correspond to 'equal opportunities' for girls and boys (Vertinsky, 1992).

Why has the 'equal access' enacted by Title IX not ensured equal opportunities for girls and boys in PE and the sports arena in the USA? Unequal gender power relations are structured in institutions, organisations, and practices, according to Vertinsky (1992). In her research on the history and culture of gendered practices in sports, Vertinsky pointed out how biological arguments have often been used to explain gender differences and to maintain a gender/sex binary in PE and sports. She argued that by treating sex as natural categories, gendered assumptions in the PE classroom reproduce male dominance and dictate girls' and boys' participation in physical activities. Transforming the patriarchal nature of the PE curriculum is a challenging task however, precisely because of the deeply rooted beliefs about biological influences on gender within the sport-based PE curriculum. As researchers in the United Kingdom have argued more recently, girls' limited or negative experiences of sport can constrain their physical development and physical-activity levels across the lifespan (Gorely et al., 2003; Flintoff and Scraton, 2001).

In the United Kingdom, since the beginning of the 1980s, women's growing presence in the workplace and education has paralleled the enactment of sex-discrimination and equal-opportunity legislation. The National Curriculum of 1989 in England and Wales was introduced with the premise that implementing a 'common curriculum' would ensure 'equal opportunities for all pupils' (Coppock et al., 2006, p. 69). The commitment to equal allocation of opportunities and resources for girls and boys in school was particularly relevant to subjects such as PE, science and technology, since those school subjects had been traditionally constructed as boys' domains 'irrelevant' to girls. With regard to the National Curriculum for Physical Education in schools, 'the need to avoid stereotypes and extend pupils' capabilities and range of interest beyond conventional horizons' (DES, 1991) was emphasised. School sport and PE, thus, were considered crucial sites for questioning, challenging stereotypes, addressing pervasive gender discrimination, and providing equal opportunities for girls (Lines and Stidder, 2003). Despite the hope that implementing equality policies would wipe out inequalities between girls and boys, assumptions about gender have not been eradicated in educational institutions (Francis, 2009).

Whereas the educational move towards gender equality was supported by governmental policy and the National Curriculum in the 1980s, the promise of ensuring equal opportunities was never fulfilled. The PE curriculum has remained mostly gender-segregated, differentiated on the basis of gender as a biological difference between girls and boys (Green and Scraton, 1998; Lines and Stidder, 2003). A clear gender distinction between sport-competitive, organised team sports as traditionally masculinising, and 'boy-appropriate,' in opposition to recreational, leisure-oriented sports, or 'girl-appropriate,' remains embedded in schools and in wider sport contexts (Cockburn, 2001; Coppock *et al.*, 2006; Hargreaves, 1994). For instance, Cockburn (2001) argued that netball, a popular sport among young women in the United Kingdom, implicitly reproduces the widespread stereotype that 'girls are often assumed to be more suited to netball, simply because they are girls and not because they are necessarily better than boys' (p. 71).

As a result of the dominant discourse of netball as a feminising sport practice, girls are encouraged to engage in it and they, themselves, normalised by such gendered discourse, often choose to participate in it. Rather than challenging and destabilising gender-appropriate physical activities, the inclusion of netball in single-sex female PE classes and the exclusion of football, for instance, reproduces the gendered hidden curriculum. In local school practices, the hidden curriculum maintains traditional sports such as football in a male domain and netball in a female one. The inherent problem with single-sex PE practices is that they ultimately work to naturalise and thus fix the gender/sex binary, by sustaining the traditional construction of gender-appropriate physical activity, and feminine versus masculine behaviour. The hetero-normative discourse of gender/sex implicitly operates to maintain the gendered order of sports, where young women might occupy a marginal position in 'real' sports, such as men's football, a dominant sport in the media. However, the media representation of men's football holds girls' centred position in 'minor' sports such as netball. Different from football, however, netball remains a sport absent from mainstream national and global sport media.

Despite governmental policy and sustained academic efforts, young women have limited opportunities and choices to fully develop their potential physicality in the local context of school PE and sport; young women's making sense of themselves in sport often remains confined to gendered ideals. Although gender is neither a homogeneous nor a biological category, and gendered identities are not fixed, culturally constructed gendered ideals implicitly reproduce 'feminine and/or masculine appropriate' practices of the body in and outside of school (Paechter, 2003). Maintaining gender-appropriate activities 'naturalises' the gender/sex dichotomy, intimately affecting the ways young people construct their identities and learn how to display feminine- or masculine-appropriate behaviour in sport, recreation and fitness. Netball, for example, becomes a feminine-appropriate pedagogical practice, different from and in opposition to football, which is presented as a masculine-appropriate sport.

Women's exclusion from sport: an issue resolved?

Early research on the hidden curriculum aimed to reveal gender issues embedded in PE and sport with a view to exposing the similar ways women face obstacles to opportunity because of their gender. More recently, researchers have attempted to demonstrate that girls and boys negotiate, take up, and/or reject gendered discourses of sport in a variety of ways by displaying a range of 'masculine' and 'feminine' behaviours (Azzarito and Katzew, 2010; Ronholt, 2002). These more contemporary approaches aim to reveal the hidden curriculum by challenging and disrupting the notion of gender as a homogenous category. Theory underlying this research, rejects the view that 'male' and 'female' are dichotomous categories, and instead posits 'genders' as fluid, malleable, socially constructed categories. Girlhood, from this view, is not a unitary notion, but performed by female adolescents in a wide range of ways based on the kinds of choices, opportunities and agency available to them.

While young women continue to be excluded (and might exclude themselves) from PE classes and school sport at the local level, at the global level, contemporary media accounts of new femininities have challenged such views. Recently, media representations of women in sport have disrupted gendered practices and stereotypes, promoting neo-liberal discourses of women's achievement and choice in sport (Heywood, 2007). Discourses of femininity have historically fixed girls to a 'naturally' weaker and more fragile body than men's, but emerging discourses of powerful, confident and successful girls in sport have challenged such traditional discourses of 'womanhood' (Dillabough et al., 2008). Different from some researchers' contemporary interest in 'talking gender' (Evans and Penney, 2002), it could be argued that to 're-think gender,' the complex ways in which globalisation has produced new discourses of achieved gender equality (Blackmore, 2009) must be taken into account.

The hidden curriculum at the local level of school PE and sport needs to be extended to the global arena. In particular, the new hidden curriculum is complicated by the marriage between neo-liberal discourses of equality and media representations of certain new ideals of successful, valuable and healthy feminine corporeal appearances. Neo-liberal discourses of achieved equality, while they explicitly carry on a commitment to equal 'fair treatment' and the 'meritocratic progress' for men and women (Coppock et al., 2006, p. 14), also promote narratives of gender-neutral opportunity emphasising individual accomplishment, self-responsibility, individual freedom and ambition. Such discourses work as regulatory regimes and practices suggesting that access to social and economic success is equally and globally available for *all* women (Burns, 2008).

Globalisation and its hidden curriculum puts forward a new gender order buoyed by neo-liberal narratives of achieved equal opportunity and choice in education, society and sport. In Connell's (2000) terms, 'Neo-liberal politics has little to say, explicitly, about gender. It speaks a gender-neutral language of "markets," "individuals," and "choice"' (p. 51). The 'gender-neutral' individual is, then, indifferently a man or woman, who is mobile, flexible and successful in the new global economies (Blackmore, 2009). The qualities of self-making and self-invention that sport promotes are central in producing the neo-liberal subject; a subject who can successfully meet the challenges that the new economies present to young girls, for instance. Discourses of new femininities in the new global gender order inscribe the ideal 'feminine as a bourgeois sign in new ways' (Walkerdine and Ringrose, 2006, p. 33). Discourses of female success through self-invention and individual enterprise operate to celebrate upward mobility and achievement in society through education, sport and consumption. In the contemporary global context and in discourses of new femininities, white middle-class girls, according to Burns (2008), represent the 'ideal clients' for the global production of neo-liberal subjects: girl-citizens, who are hard workers, flexible, creative and competitive in the global market.

Feminists' ongoing struggle against gender discrimination and for the promotion of gender equity seems outdated in the new global order, a useless political struggle according to post-feminists. Upheld by neo-liberal trends, post-feminist discourses celebrate girls' achievement in schools (Walkerdine and Ringrose, 2006), media representation of female empowerment and success in and through sport (Azzarito, 2010). Privilege and privileged positions in Western global society are granted to some women through the effects of whiteness and social class, which allow them to take up gender-neutral discourses in the name of post-feminism. In the context of sport, with an increased intensification of global networks, visual communication, and representation, media imaginings of sporting women tends to echo and epitomise the image of sporting men. Sporting women are like men, increasingly panoptised as successful, active, self-inventing and skilled sporting bodies. In the global society, through this new hidden curriculum, young girls are thought 'to construct their bodies and their lives alongside discourses of self-esteem, self-help, healthism, and post-feminist discourses such as "girl-power"' (Burns, 2008, p. 353).

The media circulation of the 'new girl' in sport, modelled after 'the girl-power' movement,[1] puts forward the image of an athletic, self-made, cosmopolitan, versatile femininity in a global landscape. This type of girlhood represents girls who learn how to be successful in the society through their high achievement in education as well as in sport (Azzarito, 2010). Sport thus provides relevant practices for learning self-management, allowing girls to construct themselves as successful citizen-subjects in the global marketplace. For instance, football, as celebrated by popular movies such as *Bend It Like Beckham* offers a media site for *all* girls to fantasise about and aspire to become footballers. The emergence of the 'new girl' in sport, to some extent represented by the two female main characters in *Bend It Like Beckham*, engenders and honours white ideals of the highly successful, confident, assertive and skilful girl in sport (Giardina, 2003), ideals that post-feminists put forward to celebrate the death of feminism.

'Other' kinds of girls in sport and the 'risk' of not becoming the 'new girl'

The illusion of achieved gender equality makes visible the inclusion of a very small portion of women in sport, however; while it simultaneously hinders the reality of many 'Other' women who continue to be excluded (Harris, 2004). While providing positive and powerful images of women in sport, such media representations of the new girl in sport disguise issues of gender inequalities that still inform the everyday practices, realities and experiences of many women in local sites of sport and school. Today, the role of gender in girls' experiences of sport should be contextualised within emerging global discourses of young women 'at risk' on the one hand, and new femininities on the other. In the United Kingdom, for example, young ethnic minority women (see also Chapters 1 and 8, in this volume), and women of lower socio-economic classes, are identified as being more likely to be unhealthy and less likely to engage in sport and recreation than white wealthy or middle-class women (UK Sport, 2006). Notably, South Asian girls are identified as the least likely of all the different ethnic groups to participate regularly in sport; a cohort of girls 'at risk' of inactive lifestyles (Nazroo, 2003). Although some researchers have attempted to problematise why it is that sport plays such a marginal role in the lives of South Asian adolescent girls and the 'fact' that they tend to be inactive (Fleming, 1994; Kay, 2006; Walseth, 2006; Walseth and Fasting, 2004), it seems that sport is disconnected from their sense of self, sense of agency and cultural upbringing. In many cases, due to a lack of economic and educational resources, sport simply continues to remain a site of exclusion for girls (Azzarito and Sterling, 2010; Fleming, 1994; Scraton, 2001).

Importantly too, the stereotypical construction of South Asian girls as 'passive' or 'subordinated' by family in the home might significantly inform the ways South Asian girls are (mis)represented in sport. Their invisibility in the media narrative of sporting bodies heightens this gendered and racial stereotypical view (Scraton, 2001). As Harris (2004) cautions, the 'at-risk minority is then treated as an aberration, of concern chiefly because it constitutes a threat to society. This minority is often then, marked as *different* from the norm, pathologized, criminalized, and punished' (p. 36). The youth-at-risk discourse fixates ethnic minority girls as 'different,' framing their subjectivity as potentially lacking self-responsibility and failing to achieve new feminine ideals of normalcy; a subject position that calls for surveillance and intervention (Blackmore, 2009).

Both media texts and public health discourses that designate South Asian girls as potentially at risk are complicit with the global 'hidden curriculum' by making visible 'successful' bodies in health and sport that young people read and learn. Media images function as new pedagogies (Kenway and Bullen, 2008), offering powerful sites of learning for young people beyond the traditional space of the local school. With regard to women in sport, global media fabricates a hidden curriculum of new femininities. The implications of the neo-liberal discourse of new womanhood are clear: young women who struggle to adhere and perform these globally fabricated ideals of the neo-liberal female subject in sport may be excluded from high-status feminine subjectivities and, moreover, are responsible for their potential 'failure.' Implicitly, in opposition to new sporting girls, 'Other' kinds of girls are deemed as a 'problem' or 'disadvantaged.'

While their femininity may be expressed in different ways from South Asian British girls, girls from white working-class backgrounds are less likely to be physically active (UK Sport, 2006). At the same time, they are also more likely to struggle to adjust to white middle-class girls' values and attitudes (Francis and Skelton, 2005). The values and attitudes that constitute contemporary 'feminine' middle-class performance (e.g. ambition, competition, drive, individualist values) facilitate middle-class girls' achievement in education as those values tend to be privileged in school. Moreover, with the global circulation of the new girl in sport, traditional masculine attributes such as competition and drive are promoted and valued through sport. Working-class girls' resources and their performances of femininity may be distant from new normative qualities of reinvention necessary 'to obtain the bourgeois success of the middle class girl' (Walkerdine and Ringrose, 2009, p. 33). While working-class girls are yet 'under-achievers' in school compared to middle-class girls (Francis and Skelton, 2005), in many cases, sport also remains a site of exclusion for working-class girls. This is because of limited economic resources they have available in order to fully and broadly engage with physical culture in their daily lives (Hargreaves and Vertinsky, 2007). Whereas girls' choice of sport is not gender-neutral, their gendered performance in sport is, indeed, mediated by social class and race/ethnicity.

Given the enduring gendered practices in local sites of sport and school physical education (PE) (Azzarito and Solmon, 2009; Gorely *et al.*, 2003; Lines and Stidder, 2003; Oliver *et al.*, 2009), which simultaneously co-exist with and contradict emerging, powerful images of new femininities in sport, researchers' attention to issues of gender(s), sport and exclusion is critically important to achieving more equitable physical-activity practices. Further research, therefore, should interrogate the complex ways in which issues of gender(s) and exclusion implicitly and explicitly operate in local pedagogical sites in the context of globally produced new femininities. Moreover, seeking to understand how emergent femininities in sport might be reconceptualised against a post-feminist panorama is central to contemporary debates about issues of exclusion/inclusion. In particular, critical questions should problematise the following: What types of girlhood have access to traditional sporting or 'masculinising' practices, which are nowadays represented by neo-liberal discourses of girlhood as pathways to health and success for the 'New Woman' in sport?

Through the narrative of a young South Asian woman, Zahra, a participant in a large visual ethnography in school PE classes, I discuss how the local/global hidden curriculum can inform young women's ways of speaking, experiencing, and seeing themselves in sport. Zahra's embodiment of sport manifests her negotiation of discourses of sport and gender, revealing the ways she is normalised but, at the same time, resistant to the gendered order of football and netball in and outside of school. Although I describe Zahra as 'South Asian' in this chapter, the use of this umbrella term does not aim to treat race as a homogeneous category producing a 'false universalism' (Fleming, 1994). The discussion of 'South Asian' girlhood throughout this chapter is particularly focused on South Asian girls whose social, economic, or educational resources limit or prevent their engagement in certain sports. In the discussion and analysis that follows, I strive to recognise the subjective differences of cultural practices, upbringings, experiences and religiosity among British individuals with immigrant backgrounds.

The myth of achieved gender equality in sport and the gendered reality of school physical education: Zahra's embodied experience

The narrative of Zahra included below is taken from a visual ethnographic research project conducted in the Midlands region of the United Kingdom, and sponsored by the Economic and Social Research Council.[2] The research project gave young people in predominantly diverse, inner-city schools an opportunity to present their engagement with physical activity visually, through digital photography, and verbally, through interviews with researchers. Zahra is a young South Asian girl who regularly and enthusiastically participates in single-sex female PE classes with her classmates, and, who, as she reiterated during her interviews, really enjoys physical activity. Zahra sees herself as 'very sporty.' When the interviewer asked her which school subjects were her favourite, Zahra replied:

Zahra: I like maths because I get A stars on that so, and I like PE . . . I try to do every sport, it's better, it's more fun!
Int.: And which one is your favourite?
Zahra: I think netball . . . because you have to run around as much as in football, but you get to like pass the ball really fast, and the game goes really fast . . . a lot of people love netball.

Zahra seems very engaged in PE, and her talk about sport during the interview particularly centres on comparing netball and football. Quick passing and running are critical features of football which, for Zahra, seem to represent the basis for a comparison to netball. Netball, according to Zahra, is a very popular sport in England, especially among girls, whose participation in netball is encouraged and supported by PE teachers. Zahra explains:

Int.: Do both boys and girls play it [netball] here in England?
Zahra: I'm not sure about boys, but I think girls . . . the girls on the netball team are really, really good. . . . They've been playing it for years.

As Cockburn (2001) found ten years ago describing the larger context of young women and sport in the United Kingdom, in Zahra's school, netball was delivered consistently as a core unit in the PE curriculum through the secondary-school years in girls' single-sex PE classes. When girls are channelled into the practice of netball through school PE, netball works as a gendered hidden curriculum to normalise, discipline and regulate young women to the ideals of 'proper femininity' upon which netball is constructed (Cockburn, 2001). The gendered social construction of netball as a popular 'girls' sport in England increases young women's participation in this sport, because it offers a women's space in and through which girls can still be 'appropriate girls.' The hidden curriculum in PE, in this case, maintains girls' marginal engagement with football, by providing them with an alternative (netball) to what is still viewed as a male domain (football).

Nonetheless, what emerged during Zahra's conversation with the interviewer was her negotiation and re-positioning of herself within discourses of football, netball and gender. Young people speak from their own perspectives, their experiences, and the realities they inhabit and construct in 'gendering themselves' through sport (Azzarito and Katzew, 2010). Although Zahra initially defined netball as her favourite sport, later on, recalling prior experiences in primary school, she defined herself as a 'footballer':

Zahra: *I'm really sporty.* I like all different kind of sports, like football and netball . . . primary school . . . I used to play since I was really small. I like being goalie, it's fun! I was in year one when I started playing football, then I played all the way through year six, and sometimes when I was in year seven and eight, I used to go to the park and play with my family.

Int.:   Did you ever play football with boys?

Zahra: In primary school, our team was mixed. It was mostly boys, but it was me and my other friend who was in it as well.

Int.:   Why don't you play football now?

Zahra: *They don't play it in this school, like, much.* . . . I haven't played it for a long time, but, I can still play because you don't have to run around, you do run around but you kinda stop, and you just, because I play goalie so I don't really run around a lot.

Int.:   You said it's quite easy being the goalie?

Zahra: I was taught by the boys in primary school.

Although Clark and Paechter (2007), drawing from the Football Association's (2005) report, suggest that, 'football has overtaken netball as the most popular sport for women in England' (p. 264), netball remains central in the female single-sex PE curriculum, as Zahra's narrative exemplifies. In Zahra's school context, for instance, PE teachers don't offer football as a core curriculum unit in the single-sex female curriculum after Year 9, instead delivering core curriculum units, such as netball, rounders (a field game, similar to softball) and trampoline. Football, however, is a core unit for the boys' PE curriculum throughout the secondary school years in the boys' single-sex 'sister' school located next to Zahra's school. Although implementing equal-opportunity policies aimed to 'treat everybody the same' (Coppock *et al*., 2006), and even single-sex PE initial teacher training (PEITT) institutions were removed after the mid-1980s in the United Kingdom, single-sex practices in PE persist in secondary schools (Benn and Dagkas, 2006). Mixed-sex provision was practised in the primary school where Zahra learned football. Despite her positive bodily remembrance of football as learned and played with boys in primary school, experience that solidly informs her identity as a 'footballer,' her body experiences in secondary school prevent her from further developing that aspect of her identity by narrowly framing her subjective experiences with the gendered dimension of feminine-appropriate practices. When talking about football and her learning experience, including learning with and through boys' teaching, not once during the interview did Zahra reveal feeling threatened by her engagement with the 'masculine pursuit' football represents (Clark and Paechter, 2007). Gender is not a homogeneous, natural category, but individual girls and boys take up genders in fluid, multiple, and contradictory ways (Azzarito and Katzew, 2010). Zahra's taking up a female footballer identity might be influenced by her engagement with global messages about new, empowered femininities.

Zahra's embodiment of football is perhaps informed by her reading and interpretation of sport as portrayed by the media; she points out that *Bend It Like Beckham* is one of her favourite movies because it is about sport, and especially about 'girls who play proper football.' Despite her memories, aspirations and fantasies about football, the reality of her school PE classes brings to light the lack of opportunities the hidden curriculum produces. Although girls' participation in sport has increased and girls such as Zahra, more and more, can imagine themselves as 'very sporty' or even as footballers, football, including football instruction in local school communities, for the most part remains a public, male domain.

As Zahra further explains, while she wishes she could play football, no football clubs are available close to her home or at school. Yet, she still sees herself as being active with her family members and enjoying recreational activities at home and in parks; as she explains:

> I go out a lot, I don't really stay at home like every day. I just go out and walk, or go and do something because I don't like sitting down and doing nothing ... I always try and do something active. I like walk around in the house, or go out in the garden and play or something. When I go to the park with my little sister, we run around and play on the swings and everything.

Interestingly, while Zahra speaks of herself as being very sporty, her visual diary of her physical-activity experiences gives a different picture of her everyday life. These images, for instance, capture the discrepancy between her verbal narrative centring on football and netball – a sporty self – and her visual representation of someone who engages in recreational, leisure activities with her little sister in her garden and/or parks.

Figure 5.1 Zahra's little sister at the park

Figure 5.2 Playing with Zahra's little sister in the garden

Figure 5.3 A walk in the nearby park with Zahra's little sister

When the interviewer probed these differences, Zahra responded:

Int.:   You talked about football quite a bit, but you didn't include any pictures of . . . I mean there are no pictures of sports or things like football. Is there a reason why you didn't include these pictures?

Zahra: I've lost my football. I've lost my football so I couldn't take any pictures of it.

Zahra's conflictual embodiment symbolises the contradiction between her memories and dreams, and the everyday realities of gendered physical activity practices in schools. As Zahra's narrative demonstrates, neo-liberal discourses of achieved gender equality and post-feminist positions fail to consider the structural inequalities, and particularly the economic, educational and social barriers that many women face in their localities and that inhibit them from fully enjoying, appreciating and experiencing sport.

Conclusion

Despite the proclamation of achieved gender equality that the media often celebrate when delivering images of 'new,' successful young women in sport, images endorsed by post-feminist discourses, the gender gap in and outside of school PE and in the wider context of sport remains. The post-feminist illusion of achieved gender equality circulated in the global arena diverges from the realities of many local school PE and sport contexts, where gendered practices have not been dismantled. In the United Kingdom, although researchers have attempted to understand why so few South Asian women participate in sport, these attempts need to take into account how the ongoing hidden curriculum in local and global contexts of sport shapes, constrains and defines young women's bodies. It has been central to the aim of this chapter, therefore, to make visible how the hidden curriculum at the local level intertwines with neo-liberal discourses of new femininities in sport. It offers Zahra's narrative to show the complicated, yet implicit ways, cultural, educational and structural gender inequalities inform and frame young women's physicality.

Further this chapter demonstrates how ongoing pervasive attitudes about 'gender-appropriate' practices and single-sex sport practices impact young women in sport, ultimately maintaining the exclusion of women from certain sports. In subtle ways, the absence of women of different ethnicities in sports such as football maintains the stereotypical construction of girls of different ethnic backgrounds as passive and non-athletic. Moreover, it lays blame on the girls themselves for making inappropriate choices in sport. Zahra's narrative, and the narratives of other South Asian young women's engagement with physical activity, as demonstrated elsewhere (Azzarito and Katzew, 2010), suggest that in spite of neo-liberal and post-feminist discourses celebrating new femininities, the local practices of sport and sport-based PE remains, for the most part, are either gendered or available to only some young women who, because of their social, economic and educational resources, can adhere to and/or perform the emerging discourses of successful girlhood to fit the new global order (Harris, 2004).

Thus, discourses of new femininities circulating in global media offer successful, powerful images of women constructed around 'masculine pursuits' (Francis and Skelton, 2005) that appeal to younger women. But media representations operate to privilege only certain types of success, upward mobility and consumption through education and sport. At the same time, young women's participation in physical activity continues to be normalised and regulated by the hidden curriculum of their local contexts. Contemporary discourses, embraced by post-feminists, adopt a gender-, social-class- and racial-neutral language, a neo-liberal discourse claiming that women's significant advancement in society is the result of successfully implementing equal-opportunity reforms and policies. These neo-liberal positions produced by the global hidden curriculum implicitly function to occlude the multi-layered structural inequalities, such as those evident in Zahra's narrative, embedded in the localities of many women's everyday lives. Simultaneously, they deny the need for a feminist agenda to promote the advancement of *all* young women in all public spheres.

Notes

1 Modelled after the British pop group Spice Girls and Lara Croft, and inspired by the DIY (do it yourself) punk philosophy, 'Girlpower' is a post-feminist movement. In the early 1990s, Girlpower became a popular movement in the United States and the United Kingdom and aimed to portray girls as equal to boys. It also promoted a new type of girlhood represented as attractive, independent, successful, confident, self-determined, self-inventing and driven by individualistic ideals.
2 The ESRC is the UK's leading organisation for research funding in the social sciences that tackles pressing social issues such as poverty, health and education.

References

Azzarito, L. (2010) New girls, transcendent femininities and new pedagogies: Toward girls' hybrid bodies? *Sport, Education and Society*, 15: 261–275.
Azzarito, L. and Katzew, A. (2010) Performing identities in physical education: (En)gendering fluid selves. *Research Quarterly for Exercise and Sport*, 81(1): 25–37.
Azzarito, L. and Solmon, M.A. (2005) A reconceptualization of physical education: The intersection of gender/race/social class. *Sport, Education and Society*, 10: 25–47.
Azzarito, L. and Solmon, M.A. (2009) An investigation of students' embodied discourses in physical education: A gender project. *Journal of Teaching in Physical Education*, 2: 173–191.
Azzarito, L. and Sterling, J. (2010) 'What it was in my eyes': Picturing youths' embodiment in 'real' spaces. *Qualitative Research in Sport and Exercise* (Special edition on Visual Methods in Physical Culture), 2: 209–227.
Bain, L.L. (1975) The hidden curriculum in physical education. *Quest*, 24: 92–101.
Bain, L.L. (1985) The hidden curriculum re-examined. *Quest*, 37: 145–153.
Benn, T. and Dagkas, S. (2006) Incompatible? Compulsory mixed-sex physical education initial teacher training (PEITT) and the inclusion of Muslim women: A case-study on seeking solutions. *European Physical Education*, 12: 181–200.

Blackmore, J. (2009) Globalization, transnational feminism and educational justice. In Zajda, J. and Freeman, K. (eds) *Race, Ethnicity and Gender in Education. Cross-cultural understanding.* London: Spinger, pp. 3–29.

Burns, K. (2008) (Re)imagining the global, rethinking gender in education. *Discourse: Studies in the Cultural politics of Education*, 29: 343–357.

Clark, S. and Paechter, C. (2007) Why can't girls play football? Gender dynamics and the playground. *Sport, Education and Society*, 12: 261–276.

Cockburn, C. (2001) Year 9 girls and physical education: A survey of pupil perceptions. *Bulletin of Physical Education*, 37: 5–24.

Connell, R.W. (2000) *The Men and the Boys.* Sydney: Allen and Unwin.

Coppock, V., Haydon, D. and Richter, I. (2006) *The Illusion of 'Post-feminism.' New women, old myths.* Abingdon, Oxon: Taylor and Francis.

DES (1991) *Physical Education for Ages 5 to 16. Proposals of the Secretary of State for Education and Science and the Secretary of States for Wales.* London: HMSO.

Dewar, A.M. (1987) The social construction of gender in physical education. *Women's Studies International Forum*, 10: 453–465.

Dillabough, J., McLeod, J. and Mills, M. (2008) In search of allies and others: 'troubling' gender and education. *Discourse: Studies in the Cultural Politics of Education*, 29: 301–310.

Evans, J. and Penney, D. (2002) Talking gender. In D. Penney (ed.) *Gender and Physical Education. Contemporary issues and future directions.* New York: Routledge, pp. 13–23.

Fernandez-Balboa, J.M. (1993) Sociocultural characteristics of the hidden curriculum in physical education. *Quest*, 45: 230–254.

Fleming, S. (1994) Sport and South Asian youth: The perils of 'false universalism' and stereotyping. *Leisure Studies*, 12: 159–177.

Flintoff, A. and Scraton, S. (2001) Stepping into active leisure? Young women's perceptions of active lifestyles and their experiences of school physical education. *Sport, Education and Society*, 6: 5–21.

Francis, B. (2009) The nature of gender. In Skelton, C. Francis, B. and Smulyan, L. (eds) *Gender and Education.* London: Sage Publications, pp. 7–17.

Francis, B. and Skelton, C. (2005) *Reassessing Gender and Achievement.* London: Routledge.

Giardina, M. (2003) Bend it like Beckham in the global popular. Stylish hybridity, performativity and the politics of representation. *Journal of Sport and Social Issues*, 27: 65–82.

Gorely, T., Holroyd, R. and Kirk, D. (2003) Muscularity, the habitus and the social construction of gender. Toward a gender relevant physical education. *British Journal of Sociology of Education*, 24: 429–448.

Green, K. and Scraton, S. (1998) Gender, coeducation and secondary physical education. In Hardman, K. and Hardman, K. (eds) *Physical Education: A Reader.* Aachen: Meyer and Meyer, pp. 272–289.

Hargreaves, J. (1994) *Sporting Females. Critical issues in the history and sociology of women's sports.* London: Routledge.

Hargreaves, J. and Vertinsky, P. (2007) *Physical Culture, Power, and the Body.* London: Routledge.

Harris, A. (2004) *Future Girls. Young women in the twenty-first century.* London: Routledge.

Heywood, L. (2007) Producing girls. Empire, sport, and the neo-liberal body. In Hargreaves,

J. and Vertinsky, P. (eds) *Physical Culture, Power and the Body*. London: Routledge, pp. 101–120.

Lines, G. and Stidder, G. (2003) Reflection on the mixed- and single-sex PE debate. In Hayes, S. and Stidder, G. (eds) *Equity and Inclusion in Physical Education and Sport. Contemporary issues for trainees, teachers and practitioners*. London: Routledge.

Kay, T. (2006) Daughters of Islam: Family influences on Muslim young women's participation in sport. *International Review for the Sociology of Sport*, 41: 357–373.

Nazroo, J.Y. (2003) The structuring of ethnic inequalities in health: Economic position, racial discrimination, and racism. *American Journal of Public Health*, 93: 277–284.

Oliver, K.L., Hamzeh, M. and McCaughtry, N. (2009) Girly girls can play games/las minas pueden jugar tambien: Co-creating a curriculum of possibilities with fifth-grade girls. *Journal of Teaching in Physical Education*, 28 (1): 90–110.

Paechter, C. (2003) Power, bodies and identity: How different forms of physical education construct varying masculinities and femininities in secondary schools. *Sex Education*, 3: 47–59.

Ronholt, H. (2002). 'It's only the sissies . . .': Analysis of teaching and learning processes in physical education: A contribution to the hidden curriculum. *Sport, Education and Society*, 7: 25–36.

Scraton, S. (2001) Reconceptualizing race, gender and sport: The contribution of black feminism. In Carrington, B. and McDonald, I. (eds) *'Race,' sport and British society*. London: Routledge, pp. 170–187.

Scraton, S., Fasting, K. and Pfister, G. *et al.* (1999) It's still a man's game? The experiences of top-level European women footballers. *International Review for the Sociology of Sport*, 34: 99–111.

Theberge, N. (1987) Sport and women's empowerment. *Women Studies International*, 10: 387–393.

UK Sport (2006) *Women in Sport. The State of Play 2006*. Online: www.uksport.gov.uk.

Vertinsky, P.A. (1992) Reclaiming space, revisioning the body: The quest for gender-sensitive physical education. *Quest*, 44: 373–396.

Vines, G. and Bieke, C. (1987) A sporting chance: The anatomy of destiny. *Women's Studies International Forum*, 10: 337–347.

Walkerdine, V. and Ringrose, J. (2006) Femininities: Reclassifying upward mobility and the neo-liberal subject. In Skelton, C., Francis, B. and Smulyan, L. (eds) *Gender and Education*. London: Sage Publications, pp. 31–46.

Walseth, K. (2006) Young women and sport: The impact of identity work. *Leisure Studies*, 25 (1): 75–94.

Walseth, K. and Fastin, K. (2004) Sport as a means of integrating minority women. *Sport in Society*, 7 (1): 109–129.

Weedon, C. (1997) *Feminist Practice and Poststructuralist Theory*. Malden, MA: Blackwell Publishers Inc.

6 Ability as an exclusionary concept in youth sport

Peter J. Hay

Introduction

In this chapter I will offer a socially critical explanation of two key ways in which the concept or notion of ability can influence the engagement and progress of children and young people in sport. In the first instance I will focus on the exclusionary consequences of common and prevailing understandings of ability and their notable influence in numerous talent identification processes. Second, I will offer an alternative social construction conception of ability to demonstrate the arbitrary nature of ability and its potential for influencing the inclusion and exclusion of young people in a movement culture such as sport.

Ability in sport is a concept that people tend to take for granted. For this reason traditional conceptions of ability seem to have largely gone unchallenged and have, therefore, prevailed in the field. These conceptions of ability are almost always associated with the factors that differentiate between people. They represent the privileging of a certain understanding of ability rather than the existence of only one concept or paradigm. That is, ability can also be viewed in a normative sense as competence, entailing the display and development of capacities that most people possess and that can support their participation in sport (e.g. the ability to run or walk or throw). The enduring manifestation of a view of ability as differing degrees of talent or capacity to perform in sport, rather than as competence, is perhaps a consequence of its comfortable congruence with the practices and cultural characteristics of sport. These include the keeping of scores, the awareness of winners and losers and the celebration of and fascination with sporting excellence.

Several researchers have highlighted the way in which certain cultural practices associated with sport act to privilege some people while others are marginalised or excluded (e.g. Azzarito and Harrison, 2008; Collins and Kay, 2003; Elling and Knoppers, 2005). These practices and discriminatory consequences have been evident in relation to the effects of certain values, beliefs and expectations within sport on the participation of women (Elling and Knoppers, 2005; Gorely *et al.*, 2003), of different races (Scraton *et al.*, 2005), and of different social classes (Green *et al.*, 2005; Wilson, 2002). While the notion of ability as an explanation for inordinate participation and performance rates of certain racial groups in sport has been critiqued in the past (e.g. Hoberman, 1997), a greater focus on the way in which abilities are conceived of and contribute to the exclusionary outcomes of sport is warranted.

Biological bases of ability

Traditional and common understandings of ability in sport are largely homologous with conceptions of intellectual or cognitive ability and tend to be situated within discussions about the relative contributions of one's genetic constitution and environmental conditions (Sternberg, 1998). However, recent advances in gene technology and knowledge, and the arguable pre-eminence of the physical sciences in the field of human movement studies (or kinesiology) has resulted in the privileging of a 'nature' explanation, where ability is viewed as fundamentally dependent upon one's genetic and subsequent biological composition (Manning, 2002; Paul *et al.*, 2006). The environment is inadvertently positioned as a subordinate rather than equivalent factor affecting the realisation and promotion of latent potential.

From the outset, a biological view of ability is exclusionary because its first and fundamental assumption is that the characteristics used to distinguish between the sporting performances of individuals can be viewed objectively and as the outcome of natural factors. This can promote a deterministic regime of truth where one's place and progress in sport, and another's limitations in or exit from sport, can be viewed as the outcome of natural selection. Other possible factors for differences in performances and experiences, such as the opportunity for participation, access to resources and facilities, and cultural impediments are largely overlooked. The exclusionary effects of this conceptualisation of ability are perhaps most readily evident in the measurement, identification and recognition of high ability or 'talent.' In this process, supposedly objective measures of physical capacity are treated as worthwhile predictors of talent and future sporting success. Those who are 'identified' as being most likely to be successful in a particular sport on the basis of certain physical characteristics (such as power to weight ratio, anthropometric measures, muscle type, etc.) are given special coaching attention, support and encouragement, that those who are not recognised as able have comparatively limited access to these.

Measuring ability

It is not surprising to find that in much the same way as a belief in the innate or genetically based nature of intellectual capacity gave rise to psychometric measures of an intelligence quotient (IQ) (White, 2006), belief in the biological basis of ability in sport has given rise to talent identification programmes. Considerable resources are invested into identification programmes in an effort to identify 'talented' sportspeople at a young age in order to secure their engagement in a particular sport and to develop their potential (Vaeyens *et al.*, 2008). These programmes are based on the proposition that certain physical and, to a lesser extent, psychological attributes correlate with optimal performance in certain sports (Bailey and Morely, 2006). It is assumed that a child's latent potential to achieve in particular sports can be identified through a battery of measurements focusing on the anthropometric, physiological and psychological characteristics of young people, and subsequently fostered (Pienaar *et al.*, 1998; Reilly *et al.*, 2000; Abbott and Collins, 2002). Notably, in recent developments, increasing attention has been directed towards the identification of an individual's genetic make-up to predict their likely success in various types of sports (Miah and Rich, 2006). Miah and Rich (2006) warn that genetic tests such as the ACTN3 Sports Performance Test, which can apparently indicate whether 'you, or your children, may be genetically predisposed toward sprint/power events, or towards endurance sporting *ability*' (Genetic Technologies, 2010, emphasis added), could become an integral tool for talent identification and development in sport.

There are numerous approaches to and models for talent identification (see Chapter 12 where Côté and colleagues offer further explanations on talent identification, youth and inclusive practices). Some models do highlight the importance of social and cultural learning in the realisation of and belief in the existence of certain abilities (e.g. Bailey and Morely, 2006). Fundamentally, however, the focus of these measures is the differentiation of the more physically able from the less physically able. Because of their often direct connection with a biological view of ability, the talent identification approaches that focus primarily on the genetic, anthropometric and/or physiological characteristics of an individual are arguably the most exclusionary technologies of ability. They represent value judgements about the relative worth of particular bodies and their constituent parts. It is as if the measurements of the various parts provide sufficient information about a possible future in the absence of sufficient information relating to the whole of the person in the whole of their social and cultural context. To demonstrate the way in which these forms of measurement can act in such an exclusionary manner, I will focus on one 'emerging' measurement of potential ability in sport – the 2D:4D ratio.

2D:4D ratio

Several researchers have drawn attention to a statistical relationship between the length ratios of a person's second and fourth fingers and a myriad of human biological and behavioural factors such as foetal growth, autism, hand preference, musical ability, sexual orientation, fertility and one's sporting ability (Lutchmaya *et al.*, 2004; Manning and Taylor, 2001). Male and female ability in numerous sports, particularly those involving significant running demands such as soccer and athletics, have been correlated with low 2D:4D ratios (e.g. Manning, 2002; Paul *et al.*, 2006). The ratio is determined by dividing the average length of a person's two index fingers (2D) by the average length of their two fourth fingers (4D). Obviously, the larger the fourth digit is relative to the second digit, the smaller the 2D:4D ratio will be.

While the statistical relationship between this ratio and sporting ability is well reported, the explanation for the relationship has been somewhat speculative.

Researchers have suggested that the 2D:4D ratio may correspond with prenatal and adult testosterone levels initially on the observational basis that the ratio is fixed at birth, remains constant during life and is generally lower for males than females (Manning and Taylor, 2001). Correlations between measured foetal testosterone levels and 2D:4D ratios appear to support this view (Lutchmaya *et al.*, 2004). In terms of sporting ability, it is thought that high prenatal testosterone promotes the growth of the right hemisphere of the brain which facilitates visual–spatial function so that people with small 2D:4D ratios are more spatially aware and responsive in game contexts. A second explanation is that prenatal testosterone conditions are likely to be significant antecedents to the development and stability of the vascular and muscular systems, thereby supporting advanced displays of strength and endurance.

The reported correlation between an individual's 2D:4D ratio and their ability in sport, as well as the simplicity of its measurement, positions the ratio as a 'tantalising' prospect for the identification of talented individuals at a pre-competitive stage (Paul *et al.*, 2006). Although it is unlikely that such a measure would be instituted independently of other factors (e.g. Bailey and Morely, 2006; Vaeyens *et al.*, 2008), it could nevertheless be an influential factor and a key contributor to the exclusionary effects of the ability conceptualisations that underpin it.

To illustrate, albeit anecdotally, the possible effects of such measures on youth opportunity in sport allow me to account an interaction I had with a friend of mine during the writing of this chapter. I shared with my friend the information I had been reading about the relationship between one's finger ratio and their likely abilities in sport. This person's immediate reaction was to check the lengths on my newborn baby boy's fingers, arriving at the conclusion that he was unlikely to be a high-level sportsman so his efforts might best be directed elsewhere. In this instance, judgements were already being passed on my son's suitability for and likely success in sport on the basis of a quick glance at his fourth and second fingers. The supposed innate nature of ability and the potential for objective determination had already begun its exclusionary work before my son could even crawl! My friend's reaction to the 2D:4D ratio revealed her underlying belief in the naturalness of ability, her confidence in a supposedly objective measure of talent, and a belief that involvement in sport (or other cultural activities) should be informed by one's likely success therein. Moreover, her response was consistent with the predictions of Miah and Rich (2006) who proposed that 'once the capacity to test is out there; it will be very difficult to prevent the determinist connotations that seem to pervade the lay perceptions of genetics (or associated understandings of ability)' (p. 265).

The determinism spoken of by Miah and Rich (2006) is underscored by a belief in the efficacy of narrow, biological but supposedly objective measures of ability. This belief may fuel parents' or coach's expectations of the child's future and inform their thinking and decisions about suitable fields of endeavour as well as redundant fields of engagement. Thus the child's body or (or more specifically, measurable elements of their body) become important signifiers or texts of not only these potential futures but also the courses of action appropriate to the presumed futures.

An enterprise of partiality

Determinism of the type described above, coupled with the disproportionate attention and encouragement that is given to some and not others on the basis of measured outcomes, works in both overt as well as subtle ways to exclude from sport. These measures and their rationales represent an enterprise of partiality where some facets of bodies are privileged over others. The body itself is objectified in a manner that results in the privileging of the object over the person and the social and cultural contexts in which a person lives and where their bodies communicate meaning and are read by others. In this scenario, discriminations between individuals are made on the basis of these privileging technologies. The proposed significance of the male hormone testosterone as the key factor in the differentiation of potential sporting capacity promotes an exclusionary factor that has distinct gender implications. The logical assumption from this explanation is that males have greater abilities (or more latent talent) than females and that these differences are the consequence of 'natural' factors. An expectation of the superior performances of males over females may be promoted and may foster inordinate attention to the performance optimisation of male youths. This would be at the expense of commensurate expectations of and attention to the involvement and performances of female young people.

At a simpler but no less significant level, the instigation of talent identification programmes can emphasise and promote performance over participation, and also distinction over similarity within youth sport. It communicates these values and priorities in sport both to those who are privileged and to those who are marginalised by the identification processes. While 'participation' would certainly not be discouraged, it appears to be less important than the pursuit and realisation of 'performance excellence.' So what might be experienced or learnt by children and young people in and about a sporting culture that foregrounds excellence over participation? The sport opportunities of some young people may be narrowed too early on the basis of their anthropometric or genetic suitability for a particular sport. Some children may learn that they are not well suited for sport or that alternative cultural avenues are perhaps more appropriate to pursue. Notably, a message of encouragement for all to participate and enjoy sport is marginalised.

The biological view of ability has been prominent in the field of sport. Its prominence is arguably attributable to its promotion by those who benefit from such conceptions (Hay and lisahunter, 2006) and to an absence of an alternative conception of ability. In the section that follows, a 'social construction' view of ability will be described which not only allows for an understanding of the way ability can contribute to exclusion from sport but which also provides a framework for considering how ability can be viewed and operationalised in more inclusive ways. Significantly, a social construction view of ability challenges the notion of its genetic basis, recognising that in fact our understandings and observations of abilities are formed through complex social processes, drawing on multiple sources of information.

A social construction of ability and exclusion

In recent years several researchers in the field of health and physical education have argued that traditional conceptions of and assumptions about ability are contestable (e.g. Evans, 2004; Wright and Burrows, 2006; Hay and lisahunter, 2006). Evans (2004) noted that PE had become 'disembodied,' reducing discussions about the nature of PE 'to a dribble of *unproblematic assumptions* either about motivation and health-related behaviour, or "fitness", or *"talent" for "performance"* in the interest of health and/or participation in *organized sport*' (p. 96, emphasis added). He complained that very little critical attention had been given to the concept of ability which underpinned these assumptions, or to understanding the way in which the notion of ability has been complicit in the perpetuation of inequities in PE. The same complaint could arguably be levelled against the field of sport.

In response, Evans (2004) proposed an alternative social construction conceptualisation of ability, drawing on the social theory of Pierre Bourdieu. His work, and the work of others (e.g. Evans and Penney, 2008; Hay and Macdonald, 2010) has drawn attention to the arbitrary nature of ability and its contribution to inequities in PE and sport. Evans argued that the embodied dispositions of a person, which Bourdieu described as their habitus, could be perceived as abilities when 'defined relationally with reference to values, attitudes and more prevailing within a discursive field' (Evans, 2004, p. 100). Further to this, Evans observed that one's identification as 'able,' or 'talented,' served as a form of cultural 'capital' that could be traded for other forms of capital such as high achievement grades in a school subject, or selection for culturally esteemed sporting teams or programmes. A brief description of the concepts of field, habitus and capital will assist in explaining the social construction of ability and the way in which such constructions can act to exclude young people from sport and other spaces of physical culture.

The notion of *field*, Waquant suggests, is 'the central organizing concept' (1989, p. 38) of Bourdieu's work. A field is a social arena of practices and relationships between people that is marked by a set of organising forces and principles that are imposed on all who enter and operate within the field. For example, a family, a PE class, a cricket team, a school system could be considered fields because they are observable as social arenas with characteristic practices and relationships. Each field, through the social structures and operations represented in that field generates and consolidates the values and beliefs of the field and rewards the adherents. Those with the most power in the field have the greatest influence over the conditions of practice within it, including the divisions and nature of the space (Bourdieu, 1989). The notion of field thus allows for the conceptualisation of each person's position in all spaces of competition within the field (Bourdieu, 1985). Position, defined by the relations between agents, 'determines the actual or potential powers within the different fields and the chances of access to the specific profits that they offer' (Bourdieu, 1985, p. 197).

'Habitus' refers in Bourdieu's work to 'systems of durable, transposable dispositions, structured structures predisposed to function as structuring structures, that is, as principles which generate and organise practices and representations' (1990, p. 53). In other words, as Noble and Watkins (2003) summarised, habitus can be understood 'as the dispositions that internalize our social location and which orient our actions' (p. 53). A person's habitus operates largely below the level of consciousness and is constituted through their historical interactions and experiences in different social contexts. Significantly, for Bourdieu (and indeed the social construction conception of ability), habitus is embodied and thereby manifest in our actions, appearances and what he described as our bodily *hexis* – posture, manner, accents, etc. (Bourdieu, 1977). Shilling (2004) further describes the significance of the body in society, and society in the body, by suggesting that it 'is the experiences and appearances of the body that reveal the deepest dispositions of the habitus' (p. 475). Hunter (2004) expands this understanding of the embodiment of habitus by suggesting that the body is 'paramount in reading an individual, categorizing and positioning them within a field' (p. 176).

The notion of 'capital' offers a perspective on the ways in which a person's resources (or personal characteristics constituted in habitus) are privileged, marginalised, traded and acquired in a field (Bourdieu, 1986). The structure of the field legitimates and reproduces what resources may operate as *capital* in the field, and how capital might be allocated. Broadly speaking, Bourdieu identifies three principal forms of capital – economic, social and cultural capital. The latter two forms of capital are perhaps less tangible than economic capital (one's financial state), but are no less significant in the impact their possession has on the possibilities for people in the field of sport. Social capital can be understood as possession of relational networks that allow the individual to maximise opportunities to acquire and trade other capitals (Bourdieu, 1986). These connections could include relationships with coaches, certain team members, and family members of sporting renown. Cultural capital refers, broadly, to a form of value associated with one's possession of culturally authorised resources. Bourdieu (1986) explained that cultural capital could be realised in three forms: in the *embodied* state (dispositions of the mind and body, that is, how one acts and looks); the *objectified* state (in the form of the possession of culturally valued goods); and in the *institutionalised* state (largely in the form of educational qualifications). Furthermore, one species of capital can be traded for other capital/s. In regards to Evan's social construction of ability proposition for example, valued physical appearance (which can be viewed as embodied cultural capital) may be transacted for the capital of high-ability recognition in sport. That is, possession of physical capital can be used inadvertently or deliberately to gain other forms of capital such as high-ability recognition.

Constructing abilities

Having established the theoretical reference points for the social construction of ability in sport, it is now possible to consider the processes involved and its value in explaining inclusion and exclusion in sport. The first thing to note about the social construction of ability is that it is a complex process dependent upon the interactions of multiple factors. That is, this view rejects the reduction of sporting ability to a genetically determined set of physical properties. Instead, it promotes an awareness of the constituting elements of the sporting fields in which ability recognition occurs, and the effects of field practices and relationships on one's value (or ability) in the field. This is not to say that a person's genetic or biological make-up is not a factor in the realisation and recognition of their ability, but rather that it is repositioned as one of numerous factors.

Given the centrality of playing fields to sport, Bourdieu's concept of field is a useful place to begin demonstrating the construction of abilities in sport. Bourdieu (1989) explained that the boundaries of fields were simply the limits of their influence on a person. Thus, different sports may be viewed as fields, and even different sites of engagement within a single sport may be viewed as different fields. Consider, for example, the field of a secondary school soccer programme for boys. This field may be marked by several overt structures such as the uniforms students are expected to wear, training practices students are engaged in, game times and spaces, training times and spaces, etc. The field will also be constituted by the people operating within it, their gender and ethnicities, and the extent and nature of their relationships with each other. Coaches, players of different positions, managers, parents, would thus be likely contributors to the field of the school soccer programme. Significantly, the practices and relationships within this field establish and often perpetuate certain values, beliefs and expectations that may also be considered structuring features of the field. Values such as winning at all costs, competition, and aggression may be promoted through the content and modes of communication between coaches and players. These might include certain training activities that promote aggressive play, the rewarding of players through preferential treatment, and attention to those who demonstrate and promote these values, beliefs and expectations.

According to Evans (2004) and others (e.g. Hay and Macdonald, 2010), the values, beliefs and expectations of fields shape what it means to be 'able' and thus who is considered able. Specifically, Evans argued that people were viewed as able or otherwise depending on how elements of their habitus were recognised or valued within fields. That is, the dispositions, attitudes, perceptions, appearances and actions of one's habitus are read and valued in particular ways within fields and shape the nature of one's engagement and place in the field. For example, a Caucasian boy (let's call him, Gerard) who engages in the field described above (constituted by values such as winning at all costs, competition, white Caucasian coaches, etc.) in a competitive and aggressive manner, and has an athletic appearance supplemented by the latest equipment and clothing, may be viewed as more able than an Asian boy (Noc) who has similar skills but is less assertive in the game and the field more generally, who appears relatively overweight and possesses an incomplete soccer kit. In these instances, nothing is known about the genetic or fundamental biological make-up of these boys, yet judgements are made by coaches and other players about their abilities as if they were natural.

Some would argue that this is an overly simplistic conclusion to make and that an astute coach would not only be able to see beyond the appearances of an individual, but would refrain from making a judgement about ability until seeing the player in action. Indeed, it is overly simplistic to assert that the mere appearances of an individual would be attributed as ability. In fact, as Hay and Macdonald (2010) have demonstrated, the process involved in arriving at such conclusions is, in fact, quite complex. The concept of capital provides a useful language and framework for understanding and describing this complexity. A starting point is to view the fields as sites or contexts in which certain transactions occur. The structures of the fields (and their constituting and circulating discourses) determine the currencies and currency values for the transactions. In this regard, the elements of an individual's habitus are personal resources that operate as capital, where they are so valued. Capital can be transacted for other capital/s, used to access sites in which transactions may occur, or further capital may be acquired. Notably, Bourdieu proposed that one's power in the field (and hence influence over the constitution of the field) depends on the volume and species of personal capital.

Participation in sport is a practice or behaviour that is particularly and peculiarly value-laden. There are expectations regarding an individual's actions, appearance and attitude, the displays of which can be used to distinguish one person from another. In the soccer example, Gerard's aggressive and competitive dispositions, his athletic appearance, and possession of a complete and coordinated soccer kit are embodied and objectified cultural capitals that may be transacted for the capital of high-ability recognition. That is, the expectation of high ability may be realised on the basis of appearance and disposition. In the first instance, however, these observations are more likely to grant him *privileged* access to playing spaces in which ability transactions could be made and where his skills could be recognised by those positioned in the field to confer ability identification (i.e. in this case the coach). Noc's soccer capacities are likely to be less well recognised or transacted as ability because his appearance is less typical of the field and he is less aggressive and assertive in the game and associated training activities. His comparatively limited capital means he is likely to experience greater difficulty in accessing spaces in the field where his skills can be observed. Furthermore, he is less likely to be noticed by those who have influence in the field; those who perpetuate their constituting values, beliefs and expectations and who also make judgements about the abilities of the field 'players.'

The complexity of the construction process is further manifest through the reality that the habituses of participants themselves contribute to the structures of fields. Hay and lisahunter (2006), for example, noted that the behaviours and orientations of high-ability students in PE promoted the values and structuring activities of fields that maintained their personal resources as capital, and thus their power and place as high-ability participants. In the soccer example, the aggressive play and engagement with other aggressive soccer players would consolidate aggression as a defining value of the field and thus Gerard's value or ability in it. Bourdieu also used the term 'symbolic violence' to describe the way in which people of marginal status within fields (such as lower-ability youth) actively contribute to their own marginalisation and the privilege of others through their tacit acceptance of their ability and place as if it is normal or natural (Bourdieu, 1989, 1990; Wacquant, 1989). Significantly, the belief that the constructed abilities are biological or genetic contributes to the actions and outcomes of symbolic violence as it further promotes the assertion that the ability differences in the field are natural rather than the complex outcome of cultural and social factors. In these instances the opportunities to challenge the field and promote the inclusion of more people is undermined. Certainly, it is unlikely that an individual's perceptions of their own ability would be formed on the basis of experience in a single field. However, the notion of symbolic violence reminds us that the field of sport can affirm or challenge these perceptions of habitus in ways that can be either exclusionary or inclusionary.

The processes described above highlight that the exclusionary work of ability is evident in both the manner of its construction as well as in the outcomes of its identification. In terms of construction, a person's ability could be understood as more dependent upon the volume and species of their capital than on their genetic make-up. The significance of capital to ability and an individual's place within the field of sport is affirmed by Bernstein (1990) who described the differential identification of abilities as synonymous with class relations. That is, such differences in abilities are inequities in the 'distribution of power, and in the principles of control between social groups, which are realised in the creation, distribution, reproduction, and legitimation of physical and symbolic values that have their source in the social division of labour' (p. 13). Ability in this regard is the outcome of reading and assignment of meaning to particular bodies in particular ways that have field-specific implications for the power and opportunity available to young people operating within them. This emphasises the arbitrary nature of ability (Evans *et al.*, 2007) in that it depends on the values, beliefs and associated expectations of the field. The implications, of course, are that more or different people will be considered able in different fields depending on the constitution of the fields, the implications that constitution has for what and whose resources may operate as capital, and the transaction possibilities that are evident.

Challenging the exclusionary consequences of ability

Having demonstrated the way prevailing and traditional conceptions of ability in sport can foster youth exclusion, and having articulated a social construction conceptualisation of ability in sport, the challenge of intervening in these potential exclusionary outcomes remains. This is a considerable challenge because belief in the genetic nature of ability and the differentiations it assumes appear to be well entrenched in the psyche of the broader sporting community. Furthermore, making distinctions between people or groups through the recognition of 'place getters' or 'winner and losers' is very much a defining characteristic of sport. Thus, while a 'competency' rather than 'performance' understanding and appropriation of ability (where capacities for widespread participation are emphasised and celebrated) would no doubt challenge the exclusionary work of ability conceptions, reforming the understandings of all the stakeholders in the broader field of sport is an aspiration that is unlikely to be realised.

An alternative and arguably more promising direction for action is the training of those who are most influential in the maintenance of the structuring discourses of sporting fields. By challenging the understandings and practices of coaches and teachers, the field dynamics that result in certain exclusionary configurations of ability can be contested. This could well lead to broader and more inclusive understandings and recognitions of ability in sporting contexts. Challenges to the understandings and practices of coaches and teachers in relation to ability could be an element of coach training and development as well as teacher preparation in Physical Education Teacher Education (PETE) programmes. Specifically, this could involve the engagement of coaches and teachers in experiences that actively trouble the practices, beliefs and expectations that unduly marginalise some players and privilege others, and experiences that promote the reflexive capacities of coaches. In regard to reflexivity, I refer to the self-analysis and awareness of personal beliefs, values, history, etc., and the unavoidable impact of these factors on perceptions of and interactions with others. Enhancing the reflexive capacities of coaches is no doubt a radical proposition; however, it may aid coaches in their understanding of the influence they have over youth participation and opportunities in sport. In turn, this might broaden the recognition of abilities in sporting fields and enlarge the opportunities for all participants to access sites for the recognition of ability. Ironically, such capacities may also enable coaches to more accurately discriminate between actual skills and other 'capitals' affecting the realisation of ability recognition in sport.

Conclusion

This chapter has sought to demonstrate the way in which traditional views of abilities in sport and their associated identification techniques can have an impact on the sporting engagements of children and young people. These enduring views and identification techniques are exclusionary because the differences in a young person's potential, progress and performance in sport are largely assumed to be the outcome of natural and largely measurable factors. As a result, other social and cultural factors for differences in sport performances and experiences are largely overlooked. It was argued in this chapter that a social construction view of ability provides a more integrated perspective on the way abilities are both defined and recognised in the social fields of sport.

In concluding this socially critical engagement with the concept of ability in sport, it is helpful to declare that it was not the intention of this chapter to position sport as inherently good or bad. Certainly sport and PE provide potential avenues for the promotion of widespread participation in physical activity. However, it is not too difficult to demonstrate how the structures, practices and discourses that define and shape the nature of sport can mitigate this potential. The purpose therefore of this chapter was to draw attention to the way in which ability contributes to the exclusionary work of sport so that these factors can be challenged and so that socially just practices can be promoted. Nevertheless, critical texts such as these are largely powerless in and of themselves to effect change. Rather, change depends on the open-mindedness and subsequent convictions of those in positions of power within fields of sport, who are willing and able to challenge existing practices and beliefs. May they be found and may they be successful.

References

Abbott, A. and Collins, D. (2002) A theoretical and empirical analysis of a 'state of the art' talent identification model. *High Ability Studies*, 13 (2): 157–178.

Azzarito, L. and Harrison, L. (2008) 'White men cant's jump:' Race, gender and natural athleticism. *International Review for the Sociology of Sport*, 43 (4): 347–364.

Bailey, R. and Morely, D. (2006) Towards a model of talent development in physical education. *Sport, Education and Society*, 11 (3): 211–230.

Bernstein, B. (1990) *The Structuring of Pedagogic Discourse, Vol IV: class, codes and control.* London: Routledge.

Bourdieu, P. (1977) *Outline of a Theory of Practice.* Cambridge: Cambridge University Press.

Bourdieu, P. (1985) The social space and the genesis of groups. *Social Science Information*, 24 (2): 195–220.

Bourdieu, P. (1986) The forms of capital. In Richardson, J. (ed.) *Handbook of Theory and Research of the Sociology of Education.* Westport, CT: Greenwood, pp. 241–258.

Bourdieu, P. (1989) Social space and symbolic power. *Sociological Theory*, 7 (1): 14–25.

Bourdieu, p. (1990) *The Logic of Practice.* Cambridge: Polity Press.

Collins, M.F. and Kay, T. (2003) *Sport and Social Exclusion.* London: Routledge.

Elling, A. and Knoppers, A. (2005) Sport, gender and ethnicity: practices of symbolic inclusion/exclusion. *Journal of Youth and Adolescence*, 34 (3): 257–268.

Evans, J. (2004) Making a difference? Education and 'ability' in physical education. *European Physical Education Review*, 10 (1): 95–108.

Evans, P. and Penney, D. (2008) Levels on the playing field: the social construction of physical 'ability' in the physical education curriculum. *Physical Education and Sport Pedagogy*, 13 (1): 31–47.

Evans, J., Rich, E. and Allwood, R. (2007) Being able in a performative culture: Physical education's contribution to a healthy interest in sport? In Wellard, I. (ed.) *Rethinking Gender and Youth Sport.* Abingdon: Routledge, pp. 51–67.

Genetic Technologies (2010) *ACTN3 Sports Gene Tests.* Online: www.gtpersonal.com.au/index.php (accessed 16 March 2010).

Gorely, T., Holroyd, R. and Kirk, D. (2003) Muscularity, the habitus and the social construction of gender: towards a gender-relevant physical education. *British Journal of Sociology of Education*, 24 (4): 429–448.

Green, K., Smith, A. and Roberts, K. (2005) Social Class, Young People, Sport and Physical Education. In Green, K. and Hardman, K. (eds) *Physical Education: Essential Issues.* London: Sage, pp. 180–196.

Hay, P.J. and lisahunter (2006) 'Please Mr Hay, what are my poss(abilities)?': legitimation of ability through physical education practices. *Sport, Education and Society*, 11 (3): 293–310.

Hay, P.J. and Macdonald, D. (2010) Evidence for the social construction of ability in Physical Education. *Sport, Education and Society*, 15 (1): 1–18.

Hoberman, J. (1997) *Dawin's Athletes. How sport has damaged black America and preserved the myth of race.* Boston: Houghton Mifflin.

Hunter, L. (2004) Bourdieu and the social space of the PE class: reproduction of doxa through practice. *Sport, Education and Society*, 9 (2): 175–192.

Lutchmaya, S. Baron-Cohen, S. and Raggatt, P. *et al.* (2004) 2nd to 4th digit ratios, fetal testosterone and estradol. *Early Human Development*, 77 (1–2): 23–28.

Manning, J.T. (2002) The ratio of 2nd to 4th digit length and performance in skiing. *Journal of Sports Medicine and Physical Fitness*, 42 (4): 446–450.

Manning, J.T. and Taylor, R.P. (2001) Second to fourth digit ration and male ability in sport: implications for sexual selection in humans. *Evolution and Human Behaviour*, 22 (1): 61–69.

Miah, A. and Rich, E. (2006) Genetic tests for ability?: Talent identification and the value of an open future. *Sport, Education and Society*, 11 (3): 259–273.

Noble, G. and Watkins, M. (2003) So, how did Bourdieu learn to play tennis? Habitus, consciousness and habituation. *Cultural Studies*, 17 (3/4): 520–538.

Paul, S.N., Kato, B.S. and Hunkin, J.L. *et al.* (2006) The big finger: the second to fourth digit ration is a predictor of sporting ability in women. *British Journal of Sports Medicine*, 40 (12): 981–983.

Pienaar, A.E., Spamer, M.J. and Steyn, H.S. (1998) Identifying and developing rugby talent among 10-year-old boys: a practical model. *Journal of Sports Sciences*, 16: 691–699.

Reilly, T., Williams, A. and Nevill, A. *et al.* (2000) A multidisciplinary approach to talent identification in soccer. *Journal of Sports Sciences*, 18 (9): 695–702.

Scraton, S., Caudwell, J. and Holland, S. (2005) Bend it like Patel: centering race, ethnicity and gender in feminist analysis of women's football in England. *International Review for the Sociology of Sport*, 40 (1): 71–88.

Shilling, C. (2004) Physical capital and situated action: a new direction for corporeal sociology. *British Journal of Sociology of Education*, 25 (4): 473–487.

Sternberg, R.J. (1998) Abilities are forms of developing expertise. *Educational Researcher*, 27 (3): 11–20.

Vaeyens, R., Lenoir, M. and Williams, A. *et al.* (2008) Talent identification and development programmes in sport: current models and future directions. *Sports Medicine*, 38 (9): 703–714.

Wacquant, L. (1989) Towards a reflexive sociology: a workshop with Pierre Bourdieu. *Sociological Theory*, 7 (1): 26–63.

White, J. (2006) *Intelligence, Destiny and Education: The ideological roots of intelligence testing.* London: Routledge.

Wilson, T. (2002) The paradox of social class and sports involvement. *International Review for the Sociology of Sport*, 37 (1): 5–16.

Wright, J. and Burrows, L. (2006) Re-conceiving ability in physical education: a social analysis. *Sport, Education and Society*, 11 (3): 275–292.

7 Sexuality and youth sport

Ian Wellard

Introduction

It could be claimed that sexuality remains a significant factor in many young people's exclusion from sport. However, although much has been written on socially constructed definitions of sexuality and its distinction from gender, within the fields of sport and physical education there has been relatively little discussion with most focusing on adults in gay sports, elite sport and physical education (Anderson, 2005; Brackenridge, 2001; Cahn, 1994; Caudwell, 2003, 2006; Clarke, 1998; Griffin, 1998; Pronger, 1990, 2000).

According to DePalma and Atkinson (2006), commenting on their ground-breaking research into sexuality in the school classroom:

> Despite its importance in terms of pupil and teacher well-being, sexualities equality remains the one area on inclusion still largely unaddressed in schools, often because of teachers' own fears and concerns.
>
> (DePalma and Atkinson, 2006, p. 333)

Part of the problem, they suggest, is the continued view that sexual orientation, as well as diverse family patterns, are not considered appropriate foci for education. Consequently, it could also be claimed that there are underlying tensions which exist in relation to the quest for achievement of inclusive practices for all young people in the face of continued refusal to accept that 'sexuality' does occur in the school setting. As Epstein and Johnson (1998) argue, schools are not only places of learning but also places where the possibilities and limitations of sexual identities are learned.

Within the context of school sports and PE there is the risk that generalised definitions of sexual identities restrict full understandings of the ways in which exclusive practices are maintained. Sexuality is most commonly addressed in terms of issues relating to homophobia. The problem with this is that focusing solely upon homophobia as a distinct form of exclusion can sometimes divert attention from the complexities of the ways in which discriminatory practices emerge, operate and are maintained. The intention in this chapter is not to distract from the hard-hitting evidence that homophobia is still rife within schools. According to the

Stonewall report (2006), almost two-thirds of young lesbian, gay and bisexual people experience homophobic bullying in Britain's schools. Instead, the chapter is mindful of the complex ways in which sexuality is presented and articulated to young people in both sporting contexts and the classroom.

It is difficult to talk of sexuality as a single unifying factor in explanations of exclusive practices and discriminatory behaviour. For instance, the experiences of gay men cannot be compared equally to that of the experiences of lesbians. At the same time, in sport, it cannot be claimed that *all* gay men are excluded in the same way (Wellard, 2009). Successful performances in sport draw upon other factors such as ability, gender, race and age (Evans, 2004; McDonald, 2006; Wellard, 2006) and it is these discourses of sexuality which operate inside and outside the classroom. Therefore, any theorising of the impact of sexuality upon participation in sports needs to be assessed in relation to a range of social interpretations of what are considered to be successful performances.

This chapter explores how sexuality is presented and experienced in a range of ways and presents the argument that it is important to incorporate broader definitions of gendered performance and the body.

Sexuality, gender and the body

When we talk about 'sexuality,' biological definitions fail to explain fully the complex ways in which it is understood and acted upon. Increasingly, there is the need to take into account the social dimensions which create understandings of what 'sexuality' entails, involves or comprises. According to Weeks (2003), sexuality has both a history and sociology, and these are concerned with

> the ways in which sexualities have been shaped in a complex history, and in tracing how sexual patterns have changed over time. It is concerned with the historical and social organization of the erotic.
>
> (Weeks, 2003, p. 17)

Recognising the social aspect of sexuality does, however, make providing generalised, working definitions complex. Sexuality is more than just a physical orientation towards another human being. Recognition of the erotic highlights ways in which sexuality is experienced by individuals, either physically or emotionally (through the senses) as well as being a guiding factor in the social organisation of many individuals through formulations of appropriate outlets for or manifestations of sexual desire.

Investigation of the way in which sexual desire is organised in contemporary society reveals, in fact, the limited ways in which sex, sexual relations and our understanding of the physical and emotional body are constructed and enacted within 'Western' discourse. Much of this limited understanding derives from biological explanations of heteronormative sex based on a dualist notion of male and female roles within a penetration/reproduction relationship (Firestone, 1979; Petchesky, 1986; Dimen, 2003). This adult-centred formulation of sexuality and the erotic leaves little room for young people, other than to view childhood as merely a 'waiting' period prior to the onset of puberty and subsequent entrance to an adult world. Within this restricted formulation of the erotic, because young people are not considered to be physically (biologically) able to take part in adult sexual relations, there is little room for exploring the possibilities of the body, or as Pronger (2002) describes, the 'puissance' to be found in the human condition. The question arises, where does this leave the young adult or child? Are they completely devoid of sensuous feelings or awareness of sexuality? Or are they, as most adults would like to think, oblivious to it? Although a potentially controversial and uncomfortable debate, consideration of the broader definitions of the erotic which incorporate the sensual capacities of the physical body opens up the possibilities for looking beyond the margins of current thinking about what certain bodies should be doing.

Post-structuralism and feminist thinking have influenced the way we think about gender and have forced us to tackle uncomfortable questions. In particular, more recently, queer theory has added to this research by bringing sexuality into the foreground. Where feminists have used gender as an absolute filter for exploring knowledge construction, queer theory highlights a focus on sexuality (Eng, 2006). Consequently,

> since queer theory is focused on sexuality issues, unquestioned/presupposed heterosexuality has been highlighted as a powerful discourse, which silences sexual practices that could challenge heterosexuality as the hegemonic norm.
>
> (Eng, 2006, p. 51)

A useful overview of queer theory and sport is provided by Sykes (2006) in which she sums up the ways in which queer theory has helped thinking about:

1   The construction of heterosexuality.
2   Heteronormativitiy which aligns the dominance of whiteness and late capitalism with heterosexuality.
3   Relations between hetero and the other.
4   Theories and practices that place queerness at the centre in order to transform homosexual, gay, lesbian theory into a general social theory (Sykes, 2006, p. 16).

Performances of sexuality

Much of this theoretical approach has been shaped by the work of Butler (1993) who describes how normative gender is produced through language and how, in consequence, bodily performances create a social demonstration of normative behaviour. However, rather than being a theatrical performance or reproduction of learned existing and set social practices in the interactionist sense (Goffman, 1972), these bodily performances constitute a discursive 'act' and so, for Butler, power is formed within these acts. For Butler, performance presumes a subject is already at hand or in existence whereas performativity contests the very notion of the subject and has the ability to create meaning. For instance, the term 'limp wrist' conveys meaning in terms of a social understanding of an inferior form of masculine performance rather than, literally, a physiological act. The notion that a limp wrist constitutes a failed form of masculinity is therefore a social construction which remains embedded in social understanding (of 'normal' masculine and feminine behaviour) through constant reinforcement, or performativity, which establishes it as legitimate.

Butler starts with the Foucauldian premise that power works, in part, through discourse to produce and destabilise subjects but goes on to contemplate performativity (particularly in speech acts but also through bodily performance) as the aspect of discourse which has the capacity to produce what it names (Butler, 1993, p. 225). Performativity is based on an expectation of what is considered gendered behaviour. Thus, the expectation ends up producing the very phenomenon that it anticipates. Butler also notes that performativity is not a singular act but a repetition or ritual, which achieves its effects through its naturalisation in the context of a body.

Continuing with the work of Butler, she presents the argument that in the case of heterosexuality, or any other dominant form of ideology, crafting or determining a sexual position always involves becoming haunted by what is excluded (Butler, 1994, p. 34). The more rigid the position and the greater the reluctance to accommodate alternative forms, the more likely it is that a problem is created where the stance needs to be defended, invariably by becoming hostile to those alternatives. Thus, for Butler, the greater the binary distinctions which promote social understandings of male and female as separate and opposite gender positions, the greater the intolerance generated through these practices. This can be seen in contemporary heteronormative practices and in the way institutional practices shape social understandings of the body. For instance, the social understanding of pregnancy, which is associated with a biological understanding of gender rather than a discursive framework, produces acceptance of it being a feminine space (Butler, 1994, p. 33), not only literally, in areas such as maternity wards, but in associated roles such as the care of younger children in infant and primary school settings. The same could be applied to sport, where the discursive framework rationalises it as an arena where male physical activity and performance are considered 'natural' in comparison to women's sporting performance. Butler is critical of the discursive framework which positions heterosexual men in a binary opposition to women. The binary also positions gays as opposite to heterosexual men and alongside women. Such a distinction also creates a normative understanding of the heterosexual male as superior to women and gays.

For Butler, as well as what could be considered the crux of queer theory, transformative possibilities are to be found in queer acts which provide the opportunity to oppose and de-stabilise normative understandings of gender behaviour. Through repetition and continued citing through speech acts, production occurs. Thus, performativity is, for Butler, 'the vehicle through which ontological effects are established' (Butler, 1994, p. 33). However, the silences in relation to sexuality which operate within the classroom (DePalma and Atkinson, 2006) lessen the opportunities for alternative interpretation to emerge or be exposed. Therefore, the onus is on teachers and practitioners in sport and physical education settings to confront and challenge instances of exclusion. Awareness in itself does not necessarily mean that a form of exclusion, such as homophobia, is automatically eradicated.

Sexuality and sport

Sport interacts powerfully with discourses of sexuality. It provides outlets for a variety of erotica because the body is 'spectacle' (Guttmann, 1996) and the ways in which bodily movements are demonstrated. It is not only the corporeality of sport that can be considered erotic, narratives of sporting contest are also open to erotic interpretation. In traditional sports, the popular understanding of the professional sports*man* is one of athleticism, strength, virility and attractiveness. This is promoted as the ideal form of masculinity, not only for men to aspire to, but for women to find attractive. The athlete's image is constructed through a discourse of physical and bodily performance. Most professional sports, particularly football, boxing and rugby, are highly physical, often involving contact with other bodies and there is usually a practical requirement to be physically strong. In traditional sports, there are also expectations for exhibitions of hegemonic masculinity on and off the field; for example, excessive drinking and brawling. Sport, therefore, provides not only a site for learning social codes relating to gender but can also be considered a prime site where hegemonic masculinities are made and remade (Wellard, 2009). Consequently, sport is a significant part of a social arena in which masculinities and femininities are constructed, learned and structured in relations of domination and subordination (Butler, 1993; see also Chapter 5).

In this contemporary 'Western' version of normative gender behaviour, sport has been considered as a place where a young man learns about the values of competition, valour, gentlemanly behaviour and ways to treat those who do not (or should not) possess sporting prowess, in particular, women, gays, the disabled and the old (Park, 1987). According to Park, however, the emphasis upon specific masculine performances produces conflict in later social relations during adolescence when the young male sports player may have to confront sports women or gay sportsmen. The implication is that there is little accommodation for, or acceptance of, alternative gender and sexuality within mainstream sports unless they resemble expected forms. Probyn's (2000) example of Ian Roberts, the Australian professional rugby player who 'came out' in public at the end of his career, demonstrates how any stigma of 'gayness' surrounding his masculine identity was overshadowed by his ability to perform outward displays of hegemonic masculinity. According to Probyn, Roberts, was accepted because his masculinity was not compromised by 'gayness.' His physical and bodily displays were predominantly grounded in Western, heterosexual understandings of male performance and the male body. He had little to be 'ashamed' of and, in turn, the normative presentation of his body negated any shame to be derived from being gay. Although the case of Roberts was heralded as a sign of increased social acceptance of gay *men* in professional sport, the social fear of displaying what is considered to be subordinated masculinity was not challenged. Indeed, if taking into consideration Robert's bodily performances, it could be claimed that little had troubled the continued presence of a hegemonic masculinity informed by heterosexuality.

By acknowledging that sexuality is influential in the social processes which impose upon the physical body, it is essential that any exploration of sporting bodies and inclusion does the same. For it is particularly in sport that performances of sexuality are played out continually through socially determined constructions of hegemonic masculinity and are constantly put to the test. The focus in sport on presenting performances which resemble 'real men' continues to reinforce a sexual hierarchy with heterosexual women and gay people considered in a subordinate position to those performances which represent heterosexual men. Yet, this issue is not necessarily always as clear cut. In the case of gay men for example, Segal (1997) suggests that 'the fine line between "true" masculinity (which is heterosexual) and its opposite (which is not) have been increasingly transgressed' (Segal, 1997, p. 150) by the gay (male) community in its assimilation of hegemonic masculinity. Segal sees this in the way many gay men have adopted a 'supermacho' style based on traditional images of the heterosexual male. This has led to an increase in outward bodily performances, such as body-building, macho posturing and the growth of gay sports that seek to emulate heterosexual sports.

In the case of gay sports, there has been a dramatic rise in organised sporting events and competitions specifically for gay people (Pronger, 2000; Symons, 2010). However, the increase does not necessarily mean that all gay (and transgender) people are accommodated equally. Pronger (2000) suggests that the emancipatory power that appeared initially within the gay and lesbian community, particularly in its approach to sport, has been quelled in recent years through the attempts to 'normalise' and become part of mainstream sport. Although Pronger acknowledges advances in the cause of the lesbian and gay movement, making it more visible and transforming sport from its history of systematic oppression, he suggests that it is debateable whether mainstream sport is a truly welcoming environment for sexual minorities. He writes,

> I suggest that the progress of L&G community sports, seen in the light of the socially transformative ambitions of some of the historical streams of the G&L movement, has been more about dominant socio-cultural systems (including sports) appeasing, co-opting, indeed diffusing the transformative possibilities of the sexual margins than it has been about increasing human freedom.
>
> (Pronger, 2000, p. 225)

Importantly, Pronger demonstrates ways in which the possibility of challenging discriminatory practices, within sport and other social spaces, is limited by certain power systems which tend to maintain unfair positions of power. In sport, homosexuality has traditionally been organised as negatively and prohibitively other to mainstream (heterosexual) sport. In gay community sport, particularly in North America, a liberal approach has been adopted which seeks to provide access to the mainstream for lesbians and gays rather than confronting or challenging its core ideals. Although Pronger believes that gay sports have provided lesbian and gay people with the opportunity to enjoy sports in an inclusive and safe environment, ultimately it has made these people conform to the established norms, particularly those based on oppressive male heterosexual codes and a continued demarcation between men and women.

At face value, the Gay Games can be seen to be a successful mega-event, with its own emerging history (Symons, 2010). However, for all the good intentions of the Gay Games and the gay sports movement there is still a noticeable absence of the wide range of ages, abilities and bodies which constitute the broader gay community. This reflects the continued invisibility and exclusion of many other 'types' of body from mainstream sports and suggests a failure to recognise 'other ways of being' (Hunter, 2004), which have the potential to ultimately enrich society.

Sexuality, school sport and physical education

In terms of school sports and physical education, it is precisely these adult-formulated discourses and performances of normative gender and sexuality, described above, which are played out in the classroom and playground. Consequently, there is little (if any) room for other ways of being to be expressed or experienced. Particularly in the context of school sports, the options become simple – either fit in or don't; although the consequences for not fitting in present far more hurdles. As Vicars (2006) graphically explains in reflections about his school experiences, not conforming to the social expectations of gender was accentuated in PE lessons. He writes,

> My shivering, bespectacled and disinterested frame did not endear me to my team members or the PE teacher as I repeatedly failed to rehearse narratives of hegemonic masculinity within these public performances and rituals of the body.
>
> (Vicars, 2006, p. 352)

I have argued elsewhere (Wellard, 2009) that focusing solely upon sexuality does not fully explain the many contrasting lifestyles and practices experienced in contemporary masculinities, rather it needs to be read through social understandings of the gendered body. Much of what is relevant in the lives of young people is a shared understanding of what is considered to be appropriate bodily performance. High status is continually ascribed to the active, able-bodied, athletic male body which, in turn, subordinates other bodies, particularly those which are associated with physical weakness. Heterosexual masculinity is culturally signalled by specific bodily practices. Lack of prowess provides an indication of 'failed' gender to the extent that, regardless of sexual orientation, this is articulated as homosexual behaviour or feminine behaviour. For example, Redman (2000) in his study of teenage schoolboys noted that 'unmasculine' physical performances were cited as a key indication of 'queerness' by the boys, rather than any explicit knowledge of a boy's sexuality. Similarly, Frosh *et al.* (2002) in their interviews with teenage boys found that accusations of homosexuality (and often subsequent bullying) were based, initially, upon outward physical signs which expressed a deviation from the limited margins of hegemonic masculine performances.

School experiences of sport and physical education play a significant part in developing a sense of masculine identity as well as laying the foundations for future participation in adult sports. Paul (34), for example, was one of many men I interviewed in my research exploring constructions of masculinity and the body within the context of sport (Wellard, 2009). He told me how during his schooldays he had been subjected to taunting and, on occasions, experienced hostility because of his inability to present a particular version of masculinity based upon the body. For instance,

> I remember the first, when I joined junior school and er they wanted me to play football. I cried and cried and cried and tried to get my mother to write me a letter so I didn't have to play . . . Erm, cos I knew I was going to get picked on. It was going to put me in the spotlight, I couldn't kick a ball, therefore I was going to be called a poof and, you know, I'd get all the aggression from the other boys . . .

> I kind of . . . I suppose was fed up with it . . . fed up with all the bullshit you get from the sports teachers, you know they were quite bolshy and they gave boys nicknames, er and you just wanted to get away from characters like that, you know, they, a friend of mine, they called 'Doris,' one kid they called 'stickweed.' It was kind of like subtle, or just humiliating the kids.

Many of the men told me that they were not aware of their sexuality at that stage, but aware of their bodily presentation as being different in comparison to the other boys. In this way, Paul's understanding of his bodily performance shaped the perception of his identity in the form of 'failed' masculinity. The nicknames, either feminised, such as 'Doris,' or a body type 'stickweed,' established meaning in terms of their opposition to orthodox understandings of normative masculinity. Many of the men in the sample, especially those who experienced school sport unfavourably, mentioned their teachers, in particular the male PE teachers, who would instigate bullying through name calling and encouraging specific behaviour which was associated with male sporting performance; for example, 'get stuck in,' or 'stop acting like a girl.'

Paul, like many other young people, developed an understanding of his subordinated masculinity through the reactions of other boys and men, and it was in sporting contexts that his inability to perform expected sporting masculinity was highlighted. Sport, therefore, can be seen as a prime site for illustrating the way conventional masculinity is reproduced through heteronormative understandings of bodily performance. At the same time, however, it is important to recognise that many other boys (whether gay, straight or unsure) are more able to invest in socially accepted heteronormative versions of masculine body practices, depending upon their ability to perform hegemonic masculinity. In other words, it is sometimes easier to 'act straight' rather than risk possible social exclusion.

To an extent, it could be claimed that the situation is even more complicated for women who take part in sport – whether they are gay or straight. As Caudwell (2003) documents in her research into women's football, the range of identities available and consequent implications for adopting particular identities is problematic and often creates further barriers to participation. However, the overriding message for the women in this study was the association of lesbianism with participating in football, regardless of sexual orientation, which reflects broader understandings of a complex, gendered hierarchy within sport.

The examples above provide support for Butler's (1993) use of sexuality as a means to highlight the normative practices found in understandings of gender. For her, and importantly for any critical analysis of sporting structures, homosexuality demonstrates a contrasting performance of accepted gender and, with it, the idea that alternative sexual practices have the power to destabilise heterosexual hegemony.

In relation to school sports, there have been recent insightful critiques of the knowledge generated about what children should be doing with their bodies (Evans *et al.*, 2004; Gard and Wright 2005; Kirk, 2006) and how they should be benefitting from taking part in physical activity. There continues to be, however, a slippage at policy level (and in many branches of academic sport and health-related discourse) between what is considered appropriate sporting activity for children and sport for adults. There are also similarities between adult and children's sport in what happens in the formulation of children's gendered identities. As Renold (2007) points out, in her study of primary school performances of masculinities:

> there is a lack of research that scrutinizes the specificities of age and generational dynamics in the formation of young masculinities or that fully problematizes the appropriateness of adopting adult – defined notions of hegemonic masculinity to make sense of young boys' constructions of 'boyness.'
>
> (Renold, 2007, p. 276)

In sport, in particular, there is a view that children go through a rite of passage to adult sport, where adult sport is considered a 'natural' progression, particularly for young boys (Wellard, 2009). Much of this understanding of children making a transition to adult sport is reinforced not only through social interpretations of the biological body (Synnott, 1993) but also through the structures put into place to manage the physical maturation of young people within the school place and beyond.

In many countries the education system is structured around a move from junior or primary schooling to secondary education which coincides with the onset of puberty. This transition marks out a shift to an adult-focused, more 'serious' approach to the development of young minds and the adoption of appropriate gendered roles within the heterosexual matrix (Butler, 1993). This is particularly evident in school-based sport and physical education where there is a marked shift from play-oriented physical activity at junior level to more structured, competitive sports at secondary level. Interestingly, in her study exploring the attitudes and feelings of children towards physical education during the transition from primary to secondary schools in the UK, Dismore (2007) found that the general enjoyment of physical education did not automatically stop in the first year of secondary school. Rather, enjoyment was lost through the practices and focus of provision for PE and school sports which shifted the emphasis to more adult-centred, competitive sports, taught by skilled, specialised PE staff. The focus in secondary school became more 'ability' and performance based and, ultimately, made the children reflect upon their bodies in terms of whether they felt 'able' to take part or not (Wellard, 2006). In addition, the hidden curriculum of physical education (Fernandez-Balboa, 1993; see also Chapter 5) along with ideologies of the body dominant within the school system (Evans, 2004) make it difficult for many young people to continue enjoying physical activity or feeling that they have the requisite ability.

Central to these dominant discourses are the continued binary distinctions between male and female and the invisibility of alternative forms of sexuality. For many, these discourses generate understanding of the social body as one of potential shame (Probyn, 2000). Sexuality, in this equation is therefore constructed in terms of its relationship within a heteronormative discourse. The result is that the general enthusiasm for and enjoyment of physical activity and organised sporting activities expressed by the majority of younger children is lost by a significant number in their transition to secondary schooling. It is not surprising that those who tend to 'drop out' from sport are those that do not want to adopt (or negotiate the consequences of enacting) the expected masculine performances considered necessary for continued participation.

Conclusions

Although there are well-documented and obvious benefits to be gained from taking part in sport, the problem remains that for young people there is a blurring of the messages they receive. In most cases sport is presented (by adults) as a wholesome, unproblematic, healthy physical activity in which they should take part. However, within this (on the surface) 'child-friendly' space, the conflicts between play and competition, gendered and sexual divisions and the developing physical body are not fully explained. Consequently, for young people, the restrictive belt of the heterosexual matrix is pulled ever tighter.

Opportunities to engage in sport are dictated by adult formulations of rules and fair play, while for young people there is little freedom to negotiate the rules. As they are not adults (in both social and legislative definitions), young people are told by parents and teachers when and how they can take part. Yet, whereas adults are able to pursue more challenging physical thrills in sport and leisure activities, much of which relates to a quest for physical experiences in sport which produce euphoric states and adrenalin rushes (Booth, 2009), it is difficult for young people to 'search' for these thrills. Ultimately, it is a failure to recognise that young people also inhabit the adult world but are limited in how they can occupy it. The point being made here is that it is often forgotten that the world which young people inhabit is more restricted than an adult. So, whereas the option to take part in a sporting activity can be made independently by an adult (for instance choosing to join a women's football club or a gay rugby club), this is not the case for young people. In particular, the school setting where much of sporting activity is experienced is, ultimately, regulated by adults. The implication here is that it is even more important to provide an inclusive environment.

Indeed, although the school classroom may be considered to be a space specifically designed for children and young people, the adult discourses still dominate within it. For instance, as Renold (2007) points out, in their classroom interactions, young people constantly re-enact sophisticated sexualised adult discourses, such as being a 'stud' or 'girly girl' and learn (hetero)normative expectations of gender performance. Consequently, sexuality *IS* a major issue in young people's lives. It operates through exposure to the adult discourses of the gendered and sexual body which prevail within the classroom and within other sites of sport.

A broader awareness of sexuality has the potential to open up an untapped arena of sensuous experience which could allow young people to develop a greater understanding of their own physical literacy – but only if we extend the (heteronormative) boundaries of thinking about the body. However, while the restrictive discourses which DePalma and Atkinson (2006) and Renold (2007) highlight remain, there will be limits upon the ways in which concepts such as sexuality, the erotic and bodily pleasure are formulated, particularly within the spaces of youth sport. For instance, in my investigation into male physical education teacher trainees (Wellard, 2007), I found that an irrational fear of dance had been developed by the men through their previous experiences of sport as well as exposure to general gendered discourses which equate dance with failed sexuality. The result was that a narrow view of sport and the body had ultimately restricted the men's full potential for development of pedagogical skills and their own physical literacy, in particular in the way that they constructed understandings of the gendered body and how boys and girls might participate.

It is argued, therefore, that sexuality is one important aspect to be considered when exploring the many ways that young people are 'excluded' from taking part in traditional sports and, ultimately, enjoying the full potential of their bodies. It is often assumed that the practices which operate in sport are less problematic than the individuals who would like to participate. In other words, the message is that sport is not the problem, but rather the people who do not 'appear' to fit in (such as girls, the disabled, the elderly). In the context of childhood, expressions of alternative sexuality are less obvious and only visible in comparison to other forms of exclusion. However, rather than assume sexuality is not an issue, as Hunter (2004) suggests, it is better to challenge the practices which make impossible other ways of being and arguably result in oppressing, marginalizing or alienating young people from positive orientations to themselves and physical culture.

(Hunter, 2004, p. 175)

In the case of sexuality and youth sport, we cannot talk about a school as being a place of inclusion in one sentence and then ignore a blatant form of exclusion in the next.

References

Anderson, E. (2005) *In the Game: Gay Athletes and the Cult of Masculinity*. New York: State University of New York Press.

Booth, D. (2009) Politics and pleasure: the philosophy of physical education revisited. *Quest*, 61 (2): 133–153.

Brackenridge, C.H. (2001) *Spoilsports: Understanding and preventing sexual exploitation in sport*. London: Routledge.

Butler, J. (1993) *Bodies that Matter*. New York: Routledge.

Butler, J. (1994) Gender as performance: an interview with Judith Butler. *Radical Philosophy*, 67: 32–39.

Cahn, S. (1994) *Coming on Strong: Gender and Sexuality in Twentieth-Century Women's Sport*. New York: The Free Press.

Caudwell, J. (2003) Out on the field of play: Women's experiences of gender and sexuality in football contexts. In Wagg, S. (ed.) *British Football and Social Exclusion*. London: Frank Cass.

Caudwell, J. (2006) *Sport, Sexualities and Queer Theory: Challenges and Controversies*. London: Routledge.

Clarke, G. (1998) Queering the pitch and coming out to play: lesbians in physical education and sport. *Sport, Education and Society*, 3 (2): 145–160.

DePalma, R. and Atkinson, E. (2006) The sound of silence: talking about sexual orientation and schooling. *Sex Education*, 6 (4): 333–349.

Dimen, M. (2003) *Sexuality, Intimacy, Power.* New York: Routledge.

Dismore. H. (2007) The attitudes of children and young people towards physical education and school sport, with particular reference to the transition from Key Stage 2 to Key Stage 3. Unpublished PhD, Canterbury Christ Church University.

Epstein, D. and Johnson, R. (1998) *Schooling Sexualities.* Buckingham: Open University Press.

Eng, H. (2006) Queer athletes and queering in sport. In Caudwell, J. (ed.) *Sport, Sexualities and Queer Theory: Challenges and Controversies*. London: Routledge.

Evans, J. (2004) Making a difference? Education and 'ability' in physical education. *European Physical Education Review*, 10 (1): 95–108.

Evans, J., Davies, B. and Wright, J. (2004) *Body Knowledge and Control.* London: Routledge.

Fernandez-Balboa, J-M. (1993) Socio-cultural characteristics of the hidden curriculum in physical education. *Quest*, 45 (2): 230–254.

Firestone, S. (1979) *The Dialectic of Sex: The case for feminist revolution*. London: The Women's Press.

Frosh, S., Phoenix, A. and Pattman, R. (2002) *Young Masculinities*. Hampshire: Palgrave.

Gard, M. and Wright, J. (2005) *The Obesity Epidemic: Science, morality and ideology.* London: Routledge.

Goffman, E. (1972) *Encounters.* Harmondsworth: Penguin.

Griffin, P. (1998) *Strong Women, Deep Closets: Lesbians and homophobia in sport.* Champaign, IL: Human Kinetics.

Guttman, A. (1996) *The Erotic in Sport.* New York: Columbia University Press.

Hunter, L. (2004) Bourdieu and the social space of the PE class: reproduction of doxa through practice. *Sport, Education and Society,* 9 (2): 175–192.

Kirk, D. (2006) The 'obesity crisis' and school physical education. *Sport, Education and Society,* 11 (2): 121–134.

McDonald, M. (2006) Beyond the pale: whiteness of sport studies and queer scholarship. In Caudwell, J. (ed.) *Sport, Sexualities and Queer/Theory.* London: Routledge.

Park, R.J. (1987) Biological thought, athletics and the formation of a 'man of character' 1830–1900. In J.A. Mangan and J. Walvin (eds) *Manliness and Morality. Middle-class masculinity in Britain and America 1800–1940.* Manchester: Manchester University Press.

Petchesky, R. (1986) *Abortion and Woman's Choice: The state, sexuality, and reproductive freedom.* London: Verso.

Probyn, E. (2000) Sporting bodies: dynamics of shame and pride. *Body and Society,* 6 (1): 13–28.

Pronger, B. (1990) *The Arena of Masculinity.* London: GMP Publishers.

Pronger, B. (2000) Homosexuality and sport – who's winning? In McKay, J. Messner, M. and Sabo, D. (eds) *Masculinities, Gender Relations, and Sport.* London: Sage.

Pronger, B. (2002) *Body Fascism: Salvation in the Technology of Fitness.* Toronto: University of Toronto Press.

Redman, P. (2000) 'Tarred with the same brush': 'homophobia' and the role of the unconscious in school-based cultures of masculinity, *Sexualities,* 3 (4): 483–499.

Renold, E. (2007) Primary school 'studs': (de)constructing young boys' heterosexual masculinities, *Men and Masculinities,* 9 (3): 275–298.

Segal, L. (1997) *Slow Motion; Changing Masculinities, Changing Men.* London: Virago.

Stonewall (2006) *The School Report: the experiences of young gay people in Britain's schools.* London: Stonewall.

Sykes, H. (2006) Queering theories of sexuality in sports studies. In Caudwell, J. (ed.) *Sport, Sexualities and Queer Theory: Challenges and Controversies.* London: Routledge.

Symons, C. (2010) *The Gay Games: A history.* London: Routledge.

Synnott, A. (1993) *The Body Social.* London: Routledge.

Vicars, M. (2006) Who are you calling queer? Sticks and stones can break my bones but names will always hurt me. *British Educational Research Journal,* 32 (3): 347–361.

Weeks, J. (2003) *Sexuality.* London: Routledge.

Wellard, I. (2006) Able bodies and sport participation: social constructions of physical ability for gendered and sexually identified bodies. *Sport, Education and Society,* 11 (2): 105–119.

Wellard, I. (2007) *Rethinking Gender and Youth Sport.* London: Routledge.

Wellard, I. (2009) *Sport, Masculinities and the Body.* New York: Routledge.

8 The embodiment of religious culture and exclusionary practices in youth sport

Symeon Dagkas and Tansin Benn

Introduction

This discursive chapter will address the issue of the embodiment of religion and culture in sport and physical education. It will explore ways in which religion and culture can lead to exclusion from and through sport, particularly for Muslim girls and young women. The embodiment of everyday religious and cultural practices will be critically examined at their interface with sport participation. The discussion draws on voices from participants in selected research projects, notably the 'BASS project'[1] (Benn *et al.*, 2011a; Dagkas *et al.*, 2011; see also Jawad *et al.*, Chapter 14). The project was conducted in a UK city that is home to almost one in ten of all Muslims in the country and has the second largest population of Muslims, predominantly of Pakistani and Bangladeshi heritage (Abbas, 2006).

As has been highlighted in other chapters in this book, the complex interplay of identities provides one explanation for the finding that ethnic minority girls have the lowest participation rates in many physical activity settings (Ahmad and Bradby, 2007). Despite global advocacy for the benefits of physical activity, physical education and sport for young people's spiritual, mental and physical development (Bailey, 2009), Muslim women and girls have fewer opportunities to participate in sporting contexts compared to their contemporaries (Carroll and Hollinshead, 1993; Kay, 2006).

Muslim girls tend to be marginalised from participation in both formal schooling and community sport contexts (Benn, 1996; Kay, 2006; Benn and Ahmed, 2006). This has resulted in them becoming the focus of struggle for critical feminists, both Western and Islamic (Hargreaves, 2000; Knez, 2010; Jawad *et al.*, 2011). Moreover, the rhetoric of religious freedom in Europe is somewhat undermined by rising Islamophobia fuelled by extremist terrorists attacks in the Western world. Prejudice and discrimination, centred notably on followers of Islam, has led to the 'racialisation of religion' (Benn *et al.*, 2011a) and a tendency for intersections of disadvantage located in ethnicity, religion and gender to lead to the marginalisation of Muslim people living in the Western world. For these reasons, it is of paramount importance to address the 'Othering' (Macdonald *et al.*, 2009) of Muslim youth in youth sport settings that can both exclude and subordinate people who do not appear to 'fit' into the mainstream.

An example of the complexity of exclusion processes is seen in the difficulties encountered in attempting to distinguish between pseudo-religious reasoning and authentic religion. The former tends to originate in prevailing cultural attitudes and behaviours and it is sometimes used to disadvantage girls and women. The challenges resulting from the contested interpretation of religious texts and the pursuit of authentic Islam cannot be underestimated (Jawad, 1998). To address notions of disadvantage in the case of Muslim girls and women, Islamic feminists' work is helpful because 'interrogation of girls' and women's oppression is approached from a "faith-based" position, engaging scholars in reinterpretation of authentic Islam through holy texts that have been used to disadvantage Muslim women' (Jawad *et al.*, 2011, p. 25). In reality, there is nothing in these texts that forbids participation in physical activity by girls and women, but there are references to 'body modesty' that we will consider in more detail later in this chapter.

Popular perceptions of Muslim girls and young women as lacking interest in sport participation (Carroll and Hollinshead, 1993) have contributed, albeit unconsciously, to the development of exclusion pedagogies, especially in structured PE/sport environments. In many cases, such 'exclusion practices' have resulted in non-participation in physical education classes and school sport by some groups, as documented in recent empirical studies (Kay, 2006; Walseth, 2006). Reflecting on accounts expressed in this volume, we argue there is an urgent need to examine 'exclusion' more closely. This analysis could lead to more complex understandings of exclusion, thus eschewing the simple binary of 'exclusion and inclusion' in/from/through sport. Another approach could be to adopt a feminist, critical, post-structuralist approach to understanding exclusion through the eyes and voices of Muslim girls themselves (see, for example, Chapter 5).

The intention in this chapter is to increase understanding of cultural and religious practices and their effects on the inclusion/exclusion debate for Muslim girls in sporting contexts. It is written from a standpoint of 'fluid positionalities' (Hamzeh and Oliver, 2009, p. 1) and subjectivities (personal views of lived realities) that many Muslim girls and young women embody and which are often disregarded in the cultures of sport, physical education and physical activity.

Embodiment of religious culture

Islam has been acknowledged as the second largest religion in the world and the fastest growing in Europe (Fekete, 2008). Global migration patterns have contributed to increasing diaspora communities in the Western world. 'Cultures of hybridity' (Dagkas and Benn, 2006, p. 22), for those in diaspora contexts, reveal the fluid management of identity in relation to specific contexts; for example, where the centrality of the body and different cultures of physicality have different levels of significance and meaning.

Attention to the concept of *embodiment* of religion and culture 'acknowledges the material, physical, biological as well as the social whole of the "lived body"' (Garrett, 2004, p. 14). Socio-cultural, historical and economic factors impact differently upon young people's discursive practices towards sport and physical activity. Analysis of the ways in which Muslim girls live through Islam, and their degree of Islamisation, needs to be considered in any research on girls' positionalities towards sport and physical activity.

According to Benn (2009, p. 52)

> faith is embodied in the sense that presentation of the body, appearance, physicality, social interaction and behaviour are integral to religious identity, to lived reality of the daily embodiment of religious belief. Embodied faith reflects outward manifestations inseparably connected to internalised belief.

'Bodies are both inscribed with and vehicles of culture' (Garrett, 2004, p. 141), which means there are multiple ways in which both social and religious values are embodied. Outward manifestations of the religion and culture, such as dress codes and social interaction rules, are rooted in particular values, beliefs and behaviours concerning the body. In some physical education and youth sport discourses, tensions can arise where there are differences between learners and teachers/coaches in values attached to dress and social interaction.

Questions can be asked about the extent to which teachers, coaches and sport organisers understand the full implications of diversity in religious and cultural expression. Are they willing to listen and change pedagogies and practices where feasible? What level of importance do they place on changing to meet diverse needs? What are the gains and losses in making such changes? What can be learnt from the little-heard 'Muslim women and sport discourse' about the realities of those who have been successful sportswomen at every level, in many countries of the world, and in a variety of sporting arenas including the Olympic Games (Pfister, 2010; Benn and Dagkas, in press)? For example, many Islamic countries have compulsory physical education for girls and boys, and facilities allow freedom of physicality in appropriately structured learning environments (Benn *et al.*, 2011b). Providers and policy makers in non-Islamic countries might be puzzled by the apparent diversity within Islam, so issues related to embodiment are discussed further with special reference to the wearing of hijab (head covering), appropriate Islamic dress codes and sex segregation.

Jawad (1998, p. 99) maintains that 'factors including globalisation, increased migration patterns and the development of new Diaspora, have led to Islam being experienced differently within Islamic groups throughout the world.' Dagkas and Benn (2006) have noted that individuals can negotiate the expression of their religious identity in the sporting arena. It is important, however, to identify ways in which being Muslim can be influenced by other factors such as family, community, culture and expectation. Such factors need to be taken into account to avoid the tendency to attribute non-participation in sport to the religion alone.

The issue of body modesty, which is an Islamic requirement, necessitates attention to body covering, often most visibly expressed in women's adoption of hijab and practices relating to gender relations post-puberty. For some women and their families, sex-segregation is viewed as vital for participation in physical activity, although there is nothing either in the Quran or the *Hadith*[2] stating explicitly that strict segregation between the two sexes is required (Jawad *et al.*, 2011). The wearing of hijab is also a contested site of religious and cultural conflation, where there are different opinions, religious views and lived realities found around the world. Not all Muslim women wear the hijab; some are coerced into wearing it (e.g. in Iran and Saudi-Arabia), whilst others are forbidden from wearing it (e.g. in some contexts in France and in competitive sport in Turkey) (Koca and Haciosoftaoglu, 2011). In the UK, however, the wearing of the hijab is usually a matter of personal choice. For some Muslim women, the hijab represents the personal embodiment of a commitment to faith, which has become both public and symbolic (Kay, 2006). For others, who choose not to wear hijab, faith remains internalised and private (Jawad *et al.*, 2011).

Hijab can be regarded in a number of different ways. For many Muslim girls and women, hijab is a symbol of honour connected to faith and an expression of respect for the Islamic requirement to cover the hair. For others, hijab is regarded as a symbol of oppression or repression, or a symbol of rebellion against Western values (Fekete, 2008). According to Hamzeh and Oliver (2009), the hijab is a spatial divider between places and a protector from forbidden practices, as well as being a visual barrier between the body and the sight of another. As Benn *et al.* (2011a) point out, while most people in the world cover parts of their bodies for reasons of modesty, attention to this practice is highly significant in Islam and in the lives of many Muslim women. In short, hijab brings visibility of faith which results in solidarity and approval from some and, particularly in diaspora communities, alienation from others.

While sport providers and policy makers in the democratic West cannot deny the basic human right to have and express a religion, accommodating different dress codes or considering sex-segregated environments can be problematic. Since the dominant equity discourse is for inclusion, it is essential to acknowledge the very real significance of religion in the lives of some people, accept diverse ways in which Muslim girls and women embody their faith, and seek ways to accommodate the religious needs of these people. The significance of the school as the main, and sometimes the only, environment in which some young Muslim girls will experience physical activity and sport cannot be ignored. Despite good practice in some youth sport arenas (see also Chapter 14), in some cases Eurocentric curricula (Macdonald *et al.*, 2009) and pedagogies have created impasses between educators and Muslim girls (Dagkas *et al.*, 2011).

Macdonald *et al.* (2009: 14) stress the need for teachers to engage more with young people and their families and to understand their core values in order to avoid acts of separatism and 'Othering.' 'Othering' means treating difference between people hierarchically – for example, in terms of superiority and inferiority – thereby dismissing the needs of others as invisible or unimportant. Recent research has attempted to address these issues by focusing on the voices of those engaged in seeking resolutions where tensions regarding issues of exclusion arise. In order to illustrate this point, a flavour of multiple voices from the 'BASS project' is interesting (for more see Chapter 14). Problems arose in the educational provision of a major city in the UK because of the increasing trend for Muslim girls to be withdrawn from physical education lessons. Data are abstracted that capture positionalities and subjectivities from recordings of the voices of Muslim girls, parents and teachers/providers, and representatives of the Muslim Council of Britain. The intention here is to illustrate a nexus of dispositions and subjectivities regarding religion, culture and physical activity and to outline one way of seeking negotiation, increased understanding and improved pedagogies of inclusion.

Voices and positionalities

We reiterate that the emphasis here is not on problematising Muslim girls but on examining systems, policies and practices that result in the exclusion of some Muslim girls from participation in sport, physical education and school sport.

Voices of teachers and headteachers

Data from the schools in these studies confirms that where accommodation of specific needs could not be found, the result was young people who just 'did not take part in PE at all' (PE teacher, interview). In other cases, Headteachers reported that some girls 'were collected by their parents at the start of the (PE) lesson and returned to school at the end' (headteacher, interview). Issues of modesty were evident in most of the voices from the teachers in our studies: 'We have had pupils who refused to take part because arms and legs could be seen' (headteacher, interview).

The issue of single-sex spaces arose and could be identified as a key factor in the development of 'pedagogy of exclusion.' Additionally, in some cases teachers' lack of knowledge and patchy awareness of Islamic requirements for modesty contributed to the gaps between physical education practices and the girls' embodiment of religious and cultural values. As some of the physical education teachers explain in interviews:

If there are any specific Islamic requirements we are not aware of them.

(female teacher)

Sometimes I struggle to address the implications of religion on my students' behavior and performance . . . Especially during Ramadan [religious festival].

(male PE teacher)

This is an increasingly diverse society that we live in – trends change as knowledge does – we [PE teachers] should be educated to be able to accommodate the needs of our students.

(male PE teacher)

Some teachers expressed a desire to be clearer about the distinctions between religious versus cultural requirements and interpretations. Concerns were expressed that initial teacher training was an inadequate preparation for learning environments that included diverse ethnicities and multiple faiths. Issues raised included concern for appropriate dress codes, religious requirements and provision of single-sex environments with, in many cases, argument for same-sex staffing. In addition, gaps in knowledge and understanding of parents regarding the value, status and benefits of physical education were identified by some teachers:

> Parents need to be aware of the fact that physical education is compulsory and what physical education actually is in a school.
>
> (female headteacher)

Voices of Muslim girls

In all the responses found in the studies, a common issues raised by the girls was that they considered physical education to be an enjoyable part of their school curriculum. As is illustrated below, this was particularly noticeable in those schools where religious requirements were met and both body modesty and sex segregation were part of the school ethos. There was much enthusiasm for the range of activities on offer in PE with some understanding of their importance as part of a healthy lifestyle. As one girl explained: '[physical education] is fun, gives us more exercise – keeps us healthy, gives us stronger bones.' Overall, our data from primary schools revealed that students' responses were largely positive about attitudes to physical education and school sport and its life-enhancing potential. Many secondary school pupils shared the positive experiences of the primary children in broad activity areas. For some Muslim girls, the hijab and arm/leg coverage were essential to retaining their embodied faith while participating: 'I cannot participate comfortably without hijab' (Muslim girl). Being persuaded or forced to transgress from what she perceived as a religious obligation created tension between her sense of religious identity and school practices (Western practices). In many cases, girls' embodiment of faith mirrored those expressed in Hamzeh and Oliver's (2009) study where it was noted that the interpretation and the embodiment of the hijab has three dimensions: 'dress; mobility to/in public spaces; and physical activities in public spaces' (p.12). It is the interlocking of these interpretations and embodied practices that can create tensions and that can provide a platform for exclusionary practices.

Interview data indicated that secondary school Muslim girls (aged 11–16) were much more conscious of the influence of their parents' views and religious and cultural imperatives than primary-aged Muslim girls. Referring to delivery of dance as part of her physical education curriculum, one girl explained: 'parents will give permission for girls-only dance.'

Many Muslim girls participated in PE wearing 'mix and match' kit. This kit has some Islamic features, such as optional hijab and tracksuit bottoms with short-sleeved tops, as illustrated in the photographs from one school used in the guidance document (BCC, 2008). In this particular school, young people on the school council had designed flexibility and choice in their kit policy (see also Oliver *et al.*, 2009; and Chapter 11). Other Muslim young people chose not to wear any outward manifestation of faith, preferring a private, internalised approach. Some had little time for peers who spoke out against PE, as two Muslim girls explained in a group interview context:

> *Sam:*   I think some girls just kick up a fuss because they don't want to do PE.
> *Farooq:*   Yeah I agree, If they don't like mixed-sex PE they should have chosen an all-girls' school.

The above views demonstrate little empathy with the need expressed by some girls for the accommodation of the embodiment of religion. Furthermore, as we see below in an extract from an interview with a Muslim girl (discussing the issue of some Muslim girls' decision to opt out of PE lessons), some girls were happy with the school's policy to remove the hijab from PE:

> I think the whole scarf business . . . Some girls get angry because they are told they have to take their headscarves off for physical education for health and safety reasons – some girls get upset – I think that's what holds girls back in physical education. Here there is no choice.

Another girl discussed managing movement through open spaces into the 'male-free' physical education space:

> I don't see that there is any problem because there are just girls (in the sports hall) – if we have to cross public spaces we are allowed to wear them until we get into the hall. To be honest for some it is just an excuse not to do it.

Lived realities and discourses captured the diversity of voices in and between Muslim communities. These voices span Muslim young women who participate happily in established physical education/school sport contexts; those requesting modest clothing for participation (e.g. wearing of hijab and tracksuits); and those requiring gender segregated spaces for freedom of participation. It is in this sense that we argue that religious identities are neither static nor fixed within communities, but are dynamic, fluid and closely related to cultural and societal factors. According to Benn *et al.* (2011a) 'action in pursuit of preferences for opportunity to participate in sporting activities and retain adherence to religious identity, demonstrate such agency.'

Voices of parents

Parents expressed conflicting views on the delivery of PE and school sport. In many cases, these conflicting views identified confusion between embodiment of religion and culture and, often, exclusion. In the following quotation, a Muslim headteacher tries to explain the difficulty that many diaspora parents find in

distinguishing cultural heritage and Islamic requirements, leading them to perceive some practices as exclusionary:

> From our point of view [headteacher] – a lot of parents . . . find it difficult
> to separate the principles of Islam from their cultural heritage . . . [From our
> point of view] we are educating British Muslims and that's what the mission
> statement and aims and objectives clearly state – to provide the national cur-
> riculum within an Islamic framework. So we have tried to help parents to
> separate their cultural understanding of Islam from Islamic principle . . . once
> they see the differences and they understand the boundaries of Islamic values,
> they are able to make that shift.

Lived realities encompass diversity in the embodiment of faith and, more importantly, of culture and it is clear from the statement above that, once parental
education is established, gaps can be bridged, benefits understood and practices
differentiated. Many parents in the project expressed views that could be understood as battles between cultural values, religious views and Western trends which,
in many cases, lead to exclusion, non-participation and withdrawal of girls from
physical education and school sport. 'Pedagogies of exclusion' that stemmed from
cultural interpretations of religious texts were clear in many parental statements
about the delivery of physical education in schools. Conflicting views that reflect
these arguments were evident in parental group interviews (all female parents):

> My daughter goes to a single sex school with all female teachers – I don't
> have a problem and my daughter can wear anything.
>   My daughter goes to a school where they force them to do physical educa-
> tion. The teachers make them take off their headscarves and they do not under-
> stand that we are not happy about that . . . dress sense should be respected.
>   I don't like my daughters running and swimming; it is against our culture.
> Also they may run out of breath and this might cause asthma. Girls are not
> made for running. The school is not going to do what we want them to do, they
> do not listen to us, and they must think physical education is a good thing. I do
> not agree . . . I have never done any sports in my life. It is not in our ways.

This range of responses illustrates the lack of congruence in views about the value
of physical education and sporting activities within communities. Parents also
recognise the differences within their own communities. Some linked the differences to degrees of religiosity.

    Again, such polarised views indicate the complexity of negotiating outcomes
to improve inclusion.

Where are the role models?

A further problem with discourses of inclusion and exclusion pedagogies in
physical education and youth sport cultures is that people in the most powerful

positions (researchers/knowledge makers, policy makers, providers, teachers and coaches) are predominantly white, non-Muslim, able-bodied and members of the host, not the diaspora communities. This indicates that some young people also are denied access to key higher education and vocational opportunities in the field.

Inevitably in a monograph concerned with pedagogies of inclusion and exclusion, there is a focus on educational contexts. In particular the focus is on policies and practices that create, or conversely deny, the provision of a welcoming and supportive learning environment for all young people, especially those from under-represented class, gender, disability and ethnic minority groups. Paradoxically, in a society which celebrates the myth of sport as the ultimate avenue of success (Commission of the EC, 2007) and upward social mobility, the Training and Development Agency recently revealed that physical education has the lowest figures – 3 per cent – for recruitment and retention of black and ethnic minority teachers compared with teaching generally – 11 per cent (Flintoff, 2008). Prior to Flintoff's work, very little attention had been paid to understanding the reasons for these figures. One exception was Benn (1996) who raised the issue of prejudice, discrimination and exclusion pedagogies in physical education teacher training in the UK for Muslim students of Asian and African heritage. Even in the sport of football, where 25 per cent of players in the English premier league are black, only two out of ninety-two managers of English clubs are black (Kessel, 2010). This sport context phenomenon is not new; for example, there is a long history of American, then UK research on the 'glass-ceiling' for black athletes who could not break into careers and more powerful positions in their field (Coakley, 1997). Why then is there little evidence of change?

With very few exceptions, higher education institutions and powerful sports governing bodies are notably silent in self-critical discourse on equity. Even if unintended, these bodies fail to recognise pedagogical policies of exclusion in the process of recruiting and educating future teachers and coaches. Failure to recruit potential leaders from minority populations perpetuates failure to develop role models in positions of power, resulting in a downward spiral of negative reinforcement that further depresses the aspirations of potential (black) students of sport.

Arguably then, sport provision in higher education and vocational training routes is part of the problem of exclusion rather than being part of the solution. What seems to be required is a radical transformation of teacher and coach education into a model for, and a driver of, change. Critical to this endeavour is attention to the voices of those marginalised groups and ability to respond with affirmative action.

Conclusion

The lives of girls and women in Islamic, Muslim majority and Muslim minority countries vary across the world. There is a need for awareness of the complexity of multiple and often diverse influences of religion/home/school/community cultures on girls' participation in physical education, school sport and physical activity.

Context, religiosity and cultural differences affect values, attitudes and behaviours that are centred on the body, issues of modesty and physicality. Improving two-way channels of communication, dialogue and negotiation can contribute to an improved understanding of difference, leading to solutions for change where exclusion pedagogies exist.

It was clearly evident in the voices presented above that cultural values and interpretations of religion, mostly initiated by parental attitudes, stimulate the 'disciplinary mechanism' of embodiment of religion (Hamzeh and Oliver, 2009, p. 13). These attitudes are particularly influential in the lives of young Muslim girls. Interpretation and application to living faith are influenced by cultural, political and economic conditions, and it is important to understand the fluidity of positioning and adherence to religion in order to start recognising and adapting pedagogies of exclusion. The exclusion of Muslim girls and women in sport and physical activity is usually linked to meeting the needs for modesty (*al-ihtisham, inshallah and haram*[3] (own emphasis) (Hamzeh and Oliver, 2009). Improvement lies in respecting diverse positionalities, particularly in the desire for embodiment through hijab or gender segregation. Clearly, change can be challenging for providers in secular societies where sporting provision is structured and organised in line with predominately Eurocentric perspectives (Macdonald *et al.*, 2009).

Listening to young people, especially those from marginalised groups in society, and the support of Islamic studies researchers, can provide views that open contested and serious dialogue. It is important to remember that Muslim females are not a homogeneous group, as has been illustrated in this chapter and others. There are differences in the ways in which they choose to resolve religious and other cultural demands which are fluid and dependant on historical and shifting socio-environmental factors. Macdonald *et al.*, (2009, p. 9) reinforce the point, arguing that research should 'acknowledge the different cultural backgrounds and varied interpretations of Islam' in order to avoid the temptation to look for 'quick fix' solutions to problems.

For the futures of young people in youth sport cultures, there needs to be greater awareness of the interface of faith and religion. Finally, we suggest that one key to more inclusive youth sport cultures is to acknowledge the ways in which issues of race, religion, gender, class and disability inequalities reinforce one another in sport higher education and training arenas. They create structured and persistent obstacles to the achievement of a genuine teaching, coaching and administration meritocracy operating in a social climate of inclusion and equity. The relative invisibility of marginalised groups in influential vocational positions in sport is critical in terms of social justice and equity. Exclusion from education and training opportunities in sport effectively excludes from decision-making and leadership roles. Only in such positions can a more representative profession have the power and influence to contribute to the challenge for us all – to change 'pedagogies of exclusion' in youth sport cultures in schools, community sport and physical activity contexts.

Notes

1 The 'BASS (Birmingham Advisory and Support Service) project' is described in detail in Chapter 14 by Jawad *et al.*
2 In Islamic terminology, *Hadith* refers to reports, statements and narrations concerning the words and deeds of the Islamic prophet Muhammad. *Hadith* are regarded as important tools of understanding the Quran.
3 *al-ihtisham* – modesty is the virtue by which a Muslim maintains her/his moderation, humility, and respect; *inshallah* – is a central principle in the Muslim's faith of obedience to one God; *haram*, in Arabic, is a commonly used term derived from the verb *hrm*, which means made sacred and forbidden (Hamzeh and Oliver, 2009, pp. 8, 9 and 10).

References

Abbas, T. (2006) *Muslims in Birmingham*. COMPAS centre on Migration, Policy and Society, Oxford: University of Oxford.

Ahmad, W. and Bradby, H. (2007) Locating ethnicity and health: exploring concepts and contexts. *Sociology of Health and Illness*, 29 (6): 795–810.

Bailey, R. (2009) Physical education and sport in schools. In Bailey, R. and Kirk, D. (eds) *The Routledge Physical Education Reader*. London: Routledge, pp. 9–27.

BCC (Birmingham City Council) (2008) *Improving Participation of Muslim Girls in Physical Education and School Sport: Shared practical guidance from Birmingham schools*. Birmingham Advisory Support Service, School Effectiveness Team, Martineau Centre, Balden Road, B32 2EH, Birmingham, England. Online: www.birmingham.gov.uk/childrenservices.

Benn, T. (1996) Muslim Women and PE in initial teacher training. *Sport, Education and Society*, 1 (1): 5–21.

Benn, T. and Ahmed, A. (2006) Alternative visions: international sporting opportunities for Muslim Women and implications for British Youth Sport. *Youth and Policy*, 92: 119–132.

Benn, T. (2009) Muslim Women in sport: a researcher's journey to understanding 'embodied faith.' *Bulletin 55, International Council for Sports Science and Physical Education (ICSSPE)*, pp. 48–56. Online: www.icsspe.org (accessed 28 January 2009).

Benn, T. and Dagkas, S. (in press) The Olympic Movement and Islamic Culture: Conflict or compromise for Muslim Women? *International Journal of Sport Policy*.

Benn, T., Dagkas, S. and Jawad, H. (2011a) Embodied faith: Islam, religious freedom and educational practices in physical education. *Sport, Education and Society*, 16 (1): 17–34.

Benn, T., Pfister, G. and Jawad, H. (2011b) *Muslim Women and Sport*. London: Routledge.

Carroll, B. and Hollinshead, G. (1993) Equal opportunities: race and gender in physical education: a case study. In: Evans, J. (ed.) *Equality, Education and Physical Education*. London: Falmer Press, pp. 154–169.

Coakley, J. (1997) *Sport and Society: Issues and Controversies*. New York: McGraw-Hill.

Commission of the European Communities (2007) *White Paper on Sport*. Brussels (COM[2007] 391 final).

Dagkas, S. and Benn, T. (2006) Young Muslim women's experiences of Islam and physical education in Greece and Britain: A comparative study. *Sport, Education and Society*, 11 (1): 21–28.

Dagkas, S., Koushkie-Jahromi, M. and Talbot, M. (2011) Reaffirming the values of physical education, physical activity and sport in the lives of young Muslim women. In Benn, T., Pfister, G. and Jawad, H. (eds) *Muslim Women and Sport*. London: Routledge, pp. 13–24.

Fekete, L. (2008) *Integration, Islamophobia and Civil Rights in Europe*. London: Institute of Race Relations.

Flintoff, A. (2008) Black and ethnic minority ethnic trainees' experiences of physical education initial teacher training. *Report to the Training and Development Agency*. Leeds Metropolitan University.

Garrett, R. (2004) Gendered bodies and physical identities. In Evans, J., Davies, B. and Wright, J. (eds) *Body, Knowledge and Control: Studies in the sociology of physical education and health*. London: Routledge, pp. 140–156.

Hargreaves, J. (2000) *Heroines of Sport. The politics of difference and identity*. London: Routledge.

Hamzeh, M. and Oliver, K. (2009) Gaining research access into the lives of Muslim girls: Researchers negotiating *muslimness*, modesty, *inshallah*, and *haram*. *International Journal of Qualitative Studies in Education*, 23 (2): 165–180.

Jawad, H. (1998) *The Rights of Women in Islam. An Authentic Approach*. Basingstoke: Macmillan Press Ltd.

Jawad, H., Al-Sinani, Y. and Benn, T. (2011) Islam, Women and Sport. In Benn, T., Pfister, G. and Jawad, H. (eds) *Muslim Women and Sport*. London: Routledge,. pp. 25–40.

Kay, T. (2006) Daughters of Islam: Family influences on Muslim young women's participation in sport. *International Review for the Sociology of Sport*, 41 (3–4): 357–373.

Kessel, A. (2010) *The Lack of Black Football Managers is a Problem that won't go Away. The Observer*, Sunday 31 October. Online: www.guardian.co.uk/football/2010/oct/31/black-football-managers (accessed 16 December 2010).

Koca, C. and Haciosoftaoglu, I. (2011) Religion and the state – the story of a Turkish elite athlete. In Benn, T., Pfister, G. and Jawad, H. (eds) *Muslim Women and Sport*. London: Routledge, pp. 198–210.

Knez, K. (2010) Being Muslim and being female: negotiating physical activity and a gendered body. In Wright, J. and Macdonald, D. (eds) *Young People, Physical Activity and the Everyday*. Oxford: Routledge, pp. 104–118.

Macdonald, D., Abbott, R. and Knez, K. *et al.* (2009) Talking exercise: cultural diversity and physically active lifestyles. *Sport, Education and Society*, 14 (1): 1–19.

Oliver, K., Hamzeh, M. and McCaughtry, N. (2009) Girly girls *can* play games/Las niñas pueden jugar tambien: Co-creating a curriculum of possibilities with 5th grade girls. *Journal of Teaching in Physical Education*, 28 (1): 90–110.

Pfister, G. (2010) Outsiders: Muslim women and Olympic Games – barriers and opportunities. *The International Journal of the History of Sport*, 27 (16–17): 1–33.

Walseth, K. (2006) Young Muslim women and sport: the impact of identity work. *Leisure Studies*, 25 (1): 75–94.

9 Sporting fat

Youth sport and the 'obesity epidemic'

Lisette Burrows and Jaleh McCormack

Introduction

In this chapter we focus on the interrelationship between youth sport and health imperatives expressed in school-based physical activity practices, and in the beliefs and dispositions of New Zealand teachers and young people. We describe a little of the New Zealand context, then draw on ethnographic work in a secondary school, Peabody High School, to explore some of the ways in which both teachers and students are linking sport and health imperatives in their talk and practice. We argue that at a time when youth inactivity and obesity are centre-stage, more young people are being encouraged/required to play sport with some oft-unintended effects.

What has an international obsession with the weight and size of young people (Campos, 2004; Gard and Wright, 2005; Gard, 2009) got to do with youth sport? Until relatively recently, perhaps not much at all. Historically, sport has variously been touted as a vehicle for the development of social responsibility, competitive spirit, co-operation, self-esteem, morality, character and strength (Kirk, 1992). Contemporaneously, however, youth sport has been harnessed to a somewhat different agenda, re-fashioned as a crucial addition to the arsenal of 'weapons' stockpiled for the 'war' on obesity (Gard, 2004, 2007, 2008). In New Zealand, a Conservative government is arguing vociferously for the role of extra curricula and in-school sport in improving the health of the nation's youth (Key, 2008). The prime minister seamlessly draws on orthodox notions of sport as an important contributor to social and personal development while simultaneously linking sport to current health imperatives in his explanation of what his government's new initiative – Kiwisport – will achieve for children:

> The Government wants to see more Kiwi kids participating in sport so that they get the health and lifestyle benefits of better physical fitness, as well as the chance to be part of a team, find mentors, gain a taste for competition and winning, and get more involved in their communities.
>
> (Key, 2008)

This harnessing of sport to health is not unique to New Zealand. In the United Kingdom, calls for more youth sport are annexed in popular and professional discourse to obesity reduction agendas (Evans *et al.*, 2005). Similarly, in Australia, initiatives such as the Queensland Government's *Eat Well, Be Active Campaign* (2007) link sport and recreation portfolios with those of both health and education. In Canada, sport and/or physical activity programmes are proliferating in a context where physical inactivity and obesity are positioned as 'risks to both the individual body's health and to the social body' (McDermott, 2007, p. 303). Further, children and young people across Western contexts are themselves increasingly regarding their engagement in sport both as a health obligation and as a fat-busting strategy (Burrows, 2008; Fullagar, 2002; Rail, 2009).

In this chapter we interrogate the relationship between youth sport and health imperatives, including weight loss, expressed in school-based physical activity practices, and in the testimony of teachers and young people themselves. We begin by providing a sense of the New Zealand context relating to both sport and health. We envisage that many of the issues arising for young people and teachers there will resonate with those facing educators and students across global divides. Indeed, our argument is fuelled by the ubiquitous concern for young people's health (and in particular, their weight) expressed now in most regions of the so-called 'developed' world (Campos, 2010; Gard and Wright, 2005).

Second, we draw on ethnographic observations, interviews with teachers and the questionnaire responses of young people from one New Zealand secondary school, Peabody High School, to elucidate some of the ways that both teachers and students are linking sport and health imperatives (including weight loss) in their talk and practice. As part of a broader study examining how health imperatives are being taken up by schools in New Zealand (see Burrows and Wright, 2007), teachers and students were asked several questions about their understandings of health, behavioural attributes linked to its achievement and the role of schooling in alleviating broader public health concerns. Much of their commentary about these issues focused on the role of physical exercise and/or sport in health enhancement, which included an understanding of health as key to weight loss and having a thin/healthy body.

Finally, we point to some of the problematic consequences of framing sport as a health-enhancing and/or fat-busting tool. We argue that while youth sport has never provided an open-entry playing field for *all* young people, contemporary concerns about youth inactivity and obesity have created a climate where even reluctant participants are being impelled to action; yet with what effects?

The New Zealand context

New Zealanders have always thought of themselves as sporty people (Phillips, 1996). The iconic All-Blacks rugby team is pivotal in this imagery (Falcous, 2007; Hokowhitu, 2003), but so too is the geography of the country. A much-touted, clean green image coupled with an undisputed surplus of national parks, beaches and roomy backyards contributes to the vision of an outdoorsy nation; one replete with active, tough, sporty youth batting balls and running free in a land of milk and honey. Latterly, however, this wholesome vision has been disputed. Commentators variously apportion blame for an avowed decline in the numbers of young people engaged in organised sport to the proliferation of internet and videogame technologies, the emergence of a risk adverse society, and negligent parents (Fight the Obesity Epidemic, 2008). What some commentators call a 'cottonwool generation' is emerging (Wong, 2005) where children are 'protected' from engaging in physical activity experiences that were formerly part and parcel of New Zealand culture (e.g. playing alone outdoors, engaging in outdoor education experiences).

When the above concerns are linked, as they are in the public eye, to widespread anxiety over childhood obesity, the impetus for government to take action is understandable. Having just been labelled the third fattest nation in the world (New Zealand Press Association, 2008), New Zealand health officials and educators are keen to develop policies and implementation plans that will propel New Zealand youngsters off their couches and into the play spaces with which the country is so liberally endowed (Key, 2008). Sport, it seems, is yet another potential piece of armoury in the war against obesity and coddled youth (Gard, 2008).

On 11 August 2009, New Zealand's newly elected National Government launched an 82 million dollar fund to encourage more New Zealand kids into sport (Key, 2009). According to Prime Minster John Key, the previous government, a Labour-led government with a clear mandate to address New Zealand's obesity problem, had wasted good money on social marketing campaigns and other 'gadgets' designed to get New Zealanders 'off the couch' and into exercise, when what was really needed was more funding for grassroots youth sport. While few could quibble with the sentiment – that is, putting the money where the children are, funding bats and balls rather than messages – we suggest, in this chapter, that young people may not necessarily 'read' or receive governmental good intentions in the manner intended. In particular, we suggest that in a context where obesity imperatives pervade popular and professional consciousness, the mandatory call to 'sport' could, conceivably, alienate more children from an understanding of their physicality as a source of pleasure and indeed make life more difficult for those who have little interest in sport. Further, even for those whose proclivity *is* sports, the annexing of sporting practices themselves to health-related objectives is changing both the nature and the function of sport in secondary schools.

Below we endeavour to illustrate some of the aforementioned issues, drawing on ethnographic work conducted in Peabody High School. Peabody was one of four New Zealand schools we worked with in 2007 and 2008 as part of a collaborative research project designed to investigate the ways health imperatives are being recontextualised in schools across Australia, the UK and New Zealand. Students aged 12–17 years completed a questionnaire, curriculum and policy resources were collated, teachers and administrators were interviewed and detailed observations of school life and surrounds were conducted.

Sport in the life of Peabody School

Peabody is a secondary school (i.e. contains students from 12 to 18 years of age) serving a predominantly low socio-economic area and drawing its students from populations who largely identify as Maori (New Zealand's indigenous population) and/or Pasifika (i.e. students who identify with a range of Pacific Island nations). Both Maori and Pasifika peoples are widely portrayed as 'high health need' communities in New Zealand (Johnston, 2007; Tagata Pasifika, 2007). At Peabody sporting success is highly valued. Sporting achievements are regularly celebrated with ceremonies and trophies, and certificates and newspaper accounts of Peabody sporting successes grace the walls of the school foyer and classrooms. Inter-school sporting competitions are prepared for eagerly representing, as they do, significant opportunities for boosting school morale and community-wide perceptions of the school. As one Peabody teacher suggested, 'we've got such a huge sporting talent in the school! One of our local guys has just, he did my sports nutrition class and he is now in the Lions squad so he's an up and coming All Black' (teacher A).

School resources are directly channelled into supporting school sport representatives. For example, girls participating in the school first-fifteen rugby team have their own teacher aide who supports them with their school work and ensures they are prepared for rugby training. Sporting facilities are over-subscribed by students and members of the wider community. Sport, it would seem, is crucial to the community and an integral ingredient of the school's culture.

Peabody students who go on to succeed on the national and/or international arena are regularly recruited as 'role models' for successive generations of Peabody students. In an important sense, sports are perceived and used as a vehicle for promoting a 'can do' attitude amongst students. Moreover, sporting success is viewed and promoted as 'evidence' of students who, although appearing to have minimal economic, social and/or educational resources, manage to achieve despite this.

The notion that sport can and does serve as a vehicle for helping students to realise and consolidate their potential as citizens of the world is not a particularly novel one. Indeed this trope has served the popular movie industry well with numerous films (e.g. *Bend it like Beckham*, *Billy Elliot*) starring marginalised young people (via class, ethnicity and/or gender) making good through their engagement and success in sport. Further, sociological studies (e.g. Artencio and Wright, 2008) have pointed to the ways in which sport is regarded by marginalised youth as a 'way out'; a way to transcend their current life circumstances. At Peabody, this trope is seemingly alive and well. Teachers regard sport as crucial because of its capacity to help students see they can make something of themselves. It also functions to increase the mana (status) of the school amongst the broader educational community and to produce 'role models' to inspire younger generations. Students, too, display an understanding that engagement in sport can facilitate a brighter future, a better career and, importantly in the context of this chapter, a healthier (thinner) 'self.'

Young people's understanding of the relationship between health, sport and weight

In this section, we briefly foreground Peabody students' responses to questions about their health beliefs and practices. Responses were written by the students and thus we have left the, at times, unconventional spelling intact. Given the school's commitment to sport per se, its positioning as a low socio-economic index environment *and* in light of widely reported 'issues' with the health and weight of Pasifika and Maori populations, it perhaps comes as little surprise to find that, within this particular school, sport is regarded by students as inextricably linked to health and/or weight. The following responses to the question 'what are the most important things a person should do to be healthy?' illustrate the pivotal role of sport as a health enhancing tool for some of the Peabody students:

- eat right sleep right and play sports
- play sports, eat veges
- Eat healthy food and do lots of sports
- Look at what they eat and keep doing sport

The consequences of this assumed sport/health relationship for young people's practices can be seen in the tendency for many young people to self-monitor their engagement in sport. They appear to view sport as a kind of medicine or 'dosage' and to worry about the extent to which their participation in sport is 'working' in terms of their health outcomes (including weight loss). When asked how they would *improve* their health, responses from both young men and women included:

i would do extra sport
More exercise
play alot of sports lose weight
eat healthy exercise more
eat healthier, play sport!
By eating the right foods and having more physical activities, like playing sport
I would go for runs. and also go to all my trainings for sports. And eat healthy.

The actual and implied recurrence of the descriptor 'more', even in the few responses cited above, is symptomatic of a general tendency amongst children, even those who are already highly active, to believe they need to do more sport and exercise if they are to reach their health (or weight) objectives. It is as if they believe they can never do enough sport or exercise no matter how much engagement they have. As one 15-year-old Cook Island Maori Peabody student says 'I play a lot of sport and train a lot and go for jogs but still want to do more exercise.' The desire to do more and more exercise is also indicative of an understanding that health (and thinness) simply requires the 'right' dose of physical activity. When asked if they had ever thought they needed to do more exercise, many Peabody students responded 'yes' with their supporting rationales pointing to an understanding that the purpose of exercise (and in many cases, sport) is to lose weight:

When I'm lacking in my rugby games and put on 5 kg
because my weight is too big
My size
because I could see that my body is going fatter
I feel like I'm fat
so I can lose weight
my size cause I am energetic it's just that I can't be bothered
myself sometimes i think i need exercise because some of my clothes I can't
    fit
sometime I think I'm getting fatter so I when for run after school

A self-deprecatory assessment of their current selves as 'lazy' also characterised some of the Peabody young people's responses. Despite the many competing pressures on their time at secondary school (e.g. homework, exams, family obligations), young people declared that they want to exercise more for reasons such as, 'because I'm getting fat and lazy,' 'because I was starting to get lazy and gaining weight' and 'too lazy and getting fat.' This association between fat, inactivity and laziness has been evidenced in several prior studies with young people (e.g. Burrows *et al.*, 2002; Macdonald *et al.*, 2005). We suggest that in a context where sport is represented as a universal 'good,' young people's failure to do 'enough' can and does contribute to harsh self-assessments not only of their health but also of their own and others' personal capacities and dispositions. A fat body, for these students, was indicative of an inactive body, of a person that has failed to exercise and/or eat 'correctly.' When asked if they thought a person's size/shape had anything to do with their health, student responses included the following:

because if they're too big they're not eating healthy and not doing exercise
Yes i reckon it does cauze the only way you can get fat is eating too much
    and not very active but there is a disease when you get fat
Because you can easily tell when someone fat is not really healthy because
    that tells us that they don't eat healthy food and they don't get involved in
    healthy/ health activities
Because if you're big, that means you need a lot of exercise and stop eating fat
    food
if someone is too fat he/she shape is not healthy. Keep on doing Exercise

The testimonies of young people discussed above demonstrate that for these young people, at least, sport is understood to be a vehicle for health enhancement *and* an activity that can be 'taken' in doses en route to improving health and securing weight loss. In the next section we draw on Peabody teachers' narratives to explore the ways teachers too in their practices and speech acts link sport to health and weight-loss imperatives under the guise of pastoral care (McCuaig and Tinning, 2010). Indeed, we suggest that teachers' ideas about health and the practices they choose to deploy in their work with young people aim to establish a relationship between health, sport and weight that appears to be taken up readily by some of their students.

Teachers' views about students' health, physical activity, nutrition and weight

Staff at Peabody High School suggested that amongst the student population there were several students who were overweight and/or obese, and who had 'unhealthy' diets and lacked exercise. Although acknowledging that these students were very much the minority, teachers were nevertheless committed to the role their school should play in addressing these 'presumed' health issues across the entire student population. As Gard (2008) has noted, despite the often small minorities of young people experiencing severe weight-related health concerns, it has become standard practice, across the Western world, for health promotion strategies to be geared towards *all* the population. Schools, in particular, are regarded as ideal sites for reaching large numbers of young people (Burrows, 2008).

Staff offered three key justifications for the role of the school in the amelioration of health concerns. First, they believed that a child's health status affects capacity to learn. Second, improving youth health was regarded as part of the school's 'duty of care' to students, and finally, teachers suggested that tools for healthy living were integral to schooling that aims to prepare students adequately for life post-school. Fuelling these rationales were Western-centric assumptions about what 'health' comprises (i.e. exercise, a good diet and a non-fat body) together with an understanding that children at this low decile school were particularly at risk in relation to ill-health (Burrows, 2011). These taken-for-granted presumptions, in effect, afforded teachers a conceptual lens through which to view their students. In other words, whether or not the entire school population was at risk of poor health outcomes was not the issue. Instead, dominant constructions of this population as especially susceptible to poor health outcomes provided a taken-for-granted rationale for school-wide efforts to ameliorate them.

Several deliberate strategies were deployed by teaching and management staff to facilitate better health outcomes for their students. Chief among these was capitalising on intense student interest and engagement in sport. As the head of health and physical education put it, 'staff target students through their engagement with sports' (teacher A). For example, students who participated in competitive rugby games at the school spent time together before matches sharing 'nutritious' meals specially prepared by the home economics teacher. During these meals students were taught about the nutritional value of what they were eating and how nutrition can positively or adversely affect their sporting performance. Underlying many of these pedagogical encounters was a thinly veiled intention to educate these young people about obesity. On one occasion, the head of health and physical education invited representatives from a local health initiative (designed to support healthy eating and healthy physical activity within the wider community) to address students during one of their meals in order to inform them about the 'obesity problem.' On another occasion, a famous rugby player visited the students to talk about sport and nutrition: As the head of health and physical education described it:

> I said to him 'how important is sports nutrition for you?' and his words were 'well you can't do well at school if you don't do your homework and you can't play on the field if you don't eat well.' He said 'I don't get where I am today eating McDonalds every day,' so 'I could have kissed him.'

Sport training, in these instances, has been reinvented as a medium for educating students about healthy behaviours and the consequences (obesity and poor sporting performance) of not taking up these practices. Sport is also presented as a motivator to obligate them to eat and exercise 'right,' maintain the 'right' weight in order to be at their best for the team.

A particularly explicit example of the presumed health-enhancing and weight-reducing role of sport can be found in the attention paid to Peabody's first-fifteen girls' rugby team. These young women are treated to special sessions with staff from the local regional health team during which they monitor the girls' weight, discuss nutrition and, avowedly, foster the students' learning. These sessions are regarded by staff as vehicles through which to support students in their sporting and academic pursuits. At the same time, they afford important opportunities to engender health 'knowledge,' monitor weight and behaviours and develop a specific understanding amongst these students about the role of health in their lives. As was the case with the boys' rugby team the mantra, although not explicitly stated, is that students have a moral obligation at Peabody to 'work on one's health' for the sake of the team. In a similarly stealth-like fashion, the head of HPE also regards the young women's love of sport as a motivator for them to deal with 'weight issues' they face. Whilst she does not necessarily tell students that they must lose weight to be effective in their sport, she does discuss the need for students to achieve a weight that is appropriate for the particular position they occupy on the team. Her strategy is to convey to students that their bodies can be whatever shape they are, yet at the same time emphasise that strength, agility and pace are needed to succeed in rugby. By encouraging the girls to develop these capacities she 'knows' they will lose weight in the process. Whether or not students are told directly that they need to be a particular weight to have sporting success, the actions of staff in this school to monitor their weight and instruct girls to work on their bodies to achieve strength, agility and pace are likely to result in students making connections between weight and sport.

The elite sports teams are not the only groups targeted for weight loss. The practices of both the head of health and physical education and the home economics teacher indicate a pervasive concern about the body size, weight and shape of the entire school populace. The home economics teacher tackles this issue with what her students call 'strict' rules about what they should and should not eat, while the head of the health and physical education department regards sport as a vehicle for preventing an escalation in numbers of 'obese girls.' Cognisant that many of these so-labelled young women display a self-consciousness about their bodies she suggests that this makes it challenging to address the 'issue of their weight' and 'what can be done about it' (teacher A). She assumes that girls will be motivated to play sport by a desire to get thin and has developed a number of sport-based initiatives designed both to prevent girls from growing fatter and to increase their participation in PE and physical activity within the school. These initiatives include single-sex 'recreational PE' with a focus on non-traditional sports and an emphasis on participation and teamwork, and a planned girls' only fitness class. The results of several research studies in international contexts (e.g. Enright and O'Sullivan, 2010; Flintoff and Scraton, 2001; Hesse-biber, 2006; Oliver and Lalik, 2004; Wright *et al.*, 2006) would suggest that each of these initiatives would likely appeal to young women.

So what?

There are several issues that concern us with respect to this avowedly emancipatory practice of using sport as a vehicle for achieving health outcomes (including weight loss). Our first concern is what we would regard as a mistaken pedagogical intent to influence young people to lose weight using the guise of sport and health to achieve this. As Campos (2004), Blair and Brodney (1999), and Aphromor (2005) would attest, solid epidemiological evidence would suggest that weight is not necessarily correlated with the specific health issues about which Peabody teachers are concerned. Further, weight loss is not sustainable in the long term and the stigmatising effects of encouraging young people to believe that they need to lose weight are well documented (see Evans *et al.*, 2008).

Our second concern is the underlying assumption that there is a definitive and universally applicable recipe for healthy eating and sport-related exercise that will work similarly across the entire 'team' or school populace. As numerous studies have revealed, food and exercise 'doses' do not yield uniform results with children who inevitably have different body compositions, metabolic rates and so on (Blair, 2010; Campos *et al.*, 2006; Flegal, 1999). Further, research investigating young people's understanding and application of healthy food and exercise messages in their own lives (see Burrows, 2008; Burrows, 2011; Evans *et al.*, 2005) would suggest that repeated iterations of simplistic and prescriptive invocations to 'eat more fruits and vegetables' can produce anxiety and guilt among children who, for whatever reasons, fail to practise health in the ways suggested or indeed do not achieve the anticipated weight loss. Sport is an activity that many young people enjoy immensely, and turning it into another site for health promotion may expand the 'reach' of the healthy living message. On the flip side, however, to do so is emblematic of what we suggest is a gradual colonisation of youth spaces by health interests. Sport, in this regard, is no longer a site where young people can simply enjoy themselves, but rather it becomes yet another space where they are required to think about and monitor their health and, in the case of Peabody it would seem, their weight.

Further when sport is invested with so many life-affirming qualities (e.g. health, weight loss, school status, success in life, fame, a brighter future), as it is at Peabody, the potential consequences of failing to eat 'right' or exercise appropriately are not just losing the 'game' and failing at sport, but also failing the school, themselves and their futures.

The use of indigenous sporting 'role models' to convey simplistic and potentially misleading messages to young people is another issue arising in the context of Peabody pedagogies. Implicit in the rugby player's declaration, 'I don't get where I am today eating McDonalds every day' is an assumption that this is precisely what some of the cohort he is addressing do, together with a representation of himself (an elite, buffed rugby player) as the kind of person all young people would want to be, regardless of gender, disposition and ability. Implicit too in the recruiting of indigenous sporting role models is what Hokowhitu (2009) and Sharples (2007) have called a brand of 'colonizing by the colonized.' In other words, famous Maori and/or Pasifika persons are used to transmit the message that Western dietary practices and exercise regimes are the keys to salvation. In media reporting *and* expressed in many of the health campaigns to which this school community is exposed, both Maori and Pasifika people's are regularly represented as a group that has a tendency to eat too much junk food (see Spratt, 2006). Further, the 'effects' of consuming too much of food such as McDonalds' hamburgers are portrayed as even more severe for Maori and Pasifika populations than the rest of the population (e.g. Zimmet, 2008). Teachers themselves at this school also made comments reflecting their commitment to the notion that Maori and Pasifika children are most likely to eat 'bad' foods compared to their Pakeha counterparts. Indeed, in the testimony of young Maori students themselves, an expressed desire to reject what are staple culturally preferred foods was occasionally discerned. As one young man put it when asked what he would do to improve his health: 'I would have to reduce eating sweet drinks and chocolate also mutton flaps and meat.' The mutton flaps referred to in this response are staples of some Maori children's diets.

Conclusion

What can a small case study of a working-class school in New Zealand tell us about the relationship of sport to fat and health? While clearly the findings of the study reported in this chapter are not generalisable to other contexts, or even other schools in the same region, we nevertheless suggest that the motifs illuminated throughout this chapter are ones that are not unique to this school. Rather, they signal the oft-unintended ways in which ostensibly productive policies such as 'more sport in schools' may be taken up, deployed and experienced by teachers and students alike.

We have suggested, throughout this chapter, that health is in some ways regarded as a synonym for 'weight' and/or shape, as expressed in the testimonies of both students *and* teachers at this school. Prior work (e.g. Burrows, 2008; Evans *et al.*, 2005; Rail, 2009) would suggest this finding is not unique to lower decile schools, but rather symptomatic of the ways many schools are responding to the 'obesity epidemic' and harnessing sport to their desire to 'do something' about the avowedly ever fatter student populace. The troubling elements of this strategic move include the potential for young people to regard their engagement in sport as not something attenuated to fun, sociality and the joys of competition, but rather as yet another practice they must and/or should enact for the sake of their health. It is not difficult to imagine a scenario where disappointment in sport's failure to help them lose weight leads to student disengagement rather than engagement in sport.

Further, what potentially follows from this health/sport coupling, as signalled throughout this chapter, is a somewhat inevitable annexing of sport, and indeed, any kind of physical activity, to weight loss. As Rich *et al.* (2004) have repeatedly pointed out, the troubling consequences of regarding sport as a fat-busting tool include the potential for some children to cultivate dysfunctional relationships to their bodies and engage in practices that may in fact be harmful rather than productive for their health. When asked if she had ever tried to lose weight, one young Peabody girl replied, '[I] starved for about 3 days straight. Tried to cut down on my eating and started playing touch for my school.' While arguably an isolated comment, embedded in most of the responses to this question were clear indications that young people perceive weight not only as a symbol of a healthy, active body, but also believe sport and exercise have the potential to substantially change a person's body shape and weight. Both of these assumptions are hotly debated in both the epidemiological and sociological literature (see Blair, 2010; Campos, 2010; Gaesser, 2005; Ross, 2005) and furthermore may well generate both misplaced motivations for engagement in sport and considerable disappointment for young people who try to do 'more and more' physical activity yet fail to achieve the desired results.

Finally, and somewhat obviously, given that most young people, teachers and of course, health promotion advocates, seem to regard engagement in sport as a marker of a healthy person, the mandate to participate for the sake of their health conceivably positions those whose interests lie elsewhere (e.g. in alternative forms of physical expression, music, books) as not only lazy, unhealthy and irresponsible but also morally defunct.

References

Aphramor, L. (2005) Is a weight-centred health framework salutogenic? Some thoughts on unhinging certain dietary ideologies. *Social Theory and Health*, 3 (4): 315–340.

Atencio, M. and Wright, J. (2008) We be killin' them: Hierarchies of black masculinity in urban basketball spaces. *Sport Sociology*, 25 (2): 263–80.

Blair, S. (2010) Fitness, fatness, obesity, and health outcomes. Invited presentation to *The Big Fat Truth Symposium*, University of Otago, 1 February 2010.

Blair, S. and Brodney, S. (1999) Effects of physical inactivity and obesity on morbidity and mortality: current evidence and research issues. *Medicine and Science in Sports and Exercise*, 31 (Suppl.): S646–S662.

Burrows, L. (2011) I'm proud to be me: Health, community and schooling. *Policy Futures in Education* (Special edition: Politics, Pedagogy and Practice in School Health Policy), 9 (3): 343–354.

Burrows, L. (2009) Pedagogizing families through obesity discourse. In Wright, J. and Harwood, V. (eds) *Biopolitics and the 'Obesity Epidemic' Governing Bodies*. New York/London: Routledge, pp. 127–140.

Burrows, L. and Wright, J. (2007) *Health Imperatives in New Zealand Schools*. A University of Otago Research Grant study.

Burrows, L., Wright, J. and Jungersen-Smith, J. (2002) Measure your belly . . . New Zealand Children's Constructions of Health and Fitness. *Journal of Teaching in Physical Education*, 22: 39–48.

Campos, P. (2010) Ask your doctor if cultural hysteria is right for you. Keynote address at *The Big Fat Truth Symposium* 3 February, University of Otago, Dunedin.

Campos, P. (2004) *The Obesity Myth: Why America's Obsession with Weight is Hazardous to Your Health*. New York: Gotham Books.

Campos, P., Saguy, A. and Ernsberger, P. *et al.* (2006) The epidemiology of overweight and obesity: public health crisis or moral panic? *International Journal of Epidemiology*, 35 (1): 55–60.

Enright, E. and O'Sullivan, M. (2010) 'Can I do it in my pyjamas?' Negotiating a physical education curriculum with teenage girls. *European Physical Education Review*, 16 (3): 203–222.

Evans, J., Rich, E. and Davies, B. (2005) Fat Fabrications. *The British Journal of Teaching in Physical Education*, 36 (4): 18–21.

Evans, J., Rich, E. and Davies, B. *et al.* (2008) *Education, Disordered Eating and Obesity Discourse*. London: Routledge.

Falcous, M. (2007) Rugby League in the National Imaginary of New Zealand Aotearoa. *Sport in History*, 27 (3): 423–446.

Fight the Obesity Epidemic (2008) *Obesity: the facts*. Online: www.foe.org.nz/facts3.html (accessed 2 January 2008).

Flegal, K. (1999) The obesity epidemic in children and adults: Current evidence and research issues. *Medicine and Science in Sports and Exercise*, 31 (Suppl.): S509–S514.

Flintoff, A. and Scraton, S. (2001) Stepping into active leisure? Young women's perceptions of active lifestyles and their experiences of school physical education. *Sport, Education and Society*, 6 (1): 5–21.

Fullagar, S. (2002) Governing the healthy body: discourses of leisure and lifestyle within Australian health policy. *Health*, 6: 69–84.

Gaesser, G. (2005) Fit and fat, still a solid concept despite recent challenges. *Health at Every Size Journal*, 19: 54–61.

Gard, M. (2009) Friends, enemies and the cultural politics of critical obesity research. In Wright, J. and Harwood, V. (eds) *Biopolitics and the 'Obesity Epidemic:' Governing Bodies*. London: Routledge, pp. 31–44.

Gard, M. (2008) Producing little decision makers and goal setters in the age of the obesity crisis. *Quest*, 60 (4): 488–502.

Gard, M. (2007) Is the war on obesity a war on children? *Childrenz Issues: Journal of the Children's Issues Centre*, 11 (2): 20–24.

Gard, M. (2004) An elephant in the room and a bridge too far, or physical education and the 'obesity epidemic.' In Evans, J., Davies B. and Wright, J. (eds) *Body Knowledge and Control: studies in the sociology of physical education and health*. London and New York: Routledge.

Gard, M. and Wright, J. (2005) *The Obesity Epidemic: Science, Ideology and Morality*. London: Routledge.

Hesse-biber, S. (2006) *Am I Thin Enough Yet? The Cult of Thinness and the Commercialisation of Identity*. New York: Oxford University Press.

Hokowhitu, B. (2009) Foucault and culture. Presentation to Humanities *Foucault Symposium*, University of Otago, 21 May.

Hokowhitu, B. (2003) 'Physical beings:' stereotypes, sport and the 'physical education' of New Zealand Maori. *Culture, Sport and Society*, 6 (2/3): 192–218.

Johnston (2007) *Yawning Difference in Sleeping Habits.* Online: www.nzherald.co.nz/section/1/story.cfm?c_id=1andobjectid=10397743 (accessed 15 April 2008).

Key, J. (2009) *Kiwisport Initiative Good for Young People.* Online: www.beehive.govt.nz/release/kiwisport+initiative+good+young+people (accessed 11 August 2009).

Key, J. (2008) *Sport for Young Kiwis: A National Priority.* Online: www.national.org.nz/Article.aspx?ArticleID=28149 (accessed 2 April 2008).

Kirk, D. (1992) *Defining Physical Education: the social construction of a school subject in Postwar Britain.* London: The Falmer Press.

Macdonald, D., Rodger, S. and Abbot, R. *et al.* (2005) I could do with a pair of wings: perspectives on physical activity, bodies and health from young Australian children. *Sport, Education and Society*, 10 (2): 195–209.

McCuaig, L. and Tinning, R. (2010) HPE and the moral governance of p/leisurable bodies. *Sport, Education and Society*, 15 (1): 39–61.

McDermott, L. (2007) A governmental analysis of children at risk in a world of physical inactivity and obesity epidemics. *Sociology of Sport Journal*, 24 (3): 302–324.

NZPA (2010) *NZ Third Fattest Country in Developed World.* Online: www.3news.co.nz/NZ-third-fattest-country-in-developed-world---OECD-report/tabid/420/articleID/112209/Default.aspx (accessed 13 July 2009).

Phillips, J. (1996) *A Man's Country?: the image of the pakeha male, a history.* New Zealand: Penguin.

Queensland Government (2007) *Eat Well Be Active Campaign.* Online: www.eatwellbeactive.qld.gov.au/ (accessed 30 January 2007).

Oliver, K. and Lalik, R. (2004) Critical inquiry on the body in girls' physical education classes: a critical poststructural perspective. *Journal of Teaching in Physical Education*, 23 (2): 162–195.

Rail, G. (2009) Canadian youth's discursive constructions of health in the context of obesity discourse. In Wright, J. and Harwood, V. (eds) *Biopolitics and the 'Obesity Epidemic:' Governing Bodies.* London: Routledge, pp. 141–156.

Rich, E., Holroyd, R. and Evans, J. (2004) Hungry to be noticed: young women, anorexia and schooling. In Evans, J., Davies, B. and Wright, J. (eds) *Body Knowledge and Control: Studies in the Sociology of Physical Education and Sport.* New York: Routledge, pp. 173–190.

Ross, B. (2005) Fat or fiction: weighing the 'Obesity Epidemic.' In Gard, M. and Wright, J. (eds) *The Obesity Epidemic: Science, Ideology and Morality.* London: Routledge,. pp. 86–95.

Sharples, P. (2007) Tino Rangitiratanga: a key determinant for good health in Aotearoa, unpublished address delivered at New Zealand Health Teachers' Association Conference *Our Health, Our Children, Our Future*, Dunedin, 3 July.

Spratt, A. (2006) The big picture. *New Zealand Listener*, November 18–24, pp. 14–20.

Tagata Pasifika (2007) *Child Obesity in New Zealand Study.* Online: www.tnz.co.nz/view/page/410965/1448684 (accessed 2 January 2008).

Wong, G. (2005) The cottonwool kids. *Metro*, 284: 24–30 and 32–3.

Wright, J., O'Flynn, G. and Macdonald, D. (2006) Being fit and looking healthy: young women's and men's constructions of health and fitness. *Sex Roles*, 54 (9–10): 1–15.

Zimmet, P. (2008) *Diabetes: From Cinderella to Australia's Public Health Enemy Number 1, Paul Zimmet's Point of View.* Online: www.metabolicsyndromeinstitute.com/informations/experts-opinion/zimmet-2007.07.05/index.php (accessed 20 July 2008).

Part II
Moving towards inclusion

10 Young people's voices in sport

Ann MacPhail

> Like sports, some people would think maybe that physical education is something
> that you kind of have to do in school, and then people then who might think they're
> kind of sporty people and join a club, and activity . . . well, it's their choice and
> they kind of do it outside of school and in their own time, kind of like that. That one
> would be by choice and would, maybe not.
>
> (Senior level active girl, Woods *et al*., 2010)

> Well physical activity would be like swimming or, would that be sports? I'm con-
> fused, um.
>
> (Inactive girl, Woods *et al*., 2010)

Introduction

The young people's responses above to a question asking them to differentiate
between physical education, physical activity and sport conveys a certain level
of ambiguity, and perhaps this is understandable. Moreover, providing a definitive definition of sport would be illogical in a chapter that seeks to present young
people's voices on their experiences of what they construct as sport, acknowledging that sports themselves are 'contested (physical) activities' (Coakley, 2004)
and that 'sport' is more than just a physical activity. It is feasible, however, to
identify some commonalities when young people define and discuss their experiences of sport. These shared views relate to a wide range of informal and formal
recreational and fitness-related team and individual activities, competition, being
a member of a sport club, concern with improving performance, presence of a
coach and being motivated internally and/or by external rewards.

This chapter foregrounds what young people convey, using their own voices,
about their sport experiences (i.e. what they construct to be sport experiences) and
how such experiences *may* result in young people feeling included or excluded in
youth sport. Inclusion is about equal opportunities for all young people, whatever
their background, experiences and circumstances, and has tended to focus particularly on disadvantaged and under-represented young people in sport (Collins,
2004). Other authors have examined social inclusion by examining the interface
between issues of equity, equality and social justice (acknowledging that clear
definitions for each remain contested) that arise when young people feel included

in or excluded from sport (Hayes and Stidder, 2003; Penney, 2002). Arguably, exclusionary practices in sport can arise from stereotypical views and expectations of sport and resulting assumptions that not only impact a young person's (lack of) current involvement but also future participation. Moreover, it is important to remember that poverty has been identified as the core of exclusion (Collins, 2004), although there is limited evidence about the extent to which young people are either conscious of this at a young age or can clearly articulate the issue in their own voice.

The key purpose of this chapter is to allow young people's voices in sport to be heard, rather than adults' recollections of their involvement in sport as youngsters. Previous studies have reported, retrospectively, adults' reflections on the sport they experienced as a child (e.g. David, 2005). However, if sport is to be valuable and valued in young people's lives, it is imperative that the voices of young people inform and help to create appropriate, worthwhile and meaningful sporting provision. It is also important to remember that discrimination against individuals or populations in sport is extensive and well documented (Fernandez-Balboa, 2000). Concerns have been raised about issues of (in)equity in sport and the influence of the interlinking of a number of characteristics including social class, disposable income, levels of educational attainment, location, gender, ethnicity, (dis)ability, sexuality and at-risk youth.

What this means is that young people's voices are always positioned within a range of physical, social, geographical and economic factors and, moreover, that some of the potential inclusion/exclusion factors may not yet have arisen due to the young person's age and exposure to particular life opportunities. What young people convey about their experiences of sport will therefore, to some extent, be positioned by their exposure to, and experience of, different stages of sport participation. The development model of sports participation accommodates a progression from the 'sampling phase' to the 'specialising years' and then to the 'investment/recreation phase,' acknowledging that at any stage of involvement young people can choose to move to take part on a recreational basis or drop out (Côté and Hay, 2002a; see also Chapter 12). It is not always possible, however, from the available extracts of young people's voices, to match the stage of sport participation with what young people share about their experiences of sport. Coakley and White (1999) set out to explore how young people (aged between 13 and 20 years) made decisions about playing sports and how they integrated sport participation into their lives. This study remains one of the few that has deliberately set out to identify young people that reside at various points on the participation continuum (as participants in a sport programme or as a 'drop out' or 'non-participant'). The young people reported that sport participation was not a separate experience in their lives, but rather was closely tied to four factors, (1) growing up and being seen as competent, (2) sense of identity, (3) constraints associated with involvement and, (4) past experiences of sport and physical education. Aicinena's (2002) fourteen-year participant observer investigation of youth soccer in the US is evidence of an impressive level of commitment towards presenting young people's experiences of soccer. The study identifies issues around minority participation, cultural differences resulting in a Mexican-born youngster departing from the team, the demands of competing roles in sports for young people, the experiences of unwilling participants and also those excelled in sport at an early age only to become an average player as they entered adolescence.

Young people's positioning in sport

Along the sport participation continuum on which young people reside, there are varying degrees to which young people view sports as social activities that make up a part of their everyday lives (Sport England, 2005). Examining the sporting motivation profiles of a cohort of 2,510 boys and girls aged 11–14 (Wang and Biddle, 2001), five groups of young people were identified, ranging from those who were most physically active to those who were not physically active. The group that was the most physically active had more boys than girls in it and this group was found to have the highest level of physical self-worth. The group that was not physically active contained more girls than boys and was found to have the lower levels of physical self-worth. Kirk (2004) argues that these data suggest that between the ages of 11 and 14, young people's motivational profiles, and their dispositions towards active participation in sport, are well on their way to being formed. If this is the case, it heightens the need to seek, understand and learn from young people's experiences of sport in order to inform sporting practices and provision that meets the needs, interests and capabilities of all young people.

Establishing young people's access to, and maintenance in, sport

How inequality is exhibited, and how it can be identified, are discussed elsewhere, recognising that sport is not isolated from other inequalities in society and so does not exist in a vacuum (David, 2005; Hylton and Totten, 2001). Interestingly, the paradoxical nature of sport in society is evident in that while it is often presented as a tool for putting right a whole range of social wrongs (such as violence, racism, and sexism), these issues also permeate sport itself (Gatz *et al.*, 2002).

If the aim of sport is to foster 'inclusion,' then 'exclusion' (i.e. persistent barriers to participation) and its social context must be better identified and understood (Hylton and Totten, 2001). Just as is the case with adult populations, there has been limited success in gaining access to particular populations of young people who are not involved in sport in order to establish potential exclusion criteria.

While there is evidence that the number of opportunities for participating in sport for young people continues to increase (Smith *et al.*, 2004), caution needs to be exercised in making any assumption that particular populations of young people can access such opportunities. For example, we need to ask critical questions about whether new opportunities for underrepresented groups simply result in more participation by those already heavily engaged in sport by adding new options to an already impressive portfolio of sporting opportunities. While quantitative data provides us with evidence about broad patterns in young people's sport participation and highlights trends that reveal inequalities in participation (Hylton and Totten, 2001), there is a need for more qualitative data that can provide greater insight into *why* particular young people are included in, or excluded from, sport.

This chapter is concerned with providing an overview of what young people tell us, collectively, about their experiences of sport and it seeks to identify shared experiences of inclusion in, and exclusion from, sport. In order to present this overview, the chapter draws upon interpretive research in order to examine sports 'from the inside' through the experiences of the participants (Coakley and Donnelly, 1999).

As was noted earlier, there is a limited pool of studies that convey, in the voices of young people, the extent to which sport either contributes to social inclusion or marginalises and disadvantages particular groups of young people within society. Numerous studies do promote the importance of listening to young people's voices with regards to providing inclusive sport practices, yet there has been an over-reliance on studies that (1) aggregate responses without sharing the richness of the young people's voices and (2) do not disaggregate the data by different population groups. There is a tendency, for example, to group young people into the structures through which their views are accessed – for example, school or clubs – thereby failing to link young people's inclusion in or exclusion from sport to the age, gender, ethnic, social and other groups to which young people belong. While a young person's experience of sport conveys an individual perspective, the association with other young people from a similar group – for example, gender or race – can be either important or irrelevant. Certainly we can argue that there is a need to begin to identify the relationships across demographic factors; for example, the intersection of gender, race and sexuality (Oliver, 2010).

General characteristics of young people's involvement in sport

The practice of sport has the potential to have a positive impact on young people's physical, social, psychomotor and mental development. The majority of young people have high levels of intrinsic motivation in relation to sport (Sport England, 2005), with a noticeable pervasiveness and variety of activities evident in children of primary school age. As they grow older, more boys than girls take part in sport, with the gap increasing as teenage girls begin to drop out from taking part in sport (Slater and Tiggeman, 2010). Boys have a preference for more traditional and team sports, with a focus on performance, physical contact and competition, while girls favour individual and social sports (Rees *et al.*, 2007). Girls' awareness of the perceived risk to female identity that success in a physically demanding sport can bring and may (un)consciously lead to girls in the majority preferring sporting opportunities that allow them to socialise with friends (Sport England, 2005). This does not dismiss those girls whose sporting habits tend to resemble what is more commonly referred to as boys' sporting habits; that is, an investment of time and energy, in improving their performance in a chosen sport. Boys and girls who are more active in sport are more likely to be characterised by high levels of self-worth than sedentary young people (Trew *et al.*, 1999). Middle-class children are overrepresented in sports clubs, with membership in a sport club related to gender, social class and family situation (Kirk, 2004). Enjoyment has to be prevalent in sport experiences for continued participation (Sport England, 2005).

Ethnicity, social class and disability

Before sharing a sample of young people's views of their experiences of sport, it is important to remember that our understanding of the rich experiences of young people affected directly by, for example, ethnicity, social class and disability is still limited (see also in this volume, Chapter 13; Chapter 1 and Chapter 8). While it is possible to identify patterns of participation between different ethnic minority communities, and associated barriers to participation in sport (Sporting Equals and Sports Councils, 2009), data reporting young people's voice on the dynamics of ethnic relations in sport is limited. It is interesting to speculate on why this is the case. Social class and its impact on participation in sport is well documented. There is agreement that low social class, in conjunction with other social structures, creates an inequality in individuals' access to sport (Collins, 2004). However, the lack of data on young people's voice with respect to social class is limited and this may be the result of sensitivities in questioning young people about socio-economic inequities. What we do know, however, is that better opportunities for involvement in youth sport exist (as one might expect) among children from middle and upper socio-economic classes:

> The most exciting thing that ever happened to me was the first time I went skiing. And I've loved going there ever since I go every winter with my Mom.
>
> (Aileen, fifth class, first level; O'Connor, 2009, p. 116)

Disabled people participate less and undertake a narrower range of sporting activities than non-disabled people. This can be explained, in part, by a lack of support, poor access to facilities, and stereotypical and discriminatory assumptions held by non-disabled people (Fitzgerald, 2009; see also Goodwin and Peers, Chapter 13 in this volume). There is a need for more detailed narratives from this population to understand not only the intricacies of providing inclusive sport practices for disabled people but also the interrelationships with other social characteristics that affect their sporting lives.

In the next four sections of this chapter, the reader can begin to engage with the richness of insight that listening to young people's voices offers. In hearing their voices we can attempt to appreciate and understand how some sport experiences can result in young people feeling included or excluded from sport. The data sources that convey young people's voices in this chapter include written narratives and interviews. The spelling and grammar of the written narratives are reported as written by the young people and the interviews are recalled verbatim.

1 Sport and gender

Research on the ties between sport, gender and a sense of identity report consistent findings. Boys tend to report positive experiences that are fun, team based, require a certain level of physical competence and entail competition:

> The fun. The fun and competitive, both. You have to have a laugh. If it's not competitive then there is no point playing football. To enjoy it. You wouldn't say you play football to have a fight over it. If it wasn't competitive you wouldn't really bother, it's better like winning matches. It doesn't matter with me. More competitive, yeah. You get something out of it. Boxing is more competitive so you can't have fun in boxing.
>
> (Woods *et al.*, 2010)

The contradiction in the above quote where the interviewee discusses the necessity of competition but then admits that boxing is 'more competitive so you can't have fun' perhaps provides an insight into the type of competition that is preferred to that of an overtly contact sport. Girls tend to report positive experiences where they are fun and encourage friendships:

> my hobbies are football, camogie, swimming and running. My favourite one is camogie because it is great fun and you make new friends on the team.
>
> (Carol, transition year, second level; O'Connor, 2009, p. 115)

Girls tend not to identify themselves as athletes, even when they are physically active in a sport. However, it is important not to generalise too much because there are some instances where this is not the case:

> The thing I enjoy doing most is sailing. I try to be the best I can be at anything I care about, and I take sailing very seriously. I've been on the under sixteen sailing team for the last two years and both years were really good fun. I was especially pleased with my results last season because I got to represent Ireland at the European Championship. I hope to still be sailing for many years to come because I enjoy it so much and I'd like to be able to achieve a lot in this sport. Whenever I am not sailing (I've probably bored you enough on the subject!) I'm usually doing other sports or going out with my friends.
>
> (GSS, 30; MacPhail *et al.*, 2009)

The level of investment in sport noted in the above extract is found more often in the research on boys and young men, particularly in the ways that they tend to convey their identity as someone invested in sport. It is often found, for example, that boys are significant consumers of 'media sport' while girls identify a range of competing interests and experiences (MacPhail *et al.*, 2009). The following extract denotes not only a 15–16-year-old boy's desire to be a participant in sport but also his desire to be a consumer of sport in the form of the national soccer league:

I'm sitting in English class writing this note at 11.35am. I'm looking forward to our football match against [name of club]. I'm really big into sports and Im [sic.] so glad that Leeds beat Arsenal last night because that gives Manchester United (my team) a great chance to won the premiership.

(BCS, 52; MacPhail *et al.*, 2009, p. 294)

While numerous studies report girls' reasons for choosing (whether it be forced or unforced) not to take part in sport, or to drop out from sport (Slater and Tiggemann, 2010), it is important that we also acknowledge boys' drop out. Although likely to be lower in number than girls, boys also avoid participation in organised sports due to factors related to their feeling of (in)competence (Coakley and White, 1999; see also Wellard, Chapter 7 in this volume). It has also been argued that many girls are, in fact, interested in being involved in sport or physical activity, but they are disengaged from the nature, structure and opportunities of existing provision (Coakley and White, 1999). For example, they find limited opportunities to socialise with their friendship group in a non-competitive environment, and they are unhappy with sporting opportunities that tend to draw attention to their self-consciousness and perceptions of personal ability and body shape.

2 Perceived competence in sport

Young people have reported that their perceived competence in a particular sport encourages and maintains their interest in participating in that sport:

My favourite sport is soccer because I think I am a very skilful player. My greatest ambition is to be a soccer player.

(Dermot, fifth class, first level; O'Connor, 2008, p. 115)

While some young people may not yet have experienced the power that competence can have in future decisions on their personal involvement in sport, this reflection from an elite adult athlete reminds us that success is important:

My main sport was running . . . [but] I wasn't getting anywhere, I wasn't winning races. Whereas with swimming, I didn't enjoy it but I was getting quite successful. I was winning races, so it just seemed logical at the time to continue doing that, although I didn't enjoy it to begin with.

(Stevenson, 1999, p. 93)

An interesting contrast to traditional views on the importance of competence in sport was uncovered by Beal (1999) who interviewed a group of skateboarders (average age of 16 years) to gain insight into their subculture. Here it was evident that while the emphasis was on skill development, these young people attempted to downplay any association between the acquisition of skills and the value of engaging in skateboarding. As one 13-year-old boy expressed:

Well, we don't, we're not like competitive like saying, 'I can Ollie higher than you so get away from me,' and stuff like that, we're like, we just want to do a few things people are doing, and skaters help out skaters . . . and if I were to ask a good skater like some people I can skate with, like Brad Jones, he's the best skater I know in Welton, if I asked him he would like give me tips and stuff, you know on how to do it and that's just how we do it, we want to show other people how to skate.

(p. 141)

In another study, one group of sport-active boys lamented the fact that their trainer was not good at encouraging anyone who displayed low physical competence:

he would never encourage the weak players as much and then they lose confidence, they lose interest then you know that's a big thing. It's a big thing with our manager like. He's a man that will pick the good players and keep encouraging them like and the weaker players he won't. And then it's up to the players to encourage the weaker players so once the higher up players are encouraging the weaker players then they'll get on alright, but like it isn't right.

(Active boy; Woods *et al.*, 2010)

Inclusivity related to ability level

In seeking responses from over six hundred 14 to 18 year olds about what can be done to help more young people to participate in sport (MacPhail *et al.*, 2003), it became clear that making sport inclusive to all (dis)abilities was a recurring concern. The issue of being 'left out' reflected the frustration experienced by young sports participants who felt this was due to an overemphasis on elite performance. Instead, young people suggested that learners should be grouped according to ability, offering opportunities to participate in forms of competition regardless of ability. These concerns convey the need for recognition of, and attention to, individuals who want to take part but are perhaps excluded because they do not excel. Young people's continued requests for access to a wide range of sports further highlights the importance of ensuring young people can find a sport to which they are attracted, in which they can remain involved, and that caters for their individual abilities and interests.

Moving towards elite sport

'Elite sport' describes young athletes who train for a minimum of one to two hours a day, on at least five days a week (David, 2005). The intense expectations that some parents and coaches have for a young person to succeed at the highest level in a particular sport are illustrated throughout David's (2005) research. Such a reliance on retrospective data conveys that for particular individuals, as young athletes, their views and experiences of elite sport were not taken into account to prevent and protect them from harm:

We should have been able to make decisions about when we could go no further . . . I mean you know within your own body, if you're so sick that you should not be training, you should be allowed to say 'I can't come today' . . . You should be able to have a day off every week, you should be able to make decisions about your own career in sport, and about what your level of involvement would be. You shouldn't have to accept the coach's view on everything, you should be able to make your own choice on what level of sport you want to be on.

(A British female elite athlete quoted from Brackenridge, 2001 in David, 2005, p. 195)

Young people's perceived competence in a sport can also be attributed to the role that sexuality plays in encouraging an elevated or undermined status in a particular sport, resulting in young people feeling included or excluded from sport.

3 Sexuality and sport

With an interest in learning about masculinities in sport, Ingham and Dewar (1999) interviewed 14-year-old males involved in organised competitive ice hockey. The following extract highlights a particular version of macho sport from the perspective of these boys;

Interviewer:	On the team you played for, what's the thing that you admired most?
Player:	Taking shots [read: being able to take a hard hit from an opponent].
Teammate:	Your shot, your goal average, how well you can kick ass. You have to hit hard. You have to be able to put five kids in a crying position before the end of the season.
Interviewer:	Is that right? You've got to show that you're tough and can take it out there?
Player:	There's some that will call you pussy even if you do. I've put about fifteen kids down and a couple of them had to be carried off, and [he] put like five down. He [another boy] put a lot down. I mean these aren't rough hits. I mean they're not rough like in sticks up.

(p. 22)

The authors concluded that these boys were exposed to a narrow set of ideas about masculinity and that they not only strived to reproduce this in sport, but also as a basis for how they should conduct themselves outside of sport. Coakley and White (1999) support the suggestion that participation in sport is considered by young men as being associated with becoming a man. These authors found, however, from interviewing a sample of twenty-six young women and thirty-three young men aged from 13 to 20 years, that none of the young women viewed sport participation as being important in their transition to adulthood. On the other hand, the young males in Ingham and Dewar's (1999) study also articulated the elevated status that was accorded to involvement in what were considered prestige sports in high schools:

> *Teammate:*   Soccer players. No the soccer players are like the same as us – no actually they're more popular than us.
>
> *Interviewer:*   So tennis players and golfers are like . . .?
>
> *Teammate:*   Geeks! There are some popular ones who play other sports. But after that they're like geeks. That's how football and basketball players consider hockey players. [We] hockey players just look up and say 'play tennis.'
>
> (pp. 21–22)

The above extracts hint at the socialising forces that encourage young people to be involved (or not) in particular sports. The role that significant others play in encouraging young people to feel included or excluded from sport is frequently reported by young people.

4 Role of significant others in sport participation

Parents, siblings, peers, teachers and coaches have all been reported as important socialising forces in young people's entry to and continued participation in sport (Côté, 2002; Côté and Hay, 2002b; Kay, 2004; see also Chapter 12). The reciprocal interaction between young people and these socialising forces results in young people developing self-perceptions about their competence in a particular sport (Stroot, 2002). In some cases, there is evidence that socialising forces assert too much pressure on a young person to participate in club sport:

> I don't like parents and teachers telling me what to play, like, you are built for rugby so why not give it a go? Is it good to be built for rugby? . . . no.
>
> (Inactive boy; Woods *et al.*, 2010)

Young people may choose not to share the extent to which their sport experiences are pressured by significant others, yet peers sometimes observe the pressures and will talk about them. One sport-active girl talked about a friend who was active in gymnastics to the point of not being allowed to do anything else:

> her Mom has to collect her from school and bring her straight to the gym until like 8o'clock and then she comes home and rushes her homework like so like you can be kind of obsessive as well in some sports or and it's kind of like she doesn't even like it that much, her Mom wants her to be like the greatest, so you can go overboard in sport like its good to have kind of balance and try loads of different things and not just have the one thing . . . it is too bad.
>
> (Woods *et al.*, 2010)

Conclusion

Article 2.1 of the United Nation's Convention on the Rights of the Child (United Nations, 1989) declares that children should not be discriminated against on grounds of 'race, colour, sex, language, religion, political or other opinion, national, ethnic or social origin, property, disability, birth or other status.' A case has been made that there is a low level of awareness and understanding about the specific human rights issues generated by intensive training and competitive sports (Brackenridge and Rhind, 2010; David, 2005). However, a case can also be made that there is a low level of awareness and understanding about particular groups of young people and their access to, and experiences of, sport (e.g. disabled young people). There is also a need to ascertain how best to sustain the activity levels of younger children into their adolescent years and beyond. Decisions about sport participation are made continually through the life course, not just once and for all time (Coakley and Donnelly, 1999). Social conditions and structures can aid or hinder young people's involvement in sport, making certain choices more or less likely at a point in time. A recognition of the facilitators for, and barriers to, young people's involvement in sport allows sport providers (be they teachers, coaches, families, sport development officers, national governing bodies, youth workers) to strive towards providing sporting experiences that accommodate all young people:

> When young people have a voice they are much more likely to seek information about the programme in which they participate and the community context in which the programme exists. Many young people desperately need experiences that show them they can exert control over their own lives and the contexts in which they live.
>
> (Coakley, 2002, p. 27)

As teachers, coaches, researchers and policy makers we need to be cognisant of the complex mix of motives that attract and sustain, or fail to attract, young people to sport. Arguments for examining sport from the point of view of young people in relation to other aspects of their life, in order to present the realities of young people's lives, are gaining momentum (see chapters from O'Sullivan and MacPhail, 2010; O'Connor, 2009). Young people's experiences of sport are multifaceted and, external to the personal circumstances in which a young person finds themselves, the delivery of sport provision and the culture of the sporting context affect such experiences.

Andrews and Andrews (2003) call for further evaluative research of a longitudinal nature, in a variety of settings, with samples of children with different demographic characteristics. Long and Carless (2010) challenge us to extend our thinking in order to devise innovative and effective practices and methodologies to encourage young people to share their stories about sport. What we need, they argue, is to move the voices of young people from the margin to the centre:

This involves not just hearing, but actively listening to the stories with a view to facilitating change. Somewhere along the line someone has to take the step from understanding individual experiences to formulating policy and devising practice. To facilitate this important step we might promote the idea of young people as co-researchers or active partners in a research agenda which strives to engage and affect its audience in an immediate and embodied manner.

(Long and Carless, 2010, p. 223)

References

Aicinena, S. (2002) *Through the Eyes of Parents, Children and a Coach. A fourteen-year participant-observer investigation of youth soccer.* Lanham: University Press of America.

Andrews, J.P. and Andrews, G.J. (2003) Life in a secure unit: the rehabilitation of young people through the use of sport. *Social Science and Medicine*, 56: 531–550.

Beal, B. (1999) Skateboarding: an alternative to mainstream sports. In Coakley, J. and Donnelly, P. (eds) *Inside Sports*. London: Routledge, pp. 139–145.

Brackenridge, C.H. and Rhind, D. (2010) *Elite Child Athlete Welfare: International Perspectives*. Brunel: Brunel University Press.

Coakley, J. (2004) *Sports in Society: Issues and Controversies*, 8th edn. Boston: McGraw Hill.

Coakley, J. (2002) Using sports to control deviance and violence among youth: let's be critical and cautious. In Gatz, M., Messner, M.A. and Ball-Rokeach, S.J. (eds) *Paradoxes of Youth and Sport*. New York: SUNY, pp. 13–30.

Coakley, J. and Donnelly, P. (1999) (eds) *Inside Sports*. London: Routledge.

Coakley, J. and White, A. (1999) Making decisions: how young people become involved and stay involved in sports. In Coakley, J. and Donnelly, P. (eds) *Inside Sports*. London: Routledge, pp. 77–85.

Collins, M. (2004) Sport, physical activity and social exclusion. *Journal of Sports Sciences*, 22 (8): 727–740.

Côté, J. (2002) Coach and peer influence on children's development through sport. In Silva, J.M. and Stevens, D. (eds) *Psychological Foundations of Sport*. Boston: Allyn and Bacon, pp. 520–540.

Côté, J. and Hay, J. (2002a) Children's involvement in sport: A developmental perspective. In Silva, J.M. and Stevens, D. (eds) *Psychological Foundations of Sport*. Boston: Allyn and Bacon, pp. 484–502.

Côté, J. and Hay, J. (2002b) Family influences on youth sport performance and participation. In Silva, J.M. and Stevens, D. (eds) *Psychological Foundations of Sport*. Boston: Allyn and Bacon, pp. 503–519.

David, P. (2005) *Human Rights in Youth Sport. A critical review of children's rights in competitive sports*. London: Routledge.

Fernandez-Balboa, J.M. (2000) Discrimination: what do we know, and what can we do about it? In Jones, R.L. and Armour, K.M. (eds) *Sociology of Sport: Theory and Practice*. Harlow: Longman, pp. 134–144.

Fitzgerald, H. (2009) *Disability and Youth Sport*. London: Routledge.

Gatz, M., Messner, M.A. and Ball-Rokeach, S.J. (eds) (2002) *Paradoxes of Youth and Sport.* New York: SUNY.

Hayes, S. and Stidder, G. (2003) Social inclusion in Physical Education and sport. Themes and perspectives for practitioners. In Hayes, S. and Stidder, G. (eds) *Equity and Inclusion in Physical Education and Sport.* London: Routledge, pp. 1–14.

Hylton, K. and Totten, M. (2001) Developing 'Sport for All?' Addressing inequality in sport. In Hylton, K., Bramham, P. and Jackson, D. *et al.* (eds) *Sports Development: Policy, Process and Practice.* London: Routledge, pp. 37–65.

Ingham, A.G. and Dewar, A. (1999) Through the eyes of youth: deep play in Pee Wee ice hockey. In Coakley, J. and Donnelly, P. (eds) *Inside Sports.* London: Routledge, pp. 17–27.

Kay, T. (2004) The family factor in sport: A review of family factors affecting sports participation. In Sport England (ed.) *Driving Up Participation: The challenge for sport.* London: Sport England, pp. 39–60.

Kirk, D. (2004) Sport and early learning experiences. In Sport England (ed.) *Driving Up Participation: The challenge for sport.* London: Sport England, pp. 69–78.

Long, J. and Carless, D. (2010) Hearing, listening and acting. In O'Sullivan, M. and MacPhail, A. (eds) *Young People's Voices in Physical Education and Sport.* London: Routledge.

MacPhail, A., Collier, C. and O'Sullivan, M. (2009) Lifestyles and gendered patters of leisure and sporting interests among Irish adolescents. *Sport, Education and Society*, 14 (3): 281–299.

MacPhail, A., Kirk, D. and Eley, D. (2003) Listening to young people's voices: youth sports leaders advice on facilitating participation in sport. *European Physical Education Review*, 9 (1): 57–73.

O'Connor, P. (2009) *Irish Children and Teenagers in a Changing World. The National Write Now Project.* Manchester: Manchester University Press.

Oliver, K. (2010) The body, physical activity and inequity: Learning to listen with girls through action. In O'Sullivan, M. and MacPhail, A. (eds) *Young People's Voices in Physical Education and Sport.* London: Routledge.

O'Sullivan, M. and MacPhail, A. (eds) (2010) *Young People's Voices in Physical Education and Sport.* London: Routledge.

Penney, D. (2002) Equality, equity and inclusion in physical education and school sport. In Laker, A. (ed.) *The Sociology of Sport and Physical Education. An Introductory Reader.* London: Routledge Falmer, pp. 110–128.

Rees, R., Kavanagh, J., Harden, A. *et al.* (2007) Young people and physical activity: a systematic review matching their views to effective interventions. *Health Education Research*, 21 (6): 806–825.

Slater, A. and Tiggemann, M. (2010) Uncool to do sport: A focus group study of adolescent girls' reasons for withdrawing from physical activity. *Psychology of Sport and Exercise*, 11 (6): 619–626.

Smith, A., Green, K. and Roberts, K. (2004) Sport participation and the 'Obesity/Health Crisis': Reflections on the case of young people in England. *International Review for the Sociology of Sport*, 39 (4): 457–464.

Sport England (2005) *Understanding Participation in Sport. A Systematic Review.* London: Sport England.

Sporting Equals and Sports Councils (2009) *A Systematic Review of the Literature on Black and Minority Ethnic Communities in Sport and Physical Recreation.* Birmingham: Sporting Equals.

Stevenson, C. (1999) Becoming an international athlete: making decisions about identity. In Coakley, J. and Donnelly, P. (eds) *Inside Sports.* London: Routledge, pp. 77–85.

Stroot, S. (2002) Socialisation and participation in sport. In Laker, A. (ed.) *The Sociology of Sport and Physical Education. An Introductory Reader.* London: Routledge Falmer, pp. 129–147.

Trew, K., Scully, D., Kremer, J. *et al.* (1999) Sport, leisure and perceived self-compe-tence among male and female adolescents. *European Physical Education Review*, 5 (1): 53–73.

Wang, C. and Biddle, S. (2001) Young people's motivational profiles in physical activity: A cluster analysis. *Journal of Sport and Exercise Psychology*, 23 (1): 1–22.

Woods, C., Moyna, N., Quinlan, A. *et al.* (2010) *The Children in Sport Participation and Physical Activity Study (CSPPA Study).* Summary Report to the Irish Sports Council.

United Nations (1989) *Convention on the Rights of the Child*, UN General Assembly reso-lution 44/25 on 20 November. New York: United Nations.

11 Lessons learned about gender equity and inclusion in physical education

Kimberly Oliver and Nate McCaughtry

Introduction

Issues of equity and inclusion, particularly with respect to gender, have been acknowledged, debated, critiqued and struggled with from a variety of theoretical perspectives across physical education, physical activity research and scholarly writing (McDonough and Croker, 2005; McKenzie *et al.*, 2002; Oliver and Lalik, 2004a, 2004b; Trost *et al.*, 2002; Vertinsky, 1992; Wilson *et al.*, 2005; Wright, 1995). Despite two solid decades of scholarship, we continue to see multiple forms of gender inequity in schools and in physical education and activity settings (McCaughtry, 2004, 2006; Oliver and Lalik, 2004a; Oliver *et al.*, 2009; Oliver and Hamzeh, 2010). Further, we continue to see a decrease in girls' physical activity participation, despite increased awareness about and interest in rectifying forms of gender inequity that threaten girls' participation in physical activity (Gordon-Larsen *et al.*, 2001; Wolf *et al.*, 1993).

Over the years, both authors have studied issues of equity and justice in physical activity and/or physical education settings in US schools. Whereas Oliver's work has been primarily with young girls, McCaughtry's has focused on teachers. Through our individual and collaborative work, we have come to several key realizations that will frame this chapter:

- Understanding how gender inequities function in schools takes time and relationship building between teachers and students (McCaughtry, 2004; Oliver and Lalik, 2000; Oliver *et al.*, 2009).
- Understanding gender inequities means examining the entire ecology of schools and PE programs (McCaughtry, 2004).
- Attempts at gender equity reform will likely be met with resistance and requires personal resilience and adept political maneuvering (McCaughtry, 2004, 2006).
- Working directly with girls to change inequities that they believe are barriers to their enjoyment and/or opportunities for physical activity participation is not without challenges (Oliver and Lalik, 2001; Oliver and Lalik, 2004a, 2004b).
- Working to transform physical activity inequity requires that teachers and

students collaboration (McCaughtry, 2006; Oliver *et al.*, 2009; Oliver and Hamzeh, 2010).

We have organized this chapter into three sections. In the first section, McCaughtry draws on his research illustrating the arduous process for teachers in coming to view gender relations critically in schools, both in physical education and in wider school environments, and the complicated, political process involved in pursuing inclusive gender equity reform. In the second section, Oliver discusses specific instructional strategies she has used across studies to work with young girls to help them identify, critique and transform inequities that threaten their enjoyment and/or opportunities to be physically active. Drawing on our collective work, in the final section we will discuss implications for teaching, teacher education and research.

Understanding teachers and gender equity through narrative (McCaughtry)

Several years ago, I had the fortune to spend time with a high school physical education teacher named Tammy (pseudonym) who was facing many dilemmas with respect to gender in her school and was growing increasingly disillusioned with her teaching career and the role that schools played in girls' development. Guided by a general professional affinity toward issues of equity and with critical, feminist perspectives, I set about to understand this teacher's perspectives. I suspected that she had a unique story to tell and at this point I was curious.

I met Tammy one afternoon between classes at her high school and explained that one of her friends had suggested that I visit Tammy to learn more about her story. After 30 minutes with Tammy, not only did I realize that she had a noteworthy and powerful story to tell, but also that she was willing to tell it, and tell it to me. This was a bit of a surprise, as I expected her to be at least somewhat reluctant to share her perspectives with me as a white male outsider representing a higher education institution. In retrospect, I am confident that I stumbled upon Tammy at a unique time in her life; a time when she was bursting at the seams with a story to tell to someone caring who would listen and understand, and who might also have the ability to help her tell her story more widely.

Over the next four months, I visited Tammy twenty times. I spent entire school days talking with her, her fellow PE teachers, other teachers and administrators. I watched the physical education programs, sport programs, and school lunchroom. Most of all, I listened to Tammy's story of coming to see gender relations critically at her high school, and the turmoil it manifested in her as she watched helplessly at first, and later moved purposefully to change things.

During my time with Tammy, I learned several important features about gender equity in schools generally and physical education specifically, and the prospects for reforming a broken system. First, I realized the limitations of our literature in physical education. We have an enormous body of excellent work where researchers have examined how boys and girls perceive the physical education environment, researchers have offered critique of the PE settings they observe, and theorists have provided suggestions for more equitable school PE. Tammy's situation reminded me, however, that we know very little about how teachers think about gender in school PE. We, as scholars, are remarkably adept at critiquing what teachers do in the name of gender (in)equity, but have less often sought to really understand how teachers see things. Second, I learned that critiquing gender inequities is something that happens for teachers over time, and through a keen eye and significant relationships with students. Third, I learned that more experienced colleagues who maintain a status quo system of gender inequity can stifle the critique and passion of younger, reform-minded colleagues. Last, I learned that gender equity reform is deeply political and is often enacted under alternative pretenses. (For a more detailed account of the forthcoming narrative, see McCaughtry 2004, 2006.)

Learning to read gender takes time

Tammy had arrived at Reese High (pseudonym) four years prior to my work with her. Over that time, she had developed a fairly elaborate critique of gender at her school. In general, she believed that the broader school culture, combined with several practices within the traditional physical education program, sent boys and girls clear messages about gender expectations and embodiment. Specifically, these messages suggested that docility, inactivity, and appearance mattered most for girls, while boys were rewarded for physicality, aggressiveness, and 'doing things.' For example, Tammy grew to believe that wider school events such as the 'beauty walk' (see Kim's explanation later in this chapter) and the recent upgrading of the athletic facilities (which essentially doubled male physical activity and sport space in brand new facilities, and downsized female space into the older, outdated facilities) emphasized to girls the need to focus on their appearance because that is what mattered most, and that physical activity was prized most highly for boys.

Tammy also grew to believe that practices in the traditional physical education program that were conducted and treasured by her four colleagues served to reinforce these gendered messages sent to boys and girls through wider school events. She felt the exclusive focus on partially supervised, large-sided team sports allowed boys to 'push girls to the margins' of playing space and equipment. Omitting significant aspects of youth health from the curriculum (e.g. nutrition, eating disorders, body image, weight management) was further evidence of support for a culture in which boys felt prized for enacting physicality, while girls felt prized for docility and inactivity (McCaughtry, 2004). Although Tammy's critique of the gendered messages sent through these wider school events and the traditional physical education program are hardly unique to the existing literature (indeed, many have already been well documented, Flintoff and Scraton, 2006), perhaps what is most intriguing is the way in which these realizations came about.

From the beginning of our time together, Tammy was quick to explain how she saw the gendered messages at her school, but when I asked her how she came to such strong and political insights she needed time to think about it before answering. After several more sessions together, I again asked how she came to understand things the way she did. She claimed that 'time was one of the most critical factors that nurtured her perspectives.' During both her high school and college experiences, Tammy had been sheltered from disempowering gender messages and practices by strong women who encouraged equity. Tammy claimed that this sheltering led her to 'perhaps take-for-granted' the significance of issues of gender in schooling. She said:

> When I had them [her female coaches and teachers] telling us that we didn't have to be the 'pretty little girl,' I guess you stop thinking about the limits of gender. You lose it as one of your lenses for seeing the world.

She argued that it took several years at Reese before she could see how gender relations were dichotomized between boys and girls. She said:

> When you're new, you just want to survive. The last thing I wanted to think about was gender . . . plus it was just off my radar then. I came out of school empowered as a woman . . . It took time to see beyond my own feelings and into the realities of these girls.

I then asked Tammy what enabled her to make this shift in focus from surviving as a new teacher to seeing gender relations critically. She claimed that it was spending lots of time really listening to how girls understood the school and their identity that caused her to re-center her attention onto gender. She explained:

> There was so much non-teaching going on that I had huge time to talk to these girls. And then there's my coaching. You really get to know these girls when you want to see how they think about things. It's easy to see how they internalize this beauty walk crap, or see their reactions when those guys [the male students] push them off the courts . . . All I had to do was listen.

For Tammy, it was the combination of time and a willingness to listen closely to how girls interpreted their world that cemented and intensified her critique of the established gender order at Reese High.

Stymied reform

At this point, the direction of my research shifted slightly and I grew interested in understanding what Tammy had already done and would continue to do with what she had learned about the inequitable gender relations at her school. Her reactions to my questions were a mix of both frustration and excitement. She admitted that she had considered either leaving teaching altogether or requesting a transfer out of Reese High because she had grown exceptionally frustrated with her colleagues' lack of interest in the gendered messages they were sending students and their unwillingness to change their programs. For her, the other teachers were either unaware of gender at their school or perceived it to be the natural state of things. Furthermore, it was clear to Tammy that altering the traditional PE program would result in more work for these teachers who seemed to be, at heart, committed more to coaching after-school sports than to teaching PE classes. Tammy felt as though she had become the pariah of the faculty because she pointed out limitations in the traditional program and suggested ideas for reform, which were always met with vocal resistance from the other teachers. She said, 'I can't tell you how many times I've gone home and cried. I'm so tired of them giving me the cold shoulder or criticizing every idea I have.' Her status as a newer, untenured (without job security) teacher compounded her feelings of powerlessness; often being told that she 'should be happy she's got a job.'

Gender equity reform through the back door

Rather than quit or request a school transfer, the summer before I met her, Tammy had devised a plan to move her agenda forward 'under the radar.' She knew that widespread change was quite unlikely, and even small-scale change would be resisted if it were promoted as gender equity. So, for each small reform Tammy wanted to make, she considered who the key stakeholders might be and how they might interpret her request. She then devised a 'cover story' (Clandinin and Connolly, 1995) to explain and justify her request, making the request seem plausible and acceptable to the power-broker stakeholders who were the arbiters of the 'sacred story' of the school. In other words, Tammy carefully thought out which changes were doable and could be explained in a way that would appease the power brokers of the school, while under the surface they were promoting her personal reform agenda. For example, during the summer, she requested that some of the athletes be assigned to separate classes outside of the traditional, mandatory PE program which was usually taught with a sport focus in order to improve the school's athletic prowess. The principal, who took great pride in the acclaim he received from the success of his athletic teams, readily agreed. As a result of this move, Tammy would be teaching a large portion of the females enrolled in the general PE classes. From Tammy's perspective, while gender segregation was not ideal or the long-term solution, it did provide girls with an immediate safe space for physical activity where she could begin instituting and ingraining an alternative program format, which she believed would one day be sought by all students attending physical education classes.

Another example of Tammy's political maneuvering occurred through her use of guest speakers and presenters in her classes. For Tammy, it was important that girls learn to think critically about important components of young women's health such as nutrition, dieting, weight maintenance, body image, eating disorders, and over-exercising. She had learned during her earlier years of relationship building with female students that these were significant issues in their lives. She also wanted girls to see and hear from female role models in a range of careers associated with human movement and health. However, she wanted all of the PE students to attend, especially all female students in the other PE sections, but she knew she would encounter resistance from the other teachers if she shared her real reason for arranging and hosting the speakers and fairs. Instead, she offered the other teachers to send their students to her events so they could have more free time to focus on their sport coaching duties, which she knew they heavily coveted. In this way, she was able to achieve her goals of exposing students to careers and important topics in their health, without exposing those goals publically and opening herself to ridicule and resistance. Of her tactics, she said, 'All along they think I'm just making their jobs easier, or building my program [volleyball team]. They're going to wake up one day and realize that it's all changed and they never knew it.'

Reflective note

In watching Tammy's tactics, I learned that there are multiple routes to achieving gender equity reform in physical education. Of course, it can be pursued head on, through the auspices of Title IX, fear of litigation, or on moral grounds. In some contexts, this might work. But what about contexts in which the status quo system seems natural, logical, or serves to benefit more senior power brokers? What young teacher has the zeal or will to pursue unpopular reform knowing it will be resisted and is likely to create a negative work environment? Tammy's case makes clear that pursuing a reform agenda, especially one related to gender equity, is as much political as it is anything else.

Taken as a whole, Tammy's story of coming to see gender and her pursuit of equity reform highlights the need to better understand the role that teachers play in gender equity issues in physical education. From the literature, we now have a fairly good sense of how boys and girls experience PE differently, how the mechanisms of many PE programs result in inequities, and what more equitable practices might look like (see Oliver's work below). The question that emerges for us is: How can we get there in the context of real schools? The obvious answer is that teachers are the lynchpin of reform, and we must know much more about how to prepare them in Physical Education Teacher Education (PETE) programs. They need to be able to 'see' substantive social issues such as gender equity as they move into their early careers as neophyte teachers, and know how to exist, thrive, and push along change agendas within the confines and constraints of in-grained educational institutions. We must do more to examine the contexts in which gender reform is currently or has already occurred to better understand how deeply entrenched, long-standing systems of gender inequity can be changed. Simply offering strategies for more inclusive practices masks the complexities inherent in making those strategies a reality for many girls and boys in such a resistant field as school physical education. Given this, we need to offer K-12 teachers as well as teacher educators in higher education institutions more specific ways in which they can engage their students in dialogue about how they can recognize and transform systems of exclusion and begin creating more inclusive forms of physical education.

Working with girls to challenge body inequities (Oliver)

Over the past fourteen years I have developed and studied curricular topics and instructional strategies for teaching aspects of health-related physical education to adolescent girls. Working in the traditions of feminist, critical and activist research and pedagogies (Fine, 1992), my interest has been in learning how teachers can assist girls in exploring, critiquing, and transforming personal and cultural barriers that hinder their health and well-being.

I came to this line of inquiry and interest in activist research for several reasons. First, I was troubled by continual research reports documenting a decline in girls' physical activity participation. Second, I was concerned about the numbers of girls that were becoming increasingly more dissatisfied with their bodies. Third, I was concerned by the oppressive cultural representations of girls' and women's bodies. Finally, I was concerned with what seemed to be missing in health-related physical education curriculum. That is, I was worried that as girls moved into and through adolescence they were not being provided with opportunities to critically examine how they were learning to think and feel about their bodies. I was also concerned that girls were not learning strategies aimed at helping them to identify and transform their self-identified barriers that hindered their health and well-being.

When I first started as a researcher I worked with small groups of girls in the hopes of being able to analyze the girls' work at a detailed level. Eventually I began studying how to implement these types of strategies into regular-sized physical education classes in secondary schools in the US. In the process, I have learned a great deal about engaging girls in exploration, critique, and transformation as will be explained below.

Exploring girls' interests

There are three strands to the work I have done with girls. The first strand revolves around my interest in wanting to understand girls' experiences of their bodies and more recently their experiences in physical activity. I have tried to create multiple ways of working with girls to explore their interests. As a researcher, I wanted the methods that I used to gather data to be ways that teachers could also work with girls in class settings. As such I have used methods involving journal and/or free writing, the use of magazine images, the use of cameras, and the use of artistic representation as ways of working with girls to understand their lives. While these have been research methods, they are also instructional strategies that teachers can use in class settings.

Journal writing as strategy

One strategy I have used consistently over the years to understand girls' perspectives is interactive journaling (Oliver, 1999; Oliver and Lalik, 2000, 2004a). With this strategy, I have given girls prompts and asked them to write about the prompts.

For example, one of the prompts I have used in my studies is, 'document the times you notice your body. What were you doing, thinking, and feeling?' I then gave the girls a few weeks to document this type of data. Here is an example of such data from Brandi, a 13-year-old African American 8th grader.

> I'm noticing my body when I'm in band. All these pretty girls with long hair. They dress so cute and wear cute hairstyles. All the boys want them and I feel so fat and like I'm not fine like them. When I'm in class I think I'm so ugly and feel the same way too.

What I have learned from using journals across studies is that the content the girls put in their journals is often different than what they will say publicly. In girls' public talk they often discuss how 'other girls' feel or think, but not necessarily how they feel. In their journals the content almost always centers on how they, personally, feel about whatever topics we are exploring (Oliver and Lalik, 2000, 2004a). I have also found that many of the girls who were somewhat shy in group settings really enjoyed writing in their journals, finding it a more comfortable way to participate (Lalik and Oliver, 2007).

Magazine exploration as strategy

The second instructional strategy that I have used to explore girls' interests is magazine explorations (Oliver, 1999; Oliver and Lalik, 2001, 2004a). Using magazines that girls like to read vs. magazines we would select, I asked the girls to 'go through the magazines and cut out things that are interesting to them.' Next, working in groups we asked them to group their pictures into categories that make sense to them. We then used the girls' categories as a starting point for discussing how they are learning to think about their bodies.

In one of our early studies, the story of 'Fashion In' and 'Fashion Out' emerged as a result of doing a magazine exploration (Oliver, 1999). 'Fashion In' and 'Fashion Out' were the girls' terms; they were interpretive codes the girls used to describe what 'looking right' and 'being normal' were, especially for 'Fashion In.' An example derives from four girls in one study conducted in the late 1990s. According to Nicole, Khalilah, Alysa, and Dauntai, to 'look right' and be 'normal' girls need 'healthy hair,' which was hair that was 'permed, straight, and had no new growth showing.' Girls needed the 'right clothes and shoes,' which meant brand named clothes and shoes that cost a certain amount of money. Girls needed the right 'body shape,' which meant being thin and shapely enough to wear the 'Fashion In' clothes. And girls needed to 'look feminine' which meant being toned but not overly muscular and not being loud and rude.

What we learned through our use of magazines, as a research strategy, is that girls use the images they select to help them to articulate how they are learning about what culture values in women. The images helped them to explain how girls' bodies are socially and culturally constructed. The magazine explorations also created a prime backdrop to begin working with girls to critique what they were learning and how that was influencing their health-related decisions (Oliver, 1999; Oliver and Lalik, 2001, 2004a).

Supporting girls' critique

The second strand in my research involves supporting girls' critique of cultural messages/images of the body. I have studied ways of working with girls to help them learn to critique the cultural messages and images of the body that limit their health and well-being. I have always been committed to going beyond just trying to understand girls' experiences to finding ways of working with girls to help them develop what Giroux (1997) calls a language of critique. If we can help girls learn to critique cultural messages of the body, for example, they might begin to learn alternative ways of looking at things. This is the part of my research where I have had the most success. Crucial to this success is recognizing the importance of starting where girls are, not from where we think they should be or where we want them to be (Oliver and Lalik, 2001, 2000, 2004a, 2004b).

Magazine critique as strategy

One of the first ways I tried to support girls' critique was through magazine critiques. Building on the magazine explorations described earlier, I have developed a variety of tasks to help girls look at some of the images they select and then begin to classify those images that made girls feel good and those that made them feel bad about their bodies. I have also asked girls to select images that send positive and negative messages to girls about their bodies and to make judgments such as 'who benefits from these pictures and how' and 'whom is hurt by these pictures and how?' I then asked them to create posters to illustrate whom benefits and who is hurt from the pictures they selected (Oliver, 2001; Oliver and Lalik, 2004a). One girl wrote:

> Men benefit from this picture because they like to look at pretty women and women who don't look like her are hurt.

Another girl wrote:

> You might not look as good as the woman on this picture, that don't mean you're not attractive and don't get as much attention as some women would get. Some attractive women sometimes don't want to be attractive because people take advantage of you when you look like this. Plus some women wish they weren't so attractive so people can look at you for who you are, and when they do that makes you feel like you're somebody.

I have used these magazine critiques in a variety of studies. These types of tasks have allowed for small group critique through discussion as well as allowed for large class discussion. Ultimately girls were able to name how magazines are used to shape their desires and the desires of others.

Photo critique as strategy

Another instructional strategy I have used for supporting girls' critique is through the use of photography. Similar to the journal prompts, I have given girls prompts for their picture taking. My interest in photographs, in addition to cultural media, stems from my curiosity about what girls would document when they were not limited by the photos they could find in magazines.

In one of my studies (Oliver *et al.*, 2009), I worked with 10-year-old girls who had been identified by their PE teachers as a group that did not like physical activity. The goal was to work with the girls to help them to identify their barriers to physical activity and also ways in which we might assist them to challenge the barriers they identified. I started the study by giving the girls cameras and asking them to 'take pictures of things that help them to be physically active and things that prevent them from being physically active.' I then used their pictures as a starting point for a discussion. One of the groups of girls I worked with brought several pictures and talked about how the boys would not let them play during recess.

Mary, a girl in that particular study, took a picture of Maggie Mae, another girl in the same study, standing alongside the basketball court watching the boys play. She explained to us that the boys would not let her play because 'she was too tall, she made most of the goals and that made the girls beat the boys and because her skin was the wrong color.' When we asked Maggie Mae about this she said:

> The boys told me I couldn't play with them because I was a girl and I was Black . . . Some boys don't want the girls to play because they are girls and I think that's a real problem because we should all be able to do what we want to do. We should all be able to play.
>
> (Oliver and Hamzeh, 2010, p. 43)

Mary's photo stimulated a critique about what was happening at their school with respect to physical activity. During this critique, the girls used several of their photographs to verbally explain how the boys and girls interacted during recess, which was their primary opportunity for physical activity.

We have learned some really important things about using photography to explore girls' interests and support their critique. First, these girls loved the opportunity to document, visually, portions of their lives. It was a very fun task for them. But, more importantly, we learned that the pictures girls take create opportunities for them to find language to express their thoughts and feelings in ways that would not have been possible if we had simply asked them direct questions. We have learned that pre-adolescent and adolescent girls often have a great deal of knowledge, but they do not always have the language to convey that knowledge. Photos, like magazine images, help them to find the language they need to express their ideas. As researchers we have found it to be an extremely important method for understanding difficult concepts or ideas (Oliver and Hamzeh, 2010; Oliver and Lalik, 2004a).

Student-designed inquiry projects as strategy

Student-designed inquiry projects are a third instructional strategy I have developed to support girls' critique (Oliver and Lalik, 2004a, 2004b; Oliver and Hamzeh, 2010). Ira Shor (1992) talked about two types of inquiry. The first is teacher-directed and is usually around topics that have some significance to students' lives; the second is student-directed and is usually around topics that students select because of personal interest and relevance in their lives. Across the years I have used both types, although far more of my work has centered on student-directed inquiry.

In one study we were looking at how to help girls critique cultural messages of the female body. I decided to introduce a topic for inquiry, as it was one the girls had discussed at length earlier in the year. I led the girls through an inquiry project designed to critique the Beauty Walk (Oliver and Lalik, 2004b). The Beauty Walk was a school-sponsored fundraiser whereby girls were elected from each homeroom (pre-school class period designed as a time to notify students of important events or information that affects their day) to participate. In this fundraiser, girls were required to dress up in fancy prom-like dresses, and they then had to parade across the stage in a way similar to that seen in a beauty pageant. They were judged on their appearance, and the prettiest girl won 'The Beauty Walk.' Needless to say both as a woman and as a critical feminist researcher I felt this event was problematic. I wondered, therefore, if the girls had an opportunity to critique this event, whether they, too, might find it problematic.

The inquiry process involved the girls developing a survey, surveying their peers, attending the Beauty Walk to collect data, interviewing Beauty Walk participants who did not win, analyzing their data, and writing letters to the editor based on their findings. We learned several things through this study. First, if we look at this portion of the letter to the editor it is clear that the girls developed a language of critique, something that we had hoped would happen.

To Whom It May Concern:

We're writing this letter to express our concern about the Beauty Walk. We're concerned about the following: the discrimination against girls, because of racism, and how it makes girls feel about themselves. Most girls that we surveyed think the Beauty Walk is unfair to females. Some girls don't have the money to buy needed supplies . . . Racism is a big issue in the Beauty Walk. One student thinks, 'If the judges are white, a white girl *will* win. If the judges are black, a black girl *might* win' . . . In conclusion, we think that the BW is unfair. It raises one girl's self esteem by cutting down other girls' self-esteem. We don't think that should be taught in schools.

Despite the fact that the girls were able to critique the Beauty Walk, we learned that researcher-directed inquiry might not be the most effective way to engage girls in critique. Through this process I had to continually redirect their energy and focus because as Brandi so succinctly put it, 'this ain't my topic' (see Oliver and Lalik, 2004b for more).

We have also done student-directed inquiry projects (Lalik and Oliver, 2007; Oliver and Lalik, 2004a; Oliver and Hamzeh, 2010). In one study (Oliver and Hamzeh, 2010), we assisted girls who decided they wanted to do something about the boys at their school who were preventing them from participating in physical activity during recess. These girls wanted to learn more about what the problems were that prevented girls from being physically active at school so we worked with them to develop a survey they could use to learn more about this form of exclusion. Examples of questions the girls included on their survey were 'When the boys won't let you play, how do you feel?,' 'What excuses do the boys make to tell you that you can't play?' and 'How would you feel if you were treated this way?' The girls then went out and surveyed all students in the 5th grade classes to learn more about why boys were not letting the girls play. Here is a little of what they reported when they finished.

> MAGGIE MAE: I learned the excuses boys tell girls are 'you're too weak,' 'girls will get hurt,' 'you're a girly girl,' 'you're too fragile,' and 'it's a man's game.'
> MARIE: Boys don't let some of the girls play . . . they say all we do is paint our nails.
> MARIA: I learned that some boys don't let you play because you're not a boy and that you're a woman and you should stay in your place.

Finally, we have used inquiry projects in regular-size PE classes. In this particular study we wanted to learn how to implement critical inquiry into US public school PE classes. Rather than working with five or so girls at a time, we worked during PE class with approximately twenty-five to thirty girls. Drawing what we learned from the Beauty Walk (Oliver and Lalik, 2004b) study where I selected the topic, in this study we designed the inquiry around the girls' interests and planned very carefully how to help girls select topics that had personal and social interest and relevance in their lives (see Oliver and Lalik, 2004a for more).

We have learned a great deal about the power of student-designed inquiry projects as a means of supporting girls' critique. First, we have learned that girls enjoy looking critically at topics that interest them. Second, we have learned that girls value the opportunity to engage in conversations about inequity, and how this inequity influences the ways they feel about their bodies and how it influences their activity participation. Third, we have learned that by engaging girls in critical inquiry projects we create the space for girls to move toward seeking change (Oliver and Lalik, 2004a, 2004b; Oliver and Hamzeh, 2010).

We have also learned about the process of engaging girls in inquiry. First, girls are much more motivated and involved when they carefully select the topic to study, vs. when a teacher or researcher selects a topic for study (Oliver and Lalik, 2004b). Second, it is important that the girls find the topics interesting if they are to continue working through the more difficult portions of the inquiry tasks

(Lalik and Oliver, 2007; Oliver and Lalik, 2004a). Third, we have learned that it is important to allow girls to engage in social talk while they work because it is within this talk that their critique often emerges (Oliver and Lalik, 2004b). Finally, it takes a great deal of effort and time for the girls to develop their own language of critique.

For researchers, asking girls to critique, whether it is through inquiry projects or other forms of critical inquiry, provides data that illuminates the types of issues that influence girls' worlds. We have found we learn more about girls when we ask them to critique their worlds than to merely explain them. We have also learned that the content of the girls' critique has consistently highlighted the intersections of gender, race, social class, sexuality, and age. These intersections have cut across every study we have done with girls to illuminate the inequities they experience.

Supporting girls' transformation

The final strand in my research focuses on supporting girls' transformation (Oliver *et al.*, 2009; Oliver and Hamzeh, 2010). Over the years I have come to believe that girls need to learn more than how to explore and critique their worlds, particularly in relation to how they are learning to think and feel about their bodies or physical activity. I agree with Giroux (1997) and Weiler (1988) that students need opportunities to develop both a language of critique and a language of possibility.

Radical educators have been criticized for focusing students' attention on critique but not then helping them to develop a language of possibility that is required for transformation to take place. What we have noticed in our work is that we have had far more success in identifying curricular topics and instructional strategies for exploration and critique than we have had in developing transformative types of pedagogy.

In assisting girls in my projects to develop a language of possibility, my hope was that I could help these girls to be able to identify multiple ways of understanding the issues that influence how they think about their bodies and physical activity. I also wanted to help them to understand and name alternative possibilities to be deployed whenever they come up against forms of inequity. In other words, I wanted them to name possibilities for ways in which they can think about themselves and act to change their worlds in the interests of their well-being, particularly in the context of engaging in physical activity. It was when we began combining critique with real and specific possibilities for change that we made small strides toward helping girls transform inequities they identify in their lives. For example, two groups of girls with whom we worked suggested that being a 'girly girl' tended to be a barrier to participation in physical activity because a 'girly girl' does not want to 'sweat,' 'mess up her hair and nails,' 'mess up her nice clothes,' and sometimes wears 'flip flops' (Oliver *et al.*, 2009). Importantly, these girls were often strategic in performing 'girly girl' when it served their mood or inclination to take up physical activity opportunities. Sunshine, a 10-year-old girl explained:

Sometimes if I don't like the sport they are playing in PE, then I'm a girly girl.

What we realized as we listened to the girls talk about being a 'girly girl' was that for them, being a girly girl was more than 'not wanting to sweat,' or not wanting to 'mess up their hair and nails,' it was a powerful discourse that they could use to articulate one of their subjectivities and an embodiment that they could easily perform to get what they desired. However, their ability to use their 'girly girl' discourse was a double-edged sword. On the one hand, when the girls chose to not participate in activities they did not like and used being 'girly girl' as their excuse, no one would acknowledge, question, or challenge this because it fitted so well within the dominant discourse of heteronormative femininity within the larger Mexican culture of which they were a part.

On the other hand, because 'girly girl' *is* such a normalized discourse no one questioned whether there might be some other explanation to why the girls were not participating in physical activity. Sunshine explained that if girls,

felt comfortable with themselves [they] would be able to do physical activity.

What seemed to be happening initially was that the girls talked about their physical activity barriers only in relation to being a 'girly girl.' But as we listened longer, what we began to hear were stories of how the girls used their girly girl language of embodiment as a way to express additional barriers that hindered their physical activity participation. That is, the girls did not like the choices of activities available at school, did not like how the activities were played (when playing with boys), did not like getting hurt or being left out, and wanted to be able to play and 'feel comfortable with themselves.' Thus, rather than play in situations they identified as unsuitable, they chose not to participate.

Rather than viewing the girls themselves as a problem, which has often happened in physical education, we accepted their initial desires to be a 'girly girl' and worked with them to create ways to be active and girly girl simultaneously. Never once did we ask them to critique their notion of 'girly girl.' Instead, collectively, we developed a book of activities that girly girls could play. For each theme that the girls identified as part of being 'girly girl' and therefore a barrier to their physical activity we:

- made up games;
- played the games;
- decided what modifications or changes were needed to the games;
- wrote up the games using a form we designed to help structure game creation;
- tested the games with the other group of girls;
- discussed whether they liked the game and why or why not.

What I found very interesting was that the games the girls created often contradicted the very theme, or other themes with which they identified, as a reason for not participating in physical activity in the first place. For example, the girls created 'Runaway Kickball' for days that they wore nice clothes and did not want to mess them up. In this game, the pitcher rolls the ball to the kicker. The kicker kicks the ball and all members of the team run to the bases while the outfield chases after them and tries to take the flags attached to their waist. One person in the outfield has to collect the ball and get it home. The objective is for the runners to get back to home base without having their flags taken or before the ball gets back home. Each runner that makes it back to home bases without their flag being stolen earns one point for the team. Interestingly, there is no doubt that this game has the potential to mess up kids' nice clothes, and most likely the girls will also sweat or mess up their hair.

What we learned through this study was that when opportunities were presented in physical activity settings for the girls to be girly girls, it facilitated rather than hindered their physical activity participation. Thus, instead of being girls who 'did not like PE' or 'did not like physical activity,' these girls in fact did enjoy activity and noted 'girly girls can play games too.'

Conclusion

Three themes have cut across the work that we have done around understanding, critiquing and transforming issues of inequity in the hope of finding more inclusive practices in PE and physical activity setting. The first theme is that this type of work takes time.

For example, Oliver noted that supporting girls' transformation, like supporting girls' critique, takes time. What we have learned from working with girls over the years is that they have really good ideas about how to change forms of inequity that threaten their health and well-being. What they do not have are spaces in school curriculum to explore these ideas and work toward implementing the types of change they desire. As researchers, we have been able to use our expertise and positions to assist girls in working toward the types of change they desire. Nonetheless, this requires a time-intensive commitment, one we believe is necessary if we are to see real reform. Likewise, McCaughtry has also highlighted how it takes time for teachers a) to learn to see forms of gender exclusion, as well as learn b) to negotiate the political school environment in order to start slowly implementing more inclusive practices

A second theme in our collective work is that working toward inclusive practices requires a commitment from both teachers and students. It is not something that teachers can do without their students, and it is certainly not something that students can do alone. The willingness for both teachers and students to listen to and respect each other is vital to understanding ways that help facilitate finding more inclusive practice. Had Tammy not been willing to listen to her female students over time, she would not have come to the realization that the more male-dominated forms of physical education curriculum and pedagogical practices were not meeting the needs of her students in physical education. The same is true in Oliver's work with girls. Her commitment to listening to her research participants and attempting to respond to what she was hearing has gone a long way toward finding specific strategies teachers can use to help girls explore, critique and transform forms of inequity in physical education/physical activity settings.

Finally, none of this work, whether it is with teachers or with students, has been without challenges. In fact, the challenges in our work have presented multiple opportunities for both of us, as researchers, to better understand both exclusion and inclusion in physical education and physical activity settings. As we have worked with our research participants over time, the challenges that we have experienced have forced us to spend more time, listen longer and in more subtle ways, and struggle to find ways to transform the environments we work in. We believe that if researchers, teachers, and students are committed to inclusive practices, then they will have to work together through the challenges that arise. This common goal becomes what bonds them together and allows for change to take place. Ultimately, that is the goal: more inclusive curricula, more inclusive pedagogical practices, and more inclusive physical activity environments.

References

Clandinin, J.D. and Connolly, M.F. (1995) *Teachers' Professional Knowledge Landscapes.* New York: Teachers College Press.

Flintoff, A. and Scraton, S. (2006) Girls and PE. In D. Kirk, M. O Sullivan and J. Wright (eds) *An International Handbook on Research in Physical Education.* London: Sage.

Fine, M. (1992) *Disruptive Voices: The possibilities of feminist research.* Ann Arbor: The University of Michigan Press.

Giroux, H. (1997) *Pedagogy and the Politics of Hope: Theory, culture, and schooling.* Boulder: Westview Press.

Gordon-Larsen, P., Adair, L. and Popkin, B. (2001) Ethnic differences in physical activity and inactivity. *Obesity Research*, 10 (3): 141–149.

Lalik, R. and Oliver, K.L. (2007) Differences and tensions in implementing a pedagogy of critical literacy with adolescent girls. *Reading Research Quarterly*, 42 (1): 46–70.

McCaughtry, N. (2004) Coming to see gender: Implications of personal history and political pressures on identifying disempowerment for girls. *Research Quarterly for Exercise and Sport*, 75: 400–412.

McCaughtry, N. (2006) Working politically amongst professional knowledge landscapes to implement gender-sensitive physical education reform. *Physical Education and Sport Pedagogy*, 11 (2): 159–179.

McDonough, M.H., and Crocker, P. (2005) Sport participation motivation in young adolescent girls: The role of friendship quality and self-concept. *Research Quarterly for Exercise and Sport*, 76: 456–467.

McKenzie, T., Sallis, J., Broyles, S. *et al.* (2002) Childhood movement skills: Predictors of physical activity in Anglo American and Mexican American adolescents? *Research Quarterly for Exercise and Sport*, 73 (3): 238–244.

Oliver, K. (1999) Adolescent girls' body-narratives: Learning to desire and create a 'fashionable' image. *Teachers College Record*, 101 (2): 220–246.

Oliver, K. and Hamzeh, M. (2010) 'The boys won't let us play:' 5th grade *mestizas* challenge physical activity discourse at school. *Research Quarterly for Exercise and Sport*, 81 (1): 38–51.

Oliver, K. and Lalik, R. (2000) *Bodily knowledge: Learning about equity and justice with adolescent girls*. New York: Peter Lang.

Oliver, K. and Lalik, R. (2001) The body as curriculum: learning with adolescent girls. *Journal of Curriculum Studies*, 33: 303–333.

Oliver, K., and Lalik, R. (2004a) Critical inquiry on the body of girls' physical education classes: a critical poststructural perspective. *Journal of Teaching in Physical Education*, 23 (2): 162–195.

Oliver, K. and Lalik, R. (2004b) 'The beauty walk, this ain't my topic:' Learning about critical inquiry with adolescent girls. *The Journal of Curriculum Studies*, 36 (5): 555–586.

Oliver, K., Hamzeh, M. and McCaughtry, N. (2009) 'Girly girls *can* play games/*Las niñas pueden jugar tambien*:' Co-creating a curriculum of possibilities with 5th grade girls. *Journal of Teaching in Physical Education*, 28 (1): 90–110.

Shor, I. (1992) *Empowering Education: Critical Teaching for Social Change*. Chicago: The University of Chicago Press.

Trost, S., Pate, R., Sallis, J. *et al.* (2002) Age and gender differences in objectively measured physical activity in youth. *Medicine and Science in Sports and Exercise*, 34 (2): 350–355.

Vertinsky, P. (1992) Reclaiming space, revisioning the body: The quest for gender-sensitive physical education. *Quest*, 44: 373–396.

Weiler, K. (1988) *Women Teaching for Change: Gender, class and power*. Westport: Bergin and Garvey Publishers.

Wilson, D., Williams, J., Evans, A. *et al.* (2005) Brief report: A qualitative study of gender preferences and motivational factors for physical activity in underserved adolescents. *Journal of Pediatric Psychology*, 30 (3): 293–297.

Wolf, A., Gortmaker, S., Cheung, L. *et al.* (1993) Activity, inactivity, and obesity: Racial, ethnic, and age differences among schoolgirls. *American Journal of Public Health*, 83: 1625–1627.

Wright, J. (1995) A feminist poststructuralist methodology for the study of gender construction in physical education: Description of a study. *Journal of Teaching in Physical Education*, 15: 1–124.

12 Children's talent development in sport

Effectiveness or efficiency?

*Jean Côté, Colleen Coakley and
Mark Bruner*

Introduction

The documentary *Lost Adventures in Childhood* (Harper, 2009) takes a critical look at the current state of growing up in the world today. Interviews with leaders in the fields of child and evolutionary psychology, youth sport consulting, play studies, and journalism paint a grim picture of hyper-parenting and over-scheduled, over-stressed children who are severely lacking opportunities to develop creativity, freedom, and trust. We are introduced to a Canadian father who keeps tabs on his two school-age daughters by receiving their exact GPS coordinates, updated every two minutes, via the girls' cell phones. We are taken to a summer camp in the United States where a photographer takes 700–800 pictures of the campers each day to post on the camp's website for parents to see; the camp director then spends three to four hours each day fielding phone calls from parents concerned that their child looks upset or disengaged in a photo. We follow a family as they cart their two young daughters from one sport commitment to another; one of the daughters remarks about the difficulty of doing her homework in the car because of car sickness. These scenarios are in sharp contrast to images often conjured up when considering the childhoods of previous generations: children of all ages playing throughout the neighbourhood from sunrise to sunset, independent of adult supervision.

In the early 1990s, members of the International Council of Sport Science and Physical Education's Committee on Sport and Leisure proposed the daunting task of producing a book on the trends of youth sport throughout the world. The resulting book, *Worldwide Trends in Youth Sport* (DeKnop *et al.*, 1996), provides a window into the state of youth sport in twenty countries representing five continents. Upon review of the twenty national case studies, the editors present common trends (pp. 276–279) which will be paraphrased here. Sport is the most common leisure-time activity among youth worldwide. Despite the fact that the most common motives for participation are enjoyment and social connections, youth sport is becoming more institutionalized, specialized, and expensive. Adults are exerting too much influence, treating the young athletes as miniature versions of adults, having them play by rules and on surfaces designed for adult athletes. Children are joining organized sport at younger and younger ages, and are being pushed to specialize earlier in one or two sports. As the playfulness of youth sport is being replaced by seriousness, the spontaneity of sport is disappearing. Finally, it is noted that there are two distinct groups of children: those who engage in frequent, intense training and those who engage in little or no physical activity. These trends sound eerily similar to the scenarios outlined in *Lost Adventures in Childhood* and suggest an overall strategy for youth sport participation that focuses on the effective development of talent to the exclusion of the 'less talented.'

This chapter will present and discuss evidence that suggests it is important to reverse current trends in youth sport and talent development. The concepts of effective versus efficient youth sport programs will first be introduced to high-light the different foci that youth sport programs can take for the development of talent. Evidence for the value of efficient youth sport programs, that is, for those that focus on inclusion rather than exclusion of children, will be presented under the following three headings: 1) evidence against early specialization and ath-letes' selection, 2) the importance of playfulness and spontaneity, and 3) support for developmentally appropriate rules and outcomes. Building on these concepts the chapter will conclude by proposing four guidelines for youth sport aimed at improving the experiences of youth sport participants. The age group upon which this chapter is focused is youth sport participants aged 6 through 12.

Effective and efficient youth sport programs

In a review of the motor learning literature, Wulf and Shea (2002) distinguished between learning *effectiveness* and learning *efficiency*, both being important con-cepts in the study of complex motor skills and the development of talent in sport. These two concepts can be used to describe youth sport programs that have dif-ferent foci to achieve the same goal of developing talent. *Effectiveness* focuses on performance and the acquisition of motor skills independent of the cost that may be involved, while *efficiency* focuses on enhancing participation and development and limiting the psycho-social (i.e. dropout) and physical (i.e. injury) costs associ-ated with training and talent selection. The trends in youth sport summarized by DeKnop *et al.* (1996) and popularized in documentaries such as *Lost Adventures in Childhood* (Harper, 2009) indicate that youth sport programs around the world are aiming at being more *effective* in developing talent in sport, often at the exclu-sion of a majority of youth. Table 12.1 outlines the main differences in focus for effective and efficient youth sport programs.

Effective youth sport programs focus on a competence model (i.e. skill acquisi-tion) illustrated as a pyramid in which only a few can make it to the top (see Figure 12.1). This model is a reality of adult competitive sports that is characterized by a limited number of available spots in professional leagues or Olympic teams. This model suggests that earlier and increased training during childhood provides an advantage to children by allowing them to be chosen for 'select' teams, eventually increasing their chance to climb to the top of the pyramid in adult sports. Effective youth sport programs largely down-play the psycho-social (i.e. dropout, burnout, lack of enjoyment) and physical (i.e. injuries) costs associated with an increased amount of training and selection of 'talented' children. The application of a

Table 12.1 Effective and efficient youth sport programs for talent development

	Primary Focus	Secondary Focus	Success	Strategies	Outcomes
Effective Youth Sport Program for Talent Development	Performance	Participation and personal development	Winning and increased performance	Develop skills and performance in selected children	Performance-based
Efficient Youth Sport Program for Talent Development	Participation and personal development	Performance	Minimizing permanent sport dropout	Keep all children in sport Find ways to integrate everyone	Positive developmental experiences

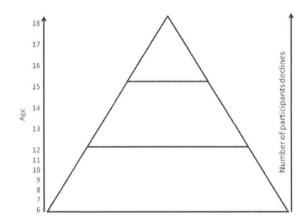

Figure 12.1 Model of an effective youth sport program for talent development

pyramid approach to youth sport programs may arguably be effective for the development of talent in sports with a large base of participants; however, it is often detrimental to the children that are progressively excluded from these programs (Fraser-Thomas and Côté, 2009). Furthermore, the identification of 'talented athletes' in selected youth sport programs is unreliable; especially when detection of talent is attempted during the prepubertal or pubertal periods of growth (see Régnier *et al.*, 1993 for a review). Yet, despite the evidence against the reliability of talent identification, and the fact that adult expert performance in sports is difficult to predict from characteristics of sport performance in childhood, the quality of effective youth sport programs continues to be measured by the performance of a few athletes who reach the top of the pyramid, while little attention is paid to young people who fail to reach an elite level of performance. For instance, Pearson *et al.* (2006) report that professional sports clubs in England continue to invest substantial resources into attempts to identify talented athletes at a young age.

On the other hand, *efficient* youth sport programs focus on including all children in sport by focusing primarily on participation and personal development (see Figure 12.2). Côté (2009) recently proposed the *coefficient of efficiency* as a measure of the internal quality of a sport program for children (ages 6–13). The *coefficient of efficiency* can be used as a measure of the quality of a childhood sport program by accounting for the dropout rate in sport from childhood to adolescence, instead of focusing on performance indicators linked to only a selected number of children. The *coefficient of efficiency* is the equivalent of an input–output ratio expressed as a percentage of the actual number of children that participate in a specific sport program at a given time (e.g. age 10) over the number of the same children that still participate in sport at a later time (e.g. age 13). A *coefficient of efficiency* of less than 100 percent from childhood sport participation to adolescence sport participation would indicate that certain children drop out of sport and are no longer available to train for elite performance in sport. Considering that performance in a given sport in childhood is a poor predictor of adult performance (Régnier *et al.*, 1993), it is important that sport programs in childhood focus on *retaining* athletes by focusing on levels of efficiency. Sport programs with a strict emphasis on early selection, skill acquisition, and training during childhood run the risk of reducing their *coefficient of efficiency* and therefore eliminating someone who, through growth, maturation, and training, later develops into an elite-level athlete. The underpinning principle of highly *efficient* sport programs for childhood is to provide space, playing and training opportunities, and equipment for a large number of children across various sports. This enables elite sport coaches to choose and select the best athletes from a large pool of motivated adolescents (Côté, 2009) by keeping children within the 'participation' pyramid of Figure 12.2.

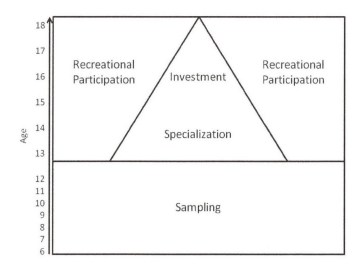

Figure 12.2 Model of an efficient youth sport program for talent development

Developmental model of sport participation

The Developmental Model of Sport Participation (DMSP) contains trajectories of sport participation that focus on the efficiency of youth sport programs by empha-sizing the importance of developmentally appropriate training patterns and social influences during childhood (Côté, 1999; Côté *et al.*, 2003; Côté *et al.*, 2007; Côté and Fraser-Thomas, 2007; Côté and Hay, 2002). The main goal of the DMSP is the inclusion of all children in sport by offering programs with equal opportunities and resources between the ages of 6 and 12. The sampling years of the DMSP provide a context of childhood sport participation that is characterized by a high amount of deliberate play and involvement in more than one sport through seasonal sport participation. The most important aspects of *deliberate play* and *sampling* are the potential contributions of these activities to motivate children to remain involved in sport and deliberately choose a recreational or elite pathway at approximately age 13 (Côté *et al.*, 2009).

In line with DeKnop *et al.*'s (1996) assertion that enjoyment is one of the pri-mary motives for youth sport participation, *deliberate play* is a form of activ-ity in sport which is intrinsically motivating, voluntary, and provides immediate gratification and enjoyment (Côté, 1999). Deliberate play may be initiated and monitored by adults or by the children themselves. Prime examples of deliberate play are backyard cricket and street football. Rules of the standardized sport are adapted to fit the situational factors, including the number of participants, their abilities, and the environment available. Deliberate play should not be confused with *deliberate practice* (Ericsson *et al.*, 1993), which is conducted with a specific outcome of improving skills and performance, is not necessarily enjoyable, and most often requires the supervision of adults.

Sampling refers to participating in a variety of activities for the purpose of enjoyment (Côté, 1999). Like deliberate play, sampling should be voluntary and intrinsically motivating. Sampling can be done among a variety of sports and with sports in addition to other extra-curricular activities. Sampling can even take place within a particular sport; for example, playing different positions or playing the sport in different contexts such as playing on an organized volleyball team and also playing volleyball on the beach, in the pool, or in the backyard with friends.

The foundational stage of the DMSP, the *sampling years* (ages 6–12) is charac-terized by a high amount of deliberate play, a low amount of deliberate practice, and participation in a variety of different sports for the sake of enjoyment. At the age of 12 or 13, youth sport participants who have experienced the sampling years typically take a decision about whether to make a greater commitment to one sport or to continue to participate in sports at a recreational level. Those athletes wishing to continue at the recreational level of sport enter into the *recreational years*, which can last throughout adulthood. In addition to the continuation of high amounts of deliberate play and low amounts of deliberate practice, participation in the recreational years may also be motivated by the health benefits of the activity. Youth who wish to reach a higher performance level will move from the sampling years into the *specializing years* (ages 13–15) and then into the *investment years* (ages 15 and up). During the specializing years, athletes will likely focus on fewer sports and although deliberate play will still be important, they will experience an increase in deliberate practice. The investment years see athletes narrow their focus onto one sport, while further increasing deliberate practice and decreasing deliberate play. It is important to note that while the performance outcomes of these two trajectories differ, both have the probable outcomes of enhanced physical health and enhanced enjoyment of the activity. The ultimate goal of the sampling years (ages 6–12) is to increase the *coefficient of efficiency* of youth sport programs by delaying selection of talent until early adolescence, thereby avoiding the exclusion of children from certain sport programs and the resulting loss of potential talent.

An alternative to the sampling years is early specialization in one sport, characterized by a high level of training in one sport during childhood, a low amount of deliberate play, and a high amount of deliberate practice. Reflecting on the scenarios from the television documentary described at the beginning of this chapter (Harper, 2009) and DeKnop *et al.*'s (1996) conclusions, there are consistent and observable trends towards early specialization programs that can be characterized as 'effective programs' designed to develop talent in sport. Yet, although early specialization programs may be effective in developing elite performance in adulthood for a very small number of children, the negative outcomes from this approach must be a cause for concern.

Evidence against early specialization and team selection

As DeKnop *et al.* (1996) reported, children around the world are being pushed to specialize in one or two sports at an earlier age. Wiersma (2000) explains, however, that there are negative physical, sociological, and psychological outcomes associated with early specialization. Wiersma suggests that early *specializers* focus on a limited pattern of skills (i.e. soccer players who never use their hands), limiting their overall motor skill development and decreasing their likelihood of participating in different types of activities later in life. Wiersma also reports that while sport provides the opportunity for sociological and psychological growth (i.e. cooperation and close peer relationships), those who specialize early spend a significant amount of their time in training and, as a result, may miss out on those benefits.

Another negative effect of early specialization is dropout. Fraser-Thomas *et al.* (2008) conducted retrospective quantitative interviews with fifty adolescent swimmers, twenty-five of whom were currently engaged in swimming and twenty-five who had recently dropped out of the sport. A distinct pattern of early specialization was found among the dropout group, despite the fact that there was no significant difference between the groups in the age when swimmers began competitive swimming. Specifically, when compared to the engaged group, dropout swimmers had participated in fewer extra-curricular activities, engaged in less unstructured swimming, and started dry land training and attending training camps earlier. Wall and Côté (2007) found similar results when conducting retrospective interviews with high-level male youth ice hockey players. The participants in this study included an active group (boys who were currently playing) and a dropout group (boys who had recently stopped participating in the sport). Results indicated similarities between the two groups in terms of participation in other activities and the amount of time on the ice in practices and games. However, members of the dropout group began off-ice training at an earlier age and spent significantly more time in off-ice training at ages 12 and 13 than the active group. This finding provides further evidence against early specialization.

With the above information in mind, it is important to understand that youth sport dropout is not always negative and can be expected as a natural result of sampling. For example, early research on youth sport dropout (e.g. Orlick, 1974) failed to follow up with dropouts after they left the sport in question, causing concern about the seemingly large number of young athletes leaving the sport. Subsequent researchers (e.g. Klint and Weiss, 1986; Lindner *et al.*, 1991; Weiss and Petlichkoff, 1989), however, recognized the importance of classifying dropouts in terms of reasons for leaving the sport and their ensuing relationship with sports (e.g. an athlete may drop out of one sport to try a new sport or concentrate on fewer sports). For example, Klint and Weiss (1986) classified dropouts into three groups:

1   *volunteer dropout* (enjoyed the sport but wanted to try a different sport or activity);
2   *resistant dropout* (wanted to participate but was unhappy in the situation);
3   *reluctant dropout* (forced out of the sport due to injury or financial reasons).

Regardless of the classification system used, it is essential to understand that dropout is neither always positive nor always negative; rather, it is important to look at the specific reasons for dropout and the behaviour that follows in terms of participation in sport or other activities. A cause for concern with youth sport programs that focus on early selection of the 'most talented athletes' and de-selection of the 'less talented' children is the unreliability of the process.

There are a number of problems with traditional methods of talent identification (Pearson *et al.*, 2006; Vaeyens *et al.*, 2008). For example, characteristics that distinguish success as an adult athlete (i.e. size or speed) may not become apparent until later adolescence. At the same time, there is no guarantee that a young athlete who possesses a desired attribute will still possess that attribute as an adult athlete. Pearson *et al.* (2006) also note that talent is dynamic and multifaceted; the characteristics of talent may be different across age groups and attempts to measure these characteristics will often overlook one or more important factors. Finally, there is the major concern that youth begin maturing at different times and rates; late-maturing athletes could be summarily dismissed through traditional talent identification methods (Pearson *et al.*, 2006). Related to this is the fact that many youth sports teams are restricted to a one-year age range. The *relative age effect*, which means that players born earlier in the cut-off year – thus being relatively older than their peers – are overrepresented, has been shown to be present in a number of sports (see Cobley *et al*., 2009; Musch and Grondin, 2001 for reviews). A recent study by Sherar *et al*. (2007) looked at both the physical maturity and the birth date of male youth ice hockey players. They followed a group of 281 players aged 14–15 years through a selection camp for a provincial hockey team. The relative-age effect was shown to be present because the percentage of athletes born in the first six months of the year increased with each selection process, culminating in 77.5 percent of the selected team being born in the first six months of the year. Additionally, when compared to the players who were cut and to a control group of their peers, the selected players were taller, heavier, and more mature (Sherar *et al*., 2007). While it is easy to make the case that the selected players were the best to represent the province at the time, the real cause for concern is the impact on the late-maturing or relatively younger players and the future success of the sport. Anthropometric data were collected from the players and there was no significant difference in the predicted stature of the selected and not selected players. In other words, though the selected players were bigger and stronger than the players who were not selected, it is likely that those differences would have disappeared by adulthood. Sherar *et al*. (2007) explain that the impact on the late-maturing or relatively younger players who were not selected is that they miss out on increased exposure to scouts, high-level coaching and the high-level competition itself (including experience dealing with the added pressures of elite sport). They also explain that although research has not yet tracked the progress of these late-maturing or relatively younger athletes, it is likely that many may leave hockey for other sports to which they may be selected for the next level, or perhaps they may leave sport completely. While this study looked specifically at male ice hockey players, this scenario is played out in many other sports, to the detriment of late-maturing and relatively younger athletes (Cobley *et al*., 2009).

Lastly, in addition to the negative consequences of early specialization and the general failure of early talent identification, there is support for sampling. For example, research on the development histories of elite athletes provides further support for sampling and against early specialization (Côté *et al*., 2007). In addition, Linver *et al*. (2009) recently looked at patterns of participation among adolescents aged 10–18 years. They found that youth who participated in sports as well as other activities had the highest levels of positive outcomes, followed by youth who participated in sports alone and lastly by youth who participated in little or no activity. This is further evidence against early specialization.

Importance of playfulness and spontaneity

It has been argued that childhood has moved indoors and the culture of play now revolves around images presented on television (Kalliala, 2006). Children are inundated with television images and presented with a view into so many aspects of adulthood that their childhood curiosity erodes. This is in addition to the fact that the actual time in front of the television is obviously time *not* outside playing. Changes in parenting are also contributing to changes in childhood play culture. There is a growing prominence of *uncertain parenting* (Kalliala, 2006). Whereas children knew where they stood with more authoritarian parenting styles common in the past, parents today are often more permissive and uncertain. These parents may wish to give their children more freedom, but they feel they cannot do that because of perceived dangers. They tend to outsource more parenting responsibilities to professionals or specialists (Kalliala, 2006).

As worldwide youth sport becomes increasingly professionalized and institutionalized by adults, playfulness and spontaneity are being replaced by seriousness (DeKnop *et al.*, 1996). There has been a long history of study on the importance of play; Huizinga (1950) explains that play is older than culture itself. Even at its simplest, most basic level in the animal kingdom, play is much more than a physical act or reflex. Despite the fact that play has been around seemingly since the beginning of time, it is ironic that play is still very misunderstood and often dismissed as unimportant. Bjorklund and Pellegrini (2002) conclude that 'behaviours are often classified as play if they appear to have no apparent immediate benefit to the actor. Yet, perhaps paradoxically, play is typically seen as serving an important function in children's development' (p. 321). Kalliala (2006) tells us that 'children don't play in order to learn, although they learn while they are playing' (p. 20). So what do children learn and how does it pertain to youth sport? Pellegrini and Smith (1998) conducted a review of literature on the functions of physical play; an aspect of play they felt was not receiving the attention it deserved in the research community. Based on the reviewed research, they hypothesize that play can improve strength, endurance, and skill movement, as well as help reduce body fat, but the functions of play go beyond the physical. Pellegrini and Smith also propose that physical play, especially rough-and-tumble play, may contribute to social development.

Specific to youth sport is the importance of *deliberate play* in development (Côté, 1999; Côté *et al.*, 2007). As indicated earlier, examples of deliberate play are backyard cricket and street football. Deliberate play is intrinsically motivated and provides immediate feedback in the form of enjoyment. But the benefits of deliberate play stretch beyond simple fun. Deliberate play encourages children to be creative, giving them the opportunity to experiment with new skills that they might be afraid to attempt under the critical eyes of coaches or parents. In *Lost Adventures in Childhood* (Harper, 2009), we watch as a youth boys' basketball team is asked to play a game for fun. A child sport consultant who is familiar with the team notes that a number of the players who are excelling as leaders and attempting new moves are not the players who usually fill these roles in the formal sport setting; the speculation is that perhaps these players 'play it safe' in front of significant adults for fear of making a mistake. Yet once these skills are attempted and eventually mastered through deliberate play, the athlete will use those skills in their play in organized games. As one example of research linking deliberate play and elite performance, Soberlak and Côté's (2003) study of elite male ice hockey players looked at the developmental history of the participants through retrospective interviews. The results showed that each of their developments followed the DMSP's pathway to elite performance through sampling. As their participation in deliberate play decreased, their level of deliberate practice increased as they passed through the specializing and investment years. Soberlak and Côté also make the connection between the innate enjoyments of deliberate play leading to continued participation which can transfer to an increased motivation for participation in the sport.

Support for developmentally appropriate rules and outcomes

In a systematic review of studies of motivation behind sport participation, Weiss and Williams (2004) found three common reasons for youth to participate in sport. The first is to develop and demonstrate physical competence, which includes learning and mastering skills, attaining goals, and physical health. The second reason is social acceptance and approval, which includes feeling part of a group and making friends. The third reason for participating in sport is to enjoy experiences, simply to have fun. In other words, youth join sports to learn skills, be good at something, be with and make new friends, be a part of a group, and generally have fun. Notice that competitive outcomes such as winning or beating opponents are not on this list. This research suggests that adults who organize youth sport ought to recognize and respect the motivations of their young athletes when developing sport programs.

The National Research Council and Institute of Medicine in the United States (NRCIM, 2002) presents eight features of positive development settings for youth activities that, if they became established, could support young people's motivation to participate in sport. The eight setting features include physical and psychological safety, appropriate structure, supportive relationships, opportunities to belong, positive social norms, support for efficacy and mattering, opportunities for skill building, and integration of family, school, and community efforts. While coaches should strive to integrate strategies to promote the eight setting features in youth sport activities, many of the features occur naturally in deliberate play. For example, a group of neighbourhood children playing basketball may use a lower hoop (i.e. modification of structure) if available to them so that their shots can reach the net, therefore increasing their success (i.e. improve efficacy) and although they may keep score, their main motivation for participating in deliberate play is enjoyment, not winning.

Guidelines for children's sport (ages 6–12 years)

1   *Increase the amount of deliberate play within and beyond organized sport.*
    It may sound contradictory to ask adults to get kids to participate in deliberate play, activity which should be voluntary and intrinsically motivating. However, children have been conditioned away from deliberate play activities, in many ways due to adult influence. These influences include the fear that parents have of giving their kids the freedom to play outside as well as the institutionalization of youth sport. Within organized sport, coaches, teachers, and programmers can reintroduce the concept of deliberate play through games in practices; in these games coaches can encourage players to try a

certain number of new moves or skills and the coach can act as a player and participate in the game. Coaches can also encourage their athletes to play with their teammates outside the organized sport setting. The onus is on the parents to give their children the freedom and encouragement to play outside their constant watchful eye.

2   *Do not cut players before age 13.*

Research indicates that attempts of talent identification during childhood are rarely successful. Selecting certain players because of a particular talent or physical characteristic necessarily excludes a potentially successful portion of the talent pool, likely late-maturing athletes. A particular mental or physical characteristic that a young athlete possesses at a certain age is not guaranteed to be present later in development. At the same time, the desired trait may not be of benefit at a later stage of competition.

3   *Encourage sampling during childhood.*

It is essential that youth sport coaches and programmers understand and appreciate the positive influence of sampling in young athletes. For example, it must be clear that instructing a young athlete to participate in baseball and soccer to improve their hockey ability is not sampling. Sampling is not simply playing different sports to gain a wider skill set or to benefit one particular sport. Rather, an integral factor of sampling is that the athlete tries different sports for fun; the positive and enjoyable experiences in different sport settings, around a new group of peers and adult leaders, contribute to benefits far beyond the physical. Coaches must resist the urge to require athletes to play particular other sports as an attempt to write the recipe for elite performance; worse yet, they must not pressure young athletes to choose one sport or participate in significant off-season training before the age of 13.

4   *Emphasize developmentally appropriate outcomes.*

Youth are motivated to participate in sport by learning and mastering new skills, being a part of a social group, and having fun. These motivations must be reflected in the goals of any youth sport program. By avoiding highly competitive outcomes and by employing modified age-appropriate rules, sport programmers, coaches, and parents can provide the positive sport experience that children need in order to increase their motivation for continued participation.

Conclusion

Drawing on the existing evidence about the psycho-social factors known to be important in youth learning of motor skills, this chapter proposed that sampling and deliberate play activities during childhood and a 'no selection' policy are the most efficient strategies to maximizing youth participation in sport during childhood and limit dropout. Despite the evidence to promote efficiency in children's sport programs, the majority of youth sport programs around the world continue to measure their success using performance measures of a few athletes. Current trends in sport programming are moving towards institutionalization, elitism, early selection, and early specialization (Hecimovich, 2004; Hill, 1988; Hill and Hansen, 1988) and the exclusion of the 'less talented.' Many sport programs are requiring higher levels of investment from earlier ages and discouraging children from participating in a diversity of activities (Gould and Carson, 2004). However, there is clear evidence suggesting that sport programs such as these may not be providing optimal environments for youth's lifelong involvement in sport and elite performance. By considering factors other than performance and skill acquisition, the DMSP allows researchers to address questions of *efficiency* and *effectiveness*. A youth sport framework that focuses on efficiency should consider the various pathways that children follow in sport. Concerted effort is required from physical education teachers, coaches, and parents to ensure youth learn skills during childhood that will allow them to continue their participation and personal development in sport at either an elite or recreational level.

References

Bjorklund, D. and Pellegrini, A. (2002) Homo ludens: The importance of play. In Bjorklund, D. and Pellegrini, A. (eds) *The Origins of Human Nature: Evolutionary developmental psychology.* Washington, DC: APA, pp. 297–331.

Cobley, S., Baker, J., Wattie, N. *et al.* (2009) Annual age-grouping and athlete development: A meta-analytical review of relative age effects in sport. *Sports Medicine*, 39: 235–256.

Côté, J. (1999) The influence of the family in the development of talent in sports. *Sports Psychologist,* 13: 395–417.

Côté, J. (2009) The road to continued sport participation and excellence. In Tsung-Min Hung, E., Lidor, R. and Hackfort, D. (eds) *Psychology of Sport Excellence.* Morgantown, WV: Fitness Information Technology, pp. 97–104.

Côté, J. and Fraser-Thomas, J. (2007) Youth involvement in sport. In P. Crocker (ed.) *Sport psychology: A Canadian perspective.* Toronto: Pearson, pp. 270–298.

Côté, J. and Hay, J. (2002) Children's involvement in sport: A developmental perspective. In Silva, J. and Stevens, D. (eds) *Psychological Foundations of Sport.* Boston, MA: Allyn and Bacon, pp. 484–502.

Côté, J., Baker, J. and Abernethy, B. (2003) From play to practice: A developmental framework for the acquisition of expertise in team sport. In Starkes J. and Ericsson, K.A. (eds) *Expert Performance in Sports: Advances in research on sport expertise.* Champaign, IL: Human Kinetics, pp. 89–114.

Côté, J., Baker, J. and Abernethy, B. (2007) Practice and play in the development of sport expertise. In Eklund, R. and Tenenbaum, G. (eds) *Handbook of Sport Psychology.* Hoboken, NJ: Wiley, pp. 184–202.

Côté, J., Horton, S. and MacDonald, D. *et al.* (2009) The benefits of sampling sports during childhood. *Physical and Health Education Journal*, 74 (4): 6–11.

DeKnop, P., Engström, L., Skirstad, B. *et al.* (eds) (1996) *Worldwide Trends in Youth Sport.* Champaign, IL: Human Kinetics Publishers, Inc.

Ericsson, K.A., Krampe, R.T. and Tesch-Römer, C. (1993) The role of deliberate practice in the acquisition of expert performance. *Psychological Review,* 100 (3): 363–406.

Fraser-Thomas, J. and Côté, J. (2009) UnderstandIng adolescents' positive and negative developmental experiences in sport. *The Sport Psychologist*, 23: 3–23 .

Fraser-Thomas, J., Côté, J. and Deakin, J. (2008) Examining adolescent sport dropout and prolonged engagement from a developmental perspective. *Journal of Applied Sport Psychology*, 20: 318–333.

Gould, D. and Carson, S. (2004) Fun and games. *Youth Studies Australia*, 23: 19–26.

Harper, S. (2009) *Lost Adventures in Childhood.* Sunday Night Entertainment in association with CTV Television Inc.

Hecimovich, M. (2004) Sport specialization in youth: A literature review. *Journal of the American Chiropractic Association*, 41 (4): 32–41.

Hill, G. (1988) Celebrate diversity (not specialization) in school sports. *Executive Educator,* 10: 24.

Hill, G. And Hansen, G. (1988) Specialization in high school sports—the pros and cons. *Journal of Physical Education, Recreation, and Dance,* 59 (5): 76–79.

Huizinga, J. (1950) *Homo ludens: A study in the play-element in culture.* Boston: Beacon Press.

Kalliala, M. (2006) *Play Culture in a Changing World.* New York: Open University Press.

Klint, K. and Weiss, M. (1986) Dropping in and dropping out: Participation motives of current and former youth gymnasts. *Canadian Journal of Applied Sport Science*, 11: 106–114.

Linder, K., Johns, D. and Butcher, J. (1991) Factors in withdrawal from youth sport: A proposed model. *Journal of Sport Behaviour*, 14 (1): 3–18.

Linver, M., Roth, J. and Brooks-Gunn, J. (2009) Patterns of adolescents' participation in organized activities: Are sports best when combined with other activities? *Developmental Psychology*, 45 (2): 354–367.

Musch, J. and Grondin, S. (2001) Unequal competition as an impediment to personal development: A review of the relative age effect in sport. *Developmental Review*, 21: 147–167.

NRCIM (National Research Council and Institute of Medicine) (2002) *Community Programs to Promote Youth Development.* Washington, DC: National Academy Press.

Orlick, T. (1974) The athletic drop out: A high price to pay for inefficiency. *Canadian Association for Health, Physical Education, and Recreation Journal*, 40: 21–27.

Pearson, D., Naughton, G. and Torode, M. (2006) Predictability of physiological testing and the role of maturation in talent identification for adolescent team sports. *Journal of Science and Medicine in Sport*, 9: 277–287.

Pellegrini, A. and Smith, P. (1998) Physical activity play: The nature and function of a neglected aspect of play. *Child Development*, 69: 557–598.

Régnier, G., Salmela., J. and Russell, S. (1993) Talent detection and development in sport. In Singer, R., Murphy, M, and Tennant, L. (eds) *Handbook of Research in Sport Psychology.* New York: Macmillan, pp. 290–313.

Sherar, L., Baxter-Jones, A., Faulkner, R. *et al.* (2007) Do physical maturity and birth date predict talent in male youth ice hockey players? *Journal of Sports Sciences*, 25 (8): 879–886.

Soberlak, P. and Côté, J. (2003) The developmental activities of elite ice hockey players. *Journal of Applied Sport Psychology*, 15: 41–49.

Vaeyens, R., Lenoir, M., Williams, A. *et al.* (2008) Talent identification and development programmes in sport: Current models and future directions. *Sports Medicine*, 38 (9): 703–714.

Wall, M. and Côté, J. (2007) Developmental activities that lead to dropout and investment in sport. *Physical Education and Sport Pedagogy*, 12 (1): 77–87.

Weiss, M. and Petlichkoff, L. (1989) Children's motivation for participation in and withdrawal from sport: Identifying the missing links. *Pediatric Exercise Science*, 1: 195–211.

Weiss, M. and Williams, L. (2004) The *why* of youth sport involvement: A developmental perspective on motivational processes. In Weiss, M. (ed.) *Developmental Sport and Exercise Psychology: A lifespan perspective.* Morgantown, WV: Fitness Information Technology, Inc, pp. 223–268.

Wiersma, L. (2000) Risks and benefits of youth sport specialization: Perspectives and recommendations. *Pediatric Exercise Science*, 12: 13–22.

Wulf, C. and Shea, G. (2002) Schema theory: A critical appraisal and reevaluation. *Journal of Motor Behavior*, 37 (2): 85–101.

13 Disability, sport and inclusion

Donna Goodwin and Danielle Peers

Introduction

The aim of writing this chapter is to question the perception that disability sport is unequivocally empowering and inherently inclusive for youth experiencing disability. We argue that sport can serve to both include and exclude young athletes and, furthermore, that there are a number of structural and socio-cultural factors that impact on the inclusion of youth experiencing disability. We will examine these issues on three interrelated planes: sport structures of inclusion/exclusion, experiences of inclusion/exclusion, and cultural contexts of inclusion/exclusion.

This chapter is written from the combined perspectives of two authors: a researcher and teacher who is an insider to adapted physical activity but who is an outsider to the disability community; and a doctoral student in the socio-cultural study of sport, who, as a retired Paralympic athlete, in an insider to both the disability sport and the broader disability communities. Both authors are working within distinctly social understandings of disability; that is, we interrogate youth sport as a means through which disability is not only included and excluded, but also (re)produced, reified, re-interpreted, and resisted.

In our examination of sport for youth experiencing disability we first interrogate the meanings of disability. Against that backdrop of understanding, we then describe sporting structures and their impact on inclusion and exclusion in sport. We next explore inclusion and exclusion sport experiences of youth experiencing disability. The final section, the cultural context of inclusion in, and exclusion from, sport is presented based upon an understanding of sport as a complex and socially constructed site that can reflect, (re)produce, and potentially resist attitudinal hierarchies, ambivalence and stigmatization. We close our discussion by reflection upon inclusion as a socio-cultural phenomenon.

Interrogating disability

Within disability, sport, and disability sport communities, there are a number of ways in which disability has been understood, problematized and, consequently, addressed (DePauw, 2000). One, widely circulated, model of disability is the biomedical model, otherwise known as the individual or deficit-based model. In this model, disability is understood to be a problematic biological abnormality or deficit that is rooted within an individual's cognition, sensation and/or physiology (Oliver, 1990; Titchkosky, 2007). In this model, politically correct person-first language describes the person *with* a disability.

Biomedical understandings affect the ways in which researchers, professionals and practitioners think about addressing the 'problem' of disability. First, because disability is understood as a biological problem, doctors and other quasi-medical staff become constructed as the disability experts who can speak to, and solve, the problem of disability (Titchkosky, 2007). Second, because disability is understood as an individual problem, the solutions to disability are also aimed at the 'problematic' disabled individuals. For example, this might include normalizing the biological abnormality of a person (e.g. surgery), normalizing the person 'with' the disability (e.g. rehabilitative sport), adapting the activities of the individual (e.g. using a walker or sports wheel chair), and, if these are not sufficient, minimally modifying the individual's environment (e.g. building a ramp to the gym) (Oliver, 1990).

In response to the biomedical model of disability, a number of alternative, social models have emerged in the past forty years (DePauw, 2000; McRuer, 2006; Oliver, 1990; Shogan, 1998). Although the specifics of these models vary widely, their shared premise is that socio-cultural factors such as negative stereotypes, expensive healthcare costs, and inaccessible architectural designs actively contribute to exclusion, poverty, unequal opportunities, and play a role in the 'disablement' of certain categories of people (Shakespeare, 2006). Some proponents of this model have chosen the alternative terminology of *disabled person*, in order to connote that it is the person who has been actively *disabled* by society, as opposed to the person simply *having* a biological 'problem.' Others find this term to be too similar to derogatory disability language that places the label before the person, and therefore prefer to use the person-first term *person with a disability*.

Social understandings of disability, like biomedical understandings, affect the ways in which we think about addressing the 'problem' of disability. First, social models tend to place a significant value on the lived experience, personal knowledge, and collective politics of those who are being disabled (Clare, 1999; Howe, 2008; Oliver, 1990). Second, because the problem is understood as social, the solutions focus on transforming disabling social structures (e.g. passing laws for accessible buildings), practices (e.g. interrogating able-bodied expertise about, and normalization of, disability), and discourses (e.g. challenging bio-medical and tragic stories), rather than on normalizing abnormal individuals (Hahn, 1984; Oliver, 1990; Shogan, 1998). In order to honor the experience, knowledge, and political struggles of those experiencing disability, a social understanding of disability, rather than the medical understanding, will guide our analysis in this chapter. Because the term *person with a disability* and the term *disabled person* are open to biomedical and derogatory readings, respectively, we have chosen to rely most heavily on the term *person experiencing disability* (Peers, 2009) to refer to those who have been subjected to medical diagnoses of disability, disabling social conditions, and/or who have claimed a disability-related identity.

Sport structures of inclusion/exclusion

There are many more interpretations and permutations of inclusion in disability sport than could be encapsulated within the simple dichotomy of exclusion versus inclusion. We present three general models for inclusion for youth experiencing disability: disability sport, mainstream sport, and innovative sport.

Inclusion in disability sport

Disability sport refers to 'sport that has been designed for or is specifically practiced by athletes with disabilities' (DePauw and Gavron, 2005, p. 8; see also Nixon, 2007). In this model, athletes who have been diagnosed with impairments participate in sporting activities that are separated from those of their able-bodied peers, and, often, their peers with different types or levels of impairment. Examples of this model are the international, multi-sport festivals of the Deaflympics[1] and the Paralympics, and their corresponding nationally and locally organized youth sport programs.

Under the Deaflympics model, Deaf sport requires that all participants have a hearing loss of at least 55 db in the better ear (International Committee of Sports for the Deaf, 2010). Importantly, there is no further segregation of eligible athletes. By contrast, Paralympic sport presents a much more complex model of inclusive segregation that is designed to provide opportunities for equitable sporting competition, and is not without controversy (Howe and Jones, 2006). At the international level, the Paralympics provides an inclusive elite sport environment for athletes who have visual, mobility and, to a lesser extent, intellectual impairments. Moreover, each individual Paralympic sport has its own specific impairment parameters that determine who can and who cannot participate, and against whom one can compete. For example, in the sport of swimming, athletes with visual impairments compete separately from those with 'functional' impairments such as cerebral palsy or amputation (IPC Swimming, 2010). In addition, a system of classification[2] is used to further separate athletes (not unlike weight classes in boxing) into a number of segregated competitions (DePauw and Gavron, 2005; Howe, 2008; Howe and Jones, 2006). The Paralympic sport of wheelchair rugby, by contrast, is inclusive of a different group of athletes: those that have been diagnosed with physical impairments to both the lower and the upper limbs (International Wheelchair Rugby Federation, 2010). This sport also uses a classification system to ensure that each team always includes athletes of various functional levels on the court at the same time.

Disability sport's very specific and varied codes of segregated inclusion affect not only youth who compete in the Deaflympics and Paralympics, but also those who participate in a host of youth-specific competitions at the international, national, regional and local levels, including the Asian Youth Paralympic Games (Tokyo 2016 Olympic Bid, 2009), intercollegiate wheelchair sport in the United States (DePauw and Gavron, 2005), and the Kent Youth Disability Games in the UK (KentSport, 2007).

Disability sport programs provide opportunities for athletes who may not find full inclusion in mainstream sport, and they provide social spaces where youth who experience disability can meet friends or mentors with similar experiences, and can participate in ways that may not require the athlete to constantly adapt to rules, equipment and values that are based on able-bodied norms (Brasile, 1990; DePauw and Gavron, 2005; Nixon, 2007). On the other hand, segregated disability sport can serve to further differentiate and stigmatize its participants. By its very existence, segregated disability sport can justify the exclusive barriers of mainstream sport and it can also be hard to access because it is often limited to urban centers where there are larger disability communities (Donnelly, 1996; Fitzgerald and Kirk, 2009; Nixon, 2007).

Inclusion in mainstream sport

Mainstreaming, within a sport context, refers to the participation of all youth within sport programs designed for, and made up mostly of, those who do not experience disabilities (DePauw and Doll-Tepper, 2000; Nixon, 2007; Smith and Thomas, 2006). At the individual level, mainstreaming can sometimes work well. For example, the learning or sensory disabilities that are experienced by some youth in other contexts may not be experienced while they are participating in some sports, as a result, these youth may feel entirely included within mainstream sport (Nixon, 2007). Other youth may experience significant disability in the context of mainstream sport, but may still find success and inclusion through a combination of adaptive technologies (e.g. hearing aids or prosthetics), high personal skill level, and the cooperation of sport leaders (Nixon, 2007).

At the institutional level, mainstreaming can occur on a variety of different levels. Some youth sport programs have endeavored to remove disabling barriers in order to integrate a wider variety of athletes into the same activities. Examples include integrated youth cricket events where all youth play together (A Very Special Cricket Tournament, 2003) and alpine skiing programs where athletes who experience a range of disabilities and abilities compete alongside each other through a system of rankings (not unlike golf handicaps) (DePauw, 1997). On another level, we see integrated youth leagues where, for example, Deaf school teams compete with teams from mainstream schools (Stephens, 2007). There are also integrated sport festivals, such as the multi-generational Commonwealth Games (Smith and Thomas, 2005), or the specifically youth-focused Canada Games (Canada Games Committee, 2007), in which select disability sports are played alongside similar mainstream sports.

Despite the above examples of mainstreamed sporting activities, and despite the plethora of international, national and regional policies and laws that mandate increased mainstreaming efforts, many youth experiencing disability remain significantly excluded from, or marginalized within, mainstream sport and physical activity programs (DePauw and Doll-Tepper, 2000; Nixon, 2007; Promis *et al*, 2001; Wolff and Hums, 2006). As Nixon (2007) argues:

People with disabilities who are capable of competing with or against able-bodied athletes may be prevented from doing so simply because they are disabled, because people in control of a sport will not make or allow appropriate accommodations of its structure, equipment, or facilities or because these people cannot or are unwilling to accept new or different conceptions of athleticism in their sport.

(p. 420)

For example, a wheelchair or prosthetic device that may allow an athlete to successfully compete in an event may be construed as either contributing to an unfair advantage or to a safety risk for others (Hutzler, 2008; van Hilvoorde and Landeweard, 2008). Similarly, inaccessible sporting venues, ablest attitudes, or the unwillingness of coaches to alter their teaching or communication styles may prevent certain athletes from participating on par with their mainstream peers (Nixon, 2007). Due to these barriers, efforts at mainstreaming can result in a kind of nominal inclusion: a mere 'placement' of youth within mainstream sport environments. Mainstreamed youth experiencing disability may be invited onto the field, but the meaningfulness of their participation may be limited if the ball is not passed to them or they are not coached (Goodwin and Watkinson, 2000). In other cases, youth may be included only as scorekeepers or as inanimate sporting objects, such as pylons or bases (Fitzgerald and Kirk, 2009; Tripp *et al.*, 2007).

Ideally, therefore, mainstreaming results in greater sporting opportunities for youth experiencing disability, as well as greater social understanding and acceptance of intellectual, sensory and bodily difference (Brasile, 1990; Tripp *et al.*, 1995). Realistically, however, many youth sport organizations have failed to develop the awareness or the willingness to create mainstream sporting opportunities that promote barrier-free and meaningful participation for all (Fitzgerald and Kirk, 2009; Nixon, 2007).

Inclusion in alternative and innovative sport

Although disability sport and mainstreaming are the two most widely practiced inclusion strategies for youth experiencing disability (Sherrill, 1997), there exists a host of other youth and multi-generational sporting programs that have incorporated features of both models, along with new, innovative strategies for meaningful inclusion. Three of these innovative strategies are: reverse integration, alternative sporting values, and meaningful choice.

Reverse integration, within this context, refers to the integration of athletes who do not experience disability into sports that are designed for, and mostly populated by, those who experience disability (Brasile, 1990; Nixon, 2007). The most celebrated example of this is wheelchair basketball in Canada, where athletes who do not experience disability play in wheelchairs alongside athletes who experience disability. A classification system ensures that individuals who experience a range of disabilities and abilities are included on the court at any given time.

The second innovation, *alternative sporting values*, refers to efforts made to change the objectives and ideals that structure sport programs and their representations. This type of innovation grew out of the critique that both mainstream and disability sport embraced, reproduced and normalized gendered and ablest ideals, including those of elitism, competition and brute strength (DePauw, 1997; Hahn, 1984; Hardin and Hardin, 2005; Howe, 2008; Promis *et al*, 2001; Shogan 1998). In response to this critique, scholars have proposed the development of sport structures that, for example:

- value the ways that one trains more than the results that one achieves (Howe, 2008);
- render the athlete's abilities visible while rendering their disabilities far less visible and relevant (DePauw, 1997; Wolff and Hums, 2006);
- focus on the outcomes of recreation, co-operation and inclusion, rather than on those of competition and elitism (Promis *et al.*, 2001).

An example of a youth sport that embraces alternative sporting values is miracle league baseball. Based in the United States, miracle league baseball is played on a terrain that is wheelchair and walker friendly, and its rules ensure that every player, regardless of the type or level of impairment, is guaranteed the chance to bat and to score in each inning (Juniors, 2009).

The third innovation is *meaningful choice*. As DePauw and Doll-Tepper (2000, p. 139) argue, 'successful inclusion requires decision-makers, including individuals with a disability, to have choice (informed choice) and to have choices.' Some organizations, such as the Special Olympics, have attempted to build meaningful choice into their sport programming. The majority of Special Olympics programming follows a segregation model, in which eligibility is dependent upon a diagnosis of intellectual disability (Special Olympics, 2010). Eligible athletes can choose to participate in open competitions in any of a wide variety of local sport programs, which tend to be based upon the alternative sporting values of inclusion, co-operation, and the 'everyone is a winner' philosophy (Nixon, 2007, p. 428). These athletes can also, however, choose to participate in, and train for, more competitive streams of their chosen sport(s). In this case, a process called *divisioning* ensures that these athletes have the opportunity to compete with and against athletes who, regardless of their specific medical diagnoses, have achieved similar athletic results (Nixon, 2007). Lastly, Special Olympics, in some regions, offer a program called *Unified Sports* in which athletes who experience disability participate alongside those who do not (Special Olympics, 2010). In this way, Special Olympics enables its athletes to choose to participate within the kind(s) of sporting environments that provide them with the most meaningful, enjoyable or challenging opportunities.

Experiences of inclusion/exclusion

An enduring theme in adapted physical activity research has been the study of impairment as 'difference' and the biomedical and socio-cultural meanings that are applied to those who experience disability. There are three key features of the relationship between an individual and the societal labelling of people:

* the constraints imposed by an able-bodied world that defines people according to medical pathology and labels them disabled;
* people managing their own biographies by constructing their own meanings of self (Williams, 1994a);
* the sense of community created through shared histories, values, and acts to resist outside influence (Goodwin *et al.*, 2009).

We explore issues of inclusion for youth experiencing disability resulting from engagement in sport and societal influences on their participation.

Disabled labeling

Disability sport settings have been identified as group contexts within which youth experiencing disability have opportunities to explore alternative identities to the socially imposed perceptions of tragedy (Groff and Kleiber, 2001; Williams, 1994a). Providing 'segregated' opportunities in which self-identified communities can congregate, develop, pursue shared goals, and create histories may not be a step backward in social justice terms (i.e. inclusion) and disability rights (DePauw and Doll-Tepper, 2000) but rather a context for the reversal of stigma, the development of positive identities, and the protection and reassurance of its members (Gill, 1997).

Disability sport can enhance self-efficacy and perceived physical ability (Martin, 2008; Martin *et al*, 1995; Page *et al.*, 2001) while increasing fitness (Wu and Williams, 2001). Similarly, youth engaged in physical activity have been reported to increase their independence and experience social connectedness (Goodwin and Staples, 2005; Goodwin and Watkinson, 2000). Taub *et al.* (1999) found that college-aged male youth experiencing disability felt that sport counteracted the stigma they experienced. There are further examples from research with adults that illustrate those who counter writing the story of disability as vulnerability and weakness. For example, female wheelchair basketball players highlighted their resistance against stereotypes of women with disabilities being weak and non-athletic (Ashton-Shaeffer *et al.*, 2001). Blinde and McClung (1997) reported that participation in sport enabled women and men to experience their bodies in new ways, to improve perceptions of their physical characteristics, to refine their physical capabilities, and to increase their sport-related confidence.

Biography management

Policies on sport and inclusion have primarily been the domain of adults and largely ignore the voices of youth (Barry, 2005). Youth 'gaze upwards' (Barry, 2005, p. 2) through a social hierarchy. Youth experiencing disability, in addition to their state of dependency on adults for protection as legal minors, are also challenged by adult-imposed perceptions of inability and vulnerability (Carnevale, 2004).

Disability sport, although still very much the domain of secondary agents, such as coaches and administrators, is a forum for self-definition. Wheelchair sport, for example, is a space where women 'can resist the dominant discourse of disability' as they experienced the benefits derived from sport on 'their identity, self-confidence, motivation, friendships, travel, health and fitness, and purpose in life' (Ashton-Shaeffer *et al.*, 2001, p. 16). Resistance to the perceptions held of female sports was further expressed by a female Paralympian who stated, 'We have a different biology and history; it is wrong to assume that we have the same sport interests and expectations as an able bodied women athlete' (Olenik *et al.*, 1995, p. 55).

Sense of community

Disability sport can create a sense of belonging, influence, fulfillment of needs, and a shared emotional connection through a psychological sense of community (Villa *et al.*, 2003).

When minority communities define group identities from within; creating feelings of community solidarity, advocacy, activism, and emancipation, positive outcomes may result (Villa *et al.*, 2003). It can be argued that disability sport is a minority community that creates, gives meaning to, establishes a unique history, and delineates customs by the authentic sense of identity of its members (DePauw and Doll Tepper, 2000). Villa *et al.* also state that community identification occurs in disability sport as the players create a counter normative respect for differences through visibility and the creation of their own forms of play.

In wheelchair rugby, for example, adult athletes spoke about the positive qualities of their community and their enhanced sense of confidence in public settings; they felt powerful, welcome, and connected to their sport community (Goodwin *et al.*, 2009). A similar sense of community was also found among youth wheelchair dancers who experienced interdependent relationships, shared responsibilities, common goals, and a sense of belonging consistent with stable communities (Goodwin *et al.*, 2004). Likewise, within the sport of wheelchair racing, elite athletes were found to support non-elite athletes with the cultural material of their sport thereby creating membership into, and enabling access to, the larger collective. Although the benefits of disability sport have been highlighted in this section of inclusion resulting from engagement in sport, it is important to note that the disability athlete voice is all but silent in the sociology of disability sport literature, which itself is very limited (Peers, 2009; Williams, 1994b). So, although sport can act to include youth experiencing disability, it can also negatively impact young athletes through established practices of prejudice, discrimination, attitude hierarchies, ambivalence, and stigmatization (Sherrill, 1997).

Cultural context of inclusion/exclusion

In this section, we interrogate how the greater social inclusion of those who experience disabilities might be analyzed and mobilized *through* sport. This inclusion-through-sport discussion is based upon an understanding of sport as a complex and socially constructed site that can reflect, reproduce and potentially resist social inequalities (DePauw, 1997; Donnelly, 1996; Sage, 1993). Correspondingly, we ask two questions of youth sport. First, in what ways does contemporary youth sport reflect the state of disability inclusion in wider society? Second, how might certain structures or practices in youth sport serve to reproduce and/or resist disability-based social inequality and exclusion?

Sport as reflective of society

The significantly lower levels of sport participation by youth experiencing disability, as compared to their non-disabled peers (Active Healthy Kids Canada, 2009; Australian Bureau of Statistics, 2009; Sport England, 2001), should not be understood as a sport-specific problem. Rather, this disparity reflects significantly lower rates of disability inclusion in many other social spheres, most notably, employment (Australian Bureau of Statistics, 2006; Bergeskog, 2001; UK National Statistics, 2004).

Furthermore, the major models that have been embraced by sport to deal with this exclusion are also reflective of the inclusion strategies embraced by Western societies as a whole. As with sport, those who experience disabilities are often *included* in society through the creation of segregated programs and structures such as separate schools, classes, housing and transportation systems (Oliver, 1990; Prince, 2009; Shakespeare, 2006). Like sport, these segregated systems remove many of the disabling barriers from essential services; however, they do so in a way that reifies 'difference' and supports medical models of disability, enabling mainstream social structures to remain inaccessible and exclusive (Howe and Jones, 2006; Oliver, 1990). Inclusion is also, however, often sought through the mainstreaming model, most notably in public education (Prince, 2009; Ravaud and Stiker, 2001; Shakespeare, 2006). This mainstreaming, much like its sports equivalent, tends to take the form of 'placing' those who experience disabilities in mainstream institutions without investing adequate financial and human resources to transform these institutions into barrier-free environments (Culham and Nind, 2003; DePauw and Doll-Tepper, 2000; Ravaud and Stiker, 2001). Within sport and other mainstreaming contexts, this enables certain individuals to integrate successfully, while simultaneously leading to the nominal inclusion, effective exclusion, and continued disablement of others who are unable or unwilling to 'normalize' themselves enough to 'overcome' the remaining barriers (Culham and Nind, 2003; Titchkosky, 2007).

The third mean by which youth sport is reflective of society is the way that those who experience disabilities, as well as their allies, have created innovative methods of re-imagining and mobilizing toward more meaningfully inclusive structures: sporting or otherwise. For example, rather than segregated accessible spaces, or integrated spaces with barriers, proponents of universal design are finding ways in which *all* new and retrofitted architecture, outdoor spaces, websites, transportation, pedagogies and technologies could be made to be barrier-free (Afacan and Erbug 2009; Burgstahler, 2007; Comden and Burgstahler, 2005; Pullin, 2009). Two other related examples are the independent living movement (US) and the disability movement (UK), wherein those who experience disabilities have mobilized resources with the aim of liberating themselves from social exclusion, cultural de-valuation, and the paternalistic control of disability industry professionals (Clare, 1999; Oliver, 1990; Peters *et al.*, 2009). Similar to sport, therefore, grass-roots innovation and mobilization are creating alternative ways of thinking about, and going about, inclusion.

Sport as reproducing and restricting disability-based exclusion

There are ways in which youth sport not only reflects, but also serves to reproduce the exclusions and inequities of disability. Youth sport, like all sport, is constructed in such a way as to enable the participation, success and normalization of those with culturally privileged bodies and aptitudes, while differentiating, devaluing and/or excluding other kinds of embodiment (DePauw, 1997; Donnelly, 1996; Sage, 1993; Shogan, 1998). For example, the rules and structures of a sport such as basketball, in its seemingly 'unadapted' form, are already adapted to privilege tall, ambulatory bipeds who can both see the ball and hear the referee's whistle. Within mainstream basketball, therefore, the success of tall, ambulatory and sensory-conforming youth, at the expense of other youth, serves to reproduce the 'naturalness' and seeming superiority of these kinds of *able bodies*.

Segregated disability sport is also implicated in this sporting logic. Although disability sport can provide opportunity for positive identity development and protection and reassurance of its individual members, at the institutional level it can reinforce ableism. The systemic differentiation of disability sport from *normal* sport, for example, serves to reproduce the idea that disability and able-bodiedness are static, dichotomous, individual-based bodily differences rather than contextual and fluctuating socially produced categories and, furthermore, that disability sport is a derivative, adapted version of *natural* able-bodied (male) sport (Fitzgerald and Kirk, 2009; Shogan, 1998). In other words, both of the most common models of *inclusive* youth sport assume a sporting logic that systemically differentiates, de-values, disables and excludes youth, while simultaneously serving to construct this exclusion and disablement as *natural*.

Despite this, there are ways in which specific athletes, practices, structures or discourses within sport can potentially serve to resist or de-naturalize disability-based exclusion and oppression. There are opportunities within mainstream sport, for example, for youth and sport leaders to begin to recognize and disassemble the socially disabling architecture, rules and attitudes that may disable certain members of their community. Similarly, there are opportunities within segregated disability sport for youth to recognize how their marginalization is shared by their teammates and, therefore, to mobilize around changing the disabling social structures, instead of internalizing the social oppression. There are also opportunities within innovative sport structures, such as integrated wheelchair basketball, to de-naturalize the dichotomy of the able and the disabled. There are even opportunities, some argue, for disabled sporting bodies to not only resist disability-based exclusion, but also to fundamentally challenge 'our socially constructed views of the body, ability, athletic performance, and sport' more generally (DePauw, 1997, p. 426).

Understanding inclusion

In summary, inclusion of youth experiencing disability in sport, recreation and leisure has been aimed at enhancing social relationships, providing meaningful supports, and providing involvement in the activities that are typical of age-matched peers who do not experience disabilities (Roberts, 2005). What is not explicit in our understanding or definition of inclusion is the inherent expectation that those whom we include will assimilate themselves, and conform to the values and aspirations of the mainstream group. As DePauw (1997) argues,

> Historically, sport has tended to reflect the dominant values, norms, and standards of a given society . . . that has privileged the sporting bodies of primarily White, heterosexual, able-bodied males from the middle and upper classes.
>
> (p. 418)

Increasingly, the counter story of sport as self-affirming, identity enhancing, and character building is being told from the perspective of youth (e.g. DePauw, 2000; Block, 1999). In such research, young people have told us that although inclusive recreational and instructional settings can be self-affirming, they can also be socially isolating, exclusionary, and result in loss of independence (e.g. Blinde and McCallister, 1998; Fitzgerald *et al.*, 2003; Goodwin, 2009; Place and Hodge, 2001). Why have the negative social experiences of inclusion in youth sport been inaccessible? We contend that three forces may have been at work:

*   ethical disregard;
*   discipline roots;
*   youth acquiescence.

Ethical disregard

Those who practice in the field of adapted physical activity and disability sport may hold to a school of thought called virtue ethics. Ethics are about 'right or wrong' or 'ought and ought not' in human behavior (Oberle and Raffin Bouchal, 2009). Virtue ethics is based on the premise that good people will make good decisions and as such it, 'appeals to our intuitive sense that one who cares for vulnerable people ought to demonstrate particular personal characteristics' (p. 11). Virtues can be learned, so if adapted physical activity and disability sport attracts people who believe themselves to be virtuous and are reinforced for their 'good work' (practice) with those considered to be tragic, the need for reflection on ethical professional practice becomes redundant and 'too posh to ponder' (Updale, 2008, p. 34). The lack of debate on ethical practice is reason for concern. Considerable and considered discussion is needed to translate ethical frameworks into meaningful actions for professional practice and the preparation of future professionals (DePauw, 2009; Goodwin, 2009).

Discipline roots

Virtue ethics may be an indication of the historical roots of adapted physical activity. Those involved in youth sport often come from the academic discipline of kinesiology, which has its historical roots in anatomical studies and the field of medicine (DePauw, 1997). The sentiment that disability is tragic (Clapton, 2003) provides a platform for interventionists to rehabilitate and normalize a problem perceived to be largely medically based (Hutzler, 2008; Peters, 1996; Wheeler, 1998). The shift in thinking away from 'normalizing' the body to one that emphasizes the socio-cultural context of how normal, and hence abnormal, is constructed has been very recent (DePauw, 2000).

Space for the concepts of personhood, autonomy, and dignity may receive secondary priority (Goodwin *et al.*, 2007) as we have become preoccupied with 'doing for' as reflected in the phrase, 'Just don't stand there, do something.' A relational ethics perspective would suggest that there is tremendous merit in the opposite of not *doing for*, as reflected in the phrase 'Don't just do something, stand there' (Austin *et al.*, 2003, p. 46). As well as doing for others, relational ethics speaks to the importance of relationship building and the need for real involvement so as 'to understand the other's situation, perspective, and vulnerability' (p. 47).

Youth acquiescence

Silent voices of youth experiencing disability involved in recreation and sport may reflect their compliance socialization rather than their recognition of the merits of their own judgment and experiential perspectives. Professional superiority creates a state of 'otherness' that perpetuates a social hierarchy (Hanford, 1993). As well as silencing that occurs through external forces, acquiescing at the hands of those who impose sanctions occurs for risk of being given a bad name, being labeled as a trouble maker, or being shunned by others (Updale, 2008).

Closing thoughts

In closing, sport pedagogy, or the intersection of instructor/coach, learner and the knowledge they produce together is fraught with ethical questions, whether applied to educational, recreational or sport contexts, is a moral activity (Goodwin, 2008). Attention to professional ethics is the responsibility of universities as they prepare career professionals in adapted physical activity and allied profession-als who contribute to disability sport as their 'pedagogical work' (Standal, 2008, p. 211). Researchers and instructors of higher education have a moral obligation and social responsibility to imbed questions of ethical practice and conduct into their teaching and share their own moral discomfort to which there is often not a clear answer (DePauw, 2009).

Notes

1 We acknowledge that the participants and organizers of the Deaflympics may not char-acterize themselves as having disabilities but, rather, as being part of a linguistic and cultural minority. Having said this, the eligibility of Deaf athletes is predicated upon a medical diagnosis of hearing loss, which creates a similar sporting structure to that of disability sport (DePauw and Gavron, 1995; International Committee of Sports for the Deaf, 2010).
2 Classification is a process whereby each athlete is assigned to a specific, hierarchical, alpha-numeric category (e.g. class S1 or class 3.5), based on their diagnosed level of impairment or their assessed level of sport-specific function (DePauw and Gavron, 1995; Howe, 2008).

References

A very special cricket tournament (2003) *Disability News and Information Service for India.* 1 (6). Online: www.dnis.org/news.php?issueid=6andvolumeid=1 andnewsid=85andi=3 (accessed 2 March 2010).

Active Healthy Kids Canada (2009) *Physical activity and inactivity* Online: Available from: www.activehealthykids.ca/ReportCard/PhysicalActivityandInactivity.aspx (accessed March 21 2010).

Afacan, Y. and Erbug, C. (2009) An interdisciplinary heuristic evaluation method for universal building design. *Applied Ergonomics*, 40 (4): 731–744.

Ashton-Schaeffer, C., Gibson, H., Holt, M. *et al.* (2001) Women's resistance and empower-ment through wheelchair sport. *World Leisure*, 2 (1): 11–21.

Austin, W., Bergum, V. and Dossetor, J. (2003) Relational ethics: an action ethic as a foundation of health care. In Tschudin, V. (ed.) *Approaches in Ethics: nursing beyond boundaries.* Woburn: Butterworth-Heinemann, pp. 45–52.

Australian Bureau of Statistics (2006) *Year Book Australia* Online: www.abs.gov.au/aus-stats/abs@.nsf/Previousproducts/1301.0FeatureArticle14200 6?opendocumentandtabna me=Summaryandprodno=1301.0andissue=2006andnu m=andview= (accessed 2 March 2010).

Australian Bureau of Statistics (2009) *Perspectives on Sport* Online: www. abs.gov.au/ausstats/abs@.nsf/Products/4156.0.55.001~Dec+2009~MaIn+Fe atures~Participation+In+Sport+by+People+with+a+Disability?OpenDocument (accessed 2 March 2010).

Barry, M. (2005) Introduction. In Barry, M. (ed.) *Youth Policy and Social Inclusion: critical debates with young people.* Oxford: Routledge, pp.1–8.

Bergeskog, A. (2001) Labour Market Policies, Strategies and Statistics for People with Disabilities: a cross-national comparison. Uppsala: Office of Labour Market Policy Evaluation.

Blinde, E.M. and McClung, L.R. (1997) Enhancing the physical and social self through recreational activity: Accounts of individuals. *Adapted Physical Activity Quarterly*, 14 (4): 327–344.

Blinde, M. and McCallister, S. (1998) Listening to the voices of students with disabilities. *Journal of Physical Education, Recreation, and Dance*, 69 (2): 64–68.

Block, M.E. (1999) Did we jump on the wrong bandwagon? Problems with inclusion in physical education. *Palaestra*, 15 (3): 30–36.

Brasile, F.M. (1990) Wheelchair sports: a new perspective on integration. *Adapted Physical Activity Quarterly*, 7 (1): 3–11.

Burgstahler, S. (2007) Who needs an accessible classroom? *Academe*, 93 (3): 37–39.

Canada Games Committee (2007) *Canada Games Media Information Package: Wheelchair basketball*. Online: www.canadagames.ca/Images/Games/2007%20Media%20Packages/FINAL%20WHEELCHAIR%20BASKETBALL%20ENGLISH.pdf (accessed 3 January 2010).

Carnevale, F. (2004) Listening authentically to youthful voices: a conception of the moral agency of children. In Storch, J. (ed.) *Nursing Ethics*. Toronto: Person Education Canada, pp. 396–413.

Clapton, J. (2003) Tragedy and catastrophe: contentious discourses of ethics and disability. *Journal of Intellectual Disability Research*, 47 (7): 540–547.

Clare, E. (1999) *Exile and pride: disability, queerness, and liberation*, 2nd edn. Cambridge, MA: South End Press.

Comden, D. and Burgstahler, S. (2005) World wide access: accessible web design. *Hudson Valley Business Journal*, 16 (2): 24.

Culham, A. and Nind, M. (2003) Deconstructing normalisation: clearing the way for inclusion. *Journal of Intellectual and Developmental Disability*, 28 (1): 65–78.

DePauw, K. (1997) The (in)visibility of disability: cultural contexts and sporting bodies. *Quest*, 49 (4): 416–430.

DePauw, K. (2000) Social-cultural context of disability: implications for scientific inquiry and professional preparation. *Quest*, 52 (3): 358–368.

DePauw, K. (2009) Ethics, professional expectations, and graduate education–advancing research in kinesiology. *Quest*, 6 (1): 52–59.

DePauw, K. and Doll-Tepper, G. (2000) Toward progressive inclusion and acceptance: myth or reality? The inclusion debate and bandwagon discourse. *Adapted Physical Activity Quarterly*, 17 (2): 135–143.

DePauw, K. and Gavron, S.J. (2005) *Disability Sport*, 2nd edn. Champaign: Human Kinetics.

Donnelly, P. (1996) Approaches to social inequality in the sociology of sport. *Quest*, 48 (2): 221–242.

Fitzgerald, H. and Kirk, D. (2009) Physical education as a normalizing practice: is there a space for disability sport? In Fitzgerald, H. (ed.) *Disability and Youth Sport*. London: Routledge, pp. 91–105.

Fitzgerald, H., Jobling, A. and Kirk, D. (2003) Valuing the voices of young disabled people: exploring experience of physical education and sport. *European Journal of Physical Education*, 8 (2): 175–200.

Gill, C.J. (1997) Four types of integration in disability identity development. *Journal of Vocational Rehabilitation*, 9: 39–46.

Goodwin, D. (2008) Self-regulated dependency: ethical reflections on interdependence and help in adapted physical activity. *Sport, Ethics and Philosophy*, 2 (2): 172–184.

Goodwin, D. (2009) The voices of students with disabilities: are they informing inclusive physical education practice? In Fitzgerald, H. (ed.) *Disability and Youth Sport.* London: Routledge, pp. 53–75.

Goodwin, D. and Staples, K. (2005) The meaning of summer camp experiences to youths with disabilities. *Adapted Physical Activity Quarterly*, 22 (2): 160–178.

Goodwin, D. and Watkinson, J. (2000) Inclusive physical education from the perspective of students with physical disabilities. *Adapted Physical Activity Quarterly*, 17 (2): 144–160.

Goodwin, D., Krohn, J. and Kuhnle, A. (2004) Beyond the wheelchair: the experience of dance. *Adapted Physical Activity Quarterly*, 23 (3): 229–247.

Groff, D.G. and Kleiber, D.A. (2001) Exploring the identity formation of youth involved in an adapted sports program. *Therapeutic Recreation Journal*, 35 (4): 318–332.

Hahn, H. (1984) Sports and the political movement of disabled persons: examining nondisabled social values. *ARENA Review*, 8 (1): 1–15.

Hanford, L. (1993) Ethics and disability. *British Journal of Nursing (BJN)*, 2 (19): 979–982.

Hardin, M. and Hardin, B. (2005) Performance or participation . . . pluralism or hegemony? Images of disability and gender in Sports 'n Spokes Magazine. *Disability Studies Quarterly*, 25 (4). Online: www.dsq-sds.org/_articles_html/2005/fall/hardIn.asp (accessed 17 November 2007).

Howe, P.D. (2008) The Cultural Politics of the Paralympic Movement: through an anthropological lens. London: Routledge.

Howe, P.D. and Jones, C. (2006) Classification of disabled athletes: (Dis)empowering the Paralympic practice community. *Sociology of Sport Journal*, 23 (1): 29–46.

Hutzler, Y. (2008) Ethical considerations in adapted physical activity practices. *Sport, Ethics and Philosophy*, 2 (2): 158–171.

International Committee of Sports for the Deaf (2010) *About.* Online: www.deaflympics.com/about/ (accessed 26 February 2010).

International Wheelchair Rugby Federation (2010) *About the Sport of Wheelchair Rugby.* Online: www.iwrf.com/history.htm (accessed 2 March 2010).

IPC Swimming (2010*) General Information.* Online: www.ipcswimming.org/Classification/GeneralInformation/ (accessed 28 February 2010).

Juniors (2009) *Sports 'n Spokes Magazine*, 35 (2): 46–47.

KentSport (*2007*) *Kent Teams Celebrate Sporting Success.* Online: www.kentsport.org/news_dis_games_june07.cfm (accessed 1 March 2010).

Martin, J.J. (2008) Multidimensional self-efficacy and affect in wheelchair basketball players. *Adapted Physical Activity Quarterly*, 25: 275–288.

Martin, J.J., Adams-Mushett, C. and Smith, K.L. (1995). Athletic identity and sport orientation of adolescent swimmers with disabilities. *Adapted Physical Activity Quarterly*, 12 (2): 113–123.

McRuer, R. (2006) Compulsory able-bodiedness and queer/disabled existence. In Davis, L.J. (ed.) *The Disability Studies Reader*, 2nd edn. New York: Routledge, pp. 301–308.

Nixon, H.L. (2007) Constructing diverse sports opportunities for people with disabilities. *Journal of Sport and Social Issues*, 31 (4): 417–433.

Oberle, K. and Raffin Bouchal, S. (2009). *Ethics in Canadian Nursing Practice: navigating the journey.* Toronto: Prentice Hall.

Olenik, L., Matthews, J. and Steadward, R. (1995) Women, disability and sport. *Canadian Women's Studies*, 15 (1): 54–57.

Oliver, M. (1990) *The Politics of Disablement.* Basingstoke: Macmillan.

Page, S., O'Connor, E. and Peterson, K. (2001) Leaving the disability Ghetto: a qualitative study of factors underlying achievement motivation among athletes with disabilities. *Journal of Sport and Social Issues*, 25 (1): 40–55.

Peers, D. (2009) (Dis)empowering Paralympic histories: absent athletes and disabling discourses. *Disability and Society*, 24 (5): 653–665.

Peters, P.D. (1996) Disablement observed, addressed, and experienced: integrating subjective experience into disablement models. *Disability and Rehabilitation*, 18 (12): 593–603.

Peters, S., Gabel, S. and Symeonidou, S. (2009) Resistance, transformation and the politics of hope: imagining a way forward for the disabled people's movement. *Disability and Society*, 24 (5): 543–556.

Place, K. and Hodge, S. (2001) Social inclusion of students with disabilities in general physical education: A behavioral analysis. *Adapted Physical Activity Quarterly*, 18 (4): 389–404.

Prince, M.J. (2009) Absent Citizens: disability politics and policy in Canada. Toronto: University of Toronto Press.

Promis, D., Erevelles, N. and Matthews, J. (2001) Reconceptualizing inclusion: the politics of university sports and recreation programs for students with mobility impairments. *Sociology of Sport Journal*, 18 (1): 37–50.

Pullin, G. (2009) *Design Meets Disability*. Cambridge, MA: MIT Press.

Ravaud, J.F. and Stiker, H.J. (2001) Inclusion/exclusion: An analysis of historical and cultural meanings. In Albrecht, G.L., Seelman, K.D. and Bury, M. (eds) *Handbook of Disability Studies*. Thousand Oaks: Sage, pp. 490–513.

Roberts, K. (2005) Youth, leisure and social inclusion. In Barry, M. (ed.) *Youth Policy and Social Inclusion: Critical debates with young people.* Oxford: Routledge, pp. 117–132.

Sage, G.H. (1993) Sport and physical education and the new world order: dare we be agents of social change? *Quest*, 45 (2): 151–164.

Shakespeare, T. (2006) *Disability Rights and Wrongs*. London: Routledge.

Sherrill, C. (1997) Disability, identity, and involvement in sport and exercise. In Fox, K.R. (ed.) *The Physical Self: from motivation to well being*. Champaign: Human Kinetics, pp. 257–286.

Shogan, D. (1998) The social construction of disability: the impact of statistics and technology. *Adapted Physical Activity Quarterly*, 15 (3): 269–277.

Smith, A. and Thomas, N. (2005) The 'inclusion' of elite athletes with disabilities in the 2002 Manchester Commonwealth Games: An exploratory analysis of British newspaper coverage. *Sport, Education and Society*, 10 (1): 49–67.

Special Olympics (2010) *Athlete Resources*. Online: www.specialolympics.org/athlete_resources.aspx (accessed 2 March 2010).

Sport England (2001) *Disability Survey 2000: Young people with a disability and sport* Online: www.sportengland.org/research (accessed 23 March 2010).

Standal, O. (2008) Celebrating the insecure practitioner: A critique of evidence-based practice in adapted physical activity. *Sport, Ethics and Philosophy*, 2 (2): 200–215.

Stephens, J. (2007) The wall of silence. *Volleyball*, 18 (3): 52–52.

Taub, D.E., Blinde, E.M. and Greer, K.R. (1999) Stigma management through participation in sport and physical activity: Experiences of male college students with physical disabilities. *Human Relations*, 52 (11): 1469–1484.

Titchkosky, T. (2007) Reading and Writing disability Differently: the textured life of embodiment. Toronto: University of Toronto Press.

Tokyo 2016 Olympic Bid (2009) *Tokyo 2009 Asian Youth Paralympic Games*. Online: www. disabled-world.com/sports/asian-youth-paralympics.php (accessed 2 March 2010).

Tripp, A., French, R. and Sherrill, C. (1995) Contact theory and attitudes of children in physical education programs toward peers with disabilities. *Adapted Physical Activity Quarterly*, 12 (4): 323–332.

Tripp, A., Rizzo, T.L. and Webbert, L. (2007) Inclusion in physical education: Changing the culture. *The Journal of Physical Education, Recreation and Dance*, 78 (2): 32–36; 48.

UK National Statistics (2004) *Focus on Social Inequalities*. Online: www.statistics.gov. uk/focuson/#social (accessed 23 March 2010).

Updale, E. (2008) The ethics of the everyday: problems the professors are too posh to ponder. *Clinical Ethics*, 3 (1): 34–36–111.

Van Hilvoorde, I. and Landeweerd, L. (2008) Disability or extraordinary talent – Francesco Lentin (three legs) versus Oscar Pistorius (no legs). *Sport, Ethics and Philosophy*, 2 (2): 97–111.

Villa, I., Crost, M., Ravaud, J.F. *et al.* (2003) Disability and a sense of community belonging: A study among tetraplegic spinal-cord-injured persons in France. *Social Science and Medicine*, 56 (2): 321–332.

Wheeler, G.D. (1998) Challenging our assumption in the biological area of adapted physical activity: a reaction to Shephard. *Adapted Physical Activity Quarterly*, 15 (3): 236–249.

Williams, T. (1994a) Disability sport socialization and identity construction. *Adapted Physical Activity Quarterly*, 1 (1): 14–31.

Williams, T. (1994b) Sociological perspectives on sport and disability: structural-functionalism. *Physical Education Review*, 17 (1): 14–24.

Wolff, E.A. and Hums, M.A. (2006) Sport and human rights. *Chronicle of Kinesiology and Physical Education in Higher Education*, 17 (2): 3–4.

Wu, S. and Williams, T. (2001) Factors influencing sport participation among athletes with disabilities. *Medicine and Science in Sports and Exercise*, 33 (2): 177–182.

14 Facilitating positive experiences of physical education and school sport for Muslim girls

Haifaa Jawad, Tansin Benn and Symeon Dagkas

Introduction

In the UK, in 2007, schools in an English, Midlands local education authority reported that increasing numbers of Muslim parents were withdrawing their daughters from physical education (PE). Reasons were related to parental concerns about schools' lack of ability to meet religious and cultural needs; for example, modesty in dress codes and sex-separation (Benn *et al*., 2011b; Flintoff, 2010). Headteachers approached the city's Advisory Support Services (BASS) requesting firmer guidelines to address the issues, hence the commissioning of the BASS study. The study investigated Muslim girls' participation in physical education and school sport from multiple perspectives and provided evidence-based guidance to inform future policy and practice. Here aspects of the study relating to emergent issues, dilemmas and solutions towards more inclusive pedagogical practices are shared. The tensions headteachers faced in their schools were between meeting the statutory requirements to deliver the English national curriculum entitlement for physical education, while safeguarding religious freedom by meeting the religious requirements of Muslim pupils.

A team of eight researchers, including Islamic studies and physical education subject specialists, city advisors, and teachers, collected mixed-methods data on experiences, issues, concerns and solutions related to participation of Muslim girls in physical education. Eight in-depth case studies were conducted across primary, secondary and Muslim state schools including interviews with nineteen headteachers and teachers (two were Muslim), focus group interviews with 109 pupils and thirty-two parents. Thirty-six young people participated in four city community/supplementary schools for Muslim communities. Thematic analysis allowed issues and concerns related to exclusive and inclusive pedagogies to emerge, and to be more fully understood by triangulating a range of perspectives: headteachers, PE teachers, pupils and parents.

The BASS Project was situated in one of two cities in the UK estimated to reach a majority black and ethnic minority population in the near future, of which the predominantly Muslim population of Pakistani and Bangladeshi heritage will be the largest group. Such knowledge further emphasises the need to pursue deeper understanding of the challenges and dilemmas faced in pursuing inclusive practices in increasingly multi-faith, multicultural societies.

'Locating the gap'

Predominantly research in this aspect of inclusion has emerged since the 1990s when the equality debate in the West moved from 'treating everyone the same' to one of seeking justice and fairness through the concept of 'equity'; that is, respecting and valuing difference (Carol and Holinshead, 1993; Sarwar, 1994). With the issue of Muslim girls' participation in physical education there is a double-bind situation between the struggle for gender equity (the rights of girls and women, Azzarito and Solmon, 2005; see also Chapter 5), and respecting difference in cultural diversity (the rights of ethnic groups). The rights of all children to participation in physical education are enshrined in global aspirations (ICSSPE, 1999). UNESCO, WHO and IOC have raised awareness of the particular role of school physical education in providing a secure, safe environment for women and girls to gain the skills, understanding and confidence to participate in lifelong physical activity. Despite this documented support for the importance of physical education, physical activity and health (Bailey, 2005), Muslim girls and women in particular are still lagging behind boys and men in terms of sporting opportunity (Dagkas *et al.*, 2011).

According to Abbas (2006) and Shilling (2008), migration patterns that have resulted in increasingly diverse societies, particularly in the West, have led to a resurgence of importance in debates about religion in recent years. Religious resurgence has not only been seen in Europe and the US but also in Africa, the Middle East, Asia and South America. Islam has become 'Europe's second religion' alongside other religions such as new forms of Charismatic Christianity and New Age paths to spiritual fulfilment (ibid., p. 150). Benn *at al.* (2011b) maintain that what has been underdeveloped in current debate is any sense of the spiritual self; for example, of religious identity and the struggles of people in different faiths for the basic human right to 'manifest one's religion or beliefs' (Human Rights Act, 1998).

Culture shapes values, attitudes and beliefs which determine behaviours and life choices. Learning about the cultures in which we live is a means of making sense of the world. Schools, physical education and lived Islam are all imbued with cultural significance through which traditions and practices are both transmitted and transformed (Benn *et al.*, 2011). For example in Britain, diverse thriving cultural dance forms are shared and celebrated in education, often in physical education where dance is currently located in the national curriculum. Cultural dance forms are acknowledged as important sites for reaffirmation, development and sharing of cultural heritage in diverse societies. Fears of sexualised body movements and associations between dance and (Western) popular culture (see also Chapter 17) make this activity area problematic in some Muslim communities (Benn, 2005).

Tensions between cultural practices of Islam and physical education have been identified, for example, in preferred dress codes, mixed/single-sex groupings, attitudes towards the body related to privacy and modesty, extra-curricular activities, Ramadan, swimming and dance activities. The Islamic requirements for modesty and privacy are not addressed in traditional school sport uniform requirements for short skirts, shorts and T-shirts, or practices such as public changing and show-ering situations. Furthermore, after puberty many Muslim families prefer sex-segregation for physical activities. While some secondary schools in the UK are sex segregated or have segregated organisation in physical education, many do not since the post-1970s drive to co-education (Dagkas and Benn, 2006). It is also important to remember that during Ramadan many Muslims fast from sunrise to sunset so energy levels and hydration are risk factors in physical education and sporting activities. Swimming can also be problematic because of the mixed-sex public nature of swimming baths, and there is no consensus in Islam about the educational value of some curriculum subjects such as dance and music. Such ten-sions can continue into adulthood with many Muslim girls choosing to opt out of physical education and sport environments.

Where school or sport environments challenge the right of young Muslim women to embody their faith the result, in too many cases, is non-participation, negotia-tion or coercion. Dominant Western school and sport models have developed in the context of perceptions of body cultures and social interaction patterns that are not shared globally. Those who pursue freedom to maintain outward manifestation of 'embodied faith' (Benn, 2009; see also Chapter 8) often as diaspora communities in non-Islamic Western countries (Kay, 2006), seek accommodation of difference as minorities in predominantly secular societies.

Negotiating change in policy and practice

The BASS Project was a collaborative research process that built bridges between research and practice in both process and outcome, resulting in the formulation of policy-orientated guidance for schools. Shared commitment to a social values approach guided volunteer participants as well as researchers who chose to engage in a study to address the impasse between religious freedom and educational prac-tices. The study involved gathering data on experiences, issues, concerns and solu-tions across city schools and multiple stakeholders. This enabled connections to be made between theory and practice that could be meaningful to those seeking solutions to current tensions. What follows is an account of the emergent areas of interest at the interface of tensions regarding Islamic culture and physical educa-tion policy and practices. To deepen understanding of tensions and solutions the voices of the stakeholders – young people, parents, teachers and headteachers engaged in the BASS study – are shared to illustrate why local negotiation of dif-ference is the most appropriate way of seeking solutions.

Evidence of pedagogical problems and solutions for the inclusion of Muslim girls in physical education

PE and body modesty

The most '*successful*' schools in providing inclusive practices (if we adopt the view that inclusion represents respect and responds to the needs of Muslim girls) were those with clear policies and senior management support for whole-school participation. Good policies contained information on school expectations and requirements with explanations, for example, of the need to meet health and safety standards.

Evidence from city primary schools indicated, particularly as children approached 10–11 years of age, that the need for privacy in changing for PE was often managed creatively. Strategies included using additional adult supervision, separate classrooms or spaces, combined classes, towelling covers, and screening to allow girls and boys some privacy. As headteachers commented in interviews:

> Because we are a primary school I think it is easier for us. We don't experience many difficulties . . . boys and girls change separately from year 1 upwards. That has a big staffing issue . . . but we want our children to have this. We use teachers and teaching supports.
>
> (Female headteacher)

> We combine classes and use spare spaces so boys and girls can change in some privacy.
>
> (Male headteacher)

The extent to which even very young children can be distressed by lack of privacy is evidenced in the following extract from an interview with a primary school headteacher:

> One or two children refused to take part in physical education. They felt it was incorrect to see other children baring their arms and legs.

Many primary schools had adopted shorts and T-shirts for physical education, and they encountered little resistance. When requested, however, schools were usually able to accommodate needs related to modesty by allowing children to wear tracksuits in order to cover their arms and legs. There was also evidence of growing accommodation of the 'wearing of hijab.' In schools that had previously banned the wearing of headscarves in all-female contexts, there were signs of a change in policy, and this is indicative of situations that were in a constant state of flux in response to changes in the dynamics of school life. The most successful 'inclusive' schools identified in this study were those where pupils had contributed to the design of kit, thus acknowledging the needs of the pupils in that school and accommodating faith-based modesty codes:

> All students are allowed to wear tracksuit trousers so that they don't need to show their legs. So the non-Muslim students do too. Likewise girls can wear tops with long sleeves and they can wear hijab, many do secure them round their head so that it's not likely to cause any problem. So we accommodate what is required for the Muslim girls to participate.
>
> (Female PE teacher)

In addition the project revealed mixed responses on issues related to specific reference to the needs of Muslim pupils in physical education policies. Most schools recognised and accommodated the requirements wherever practicable. The most evident actions for accommodation were in the schools with the highest Muslim populations but there was also recognition and accommodation in schools with less than 5 per cent Muslim pupils. The experiences of Muslim boys were also raised by some schools; although this was more evident in secondary schools. One school raised similar concerns for modesty in relation to the need for privacy in changing. The school was able to respond by building individual showering cubicles. Another example was a concern raised in a mixed school by parents about boys showing their legs. Situations were managed through meetings with parents and allowing 'respectful kit' (male PE teacher).

Secondary schools varied considerably in their organisation, some operating mixed-sex physical education and others single-sex provision. It was noted that facilities always include separate-sex changing rooms, but the problem is they often do not have individual cubicle facilities that would offer the greatest privacy. New school facilities often have dual usage for school and local community, yet it has been argued that in some cases, the needs of the local community have been ignored 'rendering them unusable for 97% of the local community' (Muslim Council of Britain). In other projects community discussions have featured highly in design:

> We are lucky to have that [sports hall] used by the school in the day and community in the evening. It was designed by the local community – separate walkway from women's changing room into the hall so they did not have to go through reception, and the ability to cover the windows so people can't see in – lots of classes for women in the community – all of which will help.
>
> (Headteacher)

In schools the importance of home liaison staff and Muslim colleagues in resolving communication problems was highly valued at primary and secondary levels. As is evident in the earlier chapters in this volume, teachers were concerned that parents did not always understand the basics of the national curriculum: 'Parents need to be aware of the fact that physical education is compulsory and what physical education actually is in a school' (female teacher). Indeed some parents believed they could withdraw their daughters from physical education for religious reasons. Exchange of information through clear school policies and induction procedures gave access to clear school/subject expectations and systems, thus fostering good relations; 'We work very closely with parents firstly to increase knowledge of the importance of physical education and sport' (female headteacher).

Secondary pupils took more responsibility for their own 'embodiment of faith' and more personal decisions on dress codes, but there was no clear consensus found (see also Dagkas and Benn, Chapter 8). For some adolescent girls in mixed-sex environments, there was little tolerance for the more radical views of peers who were perceived to be creating tensions by requesting accommodation of difference in their schools: 'religion does not stop you [referring to participation in PE]. If mixing with boys is likely to be a problem then go to a girls' school, similarly if your parents have a problem with that' (Muslim girl). Similarly, dialogue took place with a group of Muslim girls about the prospect of male coaches, and the views expressed reflect multiple positions on preferences for more modest dress or sex-segregation. Such variation in viewpoints makes it impossible to implement inflexible city-wide policies in this regard: 'We started aerobics this year – extra activities have been added and martial arts and volleyball – teachers have tried to make it more interesting – next year we are having coaches in.'

Interviewer – 'Does it matter if they are men?'

> Not for me but for some girls they wouldn't do anything in front of men – they would sit out. Sometimes we have a male teacher who has to cover the lesson – we are not really allowed to sit out – we can wear our headscarves then.

A theme that permeated the interviews with parents of secondary pupils raised issues about understanding different views focused on the importance of communicating not only with people in the schools but also in neighbourhoods; as one Muslim female parent explains:

> Be open to each other [different cultures] and communicate, be like their best friends. Open up and communicate and be positive you've got to have a good understanding of each other [people from different cultures] and your friends. Talk about different religions.

Parents who were engaged in the school as mentors, community activity participants or in other ways had more understanding of the school and were highly supportive. Parents did recognise the diversity of views in the Muslim communities and related that to degrees of religiosity. When discussing why some parents had a problem with physical education, Muslim female parents in a group interview said:

> That's because some parents are very strict.
>   Mine [daughter] goes to everything [all activities offered through PE and school sport] but there are some who will not let them go to physical education or swimming.

Both positive and negative views held by parents on the value of physical education are illustrated in discourses featuring health, empowerment and capability. Such discourses also highlight challenges faced in making sense of cultural values, often because of linguistic barriers. A group of female parents explained:

> Everyone needs to know that physical education is good for you. Muslim women have health problems . . . my daughter goes to a single sex school with all female teachers – I don't have a problem and my daughter can wear anything.

I have never done any sports in my life. It is not in our ways [referring to culture]. Also I do not have time and I don't understand English so it is not possible for me anyway.

Here the dilemmas of distinction between religious Islamic values, and cultural practices that often assume pseudo-religious status, needed to be clarified. Since the research team involved an Islamic studies scholar it was possible to draw important distinctions between religious and cultural practices for the guidance that was being prepared. A Muslim headteacher reported that she often needed to draw this distinction, using examples from the holy texts, to help parents who seemed to be confused.

Swimming

Where responsibility for the learning environment was outside of the control of the school, particularly in the use of public swimming pools, this resulted in some of the biggest tensions between Islamic and state requirements. Difficulties included those related to the public nature of pools, swimwear and the predominantly male staffing of city pools. Sometimes it was possible to negotiate an environment conducive to participation, as illustrated in this example from a state Muslim primary school:

The only physical education which isn't mixed is swimming . . . We think it is an investment worth making. . . . The swimming baths have been fantastic – supplying us with female guards and instructors and we meet with parents helping them to understand that we are working in line with what we think are the Islamic principles and are upholding them. Similarly the boys have all male staffing . . . some of the girls need to be fully covered to the ankles and can wear leggings with their leotards, it depends on what family and background they come from and different understandings. The boys wear swimming trunks, many are covered to the knees. We just allow the flexibility . . . We hire the whole pool for the school.

(Female Muslim headteacher)

The data also revealed that some primary schools continued mixed-sex swimming with the support of parents and allowed pupils to cover their arms and legs if required. A small number provided separate-sex swimming after negotiations and meetings between governors and parents. In secondary schools the issue was more prevalent because consciousness of faith embodiment practices was more prominent in the adolescent years. However, some city pools were not able to assure sex-segregated spaces – or even all-female staffing – as evidenced in the experiences of this secondary school:

the pool can't guarantee an all female environment and sometimes they have a male pool teacher. This is an issue . . . we are pushing for [same-sex staffing] across the [schools] partnership . . . saying we need more female lifeguards.

(Female headteacher)

Control of the learning situation in these examples was not in the hands of the school. The dominance of the UK's mixed-sex sport and leisure provision is at the root of this exclusion and it was evident in many pool-based activities for schools (primary and high schools) in the study. The result was non-participation for many Muslim pupils in swimming activities. In one case school, a headteacher had tried – but – failed to secure an appropriate swimming learning environment for a Muslim girl so her parents agreed to take her to a weekend women's only session in another part of the city. When the rest of the class went swimming, the parents collected the child from school and returned her at the end of that lesson time. The project revealed that this was not an isolated case and it crossed primary and secondary phases of schooling. Both headteachers and teachers expressed frustration about this impasse:

> Parents have withdrawn Muslim girls from swimming. Discussions have been followed through at parents' evenings but the school feels powerless to support the children and their parents feel angry.
>
> (Male headteacher)

> Three girls refused to go swimming. Parents were taken to the pool to see the environment but totally refused when they saw a male lifeguard. During the swimming hour these children are taken home.
>
> (Male headteacher)

For many pupils, school is the only opportunity they have to learn to swim. Ability to swim can be a life-saver but also it can be a valuable part of a long-term, healthy lifestyle.

Dance

Responses to the activity area of dance across participating schools were diverse. Sometimes, dance was regarded as a strength of the participating school whereas in other cases it was viewed negatively causing tensions in the context of values held in different Muslim communities. As was the case with other activity areas, much depended on the traditions and expectations of the school. In some schools, for example, just the mention of dance led to tensions because the predominant view of dance amongst the Muslim communities was connected to some of the sexually provocative aspects of social dance portrayed through the media. Primary schools had fewer difficulties than secondary schools. One primary teacher expressed her disappointment on arriving at her new school to find that some parents did not want their children to dance:

> One of the issues is dance [referring to tensions between Islam and PE]. I have had feedback from certain staff members and some parents who feel that dance puts shame on the family. . . . Parents want their children to be doing only Asian dance. . . . comments that girls should do dance without the boys

and that boys shouldn't be doing dance. At the end of the day dance has to be done in the curriculum and it does get done but there are discomforts with it . . . Parents bring in their views and ultimately they have a bearing on things.

(Female PE teacher)

The headteacher at the school attempted to open up opportunities for children; for example, by persisting with a project with the local ballet company despite some parental opposition. He believed that education was the place to give all children opportunities, such as those available in the rich Arts environment of the city in which they lived. He recognised that if children did not have such experiences in school, some would never have them in their lives. This illustrates a dilemma between a headteacher's aspiration for an inclusive education and parents' preferences to exclude their children from some parts of that education. Attempting to negotiate a compromise would appear to be the only possible route to resolution.

The most contentious case found in the study was at a secondary school level where a policy was introduced that meant parents who wished to withdraw their daughters from dance had to take them out of school for the period of the dance lesson. This would appear to demonstrate a breakdown in the communication. As the female headteacher explained: 'parents were adamant – no dance – the school policy on this issue is for parents to collect their child at the start of the lesson and return them at the end.' While one might admire the school's persistence to provide this activity for the majority of pupils in the school, it is difficult to understand that no alternative or compromise position could be reached for the Muslim girls in this situation.

In the face of challenges found in attempting to offer dance to all pupils, some teachers abandon dance and offer fitness activities instead. This is certainly a compromise position but it also fails to take account of the significance of dance as an Art form and as a valued community activity for many people in the UK. It also denies opportunities for dance for other students (see also Chapter 17). To overcome the problem with using the term 'dance,' one school called dance 'movement,' another used 'fitness, creative movement.' In another complicating factor, however, the lack of consensus on whether it is permissible in Islam to use music also necessitated flexible thinking in some schools. In the Islamic school, for example, percussion was used instead of music. In answer to the question 'do your children do dance here?' the female headteacher replied:

It depends how you define dance. For me dance is movement in response to music – we call it movement – it is about expressing something in movement and music provides the mood for it. We would do traditional dances . . . music again we adopt it in the way the majority of the Muslim community see as being alright. The use of percussion is most acceptable so we use that to be able to teach music and for movement response.

It can be argued that there is a need to improve reciprocal communication between the physical education profession and the Muslim community on issues such as these. According to Flintoff (2008, 2010), some teachers could be more aware of cultural sensitivities around certain forms and types of movement, and some Muslim communities could come to understand the value of physical education and activities such as dance more fully. The experience of dance in education, in that case amongst Muslim teacher-trainees, can be very different from the stereotypical notions held in the Muslim communities. Trainees discovered the educational value of dance and the diversity of choices the teacher has in terms of selection of style, starting points and accompaniment. As a result, these trainees were able to challenge misconceptions about the activity area amongst their own communities and they believed they could teach dance as a dimension of children's entitlement to a broad and balanced movement education.

Ramadan

Teachers and heads in the predominantly Muslim secondary schools in the study raised issues around awareness of changes in demands on the body and expectations in the learning situation during fasting. Three areas of sensitivity were identified: ensuring fewer or less intense physical demands were made during Ramadan, shortening the lunch hour, and swimming:

> Obviously when Ramadan is on it is always a concern for us because of fasting and that physical element, so we try and do less in regard to physical education and we take that into consideration. And obviously we respect their times when they open their fast if they are at a club or in a team.
>
> (Female headteacher)

Evidence of a range of attempts made to retain physical education during fasting but with modified expectations of physicality was found in questionnaires. One female headteacher explained: 'Prior to Ramadan we send a letter to all parents reassuring them that physical education continues but with low intensity activities. There is an opportunity for parents to contact the school if they have any worries.' Regardless of these sensitive practices, some pupils asked to be excused from physical education altogether during Ramadan. Tensions were evident, however, in the school where the policy was to shorten the lunch hour during Ramadan in order to shorten the school day. Although a popular policy with many, the unforeseen consequences for the physical education department meant that sporting clubs, usually organised at lunchtimes to ensure they were accessible to all, were cancelled for a half-term period.

The anxieties expressed by some Muslim pupils about swallowing some water accidentally in swimming lessons during Ramadan created further tensions:

> there is a major issue over swimming at Ramadan, to do with water entering the mouth . . . I feel that maybe the Imams could support us somehow . . . if you were given a cup of pool water nobody would intend to drink it. It's not done intentionally and therefore if it does pass into the child's mouth it would

be purely accidental. So I just feel that maybe some support or some clearer guidelines over swimming and Ramadan would help because that is a particular difficult time for us.

(Headteacher)

Support from local religious leaders was considered important in ensuring that the advice given to Muslim communities in the city was consistent. Evidence of good practice in this study involved sensitivity to concerns and modified physical participation requirements but continued engagement in physical education during Ramadan. Such positive approaches would appear to be preferable to adopting pedagogies of exclusion, such as withdrawal of pupils, or taking them out of school for the duration of a lesson. In addition, parental misconceptions that withdrawal from physical education is unproblematic should be challenged.

Towards more inclusive practices

The BASS study has provided evidence, from one city in the UK, about tensions in physical education pedagogies that can lead to inclusion or exclusion of Muslim girls.

The challenges headteachers faced in juggling the multiple demands of national curriculum legal requirements and the needs of all pupils, including those of Muslim children, were clearly evident. Impasse situations led to exclusive practices, such as children being removed from school premises during physical education lessons and some parents assuming it was unproblematic to simply withdraw their daughters from statutory physical education. What became clear through the study was the need for guidance to help resolves some of the tensions found. Guidance, rather than firm policy dictates, offers flexibility in local decision-making.

BASS guidance: towards inclusive pedagogies

In the BASS study, situations of exclusion were created by knowledge gaps between the teaching profession and the Muslim community. For example, there was insufficient understanding of Islamic requirements by some teachers and, among some Muslim communities, a lack of understanding about the value of physical education and the very real constraints that some schools faced. Although only based in one city in England, the evidence from this research signals a need for greater exchange of multi-layered knowledge in increasingly complex multi-faith and multicultural societies (Flintoff *et al.*, 2008).

The BASS research team's guidance focused on improving inclusive practice, sharing characteristics of *good practice*, clarifying *religious requirements*, and making recommendations for the most commonly identified areas of contention – body modesty, swimming, dance and Ramadan. The guidance also recognised the complexity of diversity in Muslim girls' and women's preferences for embodying religious belief and the multiple challenges and dilemmas headteachers, teachers and local providers can face in aspiring to meet the needs of all children in education in the UK (BCC 2008).

Good practice was identified where schools worked closely with parents and local religious leaders to address tensions. Keeping a close working relationship with parents to address tensions proved successful because it led to an increase in participation and inclusion in some case schools. Aspects of 'good practice' included:

- clarity in expectations;
- the organisation and requirements of PE communicated as part of the induction process when children first entered school;
- publication of relevant PE/school sport information for parents in the school prospectus;
- ensuring and maintaining on-going communication with parents to keep them fully informed of changes in provision and organisation.

Body modesty included attention to gender organisation and privacy sensitivities as well as appropriate dress codes. All these areas were important for Muslim young people and their families regarding participation in PE. As was noted earlier, the BASS Project revealed great diversity in the experiences and expectations of Muslim pupils across the city; some young women did not wish to cover their heads, legs or arms, while others were unhappy to participate without such covering. Positive examples of useful inclusive strategies were shared in the guidance including:

- schools producing policies in consultation with the young people;
- ensuring the same choices were made available for all children (for example in PE kit);
- meeting Islamic requirements for covering arms, legs and hair where requested especially in public playgrounds and swimming pools;
- upholding the principles of propriety, dignity and respect for all young people in guidance statements related to body modesty, uniform and changing environments.

To improve inclusion in swimming, the guidance proposed flexibility in the type of costumes allowed and attention to gender organisation to meet the needs of specific groups. The system of using local public pools meant most schools were unable to control the learning environment regarding these matters but some negotiations had led to positive outcomes. On the other hand, common barriers identified in local authority interviewees were centred on competing values, the business priority to make money and a lack of qualified women staff. The guidance recommends some changes to move forward from the position of excluding groups of the public from using city recreational facilities.

Dance is a contested area and the research revealed many misconceptions in the Muslim communities about the rationale for dance in education. The guidance recommends sharing, with parents, more information on the value, aims, diversity, benefits and distinctive contribution of dance to education. Since music can also be a contested subject in Islamic culture, it is also important to note that the teaching of dance is not dependent on the use of music, and teachers can use a variety of forms of accompaniment such as percussion, poetry, words, stories and music which can add enjoyment and atmosphere to the lesson.

In relation to Ramadan, where young people choose to fast the guidance suggests the use of more creative, inclusive pedagogies in order that young people can remain engaged in physical education in some form. For example, teachers could place emphasis on wider learning experiences such as refereeing, choreographing, recording specific movement analysis or coaching. Such activities have reduced physical demands but still offer opportunities for full learning engagement. Adaptations such as these can be made in consultation with young people to ascertain appropriate responses to individual needs.

Conclusion

Evidence from the BASS study indicated that teachers in these city schools were in need of support and guidance in order to develop ever more inclusive pedagogies for Muslim girls in physical education. It has been argued that more inclusive schools will lead to more inclusive societies resulting in a better quality of life for future generations. It is important to remember, however, that any attempts to improve social integration and cohesion must be underpinned by knowledge of context and flexibility of response because in plural societies the reality is 'fluid, spatial boundaries and overlapping cultural spaces creating a more hybrid society of re-negotiated non-essentialistic identities' (Husain and O'Brien, 1999 cited in Parker-Jenkins *et al.*, 2004, p. 93). The findings from the BASS study support Henry's (2007, p. 317) 'situated ethics' approach where 'absolute standards are rejected in favour of the requirements of a particular situation.' What 'ought to be' is negotiated, in the context in which change is sought, to bring about a consensus which inevitably 'has limits and . . . some groups will almost invariably stand outside the consensus achieved, but that consensus is an on-going construct upon mutual respect and dialogue' (ibid., p. 319).

More broadly, the challenge for teachers attempting to adopt inclusive pedagogies related to Muslim girls and women in physical education and school sport is part of a global dialogue regarding permissibility of Islam, women and physicality. In part, this is in response to the relative invisibility of Muslim women role models in the sporting field (Benn and Ahmad, 2006), at least in the Western world, and in the Western teaching profession (Benn and Dagkas, 2006; Knez, 2010). One pathway to creating new possibilities is to work with Islamic feminism, as has been explored by authors such as Jawad, *et al.* (2011). An Islamic feminist approach supports the empowerment of girls and women from within Islam (Hamzeh and Oliver, 2010), and this can be helpful in the quest to gain the support of the Muslim community for increased participation in physical activity arenas by girls and women. Through revisited interpretations of the holy texts, it is possible to substantiate advocacy for the care of the body, attention to physical development in the holistic development of young children, and advocacy for girls' and women's participation in physical activity arenas, through an analysis and understanding of religious requirements.

In addition to the acknowledgement of positive links between Islam and women's participation in physical activity, as discussed in the BASS guidance, it is also important to acknowledge 'Islam as an enabling religion.' This acknowledgement was embedded in the international 'Accept and Respect Declaration' to improve the participation of Muslim women in physical activity (Benn and Koushkie, 2008). Through a study week of international sport scholars and practitioners in Oman in 2008, the declaration emerged as a platform for advocacy. Its purpose was to persuade those responsible for sporting structures and organisations, whose regulations, policies and practices currently exclude Muslim women from sport/ physical activity participation, to make changes towards more inclusive participation environments. In line with the aspiration of the 'Accept and Respect' declaration, the BASS study offers one example of research and positive action towards the development of inclusive pedagogies for Muslim girls in physical education.

References

Abbas, T. (2006) *Muslims in Birmingham.* COMPAS centre on Migration, Policy and Society, Oxford: University of Oxford.

Azzarito, L. and Solmon, M.A. (2005) A reconceptualization of physical education: The intersection of gender/race/social class. *Sport, Education and Society*, 10 (1): 25–47.

Bailey, R. (2005) Evaluating the relationship between physical education, sport and social inclusion. *Educational Review*, 57 (1): 71–90.

BCC (Birmingham City Council) (2008) *Improving Participation of Muslim Girls in Physical Education and School Sport: Shared practical guidance from Birmingham schools.* Birmingham Advisory Support Service, School Effectiveness Team, Martineau Centre, Balden Road, B32 2EH, Birmingham, England. Online: *www.birmingham.gov.uk/childrenservices*.

Benn, T. (2005) Race and physical education, sport and dance. In Green, K. and Hardman, K. (eds) *Physical Education – Essential Issues*. London: Sage, pp. 197–218.

Benn, T. (2009) Muslim women in sport: a researcher's journey to understanding 'embodied faith.' *Bulletin 55, International Council for Sports Science and Physical Education (ICSSPE)*, pp. 48–56. Online: *www.icsspe.org* (accessed 28 January 2009).

Benn, T. and Ahmed, A. (2006) Alternative visions: international sporting opportunities for Muslim women and implications for British youth sport. *Youth and Policy*, 92: 119–132.

Benn, T. and Koushkie, M. (2008) Increasing global inclusion of Muslim girls and women in physical activity. *ICSSPE Bulletin*, 54: 22–24.

Benn, T., Pfister, G. and Jawad, H. (2011a) *Muslim Women and Sport*. London: Routledge.

Benn, T., Dagkas, S. and Jawad, H. (2011b) Embodied faith: Islam, religious freedom and educational practices in physical education. *Sport, Education and Society*, 16 (1).

Carroll, B. and Hollinshead, G. (1993) Ethnicity and conflict in physical education. *British Educational Research Journal*, 19 (1): 59–75.

Dagkas, S. and Benn, T. (2006) Young Muslim women's experiences of Islam and physical education in Greece and Britain: A comparative study. *Sport, Education and Society*, 11 (1): 21–28.

Dagkas, S., Benn, T. and Jawad, H. (2011) Multiple Voices: Improving participation of Muslim Girls in Physical Education and School Sport. *Sport, Education and Society*, 16 (2): 223–239.

Flintoff, A. (2010) Tales from the playing field: Black and ethnic minority students' experiences of Physical Education teacher education. In *Australian Association for Research in Education*, Melbourne, Australia, 28 November to 2 December 2010.

Flintoff, A., Fitzgerald, H. and Scraton, S. (2008) The challenges of intersectionality: researching difference in physical education. *International Studies in Sociology of Education*, 18 (2): 73–85.

Hamzeh, M. and Oliver, K. (2010) Gaining research access into the lives of Muslim girls: Researchers negotiating *muslimness*, modesty, *inshallah*, and *haram*. *International Journal of Qualitative Studies in Education*, 23 (2): 165–180.

Henry, I. (2007) *Transnational and Comparative Research in Sport: Globalisation, Governance and Sport Policy.* London: Routledge.

International Council of Sport Science and Physical Education (ICSSPE) (1999) *The World Summit in Physical Education: A Landmark Event*, Berlin, November 3–5.

Jawad, H., Al-Sinani, Y. and Benn, T. (2011) Islam, Women and Sport. In Benn, T., Pfister, G. and Jawad, H. (eds) *Muslim Women and Sport*. London: Routledge, pp. 25–40.

Kay, T. (2006) Daughters of Islam: family influences on Muslim young women's participation in sport. *International Review for the Sociology of Sport*, 41 (3–4): 357–373.

Knez, K. (2010) Being Muslim and being female: negotiating physical activity and a gendered body. In Wright, J. and Macdonald, D. (eds) *Young people, physical activity and the everyday.* Oxon: Routledge, pp. 104–118.

Parker-Jenkins, M., Hartas, D., and Irving, B. (2005) *In Good Faith: schools, religion and public funding*, Aldershot: Ashgate.

Sarwar, G. (1994) *British Muslims and Schools*. London: Muslim Education Trust.

Shilling, C. (2008) *Changing Bodies: Habit, Crisis and Creativity*, London: Sage.

15 Sport and youth inclusion in the 'Majority World'

Tess Kay

Introduction

There is no bigger challenge to inclusion than the deprivation experienced by the populations of the Majority World. Westernised societies may be deeply inequitable, but social and material disadvantage simply take on a different order of magnitude in the poorer nations of the globe. For these countries, exclusion through poor health is not a matter of the incremental effects of obesity and sedentary lifestyles, but of immediate exposure to the deadly impacts of infant mortality, malnutrition and global pandemics that have reduced life expectancy in some countries to less than forty years. Here, exclusion through education does not mean that some young people are disengaged from schooling and under-achieve academically, but that illiteracy is widespread among whole swathes of populations, not only undermining individual and collective economic prosperity, but also limiting their access to the information and knowledge that allows them to manage their own lives effectively. In these contexts, too, social discrimination manifests not as relative disadvantage, but as an elemental undervaluing of less powerful groups that too often ostracises those with disabilities, legitimises the undervaluing of female lives even before birth, and exposes members of lower status castes, tribes and ethnic groups to injustice, hostility and violence. Underpinning these are experiences of poverty that are not relative but absolute, manifest in poor living conditions, acute material deprivation and deficiencies in service provision and infrastructure that can foster divisive social relations.

This chapter examines the issue surrounding the use of sport to promote youth inclusion in such circumstances. It first establishes the context for sport initiatives, by examining how the concept of social exclusion can be applied in international development contexts. The chapter then provides a brief overview of the emergence of sport as an international development policy tool, and considers the types and scale of activity being undertaken, and the rationales underpinning them. Following this, it considers the type of benefits that sport initiatives offer young people, and the extent to which these may contribute to wider development goals. The chapter concludes by raising a number of questions about the appropriateness of sport for youth inclusion in international development contexts, and also considers the implications for those who carry out research into it.

Addressing 'exclusion' in international development contexts

It is widely recognised that the origins of the concept of 'social exclusion' lie in European social policy of the late twentieth century. 'Social exclusion' therefore not only has a rather short history, but also – and more significantly for international development contexts – relatively narrow cultural roots. This has implications for how we conceptualise and address social exclusion in the international development field, where, as Kahn *et al.* (2009) explain, defining what constitutes the norm, from which people are 'excluded,' is itself complex.

An extensive literature has developed surrounding whether, and in what forms, it is useful to apply a concept of social exclusion within international development. Kahn *et al.*'s (2009) web-based resource provides access to many of these debates. These recognise that concepts of exclusion and integration are culturally specific, generally reflecting analysts' own backgrounds and political traditions (Silver, 1994). In its Western countries of origin, 'exclusion' has been conceptualised primarily in relation to the welfare state and labour market, institutions which both operate in very different forms in low income states (Silver, 1994). In contrast, many developing countries lack both a comprehensive welfare state and a formalised labour market; furthermore, the exclusion of people on the basis of their race, caste or gender may be viewed by the society excluding them as 'normal.' In this context Saith (2001) questions whether the concept of 'social exclusion' can be applied in developing countries, describing how

> In the North, patterns of social integration are institutionalised and fairly clearly defined and 'social exclusion' applies to those outside accepted norms. Exclusion from participation in society is associated, for example, with loss of rights associated with work and the welfare state, long-term unemployment, and breakdown of social ties and disaffiliation (Gore, 1995). The excluded are minorities. In many developing countries however, due to structural heterogeneity, defining what is 'normal' may not be that simple'
>
> (Saith, 2001, p. 6)

Despite these differences, social exclusion is valued within international development studies as a concept that can enhance analysis of the processes that foster deprivation in low income countries. De Haan (1999) emphasises the usefulness of applying social exclusion as a theoretical concept in international development contexts so long as it is used as 'a lens through which people look at reality, and not reality itself' (de Haan, 1999, p. 5). He stresses that 'social exclusion does not connotate a particular problem such as "the new poor", an "underclass" long-term unemployed, or the marginalised as understood in a Latin-American context'; instead, 'social exclusion remains a concept, . . . a way of looking at society' (de Haan, 1999, p. 5). The concept of social exclusion has two particular characteristics that transcend specific cultural contexts: first, it is multidimensional, reflecting the reality of experiences of deprivation in low income countries; and second, it implies a focus on the relationships and processes that cause deprivation. Combining these two elements allows analysts of international development to recognise the multiple processes that contribute to exclusion, and to explore the relationships between them.

There are, therefore, some commonalities between Western conceptualisations of social exclusion and its application in development contexts. In both, social inclusion is conceptualised as complex and multifaceted, combining social, political and economic dimensions. There are, however, a number of distinctive features of social exclusion as applied to analysis of Majority World countries, reflecting not just the different realities of the social, economic and political spheres in these states, but also the processes through which they interact to impact individuals and communities. Below are listed some of the most significant of these distinguishing features.

Differences in institutional context

Majority World countries differ from the industrialised nations in many aspects of their economic, political and social institutions; for example, limited welfare provision, fluid and unstable labour markets, variable levels of democratic process, and, in some regions, high levels of political instability and poor governance including corruption. With many economic and political institutions operating in a weaker form than in Minority World countries, social institutions – families and communities – often play a more significant role in supporting individuals.

Differences in ideologies underpinning social relations

Most Majority World countries differ in two key respects from Minority countries in the ideological underpinnings of their social relations. First, most have an ideology of collectivism, as opposed to the individualisation that underpins westernised societies. This is evident in family ideologies and practices among many Majority World cultures in which family life is collectivist, membership of households is fluid and extended, and family networks have traditionally acted as social security systems, providing protection and care for the vulnerable and sick (Strobbe *et al.*, 2010). The family is central to a wider system of reciprocal social relations, with a wider array of functions than in industrialised nations. Especially in agrarian communities, families may serve as basic units of production and political representation and even as religious bodies for the worship of spiritual beings. Second, many Majority World countries are less egalitarian in their expectations of social relations than Minority World states. As well as being evident in social practice, this is often formalised in law and/or religion. Globally, marked inequalities are evident in the treatment of females, while many countries discriminate against those of 'inferior' castes, tribes and ethnic groups. Such practices are so deeply embedded historically and culturally that they normalise the exclusion of certain groups within the population from full citizenship.

Differences in the relative importance of the dimensions of exclusion

Although analysts of international development value the concept of social exclusion precisely because of its multidimensionality, they also emphasise the primacy of economic exclusion within this. As Bhalla and Lapeyre (1997) observe, 'when people are excluded from the main sources of income, their first priority is survival and a basic livelihood' (p. 430). In Majority World countries where most of the population are excluded from adequate livelihoods, the *distributional* aspect of social exclusion is therefore the most important – that is, the extent to which people lack resources. This contrasts with the situation in industrialised countries, in which the *relational* aspects of social exclusion are considered of greater significance – that is, the lack of social ties to the family, friends, local community, state services and institutions or more generally to the society to which an individual belongs (Bhalla and Lapeyre, 1997, p. 417). People in the Minority World have a minimum survival income; it is, therefore, the quality of the relationship between the individual and society which tends to be regarded as central to the phenomenon of social exclusion, rather than access to sufficient material resources.

Differences in the process of social exclusion

While emphasising the importance of economic exclusion, analysts also stress, however, the close interrelatedness of this with the political and social dimensions of exclusion. In the absence of robust systems for democratic participation, access to material resources is interwoven particularly closely with social relations. Bhalla and Lapeyre (1997) further argue that economic power underlies the ability of groups to influence government in support of their interests:

> By virtue of their incomes and assets, the rich are much more powerful and influential than the poor who, for lack of economic means, education, and so on, are poorly organized. Thus economic might enables the rich to extract from the State, civil and political rights and liberties. One may, therefore argue that economic resources enable access not only to economic goods and services but also to political goods like freedom and the ability to influence economic policies.
>
> (Bhalla and Lapeyre, 1997, p. 418)

Thus, as well as being significant in itself, economic exclusion underpins wider forms of exclusion, reflecting its multidimensionality.

Comparing how the concept of social exclusion is applied in Majority and Minority World countries is a useful exercise in highlighting how these settings differ as economic, political and social contexts. With this backdrop, the next section now examines how sport is being deployed as a tool for youth inclusion in international development contexts of this sort.

The use of sport in international development

'Sport and development' refers to the use of sport in international development work, through which the international community addresses social and economic problems in many of the world's poorer nations. These countries were previously collectively known as 'developing countries' or 'the third world' but today are more commonly referred to as the 'Global South.' This chapter adopts the alternative usage of 'Majority World,' a term intended to remind us that the poorer nations constitute by far the majority of the world's population and that they possess rich cultural traditions that are often more widely upheld than those of westernised states. At a more fundamental level, this terminology opens up the debate about the nature of 'development' itself, challenging assumptions that progression to the capitalist model of the Minority World is self-evidently desirable.

International development is politically complex and sensitive. Far from being seen as charitable benevolence, 'aid' is regarded by many as a continuing form of interference, control and cultural imperialism, through which the countries of the Minority World protect their political interests and perpetuate the structural disadvantage of those who lack power within the capitalist system. Complex power relations, therefore, underlie international development initiatives. Nonetheless, since its emergence in the mid-twentieth century, international development has become a well-established policy area, working across diverse agendas. During this time, development work has undergone significant shifts in focus and approach, reflecting the changing nature of the global economy, changing understandings of effective forms of international aid, and changing attitudes to inter-cultural relations. In its early phases, work tended to focus on economic and infrastructure issues such as improving sanitation, transport systems and communication technology, but more recently greater emphasis has been put on investment in human resources and productive social relationships. Alongside this has been a shift from international development as an externally imposed modernisation project predicated on the technical expertise and values of Minority Countries, to a stronger emphasis on partnership and collaboration which – in theory at least – allows greater scope for local interests and influence all the way from grass roots to governmental level.

These trends in international development work have increased the importance attached to the social processes underpinning poverty and exclusion. Sport therefore appears relevant to current policy approaches, because of its supposed capacity to contribute to social change. This convergence goes some way towards explaining why sport has been embraced so enthusiastically in many quarters as a tool with which to address issues of disadvantage, deprivation and exclusion. As the authors of this book have shown, in many Minority Countries sport has been incorporated in a wide array of social policy agendas that address different aspects of inclusion – for example, for diverse populations (e.g. young people with disabilities, Chapter 13) and black and ethnic minority youth (Chapter 14). The focus in sport on individuals who are disadvantaged, and on the significance of social relations for promoting or denying inclusion, parallels a similar emphasis on international development work from the 1980s onwards. While the consensus in the aftermath of the Second World War was that international development policy should focus on economic growth as a strategy to alleviate the situation of people in the world's poorest nations, the emphasis has since shifted. 'This new approach' is reflected in the eight Millennium Development Goals (MDGs), launched by the United Nations in 2000 and agreed by all of its 192 member states and by the leading development institutions of the world. The goals framed the international development agenda, identifying eight closely intertwined issues that development work must address:

1   Poverty and world hunger
2   Universal education
3   Gender equality
4   Child health
5   Maternal health
6   Combating HIV/AIDS
7   Environmental sustainability
8   Global partnership

These goals are underpinned by a common principle: they address directly fundamental aspects of the lives of poor people, especially health, education, poverty and hunger. Dealing with such deep-rooted problems requires action at multiple levels of social, political and economic systems and in a variety of contexts from local to transnational. This is, therefore, a complex policy landscape and it is helpful to recognise that sport and development projects are located within this wider policy approach and so are exposed to some of its challenges.

Sport is a relatively new addition to development work, but its use has rapidly become widespread. This reflects the perceived potential of sport to contribute to the social relations through which the MDGs may be achieved. Potentially, sport is believed to have many contributions to make to the goals, especially in policy areas where young people are a primary target. The expectations about what may be achieved through sport are similar to those attributed to it in the global North; that is, sport is believed to have the capacity to engage young people, provide positive experiences and, as a result, through these processes to contribute both to personal development (e.g. increasing self-esteem) and collective benefit (e.g. building community cohesion). Sport is, therefore, being used in policies to increase education levels, promote healthy lifestyles, support health promotion including HIV/AIDS campaigns, and confront gender inequities by empowering girls and young women.

Plotting the scale and spread of this work is a complex task. Kidd (2008) identified 166 organisations engaged in sport for development and peace projects, while Lyras *et al.* (2009), using different terms of reference, found that the number of known sport for development providers and projects had risen from around 200 in 2005 to over 1,500 in 2009. However, the form which sport and development initiatives take varies widely, from transnational programmes to small-scale grass-roots activity, and inevitably it is the projects led – or adopted – by international organisations with their sophisticated PR machines that have become most visible. The best-known instances of sport and development work include, for example, the United Nation's declaration of 2005 as the International Year of Education and Sport; the work of the international organisation Right to Play, based in Toronto and operating in multiple countries; and programmes such as International Inspirations which is the UK's 2012 Olympic legacy programme supported by a partnership of UK Sport, UNICEF and British Council. A number of in-country programmes have also gained significant exposure in policy and academic circles, through their own promotional activities and their participation in research; examples include Magic Bus in India, Go Sisters and the work of EduSport in Zambia and the Mathare Youth Sports Association project in Kenya. But in addition to these, local workers identify a whole swathe of community-initiated sport and development work that goes undetected, including that undertaken by community, education and health organisations that do not specialise in sport but find it effective in their work. The omission of such activity in published audits underplays both the scale of activity being undertaken, and the pro-active role of indigenous organisations in its initiation. Sport and development work should not be seen, therefore, as primarily the product of externally funded development investment, but as a complex jigsaw resulting from the interaction of internal and external interests.

Despite the absence of precise data, 'sport and development' is widely recognised as a growing area, increasingly applied in work addressing a range of health, educational and empowerment goals in Majority World countries. To date we do not know, however, what impacts sport may achieve in development contexts – and nor are we certain that such impacts can be captured in research. The next section draws on research in three countries to consider the extent to which sport can provide benefits which address exclusion.

Responses to sport as an international development tool

The growth of sport-based work within international development strategies has provoked extensive debate about how appropriate sport is to this policy field, and what it can be expected to achieve. The existence of a strong advocacy element, exhorting 'the power of sport,' can confuse the boundaries between what is known and what is hoped for. As a result, and despite the growing evidence base from analyses by authors such as Saaveedra (2009), Lindsey *et al.* (2010) and Mwaanga (2010), the key question of whether sport 'works' in development terms remains unanswered. There is, nonetheless, mounting evidence that sport does achieve, for some young people, a range of short-term impacts and possibly medium-term ones (e.g. Sport for Development and Peace International Working Group, 2007). Whether these impacts translate into long-term benefits, potentially engendering social change, is much less certain.

In research undertaken since 2006, the author and colleagues have examined the impacts of sport projects on young people in three separate countries – Brazil,

India and Zambia. In Brazil and India, data was obtained during one-week field visits, during which interviews and focus groups were conducted with sixty-four individuals in Brazil (nineteen adults and forty-five young people), and with thirty-eight individuals in India (seven adult workers and thirty-one young women). In Zambia, the research was conducted over a two-year period, during three one-week visits embedded within a longer research programme; twenty-two adults and twenty-eight young people took part. In all three locations, interviewees included local teachers, community workers, sports leaders and other adults, and children and young people taking part in the sports programmes. Throughout the research the emphasis was on experiential accounts rather than speculative views about sport's 'potential' benefits. Project participants were questioned about their own participation in the projects, while adult interviewees were asked for specific examples from their experience of using sport in work with local youth. The work undertaken offered three contrasting scenarios for sport in development.

Brazil

The research in Brazil provided a South American example of sport being used to work with children at risk of violence and insecurity in everyday life. It focused on the Segundo Tempo project in the Recife Metropolitan Region (RMR) in north-east Brazil, which has the highest income gap in the country. More than half of the working population is employed in the informal sector and nearly 40 per cent of its population lives in makeshift housing lacking basic services and with weak physical and social infrastructure.

The research was undertaken with youth from neighbourhoods characterised by extreme poverty and high levels of crime, drug-taking and violence. Young people had unstable family lives, low take-up of school and were at risk of becoming part of the unsafe street culture. Sport was being used as part of the Segundo Tempo ('Second Shift') project to address social exclusion among young people by encouraging their educational aspirations. Most children attended school for only half a day, but under Segundo Tempo, they could spend the other part of the day taking part in organised sport. The programme was concerned primarily with using sport to achieve a wider range of developmental outcomes including contributing to human development to improve quality of life, contributing to the process of educational and social inclusion, promoting healthy lifestyles for children and their families, reducing young people's exposure to social risk (child labour, violence and hunger), and developing children's social interaction skills and building citizenship.

India

In India the research provided an example of sport being used as a vehicle for female empowerment within an Asian society. The study was conducted with the GOAL project, a small-scale intensive initiative operating in two impoverished neighbourhoods in Delhi. Delhi, the capital of India, has an estimated population of 17 million, making it the most populous city in the world.

The GOAL project was a female-only project that aimed to empower young women to become leaders and social activists in their communities. It was run by The NAZ Foundation, a charitable organisation working to raise awareness of HIV/AIDS in India. GOAL was a relatively recent addition to the organisation's work, and was using netball as a medium to engage young women aged 13–19. The focus of the project was on sustained, intense support and education with relatively small, close-knit groups of young women. The project ran twice-weekly netball sessions supplemented by educational modules to support wider personal development. Modules covered personal issues such as hygiene, sex and sexuality, communication, and HIV/AIDS; social issues including the environment; and economic issues such as micro-finance and computing. The modules were intended to complement the health and well-being, teamwork and leadership promoted through the netball sessions.

Zambia

In the third country, Zambia, the focus was on sport as a vehicle for preventative HIV/AIDS education in sub-Saharan Africa. The research took place in Lusaka, the capital city, with projects that were using sport to deliver HIV/AIDS education to young people. At the time, nearly a million Zambians were living with AIDS, one in every six adults had HIV, and adult life expectancy was estimated at 35 years. The infection was particularly widespread among young women under 20, who were six times more likely to be infected than males. The problems of low life expectancy, poor economic productivity and high medical costs were creating imbalances at community and national level, leading to extreme poverty and a breakdown of families and wider social structures. Zambia was addressing the HIV/AIDS pandemic through strategies to reduce poverty and increase education, operating from grass roots to government level. In Lusaka, sports development non-governmental organisations (NGOs) were using sport and recreation to promote healthy lifestyles and deliver HIV/AIDS education. Through programmes of sports activities delivered primarily through peer leaders and in collaboration with schools and other community groups, the projects engaged young people and delivered a combined package of sport and life skills to direct them away from the risks of HIV/AIDS. The research obtained information from participants in the programme, peer leaders and project and community workers on the impact of the provision on young people.

Overarching sports impacts

The evidence obtained from the three studies was very positive and painted a favourable picture of sport. Despite the geographical dispersion, the reports received from young people and adult workers were also remarkably consistent. They indicated that sport may have a number of characteristics that make it a suitable vehicle for delivering some of the social outcomes attributed to it. The findings of the studies supported five claims:

1   That sport has special qualities for engaging young people.
2   That sport has special qualities for supporting and delivering educational content to young people.
3   That sport has special qualities for fostering relationships which underpinned the success of programmes.
4   That sport has an extended 'reach' and can engage some young people who are resistant to other institutions.
5   That positive experiences from sport transfer to non-sport contexts.

The special qualities of sport for engaging young people

Sport was attractive, popular and enjoyable for experienced and inexperienced participants alike, allowing programmes to tap into young people's passion and enthusiasm for sport. In Brazil, for example, one of the session leaders commented:

> I think the crucial thing certainly its sport, because they [youth] really love sports, and we provide training which makes it even more pleasurable for them, the way sports is practiced, with pleasure, with happiness.
>
> (Monitor, Brazil)

Inexperienced participants grew in confidence through mastering a sport they had not tried before; and young women gained special benefits from the new experiences of moving free physically, mastering new skills, and participation in collective activity. The physical immediacy of sport was particularly significant for engaging young people, and team sports provided a context for developing a range of personal and social skills in an experiential way through enjoyable activity.

The special qualities of sport for supporting and delivering educational content to young people

In the programmes in all three countries, sport was effective in attracting young people to educational activities. In some instances, the popularity of sport was used as a specific incentive for young people to attend school in order to be eligible to participate in the sports activities programme. Sport was also used widely as part of successful, integrated sport-education programmes. These included instances of sport being used to deliver some educational messages directly; for example, young people's experiences of being physically active in sport were used to build their understanding of health issues, while their experiences of playing team games were used to build communication and decision-making skills:

It is learning through action as well, it is not someone telling you what to do but it is showing you what happens if you don't do some things and how you can stop it happening. You will not listen to someone just telling you things so . . . sports can help with that because you have to learn for yourself.

(Pupil, Lusaka)

The special qualities of sport for fostering relationships which underpinned the success of programmes

The informal nature of sport allowed open and democratic relationships between young people and the adults who worked with them. The young people described themselves as speaking 'more' directly and asking questions to fill gaps in their knowledge. In Delhi, this provided young women (and through them, their friends and mothers) with the information about sexuality, fertility and reproduction that was necessary for them to protect and manage their bodies and lives:

It is much more comfortable, between both the sides, us and the coaches, most importantly they don't scare us, they don't scold us. Nothing is right or wrong, it's like a forum where you can come and discuss, ask your questions, share your doubts. So that makes it much more easier.

(Participant, India)

Young people also gave more credibility to what they learned from teachers with whom they had established a close relationship through sport, as illustrated in Lusaka where young people who turned away from more formal teaching were receptive to HIV/AIDS education offered through sport.

Sport had an extended 'reach'

Sport was effective in reaching some young people 'on the margins' who did not respond to mainstream provision and institutions. In Lusaka, pupils who did not usually pay attention to HIV/AIDS education did engage through sport. In Recife and Olinda, Brazil, it was also reported that sport had proved the crucial link in building relationships with young people involved in drug taking and redirecting them from that path. Sport could also elicit more active engagement than other methods. Several young interviewees in Zambia commented that the HIV/AIDS teaching offered in sports sessions was subsequently discussed by the young people among themselves; this contrasted with classroom teaching which was often barely listened to and was easily dismissed. Sport was especially – but not only – successful in engaging young men.

Sport also had extended 'reach' in the sense that the benefits delivered through sports programmes were influential beyond those who participated directly themselves. The young women in Delhi shared their new educational knowledge with other friends and their own mothers and families, and expressed their commitment to passing on knowledge. In Lusaka, there were several examples of young people passing on the HIV/AIDS knowledge they had gained through sports-based sessions to others who had not taken part:

> I wasn't at some of [the sessions], but my friends talked about it. I think it meant something to them to learn about it because we talked about it afterwards.
>
> (Pupil, Zambia)

Positive experiences from sport transferred to non-sport contexts

The research provided multiple reports of learning occurring through sport and then being transferred to other contexts. These included:

- experience of mastering sport skills leading to higher self-belief and increased aspirations (reported in all three projects, with some particularly strong examples from young women);
- developing higher confidence levels and improved communication skills through sport, which helped young people assert themselves in interactions in educational, family and other settings (everywhere, including among boys and young men in Recife and Olinda, and young women in Delhi and Lusaka);
- sport, especially team sports, building decision-making skills of use at home and in school (everywhere, and especially among young women);
- sport, especially team sports, developing relationship skills (strongly, everywhere);
- sport building discipline and self-control which transferred as a life skill.

In Delhi, particular importance was attached to the role of sport in encouraging collective action:

> One thing which is very important, these girls, during their sessions of the sports, they have developed team spirit, which is a very big thing for them. They will play a game, but team spirit is very very important for their lives. As a team they can fight for their locality, as a team they can fight for any personal issues, now they know, that single person cannot do it, anything, you have to unite, to fight.
>
> (Community coordinator, India)

The above statements summarise testimonies that came from experienced professional and voluntary workers, and from the young people with whom they work. All reported that sport was valuable as a tool for youth development, and were quite emphatic in this assertion. Many critiques of the research evidence base would, however, question the value of such accounts, derived as they are from case study research of limited scope undertaken during short-duration fieldwork. Such evidence does not always inspire confidence in policy makers, or among the academy. The question arises, therefore: can researchers reconcile the requirements to value local knowledge with meeting policy makers' requirements for tangible measures of 'impact,' while also ensuring that such analyses are located within their wider social, economic and political contexts acknowledging structural influences?

In addressing this question, one influential factor is the prominence of policy analysis as a framework for sport in development research. This typically privileges positivist forms of knowledge and methodologies that meet organisational and policy requirements for 'hard facts' (see Coalter, 2007; Laws *et al.*, 2003); for example, record-keeping of the numbers and basic characteristics of participants in sports programmes. Funding constraints usually limit the inclusion of in-depth, reflexive approaches that are better suited to unpicking the processes that underlie individuals' experiences. Small-scale, qualitative studies do clearly have limited application; however, even short-duration projects can capture insights that have value in themselves and inform other elements of a wider programme of research (Denzin and Lincoln, 2008; Laws, 2003). While the findings of the studies reported here are specific to the projects and times at which they were conducted, they illustrate the potential value of the accounts of those directly involved for our understanding of sports impacts.

The most significant requirement for understanding the potential of sport to counter exclusion in international development work is, however, the need for all such analyses, regardless of origin and ownership, to look beyond short-term, individual and local experiences and locate their assessment of impact in context. International development involves the transformation of power relations at multiple levels – and these are structural and institutional as well as individual. If change only occurs at the individual level, it may in fact do more harm than good, and may even lead to resistance and backlash. Schuler and Hashemi (1998) illustrate this in their study of a local development initiative in rural Bangladesh, which highlighted how women could be placed at risk when they challenged gender relations. One man in the study explained that 'our wives would not be beaten so much if they were obedient and followed our orders, but women do not listen to us and so they get beaten often' (Schuler and Hashemi, 1998 cited in, Muraleedharan, 2005). Cultural resistance may also be reinforced by obstacles at the organisational and policy-making levels at local, national and supranational level. In the case of gender equity, for example, Kabeer's (2003) analysis of poverty reduction policy found that, to date, international development policies had shown only limited and compartmentalised engagement. Sport for development research needs to locate its analyses of the impact of sport within such contexts.

Conclusion

As in the Minority World, sport in the context of international development offers ambiguities and complexities. There are difficulties in operating many projects, which typically rely heavily on partnership working and continuity of funding at the strategic level, and on volunteer effort – especially on the willingness of young people to act as peer leaders – at the point of delivery. Both situations pose challenges for the sustainability of even the most successful initiatives. Additionally, while sport is valued for its potential positive contributions, it can also be regarded more negatively at the micro-level for qualities such as its institutionalised competitiveness, aggression and sexism, and at the structural level for its significance as an 'export' of the global North. The reliance of many programmes on meeting the requirements of externally provided funding streams raises further questions about the autonomy of indigenous organisations to develop their sports-based work as they see fit. Together these concerns can fuel debates about whether sport is an appropriate priority for investment in countries facing fundamental issues of poverty, ill-health and hunger.

The most significant challenge facing sport and development work, however, lies deeper. Despite the rhetoric and momentum surrounding it, this dilutes the meaning – and not all studies are 'small,' researchers and policy makers do not know whether sport actually 'works.' The central challenge for academics is, therefore, how to assess the impact of sport. To address this, a number of critical networks have emerged, committed to collaborating in order to improve research quality and inform policy and practice. But like many sport and development initiatives themselves, such networks risk privileging the voices of the Minority World, and relying on culturally specific research models that reflect the values of the global North.

Western accounts of 'the impact of sport' in international development thus raise questions of legitimacy. Kay (2009) has suggested that evaluation research can be especially problematic, as these studies so frequently require researchers to privilege the positivist forms of knowledge preferred by policy makers and donor agencies. The use of these methods is particularly likely to limit local expressions of knowledge and mitigate against reflexivity, partnership and local capacity-building in research. But donor-funded sport for development projects require such data for transparency and accountability, and to counter widely acknowledged issues of poor governance. It would be naïve to expect such requirements to be removed. We may reach a more appropriate understanding of sport and development, however, if we also engage with the debates surrounding decolonising methodologies and knowledge that feature prominently in development studies. By embracing new thinking we may be able to develop a deeper knowledge of the potential of sport to address social exclusion in the context of international development.

Acknowledgements

I am grateful to Ruth Jeanes and the Leisure Studies Association for permission to draw on the themed collection of articles on sport in development that Ruth and I edited for issue 85 of the Association's newsletter. I also thank Joe Bancroft, Davies Banda, Shane Collins, Julie Fimusanmi, Ruth Jeanes, Iain Lindsey, John Morris and Jo Welford for their contributions to the primary research referred to in this chapter, and Iain, Ruth and Davies for their particular support in the work we carry out in Zambia.

References

Bhalla, A. and Lapeyre, F. (1997) Social exclusion: towards an analytical and operational framework. *Development and Change*, 28: 413–433.

Coalter, F. (2007) *A Wider Role for Sport: Who's keeping the score?* London: Routledge.

de Haan, A. (1999) Social exclusion: towards an holistic understanding of deprivation. Online: *http://webarchive.nationalarchives.gov.uk/+/http://www.dfid.gov.uk/Documents/publications/sdd9socex.pdf* (accessed 4 May 2010).

Denzin, N. and Lincoln, Y. (2008) *The Landscape of Qualitative Research*, 3rd edn. Thousand Oaks: Sage.

Gore, C. (1995), Markets, citizenship and social exclusion. In Rodgers, G., Gore, C. and Figueiredo, J. (eds) (1997) *Social Exclusion, Rhetoric, Reality, Responses.* A contribution to the World Summit for Social Development, International Institute for Labour Studies, Geneva.

Kabeer, N. (2003) *Gender Mainstreaming in Poverty Eradication and the Millennium Development Goals. A handbook for policy-makers and other stakeholders Commonwealth Secretariat/IDRC/CIDA.* Online: *www.idrc.ca/en/ev-28774-201-1-DO_TOPIC.html* (accessed 17 September 2009).

Kahn S., Stewart, F., Eyben, R. *et al.* (2009) *Social Exclusion. Governance and social development resource centre (GSDRC).* Online: *http://webarchive.nationalarchives.gov.uk/+/http://www.dfid.gov.uk/Documents/publications/sdd9socex.pdf* (accessed 28 April 2010).

Kay, T. (2009) Developing through sport: evidencing sport impacts on young people, *Sport in Society*, 12 (9): 1177–1191.

Kidd, B. (2008) A new social movement: Sport for development and peace. *Sport in Society*, 11 (4): 370–380.

Laws, S., Harper, C. and Marcus, R (2003) *Research for Development*. London: Sage.

Lindsey, I., Namukanga, A., Kakone, G. *et al.* (2010) Adventures in research: enabling community impact through sport for development research. *Leisure Studies Association Newsletter*, 85 (March): 53–57.

Lyras, A., Wolff, E., Hancock, M. *et al.* (2009) Sport for development global initiative. In North American Sociology of Sport Conference, Ottawa, Canada, November 2009.

Muraleedharan, K. (2005) *Empowering Women Inter-state Comparison of Indian Experiments.* New Delhi: Indian Council of Social Science Research.

Mwaanga, O. (2010) Sport for addressing HIV-AIDS: explaining our convictions. *Leisure Studies Association Newsletter*, 85 (March): 58–64.

Saavedra, M. (2009) Dilemma and opportunities in gender and sport-in-development. In Levermore, R. and Beacom, A. (eds) *Sport in International Development*. London: Palgrave Macmillan, pp: 124–155.

Saith, R. (2001) *Social Exclusion: The Concept and Application to Developing Countries.* Oxford: Oxford University Press.

Schuler, S. and Hashemi, S. (1998) Defining and studying empowerment of women: a research note from Bengladesh. JSI Working Paper No.3, Arligton, V.A. In Muraleedharan, K. (2005) *Empowering Women Inter-state Comparison of Indian Experiments*. New Delhi: Indian Council of Social Science Research.

Silver, H. (1994) Social exclusion and social solidarity: three paradigms. *International Labour Review*, 133: 5–6.

Sport for Development and Peace International Working Group (2007) *Literature Reviews on Sport for Development and Peace.* Toronto: University of Toronto.

Strobbe, F., Olivetti, C. and Jacobson, M. (2010) *Breaking the Net: Family Structure and Street Children in Zambia.* BWPI Working Paper 111. Manchester: Manchester University.

16 Physical education for all

The impact of standards and curriculum on student choice

Deborah Tannehill

Introduction

It should be stated that no chapter could hope to address all issues related to the impact of curriculum and curricular decisions on physical education for *all* students. This chapter is no exception, although the curriculum issues selected are those that appear most meaningful to the young people I have observed, or with whom I have worked, on two continents, and are those which reflect issues that have been prominent in research. It is my hope that the issues chosen and comments presented will cause us to think critically about how we might investigate ways of using our curricular choices to increase opportunities for and interest in physical education and physical activity. Highlighting similarities and differences from the UK to Ireland and from the US to Australia, the issues selected for discussion have been investigated in varying contexts.

There has been much discussion in recent years about how we might ensure our physical education programmes are providing young people with worthwhile and challenging opportunities. Questions have been raised about providing opportunities to learn and practise physical activity, about how we might assist practising teachers in gaining the confidence to deliver physical education in new and innovative ways, and finally how we can pose ideas on how to link our work to the community and the education of pre-service teachers. This chapter will extend these thoughts and challenge us to consider how we might examine and come to better understand some of the issues that impact physical education for all young people in our programmes. In short, if the curriculum is inappropriate, we are unlikely to be able to offer a worthwhile and inclusive programme.

Social construction of physical education

MacPhail (2004) highlights the ongoing debate that continues around the social construction of physical education and suggests it 'is based on the belief that any definition of traditional physical education is embedded in political, social, and cultural elements from a specific point in time' (p. 54). Thus, social construction is directed by what Lawson (1998) described as physical educations' managing of young people's forms of play, sport and physical activity through forced and regulated participation. The result can be programmes that alienate youth from participation rather than inviting and engaging them in worthwhile activity.

The traditional sporting model of physical education has a focus on team games delivered through a limited set of learning experiences and teaching strategies (Kirk and Kinchin, 2003; Metzler, 2000) and this is one example of a socially constructed physical education. In 1998, Lawson told us that 'physical education' and 'sport' had become synonymous both in the minds of the public and in the practice of physical education teachers. While Lawson did not question the importance of sport or its place in physical education, he does caution us that too much emphasis on sport results in the needs of some students being met and those of others neglected. For example, one outcome of an overemphasis on sport is young people who find physical education incompatible with their lifestyles, interests and what is accessible, with the result that they choose not to pursue physical activity in or out of the school setting. Indeed, Ennis (2003) argues that 'students do not find physical education coherent, relevant, or meaningful' (p. 23). From my observations and reading of the literature, I would agree with Ennis. There is evidence to suggest that few students experience a sound, sequential, or coherent physical education programme that their school years gives them sufficient opportunity to be successful. For example, 'Activities are often taught year after year, at the same time, in the same way, with little emphasis on new skills, more complex applications, or transfer to different activities or settings' (Lund and Tannehill, 2009, p. 24). Clearly such an approach can only meet the needs of very few students, while alienating and thereby excluding many others.

Serving the needs of young people

I have argued elsewhere that: 'We need to do things differently, move away from curricula that mirror only what has been done in the past, and build programmes that reflect the desires and needs of young people so that they might persist in their efforts to develop physically active lifestyles' (Tannehill, 2007 p. 3). Yet, how can we all – teacher educators, physical education teachers, or students – describe what a coherent physical education programme would look like, and would such a programme really influence students' learning and decision to participate? We might argue, for example, that a coherent curriculum would:

- be perceived by students as central to their daily lives;
- allow students to link subsequent learning experiences so that their knowledge grows and becomes richer;
- provide meaningful and important learning to students in 'real' life situations;
- allow students to explore learning by having opportunities to make sense of their lived experiences;
- make meaningful connections between the context of the school and local community;

- facilitate student application and transfer of learning to settings outside of school;
- allow students to learn through exploration and questioning;
- provide progressive and exciting challenges that move the student from simple to complex learning.

Perhaps a coherent curriculum would look something like that described by Macdonald (2003) as a postmodern physical education. Such a curriculum would be problem/task based, culturally relevant and inclusive, flexible in content and boundaries, student centred, as well as promote learning both within and beyond school boundaries, and allow for uncertainty and discovery. This would be a very different curriculum from that experienced by most young people around the world today.

Student voice

It should be obvious that physical education should provide young people with experiences that are significant and worthwhile. Collier (2006) suggests that if physical education is going to be inviting to young people and have an impact on them, curricular options must reflect students' personal interests, school culture and community resources. This suggests that we look to involve young people more intimately in the curriculum design process in terms of both what is taught and how it is taught.

The notion of including student voice in curriculum design is illustrated in a study commissioned by the Irish Sports Council (Woods *et al.*, 2010). The Children's Sport Participation and Physical Activity (CSPPA) study was initiated to improve our understanding of the role of physical activity in the lives of Irish youth and adolescents. Focus group interviews were conducted with primary (aged 10–12) and post-primary youth (aged 13–18) to exemplify some of the key themes resulting from an initial questionnaire. The interviews sought to delve into the themes further to highlight key points that might illustrate best practice with the aim of increasing young peoples' motivation to participate in physical activity (PA) and sport.

An interesting highlight in the data from boys (aged 15) was their desire to be offered variety and novel activities that were new to them and which some already enjoyed (such as tai chi, judo, hip hop and others). These boys also commented on the teacher and what, from their perspectives, would be good practice; for example, it is important to give students choice and responsibility, teachers should stop talking so much, 'let us play without interrupting,' and encourage everyone equally. Many of the older girls had slightly different insights onto physical education. For example, none of the girls enjoyed exclusion games, activities where lack of skill was very apparent or when they had no choice in what they did. Several girls talked about the boredom they felt in some activities and exclusion caused by the nature of the game. In one interview, for example, two girls commented:

'kingball, that's mostly it . . . it's just king ball,' and her friend added, 'ye, and then that only knocks people out, like not everybody's playing.'

When designing a curriculum, Tomlinson (2003) asks us to consider how we might adapt what we intend students to learn, as opposed to being very rigid in what we assume students should learn. In physical education, Cothran and Ennis (1997) encourage us to involve young people both actively and authentically in their own learning. Yet, Brooker and Macdonald (1997) suggest that student involvement in curriculum development has been limited to asking for their views on the curriculum they have experienced. On the other hand, Glasby and Macdonald (2004) suggest the idea of a 'negotiated curriculum' where students become partners in the curriculum development process. Moreover, McMahon (2007) involved primary-aged students in the process of curriculum negotiation and found that, as a result, students were more invested in and committed to the content due to increased ownership of their own learning. This could be regarded, therefore, as one route to a more inclusive physical education curriculum.

Green (2004) argues that, if physical education is intended to encourage young people to become involved in an active lifestyle then, 'PE needs to move with the prevailing tide of young people's leisure lifestyles by catering for their preferences for a wider range of activities in more informal and individual and small group settings' (p. 83). This same idea is suggested by Ennis and Cothran (1996) when they encourage physical educators to make physical education relevant to youth in ways that allow them to connect with their peers. O'Donovan (2003) agrees with both of these views when she reminds us that, 'adolescents place a lot of importance on belonging, on being included, on being "normal" and on being part of a group' (p. 239). In summary, providing young people with physical activity options that are important and meaningful to them may encourage participation both in class and into the future.

Student needs

Sagor (2002) suggests that there are a set of student needs that must be met if they are to feel successful in any activity. He defines these as follows:

C   Need to feel competent
B   Need to belong
U   Need to feel useful
P   Need to feel potent
O   Need to feel optimistic

Sagor encourages us 'to take a hard look at what is wrong about how we work with students in our classrooms' (p. 34). This is consistent with Penney and Chandler's (2000) view of the importance of teaching and instructional decisions that teachers make when delivering physical education content to young people. Similarly, Hellison (2009) has for a long time reminded us that 'we teach young people, not content' (conference presentation). He challenges us to think about how we might empower youth; teach them how to take responsibility for themselves and their well-being and then provide them with opportunities to be responsible. Building a relationship with young people and caring are at the core of Hellison's philosophy when he encourages us to take youth where they are and facilitate their growth and development in ways that are realistic and within the bounds of their context. He often cites a quote by Arthur Ashe, 'tennis is a way to reach kids and teach them things that are more important than tennis.' As I have commented elsewhere, 'While not all that we teach should be only what the students want, we must find ways to pull them in, motivate them to persevere, and provide them with what is important, relevant, and worth their time and energy to master' (Lund and Tannehill, 2005, p. 8). Examining this aspect of the curriculum process is critical if we are to meet the needs of *all* young people.

In an Irish study of a revised physical education syllabus, MacPhail and Halbert (2005) reported declining participation rates of young people in physical activity, and more specifically, physical education, especially among girls. They suggested that a solution might lie in changing the courses offered to students in physical education and also changing the pedagogy and structures that frame them. In this way, MacPhail and Halbert propose that alternative activities and an element of choice might make physical education more attractive to youth. Most noteworthy in their comments related to curriculum reform was the recognition that young people – that is, those most involved in the programmes – were not consulted in the curriculum design process at all. They suggest taking steps to add young people as participants in the design of physical education programmes. In summary, we are beginning to recognise both the importance of including student voice in the design of physical education programmes and the needs of young people including boys and girls of various ages.

Curriculum bounded within standards

In line with the thrust in education towards standards, assessment and accountability, most countries have designed a set of guidelines, or syllabi, to guide the delivery of physical education and to ensure that both the teacher and the students are held accountable. Teachers are held accountable through design of a programme that meets guidelines and students through their demonstration of achieving programme goals. For example, in Ireland there are a set of aims and objectives within an enabling structure, in the US there are standards, in Australia there are a set of syllabus strands and outcomes, and in the UK there are attainment levels. 'Demonstrates competency in motor skills and movement patterns needed to perform a variety of physical activities' is an example of a physical education standard in the USA (NASPE, 2004) and 'an understanding of the principles of fairness and tolerance in interaction with others' is included in the Irish physical education objectives. In this chapter, I use the term 'standards' to refer to all these expectations or programme guidelines.

The key problem with any set of standards is that they rarely identify the content to be taught or define how the content is delivered. Rather, as was noted by the

National Association of Sport and Physical Education (2004), standards reflect a consensus by professionals on what students should know and be able to do after participating in a physical education programme. Lund and Tannehill (2009) suggest that standards might therefore be best considered as a set of learning goals or as a framework to inform development of the curriculum. Rossi *et al.* (2009) remind us that standards documents reflect what Apple (1993) referred to as 'the voice of the state.' Further, as Collier (2006) noted, in some countries standards guide the design and delivery of physical education without consultation or input from all stakeholders.

Macdonald and Hunter (2005) note that educational policies, as expressed in standards, may 'priviledge and marginalize particular knowledge and skills . . . as materials available for developing curricula are drawn from "what is known and available"' (p. 112). Whether we agree with standards or not, at this time they are very much here and guide teachers' decisions about student learning. Some have argued that standards are overly prescriptive, yet it can be argued that because they don't prescribe exactly what is to be taught, standards do allow teachers to make informed decisions on what is most important for the students they teach and the setting in which they teach. Whatever your position on this, as I have argued elsewhere: 'Teachers must be able to interpret the standards, and make choices about how to reach them based on the intent of the standards, the context within which they teach, their own philosophies, as well as those of the students whose needs the curricula is designed to meet' (Lund and Tannehill, 2009, p. 24).

Furthermore, Rossi *et al.* (2009) make an important point about all curriculum frameworks and standards. They argue that the text of any syllabus 'will be interpreted by teachers in ways that might be influenced more by their biographic heterogeneity and the social context in which they teach than by the principles on which the syllabus rhetoric is based' (p. 87). What is clear is that in all pedagogical encounters, teachers matter, their beliefs and viewpoints matter, and their understanding of their students and the environment in which they teach is pivotal to learning.

Teacher knowledge in curriculum development

Capel (2007) suggests that 'knowledgeable physical education teachers should take a pupil-centred rather than subject-centred approach and place pupils' learning at the heart of their teaching' (p. 501). If our goal is student learning rather than simply covering content, Lund and Tannehill (2009, p. 24) identify several questions we should ask.

- What is worthy of student learning?
- What is worth student time and effort?
- What is meaningful and relevant to the lives of students?

To respond to these questions, teachers need to consider the standards and, based on their own teaching context, the needs of the students with whom they work, and 'unpack' them to determine how and through which content they might best be achieved by learners. Standards must be unpacked on two levels (Lund and Tannehill, 2009). The first level of unpacking is conceptual where the teacher interprets the main intent of each standard considering how and why it was initially developed. On the second level, teachers use their interpretations to select curriculum models and activities that will provide the learner with appropriate content and learning experiences to reach the intent of the standards. Unpacking the standards allows for what my colleague Mary O'Sullivan has labelled the FOS principle; that is, Focus On the Student. If the aim of physical education is to persuade young people to continue to participate beyond school and across their life span, we must unpack the aims and objectives in ways that meet their particular needs and interests. Designing challenging, relevant and exciting learning experiences to promote student learning and interest is the key to drawing young people towards physical activity. Investigating how this might be done is critical if we are to move forward with young people at the centre of our work.

These standards-related issues are being considered in Ireland currently as part of a large-scale review and reform of the senior cycle programme and curriculum framework. To provide context to the Irish education system it needs to be understood that post-primary education in Ireland is for students between 12 and 18 years of age and is composed of a three-year junior cycle followed by a two- or three-year senior cycle depending on whether students choose to take the optional transition year between the two programmes. This work is being overseen by the National Council for Curriculum and Assessment (NCCA). This is a significant task in a period of limited funding, and it provides an opportunity for curriculum developers to think outside the box and design something that can make a difference for all young people.

Within this senior cycle review process there are two physical education courses being developed: a non-examination curriculum framework and a syllabus for examination. The examination syllabus is committed to student learning by integrating the practical aspects of physical education with the theory that forms the basis for the content. The second course, the senior cycle framework (non-examinable) is the one where most students will reside and must be designed to include a group of young learners who differ in interests, dispositions, attitudes, talents and special needs. This new framework places the learner at the centre of the syllabus because it attempts to build on students' previous learning, draws on what we know about young people, provides students with the opportunity to make decisions on content based on what is important to them, and is inclusive for all young people (Halbert, 2009).

The planning team recognises that to achieve a programme that provides innovation, listens to students and challenges a wide range of learners is a daunting task that will be challenging for teachers and schools in its implementation. As they move through the review and reform stages, the team's intent is to involve teachers in the design of an innovative curriculum through trial of initiatives and assessment of their success with young people. Learning goals, curricular choices, instructional strategies and assessment are all a part of the curriculum development process. Involving teachers in collaborative relationships or what Kirk and Macdonald (2001) have termed 'partnerships' is essential if we are to understand the importance of not only who delivers but also how the content is delivered. Kirk and Macdonald (2001) ask us to consider the potential outcome if teachers are involved as partners in the design and maintenance of effective instructional practice that impacts teaching and learning of a new curriculum. It would appear that the Irish are attempting to do just that in their programmatic review. It is hoped that studying the impact of curriculum change as a means of determining how to better plan and implement such changes will strengthen the process as well as the outcome. In the initial stages, the Irish team is examining how physical education curriculum models might impact their work and have positive benefits for young people. One consideration the design team has discussed is how designing programmes around physical education curriculum models might meet the needs and interests of young people.

Impact of curriculum models on student involvement in physical education

There has been much written about main theme curriculum models (Ennis, 2003; Kirk *et al.*, 2006; Siedentop and Tannehill, 2000) that focus on what Lund and Tannehill (2009) refer to as 'specific, relevant, and challenging outcomes' (p. 154) and which provide more focused time for learners to be in engaged with and achieve these outcomes through active learning in a purposeful environment.

Kirk, Macdonald, and O'Sullivan in the *Handbook of Physical Education* (2006) use curriculum models as the organising framework for the analysis and review of curriculum research. The emphasis of many physical education programmes is placed on sport, so they note that it is not surprising to find that curriculum models receiving the most research attention are those that use sport as the content of the model.

In practice, choice of curriculum model should be based on the intent of student learning and achievement as well as a teacher's passion for what is important for young people (Hellison, 2009). If the goal is for students to develop the ability to design and perform a dance while working collaboratively with a dance troupe to choreograph and put their steps to music, then Sport Education would be an appropriate choice. If we want students to work as a collective to plan and experience an out-of-doors hill walking event, then choice of Outdoor or Adventure Education might prove to be an effective choice. If the intent of learning is for students to design a personal activity plan to maintain a specified level of fitness, then Fitness Education would be a logical choice of curriculum model. In each of these examples, the choice of curriculum model does not dictate the content to be delivered, the instructional format, learning experiences, or teaching strategies to be employed. These decisions will evolve as teachers examine their own preferences and interpretations of the content as well as the diverse needs and interests of their students.

As teachers make these decisions, Halbert (2009) asks us to consider that, 'choice of activity is unimportant as it is the medium through which students get the message, not the message itself.' Metzler (2005) highlighted key strategies, or instructional models for teachers to consider as they plan lesson delivery. He suggested that an instructional model includes a number of strategies, methods, styles and skills that are used to plan, design and implement a unit of instruction. Studying the various curriculum models reveals that in some cases they are most effectively delivered using a particular instructional model. Penney and Chandler (2000) contend that while often neglected, teaching is the most important aspect of the curriculum process.

If curriculum models are to be useful in designing and delivering an effective and meaningful physical education to young people then, as Kirk and MacPhail (2002) suggest, 'a systematic examination of the model in practice and its further modification and development on the basis of this research program' is essential. Situated learning with young people actively engaged with their environment might prove useful in designing curricula to meet the needs of *all* young people.

Wallhead and O'Sullivan (2005) recommend that research on different curriculum models would be well served if it examined the 'existence and nature of school-community partnerships that have been formed between curricular SE and junior sport and evaluate the efficacy of these evaluations' (p. 206). To be most useful, this examination could extend to the relationships that have been forged through other curricular models; for example, adventure, outdoor, fitness. We might ask, what has been the impact on young people and their willingness to become involved in physical activity when involved in the different curriculum models? Not unlike initiatives such as the PE, School Sport and Club Links strategy (PESSSCL) and the PE and Sport Strategy for Young People in the UK, this might well be a step towards viewing physical education in a different format that extends or begins outside the traditional school day and structured school format.

The Cultural Studies curriculum approach (Kinchin and O'Sullivan, 1999), as noted by O'Sullivan and Kinchin (in press) was developed in response to 'changing cultural and social circumstances of our times where cultural diversity and identity are becoming increasingly significant.' Its intention is for students to develop as critical consumers of sport and physical activity who can question, critique and challenge what happens in the name of sport and physical activity. It also seeks to develop students who can take action in attempting to make society aware of issues caused by biased and unfair practice (O'Sullivan and Kinchin, in press). This model is part of the discussion of the Irish team as they plan the new senior cycle syllabus.

Early work with the cultural studies approach focused on the perceptions of students and their ability to engage with issues of gender, the body and media influences in sport during a cultural studies unit (Kinchin, 1998; Kinchin and O'Sullivan, 1999; Kinchin and O'Sullivan, 2003). This approach was extended to a group of secondary teachers (O'Sullivan *et al.*, 1996) in the design and delivery of a unique social enquiry unit focused on sport. Most recently, Enright has used this model with adolescent girls in an after-school programme in an Irish secondary school (Enright, 2007; Enright and O'Sullivan, 2008, 2010). These girls progressed from being curriculum designers and evaluators to the designers of a student-led physical activity club which they coordinated and for which they advocated. While not identified as being framed in the Cultural Studies curriculum, the work of Oliver and colleagues (Oliver, 2001; Oliver and Lalik, 2001; 2004, Oliver *et al.*, 2009) share aspects of this model that are worth examining.

O'Sullivan and Kinchin (2009) challenge teachers to consider their role in the design of curricula that examine and question social and ethical issues in sport, health and physical activity. While this suggests substantial change for many teachers and their programmes, they indicate that a cultural studies approach offers a relevant and meaningful way for students to examine sport in their own lives, context and wider society (Kinchin and O'Sullivan, 2003). Wright (1995, 2000), who has long recommended alternative curricula to challenge the status quo, reports that a socio-cultural perspective, similar to a cultural studies approach, forms the basis of most syllabi in both New Zealand and Australia.

Conclusion

Timkin and Watson (2009, p. 139) argue that 'little real or substantive improvement will occur in teaching, in student learning, and specifically in the moral fiber of our lives and the lives of students (and others), without a drastic reconceptualization of our purpose as educators, and specifically as physical educators.' This chapter has argued for the importance of examining the social construction of physical education, serving the needs of the youth we teach, considering the standards guiding our programmes, being conscious of teacher knowledge and its impact on student learning, and finally exploring how physical education curriculum models might impact opportunities for all young people. A final thought is drawn from the words of Lawson (1998) who in his expose on what he describes as the looming children's crisis outlines opportunities for development of change theories and design models that can impact practice and research in physical education. He concludes that, 'the discussion has come full circle when the invitation is issued to others to imagine, design, implement, and evaluate new design models and change theories that help rejuvenate, reconstitute, and transform PE' (p. 20). That invitation is hereby extended to you, to pre-service teachers, to practising teachers and to young people in the hope that we will more effectively design physical education programmes that meet the needs of *all* children and youth.

References

Apple, M. (1993) *Official Knowledge: Democratic education in a conservative age.* New York: Routledge.

Brooker, R. and Macdonald, D. (1997) Did we hear you? Issues of student voice in curriculum innovation. *Journal of Curriculum Studies*, 31 (1): 83–97.

Capel, S. (2007) Moving beyond physical education subject knowledge to develop knowledgeable teachers of the subject. *The Curriculum Journal*, 18 (1): 493–508.

Collier, C. (2006) Models and curricula of physical education teacher education. In Kirk, D., Macdonald, D. and O'Sullivan, M. (eds) *Handbook of Physical Education*, London: Sage Publications.

Cothran, D.J. and Ennis, C.D. (1997) Students' and teachers' perceptions of conflict and power. *Teaching and Teacher Education*, 13 (5): 541–553.

Ennis, C.D., Cothran, D.J., Davidson, K.S., Loftus, S.J., Owens, L., Swanson, L. and Hopsicker, S. (1997) Implementing curriculum within a context of fear and disengagement. *Journal of Teaching in Physical Education*, 17: 58–72.

Enright, E. (2007) Can I do it in my pyjamas?: Negotiating a physical education curriculum with teenage girls. In the *British Educational Research Association Annual Conference*, London, September.

Enright, E. and O'Sullivan, M. (2008) Cos that's what I thought ye wanted to hear: participatory methods and research agendas in physical education research. In the *Researching Children's Worlds Conference*, Galway, Ireland.

Enright, E. and O'Sullivan, M. (2010) Carving a new order of experience *with* young people in physical education: Participatory Action Research as a pedagogy of possibility. In O'Sullivan, M. and MacPhail, A (eds) *Young People's Voices in Physical Education and Youth Sport*. London: Routledge, pp. 162–187.

Ennis, C.A. (2003) Using curriculum to enhance student learning. In Silverman, S.J and Ennis, C.A. (eds) *Student Learning in Physical Education: Applying research to enhance instruction.* Champaign, IL: Human Kinetics, pp. 109–127.

Glasby, P.M. and Macdonald, D. (2004) Negotiating the curriculum: Challenging the social relationships in teaching. In Wright, J., Macdonald, D. and Burrows, L. (eds) *Critical Inquiry and Problem-Solving in Physical Education.* London: Routledge.

Green, K. (2004) Physical education, lifelong participation and 'the couch potato' society. *Physical Education and Sport Pedagogy*, 9 (1): 73–86.

Halbert, J. (2009) *NCCA: Developments in senior cycle physical education.* Meeting of the Physical Education Discussion Forum. Athlone, Ireland.

Hellison, D. (2009) *Keynote Address at Physical Education Association of Ireland (PEAI) Annual Conference*, October 2–3, 2009, Tralee, Ireland.

Kinchin, G.D. (1998) Secondary students' responses to issues of gender in sport and physical activity, *Journal of Sport Pedagogy*, 4 (1): 29–42.

Kinchin, G. and O'Sullivan, M. (1999) Making Physical Education meaningful for high school students, *The Journal of Physical Education, Recreation and Dance*, 70 (1): 40–44, 54.

Kinchin, G. and O'Sullivan, M. (2003) Incidences of student support for and resistance to a curricular innovation in high school physical education. *Journal of Teaching in Physical Education*, 22 (3): 245–260.

Kinchin, G. and O'Sullivan, M. (2010) Cultural studies curriculum in physical activity and sport. In J. Lund and D. Tannehill (eds) *Standards-based Physical Education Curriculum Development*, 2nd edition. Sudbury, MA: Jones & Bartlett.

Kirk, D. and Kinchin, G. (2003) Situated learning in physical education. *Journal of Teaching in Physical Education*, 17 (4): 376–387.

Kirk, D. and MacPhail, A. (2002) Teaching games for understanding and situated learning: Rethinking the Bunker-Thorpe model. *Journal of Teaching in Physical Education*, 21 (2): 177–192.

Kirk, D. and Macdonald, D. (2001) Teacher voice and ownership of curriculum change. *Journal of Curriculum Studies*, 33 (4): 551–567.

Kirk, D., Macdonald, D. and O'Sullivan, M. (eds) (2006) *Handbook of Physical Education*, London: Sage Publications.

Lawson, H.S. (1998) Rejuvenating, reconstituting, and transforming physical education to meet the needs of vulnerable children, youth and families. *Journal of Teaching in Physical Education*, 18 (1): 2–25.

Lund, J. and Tannehill, D. (eds) (2005) *Standards-based Physical Education Curriculum Development.* Boston, MA: Jones and Bartlett.

Lund, J. and Tannehill, D. (eds) (2009) *Standards-based Physical Education Curriculum Development*, 2nd edn. Boston, MA: Jones and Bartlett.

Macdonald, D. (2003) Curriculum change and the postmodern world: Is the school reform project an anarchism? *Journal of Curriculum Studies*, 35 (2): 139–149.

Macdonald, D. and Hunter, L. (2005) Lessons learned . . . about curriculum: Five years on and half a world away. *Journal of Teaching in Physical Education*, 24 (1): 111–126.

MacPhail, A. (2004) The social construction of higher grade physical education: The impact on teacher curriculum-decision making. *Sport, Education and Society*, 9 (1): 53–73.

MacPhail, A. and Halbert, J. (2005) The implementation of the revised physical education syllabus in Ireland: Circumstances, rewards, and costs. *European Physical Education Review*, 1 (3): 287–308.

McMahon, M. (2007) 'You don't feel like ants and giants': Student involvement in negotiating the physical education curriculum. Thesis submitted to the University of Limerick.

Metzler, M. (ed.) (2000) The physical education teacher education assessment project. *Journal of Teaching in Physical Education* (Special Edition), 19 (4): 15–56.

Metzler M. W. (2005) *Instructional models for physical education.* Scotsdale, AZ: Holcomb Hathaway Publishers.

National Association for Sport and Physical Education (NASPE) (2004) *Moving into the Future: National standards for physical education*, 2nd edn. Boston, MA: McGraw Hill.

O'Donovan, T. M. (2003) A changing culture? Interrogating the dynamics of peer affiliations over the course of a Sport Education season. *European Physical Education Review*, 9 (3): 237–251.

Oliver, K. (2001) Images of the body from popular culture: Engaging adolescent girls in critical inquiry. *Sport, Education and Society*, 6 (2): 143–164.

Oliver, K. and Lalik, R. (2001) The body as curriculum: Learning with adolescent girls. *Journal of Curriculum Studies*, 33 (3): 303–333.

Oliver, K. and Lalik, R. (2004) Critical inquiry on the body in girls' physical education classes: A critical poststructural analysis. *Journal of Teaching in Physical Education*, 23 (2): 162–195.

Oliver, K., Hamzeh, M. and McCaughtry, N. (2009) Girly girls can play games/Las niñas pueden jugar tambien: Co-creating a curriculum of possibilities with 5th grade girls. *Journal of Teaching in Physical Education*, 28 (1): 90–110.

O'Sullivan, M. and Kinchin, G. (2009) Cultural Studies Curriculum in Physical Activity and Sport. In Lund, J. and Tannehill, D. (eds) *Standards-Based Curriculum Development in Physical Education*, 2nd edn. Sudbury: MA: Jones and Bartlett.

O'Sullivan, M., Kinchin, G., Kellum, S. *et al.* (1996) Thinking differently about high school physical education. In the *AAHPERD National Convention*, Atlanta, GA.

Penney, D. and Chandler, T. (2000) Physical education: What future(s)? *Sport, Education and Society*, 5 (1): 71–87.

Rossi, T., Tinning, R., McCuaig, L. *et al.* (2009) With the best of intentions: A critical discourse analysis of physical education curriculum materials. *Journal of Teaching in Physical Education*, 28 (1): 75–89.

Sagor, R. (2002) Lessons learned from skateboarders. *Educational Leadership*, 60 (1): 34–38.

Siedentop, D. and Tannehill, D. (2000) *Developing Teaching Skills in Physical Education*, 4th edn. Mountain View, CA: Mayfield Publishing Company.

Tannehill, D. (2007) Involving teachers in the design of a coherent physical education curriculum. In the *Physical Education Association of Ireland (PEAI) Annual Conference*, October, Limerick, Ireland.

Timken, G.L. and Watson, D. (2009) Teaching all kids: Valuing students through culturally responsive and inclusive pedagogy. In Lund, J. and Tannehill, D. (eds) *Standards-based Curriculum Development in Physical Education.* Sudbury, MA: Jones and Bartlett.

Tomlinson, C.A. (2003) Deciding to teach them all. *Educational Leadership*, 61 (1): 7–11.

Wallhead, T. and O'Sullivan, M. (2005) Sport Education: physical education for the new millennium? *Physical Education and Sport Pedagogy*, 10 (2): 181–210.

Woods, C., Moyna, N., Quinlan, A. *et al.* (2010) *The Children in Sport Participation and Physical Activity Study (CSPPA Study).* Summary Report to the Irish Sports Council.

Wright, J. (1995) A feminist poststructuralist methodology for the study of gender construction in physical education: Description of a study. *Journal of Teaching in Physical Education*, 15 (1): 1–24.

Wright, J. (2000) Bodies, meanings and movement: A comparison of the language of a physical education lesson and a Feldenkrais movement class. *Sport, Education and Society*, 5 (1): 35–49.

17 Dance and social inclusion

Possibilities and challenges

Michael Gard and Doug Risner

Introduction

Dance is often romanticised as a mode of existence free of the prosaic restrictions of everyday life. As such, dance artists and educators often talk about dance more as a place to escape to rather than as a vehicle for social inclusion. Despite the enthusiasm of its advocates, dance has not quite generated the rhetoric of mass physical participation in the English-speaking West, a remit that has by and large been cornered by sport. Neither as high-brow art, low-brow sexiness nor in-between fun, dance – unlike sport – is rarely seen as a socially unifying force, accessible by people across social and economic strata. There have been many attempts to popularise various dance forms and draw them into the social mainstream but, in the context of this chapter, these attempts highlight an interesting tension. If the idea of social inclusion is at least partly concerned with drawing those on the excluded margins closer to the cultural centre, attempts to involve more people in dance often stress dance's power to question, problematise and even splinter mainstream culture. For example, a number of community dance programmes aimed at boys and men in Australia have been conceived as antidotes to what its proponents saw as harmful dominant ideas about masculinity and male embodiment. In other words, in some ways, these dance programmes have sought to shake and fracture the mainstream rather than to grow and draw more people to it. So, if social inclusion is taken to mean fostering cohesion and connections between people who were previously alienated from each other, it is worth remembering that much dance expression seeks to announce, emphasise and in some cases preserve the specificity and difference of particular social (think break dance) and cultural (think folkloric dance) groups.

Perhaps what we are drawing attention to here is dance's ontological status as both art and cultural artefact. As art, the social and cultural mainstream is often the enemy of dance or at least the object of its critique. As cultural artefact, dance is a symbol of that which separates different groups. This is surely in contrast to competitive sports which, in some ways, require that geographic, social and cultural boundaries be transcended or at least channelled if the common language of organised play is the goal.

In short, social inclusion, however defined, has only very occasionally been the explicit goal of dance practitioners. This does not mean that we cannot consider the ways in which dance practices might lead to some form of social inclusion and, in what follows, we attempt to think generatively rather than narrowly about these possibilities. While there is relatively little research into the power of dance to bring about significant positive social change, we can talk with a little more confidence about the reasons why people dance and the ways in which dance is used. From this necessarily tentative starting point, if not answers, we offer examples of practical and theoretical possibility that might at least complicate and diversify our understandings of the purposes of dance.

Dance, the community *and* school education

There are a number of ways we could divide and classify dance practices or the people who engage in them. Given our own separate but overlapping interests, we propose to talk about two broad areas of dance activity: first, dance education in the contexts of schools and teacher education programs; and second, dance that happens in more explicitly artistic and professional contexts. This is a distinction that has some limitations and we use it here somewhat pragmatically in order to frame rather than constrain our thoughts.

If we put to one side people who aspire to be professional artists or those who choose it freely as a form of recreation, a difficult question about the purpose of dance arises. This is particularly so in schools where dance is seen by some educators as an important, almost taken for granted, part of a school education even though different advocates may give very different reasons for including it. For example, Buck (2006) offers an account of the historical shifts in both the philosophy and practice of dance education in schools. There is no space here for a detailed summary but, amongst other things, this history suggests there has been an ongoing struggle over the relative importance of developing artistic appreciation versus personal and/or psychological growth and, in pedagogical terms, authoritarian versus more co-operative approaches to teaching dance. In the context of a discussion about social inclusion, this history suggests that dance education's unit of analysis has most often been the individual student at the end of an imagined educative process. Although they are unquestionably linked, dance education tends to ask questions about what kind of person we want to produce rather than in what kind of society we want to live in.

There are a small number of obvious exceptions to this. First, there is a tradition that sees dance as a vehicle for addressing contentious social issues. This approach to dance education derives much of its momentum from the work of dance artists who have been relatively explicit about their use of movement to provoke thought and raise questions about the world. The challenge for educators with similar aspirations for their students becomes one of harnessing the symbolic power of movement so that movers and audiences might turn their minds or hearts to the issue being explored. There are a small number of examples in the research literature of this being attempted although these tend to do little more than describe the original educative intention and speculate about its effect on students (Ferdun, 1994; Blume, 2003; Gard, 2004). In short, there is precious little empirical support for the use of dance in schools to explicitly and effectively promote social goals, be they social inclusion or anything else. This is certainly not to dismiss this issues-based approach to dance education; we believe it has great value in helping to develop students' movement creativity, as well as giving all of us – students, teachers and artists – one more reason to dance. The point at issue here is about the often asserted – but mostly untested – ability of dance to address social problems.

There are, of course, many examples of what we might call community-based programmes aimed at reaching disenfranchised populations, communities and individuals (Green, 2000; Houston, 2005). At their root, most programmes seek social inclusion by empowering participants who are perceived as excluded from the mainstream (such as at-risk children, core city populations, persons of different ability, seniors, incarcerated populations, and the physically or mentally challenged). From a social inclusion perspective, many programmes focus on participatory community-based arts in which social transformation and urban renewal both figure prominently in projected outcomes. Participation in community-based arts in urban contexts may be understood as a gateway to activities and behaviours that stimulate local economies and nurture the establishment of healthy civic culture. While studies are limited, positive outcomes from community projects in dance education have been reported (Beck and Appel, 2003; Eddy, 2009; Ross, 2000, 2008).

However, a review of recent international scholarship analysing trends within community arts practice reveals that these studies are largely designed to validate arts outreach as a legitimate form of artistic practice, and scholars have been reluctant to criticise practitioners' effectiveness (Kuppers, 2007; Graves, 2005). In fact, it is apparent that the shift towards an 'engagement' strategy, in which artists teach classes, hold workshops and give lectures, is seen as a means to marketing live performing arts events and influencing audience reception and retention (Brown and Novak, 2007; McCarthy and Jinnett, 2001). While most scholarship fails to provide credible baseline data or resources of available, coherent teacher preparation or curricula, community-based dance programmes and their social inclusion goals provide important opportunities for interdisciplinary curriculum development and collaborative research with physical and dance educators.

It is probably fair to say that dance educators working in community-based programmes place a great deal of stock in the simple act of participation. In this context, social inclusion is assumed to flow from people coming together, working on a common problem and achieving a degree of success. This is an important point because it forces us to ask whether social inclusion is – or has – a specific pedagogy. In other words, is it enough just to involve people in social activity for us to say that social inclusion has happened? Or is social inclusion something that can be taught and achieved as a planned educational outcome? Our sense is that most dance educators would see social change as a less mechanical and rather more organic outcome of teaching dance, particularly where the dance forms being taught are social or creative.

A second strand of thinking about dance and broad social goals has problematised long-standing Western suspicions and prejudices about dance in general and boys and men who dance in particular. This is a complex social issue but, broadly, has been picked up in two ways by educators. First, there has been an essentially equity-focused concern with the forms of physical activity that schools and, in particular, physical education programmes, make available to students (Keyworth, 2001; Larsson *et al*, 2007). Despite its historical roots in various forms of creative and expressive movement, the general trajectory of physical education in Western countries post-Second World War has been towards a more instrumental rationale for movement (Kirk, 2000; Wright, 1996). We would want to make clear that an officially instrumental and 'common-sense' justification for certain forms of movement tends to obscure the social, moral and political forces shaping physical education and we will return to these shortly. For the moment, we want simply to register the point that the second half of the twentieth century signalled the growing dominance of and preference for sports and physical fitness over dance in the minds of school and university physical educators.

Equity, social inclusion and dance

Is equity the same as social inclusion? There are probably a number of ways of tackling this question but we offer what we think is a straightforward justification for considering equity here. If schools and their physical education programmes are one of the places in which we represent and reproduce our movement cultures, then the hegemony of sports and fitness officially sanctions and values the aspirations and talents of some students over others. Although haphazardly studied, there is consistent research evidence to show that the marginalisation of dance also marginalises students who want to dance (Wright, 1997; Paechter, 2000). We think this argument could just as easily be extended to students who are curious about dance and even those who are simply open to trying it. In fact, some research suggests that dance is sometimes not offered because educators assume a pervasive prejudice against it amongst students, potentially overlooking the possibility that a vocal minority is being allowed to speak for a heterogeneous majority (Gard and Meyenn, 2000).

The absence of dance is often criticised, on common-sense grounds – for example, as a matter of gender equity – school and university movement cultures that foreground sport probably cater for the movement tastes and aspirations of male students more than those of female students. However, a small number of scholars have considered the social class and ethnicity dimensions of this issue. For example, in a recent study Sanderson (2008) reported that attitudes towards dance amongst 11 to 16-year-old boys and girls in Britain varied with social class. Sanderson recommended that dance 'should be more widely available in schools so that all children and young people can have access to aesthetic experiences that have the potential to improve quality of life' (p. 485) and, further, that this dance content might best include a combination of high art and popular dance forms. Therefore, and as we have attempted to articulate throughout this chapter, there may be a place for dance in physical education that is different from educational dance's initial beginnings and development. The challenge of dance aesthetics for sport-based physical educators is, however, likely to remain a significant hurdle.

The dimension of social class highlights some of the complexities around equity, social inclusion and dance's place in the curriculum. For example, if it could be shown that wealthier students were more interested in dance than poorer students, does this mean that we should have more or less dance education? In other words, would more dance favour the tastes of more privileged students? Alternatively, if some students are disinterested in dance, does this represent a kind of social pathology that needs to be remedied? Sanderson (2008) argues that a lack of appreciation of dance amongst particular groups is both an equity and a social inclusion issue on the grounds that positive dance experiences are something all students should have access to. The idea that dance is for 'all' school students is similar to the one rehearsed by advocates of other curriculum areas, such as science and music. And yet there is a certain abstractness to some of these arguments, particularly where they start from the assumption that dance is a quasi-human right such that a life without dance is seen as somehow inferior.

The 'dance for all' philosophical position raises a number of other interesting questions related to social inclusion. For example, it will probably surprise few readers that advocates tend to make controversial, if not plainly exaggerated, claims about the problems that dance participation can address. Besides the obvious dangers that exaggeration brings, the 'dance for all' position also tends to offer a shopping list of potential benefits in a way that seems to ignore the possibility that different educational goals might require different educational interventions. For example, Gilbert (2005) claims that having a dance programme in schools will help to fight childhood obesity, improve brain function and general mental health, increase empathy and reduce violence. Our point is not to criticise educators who believe in the value of dance. Instead, we wish to highlight the way physical activity in general and dance in particular can be seen as a kind of panacea without much thought given to how, exactly, it brings about change or how it might be used differently to address different educative and social goals. Belief amongst advocates in its remedial powers is at least something that dance shares with sport.

Moving beyond equity as a dimension of social inclusion, some dance educators have turned their attention to the way movement cultures serve to construct, validate and even celebrate gender norms and identities. This most obviously raises the issue of male participation in and appreciation of dance. Here we have moved from trying to increase participation and offering educational programmes that cater for both boys and girls towards seeing dance as an embodied experience that generates critical reflection about gender. Once again this is complex theoretical and practical terrain but both of us, in different ways, have researched the reasons why some boys and men choose to dance with a view to understanding what dance means to people and, in turn, how we might draw on these meanings in order to use and teach dance in socially critical and creative ways (Gard, 2003; Risner, 2007).

If dance is a socially useful experience, one of its uses may relate to its specificity as dance. Our research suggests that some young males see creative and artistic dance as a particular way of being in the world, both as an alternative to the bodily rules of everyday life and as a way of testing and challenging one's body without the rules and violence of sport (Gard, 2006). Although they express the point in different ways, dance educators such as ourselves who think more boys and men should dance argue that our identities and the ways we learn to use our body shape and are shaped by the purposes to which our bodies are put. In Western cultures, where sport can be seen as the 'natural' form of masculine bodily expression, dance creates space for an alternative and, if nothing else, reveals the default as a choice rather than destiny.

In short, we have described dance education here as, potentially, contributing to social inclusion in two ways: first, in terms of equity – so that the movement cultures we create are able to include the talents and aspirations of more young people; and second, as social critique – such that dance, especially for boys and men, generates the space for alternative identities to be and be created. In part, this is why both of us have argued against dance advocates who have suggested making dance more like sport in order to encourage boys and men to dance. It is dance's *difference* from sport, not its similarity, that is at the heart of its potential to change people and the societies we live in.

Higher education and artistic dance

Since the early 1980s, dance programmes in post-secondary school education have tended to focus on social inclusion opportunities, both in terms of dance degree program requirements and in general education courses for university students. Most of the attention here has centred on multicultural education and its complicated discourses. For example, dance research and scholarship have sought to address alternative paradigms for understanding dance in a larger global perspective (Hagood, 2000). World dance studies today, and their related curricula, emerged from the disciplines of social and cultural anthropology (Kaeppler, 1978). Dance anthropologists in the 1970s levelled strong criticism at the implicit ethnocentrism of dance scholarship at the time challenging, primarily, the ways in which all non-Western dance was presented as 'primitive.' As a result, Western theatrical dance, particularly ballet, was positioned as the dominant dance of the performing arts (Kealiinohomoku, 1970). The ensuing years have produced significant attempts to embrace multiculturalism in dance education.

During the past decade and a half, multicultural initiatives have received considerable curricular development. Dixon (1991) highlighted evidence of African-based, Afrocentric dance influences in European culture, as well as in Eurocentric perspectives around the world, including motional concepts, cultural aesthetics and social dance forms. Her initial call for curricular revision and enhanced teacher training to include immersion in Afrocentric perspectives was supported by a number of subsequent scholars in the 1990s (Asante, 1993; Kerr-Berry, 1994a; Mills, 1994), as well as curricular innovations in institutions of higher education during the same time period. It was felt that dance, rich in cultural and ethnic forms, was particularly well-suited to address diversity and inclusion, including offerings in dance appreciation and introductory overview courses for students other than those on dance degree programmes. Yet, some dance researchers and educators focused on the need for more meaningful inclusion and integration of an African aesthetic paradigm in curricula and pedagogy (Kerr-Berry, 1994b; Hubbard and Sofras, 1998). A number of dance scholars and educators have expressed concern that multicultural approaches to dance inadequately address the bedrock goals of inclusive dance curricula. For example, Asante (1993) warned that multicultural insertion and substitution, without full integration, only rationalised a limited African influence on dance. Others, advocating global perspectives, argued for multicultural dance as valid subject matter not only in dance, but also in the humanities generally (West, 1994).

While dance scholarship has identified racism as a central component of ethnocentric bias in dance, it is clear that the persistence of such bias in spite of changing values and increasingly inclusive attitudes is a more complex problem (Asante, 1999). Using dance of the African diaspora as an example, Mills suggests,

> in dance, as in other fields, most people are inclined to maintain or reinforce existing images because people tend to perceive information in a way that is consistent with their values. The end result, as Becker posits, is that we either misperceive information that is not consistent with existing images in order to avoid any inconsistencies, thereby making us uncomfortable, or disregard the information altogether. Many times we simply cue ourselves to perceive information that is consistent with what we expect, believe, or know.
>
> (Mills, 1997, p. 141)

Mills' argument characterises the outcomes of most current multicultural efforts in post-secondary school dance: misperception of, or disregard for non-Western forms because these images are not consistent with what dance faculty and students understand as 'dance.' This Western ethnocentric perspective, dominant in post-secondary dance, situates the amalgam of African dance as 'primarily a somatic, "ethni" [sic] experience compared to an aesthetic experience . . . outside the realm of an artistic aesthetic experience' (Mills, 1997, p. 143). As such, African dance, as well as other non-Western dance forms (Lutz and Kuhlman, 2000), remains on the periphery of most dance education programmes.

The overarching tenet of inclusiveness embedded in multiculturalism also extends to include persons with different abilities. Dance education scholarship that addresses the concerns of special needs populations has its roots in the adapted physical education movement (see also Chapter 13). Recent research focuses on the social construction of disability and the ways in which differently abled bodies challenge and disrupt conventional expectations of bodies in dance. Albright (1997) exposes the implications of the body in performance and its representation of cultural identity through gendered, racial and social markings, including disability. Following notions of equitable contribution, Albright is critical of dances by disabled performers that reproduce dominant assumptions about dance, particularly aesthetics of grace, speed, agility, strength and beauty. Her argument deftly illustrates the hegemonic tendency to value and privilege the abled body, even when the focus is on inclusion, diversity and dancers with different abilities. Kuppers (2000) argues that the disabled dancing body challenges the audience to see past disability and, in so doing, to locate the social construction of disability in the spectator rather than in the differently abled body. For the most part, however, such research and performance remain on the periphery of academic dance and teacher preparation.

In summary, efforts to make post-secondary school dance more multicultural and, thereby, more inclusive, have centred almost exclusively on students' exposure to non-Western forms in order to cultivate an appreciation of someone else's cultural dance form. While this kind of exposure and appreciation can be viewed as radical and important steps towards greater inclusion, most programmes and curricula have yet to adapt a multicultural perspective or become the socially inclusive space promised decades ago in the multiculturalism movement. What post-secondary dance grapples with today is the need for greater integration of inclusion in its programmes, faculty and student populations, and pedagogies.

In order to better understand the ways in which young people engage with artistic dance, we turn to research and data that illuminate current student engagement in serious dance study and programmes conducive to empowerment through dance activity. While we are acutely aware that strict comparison or generalisation between pre-professional dance students and the general population are not straightforward, we do believe there is much to be learned from those who find significant satisfaction and empowerment in dance. In this respect, our approach provides an initial baseline for considering what other young people might find engaging and meaningful in dance activity.

Beyond multicultural efforts described earlier, dance as an instrument for social inclusion is an under-researched area in the literature. What little research there is focuses in three primary areas: social issues in dance education and training; community-based dance programmes for under-represented and marginalised populations; and advocacy pieces that promise inclusive outcomes from dance education curricula. Though limited, each of these literatures reveals potential social inclusion possibilities, while simultaneously concealing other exclusionary practices operating against inclusion in the field.

Social learning and knowing

Making dances and learning them are central components of what young dancers and their choreographers do on a daily basis. The ways in which dancers make sense, create meaning, learn and know these dances provide for rich enquiry into the social nature of dance rehearsal and performance. Though often neglected, the dancers' experience of the rehearsal studio reveals an untapped resource for theoretical and applied research (Risner, 1992).

Studies on the social nature of the rehearsal process, including consideration of young dancers and their relationships with one another, have helped the field to understand that rehearsing is not only learning steps, counts, spacing and dynamics, but also an important social means for dancers – as people – to make meaning, satisfy needs, share frustrations and exchange ideas (Risner, 1995). Dance making is an inherently collaborative activity in which movement ideas are mutually generated and refined 'with the dancers who will dance them' (Barbour, 2008, p. 45). Research into the value of collaboration for dancers and choreographers has revealed that the social context developed within the choreographic process is also significant because 'the relationships the dancers share help to define each as an individual' (Risner, 1995, p. 84). As Barbour concludes, 'Collaborative dance-making processes can function to situate all involved in a social context through which each can continue to develop relationships with others and understand themselves as part of a community of artists' (2008, p. 46).

Additionally, research has illustrated that dancers' ways of knowing are often rooted in their social connection to others in rehearsal and performance, thereby posing challenges to traditional epistemic thought that privileges distance, separation and intellectual knowledge (Risner, 2000). Other dance researchers describe this kind of social knowing as self in the group, in which individual dancers interpret the group relationship differently but see significant connections between learning and knowing the particular dance while engaging in meaningful relationships with others in the group (Critien and Ollis, 2006). Research indicates that the group self also cultivates enhanced creativity and interaction, which dancers report make the choreographic work more meaningful and expressive (Critien and Ollis, 2006). The positive influence of dancers' community and the presence of other students have been shown to be critical for learning (Bracey, 2004; Harwood, 2007). Therefore, the social nature of dance activity provides plentiful terrain for further inquiry about socially inclusive approaches.

In the following and final section we move from the collective to the individual experience of dance training and rehearsal. In particular, we return to the perennial issue of dance and its relationship to masculinity.

Challenging gender discourses: dance is for girls

The feminisation of dance as a discipline in post-secondary dance programmes, in the professional realm as well as in physical education, has been widely documented (Gard, 2006; Risner, 2009). Additionally as Sanderson (2001) has noted, 'Among dance teachers, the major limiting factor in the overall development of the subject is held to be its continued association with PE and the prevalent view that dance is an activity most suited to girls: a tradition evident in many European countries' (p. 119).

Dance, through its training, education and social meanings, has a rich history and long-time association with gender and gender roles. While dance in some cultures is seen as an entirely appropriate activity for males, and a valid vocation, the dominant Western paradigm positions dance as a predominantly 'female' activity and art form. Although the field of professional dance is generally more accepting of non-heterosexuals than the culture at large, there are many indications that male participation in Western theatrical dance education and training remains a culturally suspect endeavour for male adolescents, teens, and young adults (Risner, 2009). Because our intention is to illuminate prospects for inclusion and engagement, we believe it is important to also understand what draws youth to dance activity broadly, and then what participation in dance has to offer more specifically.

From quantitative data on gender engagement available for post-secondary study in the United States, male participation in the arts, broadly, and dance, more specifically, suggests what might be termed a challenging asymmetry in advocacy for dance activity and engagement in the masculinised realm of physical education. According to data from the Higher Education Arts Data Survey (HEADS, 2008), females comprise 65 per cent of all post-secondary students studying the fine and performing arts (visual art/design, dance, music, theatre). In fact, female students outnumber their male counterparts significantly in all arts disciplines with the exception of music (51% male; 49% female). In dance, males represent only 11 per cent of students pursuing post-secondary study. In terms of overall male participation in the arts, males in dance comprise just 1 per cent of the population.

Encouraging male participation in dance has historically involved well-intentioned but frequently heterosexist approaches. These approaches tend to idealise noteworthy heterosexual male dancers, focus on masculinist comparisons between male athletes (presumably heterosexual) and male dancers, and encourage greater male participation by minimising or ignoring the significant population of non-heterosexual males in dance. While we are somewhat sympathetic to these practical appeals for increasing male involvement, we believe these approaches are also likely to make matters worse because they exacerbate the already tenuous situation and homophobic stereotyping that boys and men in dance repeatedly encounter (Gard, 2006; Risner, 2009). In terms of charting potential strategies to enhance engagement in and social inclusion through dance, one strategy might be to theorise beginning with what we know already about male participation in the professional dance realm.

For example, in a study of seventy-five boys and young adult males pursuing pre-professional, theatrical dance study in the US, Risner (2009) investigated the lived experiences of 13 to 22-year-old males engaged in serious professional dance training. The purpose of the study was to better understand the experiences of male adolescents and young adult males studying dance at the pre-professional level (dance academies, conservatories, performing arts high schools, and university programmes) with a specific focus on male dancers' participation and attitudes. The study's empirical data were gathered from a range of dance contexts (ballet, modern dance, jazz dance and musical theatre) and sought to identify what attracts, fulfils, supports and sustains the dancing lives of young males. These findings were compared with the responses from a matched group of female dancers.

Overall, the male dancers experienced far greater stigma and social isolation as a result of their decision to pursue dance than their female peers, as well as reporting predominantly female dance training environments, they also experienced more teasing and verbal and physical harassment, and insufficient support and affirmation for their dancing from parents and male family members. They also reported that their sexual orientation was questioned and repeatedly surveilled. In contrast, female peers received most of their support from the family core (mothers and fathers). As a stigmatised and isolated group, males in the study were eight times more likely than females to report dissatisfaction with the level of social support they received.

Interestingly though, with regard to meaning and motivation in young people's dancing lives, there was much less difference between male and female dancers. The study's survey asked participants to complete the sentence, 'I dance because . . .' For both male and female dancers the most popular responses were 'Dancing is the one place that allows me to be myself,' 'I like to perform,' 'It's a creative outlet for me,' 'I like to move and the physical challenge' and 'I've danced all my life.' The similar motivations of male and females were closely tied to notions of identity, self-expression, performance and creativity and run counter to discourses that have positioned male participation and recruitment in traditionally masculine ways. Previous strategies to explain and encourage male participation in dance have often centred on drawing close parallels between sports and dance, often emphasising competitive athleticism and analogous discourses between sport and dance, while concealing boys' motivation for self-discovery and meaning in expressive artistry.

Risner's research did highlight some gender dissimilarities in desire for moving and physicality made possible in dance. Males reported 'I like to move and the physical challenge' at twice the rate of the female group. This divergence might be explained from two cursory perspectives: females may identify more closely with traditional ideals of beauty, grace and poise; males might identify more easily with athleticism and proving their worth through physical means. We are cautious about endorsing these stereotypical rationales, however, and believe that dancing for some males holds significant meaning and allows them a strong sense of connection and belonging, if only momentarily within the studio or on stage. The prospects for broader social inclusion will likely hinge upon further research on male expression, physicality and meaning in dance within larger, general populations. In particular, we would argue that the inclusion of more males in dance is more likely to be achieved by celebrating and being open about the many reasons why males dance rather than attempting to reduce these reasons down to debatable similarities between dance and sport.

Conclusion

We have attempted, tentatively, to frame ways in which dance might draw marginalised people into socially inclusive environments through movement opportunities. These opportunities are facilitated by the unique attributes of dance, especially those that offer alternatives to experiences of competitive sport. At best, the practical and theoretical possibilities illuminated here diversify our perceptions and beliefs about what dance is for, who dances and why. Though we are left with far more questions than answers, it is apparent that dance today occupies a number of contested spaces; some of which are inherent to the discipline and its stalwart questioning of the status quo and mainstream cultural assumptions.

If we can understand clearly the socio-cultural 'square peg – round hole' dilemma of dance practice, we might begin to question the traditional rhetoric about dance and inclusion. Does it really make sense, for example, the think of dance as a 'cure' for society's ills? If not, we may want to re-focus our collective energies away from the instrumental values of what dance can do for others; for example, fitness, health and wellness, reading and comprehension skills, test scores, self-esteem, and even social inclusion. Instead, our most productive efforts might best be directed towards understanding and using dance on its own terms.

References

Albright, A.C. (1997) *Choreographing Difference: The body and identity in contemporary dance.* Hanover, NH: Wesleyan University Press.

Asante, K.W. (1993) African-American dance in curricula: Modes of inclusion. *Journal of Physical Education, Recreation and Dance*, 64 (2): 48–51.

Asante, K.W. (1999) *African Dance: An artistic, historical and philosophical inquiry.* Trenton, NJ: African World Press.

Barbour, K. (2008) Sustainable dance making: Dancers and choreographers in collaboration. *BROGLA*, June: 41–51.

Beck, J. and Appel, M. (2003) Shaping the future of postsecondary dance education through service learning: An introductory examination of the ArtsBridge model. *Research in Dance Education*, 4 (2): 103–125.

Blume, L.B. (2003) Embodied [by] dance: adolescent de/constructions of body, sex and gender in physical education. *Sex Education*, 3 (2): 95–103.

Bracey, L. (2004) Voicing connections: An interpretive study of university dancers' experiences. *Research in Dance Education,* 5 (1): 7–24.

Brown, A. and Novak, J. (2007) *Assessing the Intrinsic Impacts of a Live Performance: Commissioned by 14 major university presenters.* San Francisco: Wolf Brown.

Buck, R. (2006) Teaching the dance curriculum. In Kirk, D., O'Sullivan, M. and Macdonald, D. (eds) *The Handbook of Physical Education.* London: Sage.

Critien, N. and Ollis, S. (2006) Multiple engagement of self in the development of talent in professional dancers. *Research in Dance Education*, 7 (2): 179–200.

Dixon, B. (1991) The Afrocentric paradigm. *Design for Arts Education, January/February,* 15–22.

Eddy, M. (2009) The role of dance in violence-prevention programmes for youth. In Overby, L. and Lepczyk, B. (eds) *Dance: Current selected research.* Brooklyn, NY: AMS Press, pp. 93–143.

Ferdun, E. (1994) Facing gender issues across the curriculum. *Journal of Physical Education, Recreation and Dance*, 65 (2): 46–47.

Gard, M. (2003) Being someone else: using dance in anti-oppressive teaching. *Educational Review*, 55 (2): 211–223.

Gard, M. (2004) Movement, art and culture: problem-solving and critical inquiry in dance. In Wright, J., Macdonald, D. and Burrows, L. (eds) *Critical Inquiry and Problem-Solving in Physical Education.* London: Routledge, pp. 93–104.

Gard, M. (2006) *Men Who Dance: Aesthetics, Athletics and the Art of Masculinity.* New York: Peter Lang Publishing, Inc.

Gard, M. and Meyenn, R. (2000) Boys, bodies, pleasure and pain: interrogating contact sports in schools. *Sport, Education and Society,* 5 (1): 19–34.

Gilbert, A.G. (2005) Dance education in the 21st century. *Journal of Physical Education, Recreation and Dance,* 76 (5): 26–38.

Graves, J.B. (2005) *Cultural Democracy: The arts, community and the public purpose.* Chicago: University of Illinois Press.

Green, J. (2000) Power, service and reflexivity in a community dance project. *Research In Dance Education,* 1 (1): 53–67.

Hagood, T. (2000) Traditions and experiment/diversity and change: Issues for dance in American education. *Arts Education Policy Review,* 101 (6): 21–26.

Harwood, E. (2007) Artists in the academy: Curriculum and instruction. In Bresler, L. (ed.) *International Handbook for Research in Arts Education.* Dordrecht, Netherlands: Springer, pp. 313–330.

Higher Education Arts Data Services (HEADS) (2008) *Dance Annual Summary 2007–2008.* Reston, VA: National Association of Schools of Dance.

Houston, S. (2005) Participation in community dance: a road to empowerment and transformation? *New Theatre Quarterly,* 21 (2): 166–177.

Hubbard, K. and Sofras, P. (1998) Strategies for including African and African-American culture in a historically Euro-centric dance curriculum. *Journal of Physical Education, Recreation and Dance,* 69 (2): 77–82.

Kaeppler, A. (1978) Dance in anthropological perspective. *Annual Review of Anthropology,* 7: 31–49.

Kealiinohomoku, J. (1970) An anthropologist looks at ballet as a form of ethnic dance. In Van Tuyl, M. (ed.) *Impulse.* San Francisco: Impulse Publications, pp. 24–33.

Kerr-Berry, J. (1994a) African dance: Enhancing the curriculum. *Journal of Physical Education, Recreation and Dance,* 65 (5): 25–27.

Kerr-Berry, J. (1994b) Using the power of Western African dance to combat gender issues. *Journal of Physical Education, Recreation and Dance,* 65 (2): 44–45, 48.

Keyworth, S.A. (2001) Critical autobiography: 'straightening' out dance education. *Research in Dance Education,* 2 (2): 117–137.

Kirk, D. (2000) The reconfiguration of the physical activity field in Australian Higher Education, 1970–1986. *Sporting Traditions,* 16 (2): 17–38.

Kuppers, P. (2000) Accessible education: Aesthetics, bodies and disability. *Research in Dance Education,* 1 (2): 119–131.

Kuppers, P. (2007) Straitjackets of representation. In Kuppers, P. and Robertson, G. (eds) *The Community Performance Reader.* London: Routledge, pp. 217–221.

Larsson, H., Fagrell, B. and Redelius, K. (2007) Queering physical education. Between benevolence towards girls and a tribute to masculinity. *Physical Education and Sport Pedagogy.* Online: http://dx.doi.org/10.1080/17408980701345832.

Lutz, T. and Kuhlman, W. (2000) Learning about culture through dance in kindergarten classrooms. *Early Childhood Education Journal,* 28 (1): 35–40.

McCarthy, K. and Jinnett, K. (2001) *A New Framework for Building Participation in the Arts.* Santa Monica: RAND.

Mills, G.R. (1994) Umfundalai: One technique, three applications. *Journal of Physical Education, Recreation and Dance,* 65 (5): 36–38.

Mills, G.R. (1997) Is it is or is it ain't: The impact of selective perception on the image making of traditional African dance. *Journal of Black Studies,* 28 (2): 139–156.

Paechter, C. (2000) *Changing School Subjects: Power, Gender and Curriculum*. Buckingham: Open University Press.

Risner, D. (1992) Exploring dance rehearsal: The neglected issues revealed. *Journal of Physical Education, Recreation and Dance*, 63: 61–66.

Risner, D. (1995) Voices seldom heard: The dancers' experience of the choreographic process. *Impulse*, 3: 76–85.

Risner, D. (2000) Making dance, making sense: epistemology and choreography. *Research in Dance Education*, 1 (2): 155–72.

Risner, D. (2007) Rehearsing masculinity: challenging the 'boy code' in dance education. *Research in Dance Education*, 8 (2): 139–153.

Risner, D. (2009) *Stigma and Perseverance in the Lives of Boys who Dance: An empirical study of male identities in western theatrical dance training*. Lewiston, NY: Edwin Mellen Press.

Ross, J. (2000) Art and community: Creating knowledge through service in dance. In *The American Educational Research Association*, New Orleans, LA.

Ross, J. (2008) Doing time: Dance in prison. In Jackson, N. and Shapiro-Phim, T. (eds) *Dance, Human Rights, and Social Justice: Dignity in Motion*. Lanham, MD: Scarecrow Press.

Sanderson, P. (2001) Age and gender issues in adolescent attitudes to dance. *European Physical Education Review*, 7 (2): 117–136.

Sanderson, P. (2008) The arts, social inclusion and social class: The case of dance. *British Educational Research Journal*, 34 (4): 467–490.

West, C.S. (1994) Afro-centricity: Moving outside the comfort zone. *Journal of Physical Education, Recreation and Dance*, 65 (5): 28–30.

Wright, J. (1996) Mapping the discourses of physical education: articulating a female tradition. *Journal of Curriculum Studies*, 28 (3): 331–351.

Wright, J. (1997) The construction of gendered contexts in single sex and co-educational physical education lessons. *Sport, Education and Society*, 2 (1): 55–72.

Index

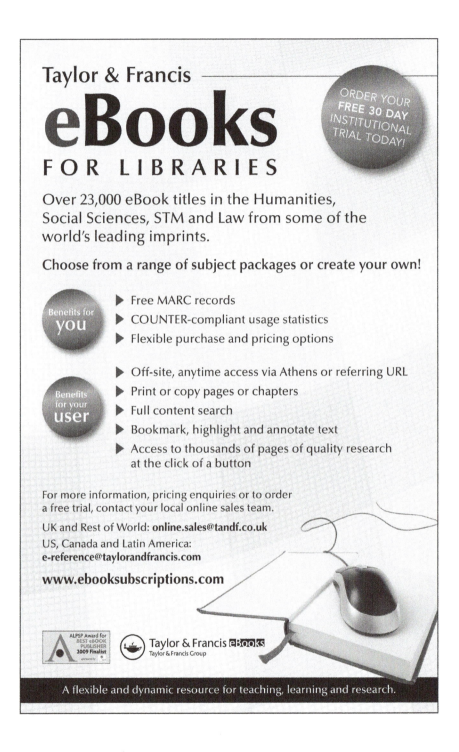

Lightning Source UK Ltd.
Milton Keynes UK
UKOW06f1807280815

257737UK00003B/140/P